CW01649737

HURRY UP NURSE MEMOIRS COLLECTION BOOKS 1-3

DAWN BROOKES

Dawn Brookes
Publishing

Paperback Collection ISBN: 9781913065645

HURRY UP NURSE

MEMOIRS OF NURSE TRAINING IN THE 1970S

2nd Edition

Dawn Brookes

Oakwood Publishing
www.dawnbrookespublishing.com

HURRY UP NURSE: MEMOIRS OF NURSE TRAINING IN THE 1970S COPYRIGHT

This book is a work of non-fiction based on the author's experiences. In order to protect privacy, names, identifying factors, dialogue and details have been changed or reconstructed.

Published by OAKWOOD PUBLISHING
www.dawnbrookespublishing.com

2nd Edition 2021

Cover Design by Dawn Brookes
Images: Adobe Stock Images

PREFACE

This book contains a collection of memories from my experiences of nurse training during the late 1970s. I trained initially as a State Enrolled Nurse and later as a Registered General Nurse in the early 1980s. The training referred to in this book occurred in and around Leicester, and the majority of experiences described occurred between 1977 and 1980.

The procedures and practices outlined throughout this book are a true recollection of my memories, as are the antics of myself and my fellow students and doctors. I loved my training, although there were trying times, some of which I have included in this book.

It took me quite a while to decide on a title for this work, but in the end I decided on *Hurry up Nurse,* as this reminded me of life on NHS hospital wards. We were always in demand, hurrying from one patient to another, and there never seemed to be enough hours in the day. I hope that, as well as sharing the hustle and bustle of working in hospitals; I've also portrayed just how much we cared.

I have tried to recreate the events, localities and conversations from my memory and notes, although I have changed the names of individuals and places to protect the confidentiality of patients and the anonymity of others. I've also mixed up identifying characteristics to further protect anonymity, and may have changed details of wards and the order of training in some instances.

It's my wish that this memoir will provide you with an insight into hospital life at the time I have written about. I am proud of myself, my friends and my colleagues for making it through those turbulent years. We were still growing up whilst coming to terms with the discipline of nurse training, and I trust this comes across. I hope you enjoy reading the book and the ones that follow.

1

THE INTERVIEW - 1977

'Why do you want to be a nurse, Miss Brookes?'

Good question, I thought. I needed a convincing answer.

'I would like to help people when they are at their most vulnerable, when they are ill,' I improvised. I could hardly say, '*A friend told me I should be a nurse because I couldn't think of anything better to do, and she wished she had finished her training.*' At least I had worked out that nursing involved caring for the sick. That declaration and interview was the beginning of the next thirty-nine years of my life. I had made a commitment to caring for others.

The selection process for entry to nurse training was an all-day affair. I had written the application letter in January 1977, and they called me for an interview in April.

Having recently turned eighteen, I hadn't endured any

tough interviews up to that point. Certainly none involving three fearsome middle-aged women dressed in starched uniforms, each in competition not to smile or put me at ease. To say it was daunting would be an understatement. The three women on the interview panel sat behind an enormous desk, shuffling papers around, occasionally tutting before firing questions at me. The questions included the one mentioned above. Worse than this was the fact I didn't really know what I was doing there. I had no clue what nursing was all about. Of course, I knew I was there for an interview. I had reached the stage of wanting to be a nurse more than anything else, if not for any other reason than that I had applied and happened to be in that room.

I had got up early that morning and dressed in my only decent clothes: a black skirt, white blouse and crinkly black jacket (my favourite) before racing out of the house. Two bus journeys later, I had walked up a long and wide finely gravelled driveway traversing the beautiful grounds lined with spring-flowering shrubs. A display of yellow drew my attention. The daffodils were well and truly in bloom. I arrived in front of a pair of large oak doors after climbing stone steps. The doors were inside an arched porch. Charles Frears School of Nursing housed external timbers facing outwards from the upper half of the building. That morning it was a forbidding Victorian building fronted by a wide gravel path and expansive lawn.

Once inside, I sat clutching the letter, inviting me for an interview, not knowing what to expect. Shortly afterwards, an administrator showed me into a room with a desk, which immediately made me feel uncomfortable, reminding me of school (my latter years at school hadn't gone well). I was now feeling nervous.

'Wait here.' The officious administrator instructed me.

About five minutes later, a rather serious looking woman came in and introduced herself as Mrs Butcher, though I was thankfully later to learn she was butcher by name not by nature. She wore a maroon uniform with a frilly hat over short permed grey hair. Mrs Butcher appeared to be in her late fifties and perched on the end of her nose were round spectacles, which she put on and off with regularity, occasionally leaving them dangling on a chain. The glasses mesmerised me. Mrs Butcher had a serious but not unkind demeanour.

'Good morning, Miss Brookes. Before the interview, "we" need to sit an entrance exam as "we" do not have the educational qualifications to be interviewed directly.' That really boosted my confidence. I was somewhat confused as to why she needed to sit the exam too, but didn't dare ask. I realised later that the "we" was the royal "we" used by experienced nurses, who repeatedly included it in their statements and questions: 'How are we today?' 'We are just going to have a little injection.' 'We are going to theatre today for an amputation, aren't we?' and so on. Many nurses were not expecting or seeking a reply to those questions at all. I bet many a patient wished the "we" really meant "we".

I was still trying to work out what the "we" meant when I noticed Mrs Butcher's mouth still moving. *Focus, Dawn,* I told myself, as I found myself daydreaming already. This had been my problem at school.

'If Dawn spent as much time studying as she did daydreaming and talking, she would do so much better.' Such statements in my reports had been a recurring theme. If only those teachers had realised the impact their words had on my poor long-suffering mother, they might have thought twice.

I pulled myself back into the present.

'After sitting the examination, *we* will have a fifteen minute break and then return to this room,' Mrs Butcher explained. 'If *we* have passed the exam, *we* will be given a formal interview.'

Next, she gave me an examination paper and told me to start the test, which I had forty-five minutes to complete. It seemed relatively simple and was based on IQ ability, mainly comprising English, Maths and problem-solving questions.

I didn't meet any other candidates on the day of my interview. I guessed they all had the required educational qualifications.

"We" did pass, and after the lengthy interview with the three women mentioned previously, they informed me I was

provisionally accepted into nurse training. Apparently I had done well in the entrance exam but was not told the exact result. Towards the end of the interview Mrs Butcher remarked on the result, and there followed some discussion *about*, rather than *with* me whether I should do a two-year course to train as a State Enrolled Nurse (SEN) or a three-year course to train as a State Registered Nurse (SRN).

I wasn't sure of the difference between the two qualifications and was not used to studying. When the interviewers saw my blank expression, they suggested it would be best for me to do the two-year training. While this meant that it would ultimately be a longer route to my eventual destination, it was the right choice, as I was not at all studious and enjoyed a hectic social life. On reflection, I'm certain I would have fallen at the first hurdle if I had done it the other way round. It's ironic that I have since spent most of my life studying.

After the interview Mrs Butcher warned me that nursing would be hard work, with long hours, difficult shift patterns including nights, lots of study with little thanks, low pay (very low pay I would have said) and that I would feel tired most of the time. I was almost on my way out of the door when she smiled whimsically and added.

'However, it is one of the most rewarding professions in the world. Many of your friends will be in jobs they hate, but it will please you to know that *you* will not be joining them.' I couldn't walk away after that.

How true those words were.

Following the interview, and with the lecture over, they sent me to Occupational Health for a medical examination. I saw a doctor first, followed by a nurse. The entire process was far too thorough for my liking, with heaps of health questions.

I was eighteen, for goodness' sake. I hadn't had time to be ill, had I?

The doctor did a lot of poking and prodding and listened to my heart and lungs; then the nurse took my blood pressure and tested my urine. The only advice I received was that my posture was poor and I should stretch my back to stop myself from getting a curvature of the spine. That sounded nasty, so I said I would try, although I'm not sure I ever did as my posture is still poor. Next, they sent me for blood tests.

It was the first time in my life I had to have blood taken, and for some reason I asked if the nurse could take it from my right arm. I thought I might faint if she took it from the left.

A stout, no-nonsense type of woman. She ignored my request.

'Don't be silly,' she snorted, and promptly took it from my left arm and yes, I did almost faint. Someone fetched me a glass of water as I had to sit down while the nurse glared at me for being such a baby. I apologised for keeping her, but inwardly I was yelling at her for not listening to me. Since then, I have never allowed anyone to take blood from my left arm. Totally illogical, but it works for me. Funnily enough, I always give patients a choice of arm for blood tests.

Finally, came the most exciting part of the day. They dispatched me to the sewing room where I was measured up for uniforms. By now, the news was sinking in and I was ecstatic and proud of myself. The process had taken up most of the day and I left having been told that, if I was successful (I think this meant if I hadn't got bubonic plague), I would get a letter giving me a start date which was likely to be in September of that year.

Wow! What a day.

When the letter arrived six weeks later, I was over the moon. I knew I'd got the place when the letter began with:

'We are pleased to inform you...'

The acceptance letter explained that I was being offered a place as a pupil nurse on a two-year training course. Training would comprise working in any or all of the three hospitals in Leicester: The Leicester Royal Infirmary, Groby Road Hospital, and The Leicester General Hospital.

I was to attend Charles Frears School of Nursing for theory and practical training in-between working on the wards, and I was to report there at nine o'clock in the morning on the set date. There was a list of things to buy prior to starting. I couldn't wait until September.

1977 was an eventful year, not just because it was the beginning of my nursing career, but there were several other landmark occasions, one being Queen Elizabeth II's Silver Jubilee. I remember the nationwide street parties, including the one I went to in Leicester; it seemed such a merry time, bringing strangers together with a sense of national pride and joy. Just before that party, my best friend Cheryl and I had met a rather odd couple who stand out in my memory for chanting in loud voices, 'WE KNOW WHERE YOU'RE GOING!' every time someone went to the toilet.

Virginia Wade won the women's Singles final at Wimbledon in front of the Queen, which seemed rather apt. It was also the year they launched the first Star Wars film. Who would have believed that the films would become so iconic?

The most poignant event of that year for me was news of Elvis Presley's tragic death, aged 42. I had idolised Elvis for as long as I could remember.

I was at home with my mum watching TV when the newsreader appeared on screen and announced: 'We interrupt this programme to bring you a newsflash. Elvis Presley is dead.'

I don't remember the rest of what he said as the tears flowed; I couldn't believe it. There were floral tributes at Graceland and a great outpouring of public grief. Subsequent days' newspapers confirmed the truth of the tragic event, and for weeks there were tributes and discussions about what had caused his death. Rumours of drugs soon emerged and the rest, as they say, is history.

Another less notable death in 1977 was that of Charles Frears himself. The man the school of nursing was named after. He was a well-known philanthropist in Leicester.

A mixture of news then, but the most exciting part of 1977 for me was that life-changing interview.

2

SIMPLE BEGINNINGS

A midwife brought me into the world at a quarter past six one wintry morning in 1959. My birthplace was a cramped bedsit in Nottingham. My brother David had been born in Lincoln eighteen months earlier. Mum and dad couldn't agree on a name for me, so the midwife made a suggestion.

'Look Mr & Mrs Brookes, as she was born at dawn, why don't you call her Dawn?' So that was it. The only error there, I recently discovered when tracing my family tree, was that my parents were not Mr & Mrs Brookes at all. My dad was still married, albeit separated from another Mrs Brookes, when my mum became pregnant with my brother. He was going through a divorce when I was born. My brother was born in The Quarry Maternity Home, a home run by nuns in Lincoln. My mum's younger sister had arranged her confinement, along with a supportive boss.

The Quarry was a maternity home where single women went to have their babies before putting them up for adoption. Many years later, I can't help but wonder whether adoption had been the plan for my brother, something my mum clearly couldn't go through with.

My parents get married in Nottingham three and a half years later.

I have vague memories of the bedsit where we lived for five years. We all slept in a double bed that dominated the room. The large Victorian terraced house had a shared kitchen, and an enormous overgrown garden where my brother and I played. We called the garden, *the jungle* – it was a paradise for two young children.

When I received a nurse's set one Christmas, it didn't release any nursing genes, but I listened to my brother's chest with the plastic stethoscope when he was injured by pirates in our jungle.

My first introduction to a hospital followed an event forever ingrained in my memory. My brother and I, along with a few friends, were out playing. It was a lovely sunny day, and one of our favourite places to play was a local wood yard near to home. The yard housed a large conveyor belt that carried wood through to a machine for cutting and shredding. We would jump on the conveyor belt for a ride and then jump off at the end just before it passed through to the shredder (more like a crusher, really). On this occasion, my brother missed his footing, and the machine dragged him through. It will come as no surprise that he was screaming.

Terrified, I ran off to fetch my mum. Fortunately, while I ran for my mum, the machine operator heard my brother's screams, turned the machine off and called an ambulance. When Mum and I arrived at the scene, there was pandemonium. Dave was wailing, and it seemed as though blood was everywhere. His left leg looked a mashed up mess. Afterwards, he remained in hospital for three months with multiple compound fractures to the leg. He was lucky to be alive. The man who worked there was extremely upset, and the next day took my brother a basket of fruit. I remember eating the grapes as Dave felt queasy. As fate would have it, I would begin my nursing career many years later on an adult male orthopaedic ward.

This wasn't the only major accident encountered in my childhood. Next up was my dad, who had been working somewhere with electrics. Heaven only knows why, because he was hopeless at DIY. He was badly electrocuted, and my Uncle Vernon came round to tell my mum. I overheard Vernon say, 'It was his rubber boots that saved him.' I determined that I would get a pair of rubber boots, as I might need them one day.

We didn't see my dad for many months as we weren't allowed to visit him in hospital. We were told his injuries might frighten us. Nothing is more frightening than a child's imagination, though, so I think it would have been better if they had allowed us to visit. On the day my dad came home, my uncle said, 'Now don't be shocked when your dad comes.' No pun intended.

The first thing I noticed was dark brown scabs covering his hands. He rushed over to me like something out of a horror movie: his face covered in scabs and bandages.

'Give us a kiss then.'

I ran away and hid. Probably not the most mature thing to do under the circumstances. Nevertheless, I was not going to kiss *Frankenstein*. We soon got used to seeing him, scabs and all, but I didn't get too close in case they came off or I caught something. I had been to Sunday school twice and heard about leprosy. Convinced that if you touched a person with leprosy, your limbs fell off, I wasn't taking any chances.

In 1965, we moved to Leicester, where my parents originated, and into our first house. I had my own bedroom for the first time in my life. The house had no running hot water and no central heating. The bathtub was in the kitchen and covered with a big wooden board used as a storage shelf. Every Sunday, the board would come off and my mum would heat water in saucepans and gradually fill the bath.

We took turns to have a bath: dad first, then mum, then Dave and finally me, the youngest. Obviously, the water was filthy and lukewarm by the time I got in, but it remained a rare treat. The toilet was outside and down the yard, so it's not surprising I learned to hold for lengthy periods of time.

We had a coal fire and once had a chimney fire. An

exciting event for us kids as the fire brigade came to put it out. Chimney fires were not uncommon in the 1960s.

Our next-door neighbour, Mrs Clarke, used to bleach the front yard and the path outside her house every weekend.

We had a family poodle. Standing out in my memory are the two litters of puppies that she delivered. Seeing the miracle of birth for the first time at the age of six was spectacular. I watched the puppies for hours on end as they fed, grew and developed, and could lose myself in this amazing world. Much later, I became a midwife, and that miracle of new life increased exponentially in my mind.

When I was ten, my best friend's brother had his eighteenth birthday party. I drank quite a few glasses of cider. Eventually, I felt peculiar and couldn't speak properly. I felt ill. Her brother's mates realised I was drunk, so they carried me home, put me on my doorstep, knocked on the door and scarpered. When my mum answered the door, I threw up in the hall. On that occasion, I think my mum knew a telling off was unnecessary. I have never touched cider from that day to this.

My brother passed his eleven plus and went to Grammar School, but because we lived in a working class area, the kids gave him a hard time. He also wore NHS glasses, a double whammy.

'Four eyes,' the local boys would taunt him, along with, 'snob, snob, toffee nose, grammar school boy,' none of which were true, apart from the fact he did go to grammar school. Whoever coined the adage 'sticks and stones, etc.' couldn't have been more wrong. Names hurt children and they can destroy teenagers. I remember my brother walking along the road one day and getting a dart thrown into his back. His only crime was his grammar school education.

I managed to fail my eleven plus and went to a secondary school, so didn't suffer the same fate as my brother. Fosse Secondary School was a struggling school for working class kids but was by no means the worst in the city. Discipline was a problem, as was alcohol and drugs. Chaos often ensued; even if you had wanted to work, it was near impossible because there were always too many distractions and too much indiscipline. Some teachers maintained more control than others.

The RE teacher was a generous man who tried to bring kindness into the school, but I remember him being attacked by one of the fifth years during a break. It was a horrible scene.

Despite the experience, I made some excellent friends at school and many of us emerged relatively unscathed.

I left school at sixteen, streetwise, but with no proper direction. I began my working life, as did my friends doing the best we could to earn a living.

3

THE 'CALL'

My childhood ambition had always been to be a professional tennis player and win Wimbledon. As my school had no tennis courts, and I stood at five foot one inch tall, I would never realise this ambition.

With a general lack of career advice from school, family expected me to work in a shop or factory, get married and have kids. Inwardly, I yearned to make something of my life, but had no idea what to do or how to go about it.

Commis Chef

After leaving school at sixteen, I bucked the trend and got a job as a commis (junior) chef. I loved the work, but the travel and shifts were challenging, as the Wheatsheaf Inn was fourteen miles and two buses away from where I lived. The job involved working two shifts a day, eleven o'clock in the morning to three in the afternoon, and then five until ten in the evening. The salary was poor, although the tips weren't bad.

I'm ashamed to say that I dated the chef, another Dave, so I could get a lift home at night. The relationship ended when I left the job a few months after starting, and I'm sure he was much better off without me. I learned how to prepare a posh prawn cocktail and could slice and decorate a melon that wouldn't look out of place at The Savoy, so the experience wasn't wasted.

Handbags

The second job, still aged sixteen, was more in keeping with expectations. I worked in a handbag warehouse at the bottom of the next street from where I lived.

While I was working there, having just turned seventeen, one of my friends decided to move to Watton in Norfolk. I had never heard of it (Watton, that is, not Norfolk) but Maria's sister Jenny lived on an RAF base because her brother-in-law was in the navy. I don't know why they lived on an RAF base. And I have to point out, if the naval authorities are reading this book, Watton is not by the sea. Her sister was living on her own with two young boys while her brother-in-law joined the crew of the *Ark Royal* for its final sailing.

Maria asked me if I wanted to join her in Norfolk, and I agreed to go.

The soundtrack of a filmed documentary of the *Ark Royal* sailing was a Rod Stewart song, *I Am Sailing.* The documentary was compulsory watching in Jenny's home.

Norfolk

We moved to RAF Watton, half a mile outside the village, about ten miles from Thetford and twenty miles from Norwich. Maria's sister was ten years older than us, and long before the smoking ban became compulsory, she banished us outside for a cigarette.

The first thing we needed to do was find a job so we could pay our way and then find somewhere else to live.

Someone told us about the opportunity to do casual labour at an onion farm not too far away. 'All you have to do is wait at the bus stop at eight o'clock in the morning, and a bus will pick you up and take you to the farm.'

I was surprised we made it to the bus stop on time, as Maria never stepped outside the door without applying enough makeup for both of us. The morning ritual included foundation, eye shadow, mascara, and thick black eyeliner. I had never really been one for daytime makeup.

'Is this the stop for the onion factory?' I asked a woman reeking of onions.

'Yeah, `twill be `ere in a minute,' she replied in a Norfolk twang. By the time the bus arrived, twenty women stood waiting at the stop. Our clothes looked out of place, as most of the women wore overalls. When we got on the bus we realised why. The stench of onion hit with force as soon as we got on. Each person had their own distinct onion smell mixed with whatever soap they used. Even the cigarette smoke didn't detract from the pungent onion aroma. Perfume and deodorants are just not designed to permeate through odour like that, otherwise ours would have helped.

Once we arrived at the farm, we followed the women to a gigantic open-air shed where we found two spaces next to each other. The idea was to peel as many onions as possible and get paid by the tray. We had imagined this would be easy and a great way to make quick money.

Not so. When the full trays appeared, there were no large onions to peel, which would fill trays in no time. An enormous woman wearing a dirty white overall and hairnet presented us with tiny onions meant for pickling. My jaw dropped to the floor. It would take forever to peel one, let alone fill a tray. We soon realised we were not very good at this (an understatement)—I had peeled around six onions by the time the lady next to me filled her first tray. This was going to be an interminable day and my eyes were already sore and watering. What was worse, I reeked of onion.

Shortly after we started work, Maria went into a panic.

'I can't see. I'm going blind,' she cried.

When I looked at her, I could see why. Her makeup had run all over her face and the more she rubbed, the worse it got. Eyeliner streaked down her cheeks along with the tears. It was cruel, but I laughed and laughed and laughed.

We had filled half a tray each by lunchtime and took a long lunch before joining the bus back to Watton. When we arrived back at meticulously house-proud Jenny's, she wouldn't let us in. She ordered us to take our clothes off and throw them straight into the wash, then she sent us to the bathroom. At least it meant Jenny didn't mind us being unemployed again.

Maria and I had more success with our second job at Travenol Laboratories in Thetford, and it paid well, even back then. Thirty-eight pounds a week was a decent salary for seventeen-year-olds. I earned less when I started nursing.

Because we were now earning a salary, we could look for accommodation as the novelty of having us was wearing off for Jenny. We found a country cottage going cheap and moved in that weekend.

A Gentle Nudge

During my short tenure in Watton, I met one of Jenny's friends, Gail, who became a lifelong friend and who must take full responsibility for me ever becoming a nurse.

Although she was twenty-nine with two young children, we got on. From there developed one of those friendships that survives the test of time; we always had something to talk about. Facilities on an RAF base are good, and although it is an unfamiliar world for us civilians, I really enjoyed going to the NAAFI (shop) and the bars and playing badminton whenever I wanted to, as I accompanied Gail. I used to go to her house and we would chat and drink coffee or wine until around midnight, as she also preferred nights to mornings.

Maria and I lived in the cottage in the middle of nowhere. Shortly after moving in, we had a row and Maria returned to Leicester soon afterwards. I opted to stay the month out and carry on working for that time. I spent some time staying at Gail's, as the area around the cottage was bleak and isolated at night.

That month, Gail told me how she had started nurse training in her youth. She never completed it because of a health scare, which turned out to be a false alarm. She always regretted giving up. It was clear she had loved it from her stories. One night, out of the blue, she proclaimed, 'You should be a nurse!'

I'm sure she could see that my life was pretty rudderless, but along with that, she wanted me to fulfil the dream she had not. Therein began Gail's mission to convince me that nursing would be a wonderful career and a rewarding profession. As I agreed I lacked direction, I said I'd give it a go, if only to shut her up. Nursing hadn't been on my radar at all and was alien to me. All I knew was that it meant working in a hospital and looking after sick people. Gail's stories were entertaining. She told me about the things she enjoyed during her training and the antics she got up to in a London hospital in the sixties.

I wish I had more philanthropic reasons for beginning

my career, but I cannot lie. It should be a vocation, a calling, a willingness to sacrifice and do-good for the benefit of humanity, and that one should have wanted to be a nurse since having a first doll and all that, but that wasn't the way I came into it. Thankfully for patients, I don't think I was any less caring.

When it came time to say goodbye, I looked forward to returning to Leicester, but I would certainly keep in touch with Gail.

She suggested I read *One Pair of Feet* by Monica Dickens, which I did, and enjoyed the sometimes hilarious descriptions of nursing in the 1950s. It couldn't be like that in the seventies, surely?

My Waterloo

I was home again. Maria was pleased to see me and spoke to me once more. The only downside was being unemployed again.

I forgot about nursing for a while and my next job came about through an advert in the local paper for an au pair in Belgium. I got the job following an interview in Slough. A week later, I was on my way to Brussels.

I said goodbye to my poor mum once more, and my dad took me to London to get the train to Dover, where I picked up the ferry to Ostend and then a train to Brussels.

My new employer Madam De Ville met me in Brussels. She drove me to Waterloo, where the De Ville family lived.

History wasn't a strong subject for me at school, but I could remember that there had been a battle of Waterloo, which was something to do with Wellington and Napoleon. The De Ville's had three monsters: Monique, aged seven, Pierre, aged five, and a baby of thirteen months called Gerard. They helped create my own personal Battle of Waterloo.

From the first moment, I knew this would not be a peaceful job. My experience of children was zilch, apart from the odd bit of babysitting.

Living in a French-speaking household exposed my pidgin French. The De Ville's insisted on speaking French the whole time (I guess it was their language). I smiled and nodded a lot while not having a clue what was going on. Mme De Ville decided I should attend night school on my evening off in Brussels to learn better French. I don't recall having any choice in the matter. The children spoke no English, and I felt lonely until my French picked up.

My room in the attic was opposite the bedroom of chief monster, Pierre. Peace evaded me night and day. These had to be the children from hell. They never did a thing they were told. Pierre was forever playing with matches. Mme De Ville spoilt them rotten (probably because she didn't have to spend any time with them). Wednesday evenings became the highlight of my week, as even taking a tram into Brussels for my evening class brought blessed relief. The teacher taught the class in French, so I often left the class no wiser than when I entered, but at least I'd got away from the mayhem of the De Ville household.

One ominous evening, Mme De Ville informed me I would be babysitting as she and her husband were going to play Bridge in Paris. After they left, I finally got the children to bed, a feat in itself. I sat downstairs to watch television, which I didn't understand. Suddenly the lights went out, and the TV switched off. Pierre came running into the room, shouting excitedly. I assumed he feared the dark, so I took his trembling hand and suggested he show me where the electric meter was, trying to calm him down. I explained that we would soon have the lights on again.

When we got to the second staircase leading to the attic rooms, I was horrified to see flames pouring out of his bedroom. I could taste acrid smoke; the fire had really taken hold, and I felt the heat. I'm not sure whether it was panic or heat from the fire causing this. There was no fire extinguisher to hand. Not that I even thought to look for one, as this was a proper FIRE and could not be tackled by a seventeen-year-old amateur. I woke Monique, who slept on the first floor, and had the foresight to grab the baby from his cot, a miracle on reflection, before running downstairs with crying children and a baby tucked under my arm.

I didn't know how to phone the fire brigade and so telephoned the lady across the road whose name and number they had written on a pad by the phone. I yelled, 'FEU, FEU!' Thank you, French teacher. Fortunately, the lady understood and called the fire brigade, who arrived within minutes. In the meantime, I corralled the children out of the house and into the street. It was a cold, black night as I recall, and the flames spilled from Pierre's window, visible from the road. The neighbour called the De Ville's back from their Bridge evening.

Chaos reigned for a few hours and when I finally got to my room that night, it was damp where the firefighters had traipsed through with hoses to use on Pierre's room. My bedroom walls were black and smelled of unpleasant charred wood; I barely slept. The following morning Mme De Ville reluctantly thanked me for saving the children's lives. Pierre's father gave him a very mild scolding about playing with matches. I would have happily strangled him.

The day after the fire, I decided to leave at the earliest opportunity. The problem was, I had no money to buy a ticket home. Thankfully, I phoned a friend who sent me a ticket home. When I told Mme De Ville, I was leaving because of the trauma of the fire. She said she had come across many au pairs who made up all sorts of stories in order to leave. *How surprising*!

A few weeks later, I was home.

Checking Out

Once home and unemployed again, I met an old school friend at the bus stop and discovered that she worked in a supermarket. She offered to ask the manager if they had any vacancies for me. A week later, I started work at Belco Supermarket. So here I was, fulfilling what destiny expected of me. There had to be more to life than this.

Determined to break the mould, having turned eighteen, I finally got around to applying for nurse training (probably in part due to Gail's nagging), and I also applied to join the WRENS at the same time. I didn't get into the WRENS because I kept showing protein in my urine, though I had no idea why, and it didn't appear again. In retrospect, it was serendipitous. I'm pleased I didn't get in. I don't think I would have liked the discipline. Nursing was bad enough, but nursing and the WRENS, I think that might have been regimental overload.

I received the letter inviting me to attend the interview at Charles Frears School of Nursing mentioned in chapter one. I'd spent two years since leaving school living like a nomad. The time had come to do something more with my life.

4

NURSE TRAINING - BACK TO SCHOOL

I really did go back to school; PTS (Pupil Training School) was classroom based. Feeling excited, it was my first day, although the excitement was mixed with nerves as I got the two buses to the Charles Frears School of Nursing once again. Even the name sounded special.

I walked up the long driveway again and entered the building. It was September 1977. I was ushered into a classroom full of eager girls, mostly my age, and found an empty desk. We were all as keen as each other and soon started chatting in groups.

'Where have you come from?' asked the girl on my left, who was taller than me (not hard as I mentioned before, I'm five foot one). She had curly brown hair and freckles.

'I live in Leicester,' I replied. 'What about you?'

'I'm from Manchester: I moved into the nurses' home on Saturday – this is Grace, she's from London.' She turned her head to the girl on her left, a blonde-haired beauty, taller than both of us. 'And I'm Sue.'

We exchanged hellos and spent the next few minutes sharing a little about ourselves. They had both left home and moved into the nurses' home, which was divided into flats, each shared by four people. They pointed out the two other girls they were sharing with sitting at the back of the class.

'That's Charlie with the dark hair and glasses, and that's Bette wearing the jeans,' Sue explained.

They were looking forward to the next few years and had already found a local pub frequented by hospital staff. Feeling fractionally jealous that I was still at home with my mum and brother while these girls would have the time of their lives in the nurses' home, I smiled. My experience of life in a nurses' home was to come a few years later in London.

'I can't wait to get to know the handsome doctors,' Grace giggled. And true to her word, she got to know quite a few: Sue and I would pick up the pieces as she fell in and out of love over the next two years. The hubbub stopped as Mrs Butcher walked into the room. She stood at the front of the class.

'Good morning, girls,' she said. *The Prime of Miss Jean Brodie* came to mind, but there was no Scottish accent. 'Welcome to Leicester and Charles Frears. My name is Mrs Butcher; I met most of you at interview but don't expect me to remember all your names just yet. I will be your classroom tutor throughout your training for the next two years. This week is an introductory week and I will let you have a timetable in a minute.'

The "in a minute" took me back to my one and only experience of being a hospital inpatient when I was a child. I was eight years old and one night I woke up with a terrible pain in my side. I crawled downstairs to get a drink of water, but my mum heard me; she got up and realised I was in a lot of pain and sat with me for a while. The pain didn't go away, so she put on her coat and said she would call an ambulance. It was around three o'clock in the morning and we didn't have a home phone, so she had to walk to the end of the road to the public telephone box and call the ambulance – not that I gave that a thought. When the ambulance came, I remember the men trying to cheer me up by telling me I was special and they were going to set off the flashing blue light to get me to hospital. I was pleased about this and managed a smile. But they didn't use the siren because they didn't want to wake people up.

Once in the hospital, a doctor examined my abdomen, and they admitted me into a bed on a children's ward. They sent my mum home, which was perhaps as well, as my brother was still in bed. I couldn't sleep as the pain was crippling me, but the doctors had decided it probably wasn't appendicitis, so they allowed me to drink. A kind nurse came.

'Can't you sleep?' she asked.

'No,' I replied.

'Would you like a glass of milk?'

'Yes, please.' I loved milk.

'I'll be back in a minute,' she said, and that was the last I saw of her. Fighting sleep, I waited and waited because I thought she would be back with my milk at any moment. Eventually I drifted off, and when I woke in the morning, there was no glass of milk.

Later that day, a nurse asked me to turn on my side while she administered what I now know was a suppository. I didn't understand what she was doing, but obeyed as a child would. The nurse then said I had to wait in bed until she came back and that she would be back "in a minute". I waited and waited again and felt desperate for the toilet, but I didn't dare get out of bed in case I got into trouble. The cramps got worse and worse; I was sweating and feeling terrible, terrified that I might mess the bed and yet frightened of getting out as I had been told to wait. Finally, I knew I could hold no longer and risked a dash to the toilet, which I found quickly and to great relief. When I got back to bed, my mum was there. I ran to her and sobbed. The nurse came and asked if I had been to the toilet. I nodded, frightened she would tell me off, but she gave me a big smile and said I could go home. I was so relieved in more ways than one.

As I remembered those events in that moment, I made a deal between myself and to future patients everywhere that my "in a minute" would mean just that. I would never allow myself to forget to go back, even if the minute stretched a little. As far as I'm aware, I kept that deal, although I guess I might not remember if I forgot! Not a brilliant start to my training, though. I had only been in the classroom a few minutes and I was already daydreaming.

'Today is the first day of your nursing career,' Mrs Butcher continued, 'and I can see that some of you are already getting to know each other.' She glared at a group of three girls chatting at the back: one of them was Bette, the flatmate of my newfound friends, who immediately stopped talking and flushed red in the face.

We would get to know that glare well. Mrs Butcher was a kind woman, but she also carried an air of authority and only had to *look* to command obedience, which must have come from her years working as a ward sister.

'Shortly, I will split you into two groups as there are forty-six of you, then we will show you around the building. Before the end of your training, I'm afraid at least ten of you will give up. We will ask some of you to leave and another ten of you will fail finals.' We stared at her, a bit stunned. I glanced around the class to see which ones were the likely drop-out candidates and noticed a few others were doing the same. I didn't dare look for the failures, and as for being asked to leave, that didn't bear thinking about.

That day they showed us around the School of Nursing that was Charles Frears. There were several classrooms with desks, clinical rooms setup with beds and odd-looking equipment, a canteen and various administration offices. Mid-afternoon Mrs Butcher gave us our whole training timetable, which included the ward placements, with dates and the School blocks and holidays. It was the most exciting part of the day, and I treasured that timetable for years to come.

We opened bank accounts for our salary to be paid in to during the first week. These days, that might not sound like a big deal, but all the jobs I'd had prior to nursing paid every Friday with cash in an envelope. I had to work an entire calendar month before I'd see any money. Most of us opened accounts with a well-known High Street bank as their staff visited us on-site to encourage us to sign up: a good ploy, as I have been with the same bank ever since. A few weeks after signing on the dotted line, I received a cheque book and a cheque guarantee card; I felt truly grown up, but didn't know how to get money out of the bank. My mum didn't get paid into a bank either, so she couldn't help. Before the development of multiple hole-in-the-wall cash machines, I used to write a cheque to myself, take it to the bank and exchange it for cash. An early cash machine appeared outside the main branch of St. Martin's in the town centre. And I would use that regularly.

Being habitually overdrawn was a nurse's lot, and I struggled financially for approximately ten years until I adapted to living on the low salary. Later, when I was doing my RGN training, I worked as an agency nurse on my days off to supplement my income, often working seven days a week.

Our training was mainly hands-on when working on the wards. During two-week blocks interspersed with eight- to ten- week ward placements, we learned theory. They implemented the Briggs report, published in 1972, in 1979, following a change of law. From then on, nurse training became less focused on the medical model and more on psychology and sociology, with the nursing process used in the USA being adopted. Project 2000 followed later, in which they trained nurses at diploma and degree level. My training wasn't perfect, but somehow the experiences gained during training helped me to deal with the challenges I faced after qualification.

In those first few weeks, I became friends with quite a few of the girls in my set and we had several nights out, but we were never a group that gelled closely enough to keep in touch for years to come, although we gelled in smaller groups. Most of us concentrated on getting through the training and qualifying.

Anatomy and physiology was hard work for those of us who had not paid enough attention to human biology at school. They taught us every human system, starting with the skeletal system. At first, the novelty helped me to concentrate, but it was hard going for someone who didn't enjoy sitting in a classroom. The saving factor was that we were all in it together and would chivvy each other along: when one of us seemed to struggle, the others would gather around and help.

We also had practical sessions, which helped break up the days. Bed-making was one of the first things they taught us in the practical rooms; not exactly vital to life, but it was a start. We had to place two chairs at the foot of the bed and we would fold back the bedding over these chairs. Two of us would stand on either side of the bed, strip it without filling the room with dust, and then remake it using hospital corners at the foot. It's sad I know, but I had been dying to learn how to do hospital corners as I had heard about them from Gail. Once learnt never forgot: I was to make thousands of beds during my career and the novelty soon wore off.

We always had fun in the practical room. There, we could let our hair down a bit and play practical jokes on each other when Mrs Butcher wasn't looking.

They taught us how to feed patients and give drinks without choking them: this was actually much more difficult on the wards. Some of the tasks we practised on each other, which always turned into a riot. Trying to give each other drinks from plastic beakers with a spout was, at times, hilarious. At first we took it all seriously but soon started messing around and instead of being gentle, offering sips, we would try to pour the whole drink down our pretend patient's throat until they spluttered and spat it out. Mrs Butcher would allow a little messing and then calm us down in an instant with one of those *looks*.

We learned how to give a bed bath using a life-sized Manikin doll – I don't think we were up to washing each other, though I'm not sure whether that would have been too embarrassing or too dangerous. The Manikins had to suffer an awful lot in our hands over the years as the tutors taught us to pass nasogastric tubes, insert urinary catheters, give enemas and so on.

As I said, the anatomy and physiology sessions were hard going, but they were necessary to help us understand what was going on with patients once we were let loose on the wards.

They gradually introduced us to the wards with a few visits prior to starting our first placement. Getting used to the odours from antiseptics and disinfectants that were used to cover those from excrement and bodily discharges was something that took time to nurture. During the first eight weeks of training, which was mostly classroom based, we took a trip to one such ward with a clinical tutor, and the first thing that struck me was the smell of hospital.

The clinical tutor escorted us behind a set of curtains to demonstrate how to give a bed bath to an actual patient. I have never forgotten the elderly lady lying in that bed, barely conscious, nor the smell of bodily fluids mixed with heat. It took every ounce of energy and concentration for me not to pass out. I had visions of myself being put onto the bed next to the patient, which focused the attention somewhat. The clinical tutor, oblivious to my discomfort, treated the patient with the utmost respect, explaining to her what was happening throughout while teaching us. As she continued with her bed bath demonstration, she must have thought I was very attentive with my fixed stare; I was trying to hold it together and not let my new friends know I might faint at any minute.

I could not remember a single word the tutor said, but I can still remember the respect and dignity she showed to that lady. This was something they taught us from the very beginning. That was one of the few times I had second thoughts about my chosen career, and I really wasn't sure I would ever make it; my first step onto a real ward and I was ready to run. This was not what it was like in books or in one of the popular TV programmes of the 60s and 70s, *Emergency Ward 10*. Where were all those glamorous people?

For our ward placements, they split us up and sent us out into the big wide world of hospital life, either alone or in twos. It was always daunting starting a new ward, not knowing anyone and not knowing the routine. When two of us from the set got sent to a new ward together, it was always a bonus, although we usually worked opposite shifts. The hospitals had staff canteens, and that was where we got to meet up. We would share food and experiences, and more importantly, offer each other the support that sometimes kept us going through tough times. Some wards were easier to settle into than others, but the worst times came when you hated a ward- and the placement seemed to last for an eternity. There weren't many like this during my training, but there were a few. This was always caused by staff and never by patients. It was when working on these wards that the support from others in the set became vital, as it stopped many of us from walking away.

My first month's salary was around eighty pounds. I needed bank loans on a rolling basis, not so different from anyone about to embark on a university education now.

I often asked myself what I was doing sitting in a classroom of forty-six girls (not one male in my training set), learning anatomy and physiology.

Mrs Butcher took us through all the bodily systems, for which I was grateful because we learnt such a lot, but I wasn't used to studying and found it difficult to get my head down.

The tutors covered the basic anatomy and physiology of the respiratory, cardiovascular, nervous, genitourinary and musculoskeletal systems, and the skin. We mastered basic observations, including temperature, pulse, respirations and blood pressures. We learned how to perform bed baths and shaves, pressure area checks, turns, lifts, wound dressings, mouth cleaning, rectal examination, enemas, fitting and emptying colostomy bags. The list is endless. The teaching was thorough, and it was all a lot more complicated than it sounds.

There was a life-sized skeleton in the corner of the practice room, and we would spend hours trying to name all the bones.

I'm not so sure the talcum powder was such a good idea, though. We would shake it liberally all over patients, especially the intimate areas, but they smelled nice. I'm surprised there aren't more nurses with respiratory diseases after breathing in all the talc that filled air. Learning in the classroom was one thing, but doing these things to real live patients was another. After two months in the classroom, it was time for the real thing.

I expect almost every nurse has nearly given up at some time during their training, and some discovered that it really wasn't what they wanted to do for the rest of their lives. Eleven people who began training in our 1977 set left and didn't complete, bringing Mrs Butcher's prediction into grim reality. What kept me going was partly remembering where I had come from, but mainly it was the fact that I fell in love with the job. I loved the patients, and I made some great friends that I kept in touch with for many years, both patients and staff.

5

NIGHTINGALE WARDS

The Leicester Royal Infirmary was the city's major hospital. It was massive and easy for a person to get lost in once inside. Although we had to wear uniform in school we hadn't had to wear the hats. That first morning, I wished I'd paid more attention to the hat lesson. We were issued cardboard hats that had to be folded like some form of origami to resemble a nurse's hat and then held together with a single plastic fixing inserted through holes. After getting it together, I had spent ages in front of the mirror trying to fix the assembled hat in place without it looking lopsided. My hat had one green stripe running around the front portion indicating to everyone who understood the ranks that I was a first year pupil nurse. Staff nurses wore the most wonderful frilly cloth hats devoid of any stripes anywhere.

My first placement was a male orthopaedic ward,

which was a Nightingale ward. Every Nightingale had a similar setup. They often mirrored each other on opposite sides of the building, with entrances via two sets of double doors.

Feeling very important in my uniform and with hat in place, I took my initial tentative steps through the first set of doors. I could hear clattering coming from the kitchen and saw the sign for a medical equipment room off to the right. Peering through the small square-glass window, I could make out stainless steel trolleys and cupboards.

'That's where we stock dressings; equipment for medical procedures like lumbar punctures; sterile packs and stuff for setting up IVs. There are also boxes full of IV fluids.' A friendly second-year student stood behind me. I knew that from the hat.

I nodded as if knowing what a lumbar puncture was.

'First day?'

'Yes.'

'Don't worry. This is a lovely ward. I'm Mary, by the way.'

'Dawn,' I answered, pleased to meet a friendly face who could show me where to go.

I followed Mary, who pointed out a side room. 'That's for barrier nursing, or any poor nurse unfortunate enough to need a bed. Sometimes patients pay to be in a side room.'

'How much?'

'About fifty quid a day, I think, but don't quote me on that.'

We passed the kitchen where all the clattering was

coming from on the left-hand side before entering through the next set of doors onto the main ward.

The clinical tutor had taken us to a Nightingale ward for the bed bath demonstration so I knew they were lengthy and wide. There was a nurse's station on the left just inside. Nurses were standing around as if waiting for something.

'Hiya,' Mary nodded to a third year. A staff nurse was on the telephone and an enrolled nurse frantically wrote in a book. 'This is Dawn, she's new.'

'Alex,' said the other girl, 'That's Staff Nurse Bingham. We'll be having a handover in a minute.'

My eyes were drawn to the marble floor, running right down to the end. 'How many beds are on this ward?' I asked.

'Forty on the main ward, six on the balcony and one side room,' Mary answered. 'It's non-stop, but you're lucky this is your first ward. The sister's great. I worked on a horrible ward when I started. It was so bad I almost packed in.'

'Which one was that?' I asked.

'I won't say, best not to put you off on your first day. There's twenty beds down each side. All Nightingales are the same.'

I discovered Mary was right as I went from ward to ward during my training. The patients faced each other and shouted across the ward to chat and banter. Especially, I discovered, on male orthopaedics. Looking up, I could see the ceiling was mega-high, and the windows reminded me of church windows but without the stained glass. They were pretty but draughty because of old-fashioned single glazing.

After we were given a handover from the enrolled nurse finishing the night shift, the staff nurse worked with Mary and they allocated me to work with Alex. A nursing auxiliary worked with another student who was nearly at the end of her first year.

'I'll give you a tour as soon as we get the morning's work done.' Alex promised.

That morning, I received a baptism of fire, working as fast as I could to keep up with Alex. We bed bathed men who couldn't wash themselves or were unconscious but out of intensive care because they could breathe by themselves. We handed bowls of hot water to young men in traction, made beds and started rounds.

A long brown table sat in the centre of the ward where we would sit and write up the Kardex at the end of each shift or before handovers. The Kardex card filing system contained each patient's nursing records inside a large metal-type clipboard about six inches wide, which opened like a stack of cards in alphabetical order. Kardex was the brand name of the company that made them.

We nurses completed the Kardex for each patient we looked after, which often meant filling in fifteen to twenty records per shift. We entered a lot of vague and meaningless information in the Kardex, such as "slept well", "no complaints", "comfortable" and "sat out".

I gleaned a few rules on the first day from Alex. 'Students are not allowed to sit at the nurses' station,' I looked towards the forbidden semi-circular desk area on the left as you entered the ward, 'only Sister and staff nurses sit there. In fact, you'll rarely sit at all.' Alex joked.

The nurses' station housed the patients' medical notes in a filing trolley on wheels, and the medicines trolley was just outside the main desk, chained to a wall. When I got the tour, Alex had promised, she showed me the sluice. To be honest, I'd already been sent there many times during the first hour to fetch or return bedpans, commodes and urinals. It was on the far left of the ward, as seen from the entrance. Here, we washed and scrubbed bedpans before placing them into a large autoclave machine which would steam sterilise the pans. I became intimately acquainted with the sluice and all its contents. As well as bedpans, the sluice contained commodes, enema equipment, urine testing tablets and test tubes, along with glass urinals.

The bedpans were made of stainless steel. Alex showed me easy ways to get them coming clean from the autoclave. We emptied and rinsed them first. The emptying was obvious, but if they weren't rinsed, they would come out of the washer clean and shiny, but we'd have to scrub the dried stuff off the base, and that was just disgusting. I wish I'd kept count of how many bedpans I dealt with on that first day alone. With most of the men in traction, they all needed daily bedpans. Having one's bowels opened regularly was a must, otherwise we had to administer something to force the issue.

As Alex asked the fourteenth patient, we helped wash and dress the same question on that first morning; she explained. 'You need to ask them every day if they had had their bowels opened, then chart it here.' Alex showed me the patient's chart that sat at the end of the bed where any inquisitive visitor could also monitor that, and other information recorded on the charts. Believe me, it wasn't always a patient's relative who would check the charts either! Initially, I found it embarrassing to ask the men about their bowel habits; after all, many of the young men on the ward were my age. "Have you opened your bowels today?" isn't the best one-liner, let's face it.

Because the bedpans were stainless steel, they were freezing cold to sit on (according to patients) unless a kind nurse ran them under hot water first. This depended on what side of bed the nurse had got out of that day.

That day and every day afterwards, we also emptied glass urinals after measuring (sometimes testing) the contents and charting the amount of urine passed. We also placed urinals in the Autoclave for washing, being careful not to drop and break any. We were less careful with the bedpans, but once you've heard the sound of a heavy stainless steel pan hitting a marble floor, you never forget it.

We helped some patients out of bed to use commodes. Alex showed me how to wash down and disinfect the pots, seats and handles in-between use. 'We also check them at the end of each shift. I'm sorry to say that as the new girl, that responsibility falls on you.'

'Great,' I quipped, although I didn't really mind what

jobs, good or bad, I was given. I was in uniform and addressed as, 'Nurse.'

The ward cleaners kept the floors, bathrooms and every surface absolutely pristine despite the age of the building. It was our job, though, to wash down mattresses, pillows that were encased in plastic and bedside lockers after we discharged patients.

Once we had finished our morning's ablutions. The cleaners followed behind, cleaning underneath the beds until they were spotless. They moved the lockers out to clean behind and underneath.

They discharged two patients that afternoon and Alex and I scrubbed the lockers with disinfectant and she showed me I had to wash every part of the bed, including all the metal and parts underneath that I didn't know existed.

In the evening, buffers came out to polish the floors. I didn't see these in action until my second day, when I worked a late shift. The buffers were part of the daily ward ritual.

During that second shift, the staff nurse allocated me the task of making and dishing out evening drinks. We offered the patients milky drinks and tea. A patient asked for a mug of Horlicks, a malted drink. Even though I'd never made it before, I thought it would be simple enough. I put two spoonfuls of the powder in a glass, then added hot milk and stirred. Were the lumps floating on top what was expected? I shrugged and handed the horrified patient his bedtime drink. One of the Nursing Auxiliaries saw my mistake and came to help.

'You mix it with a bit of cold milk first in a cup or jug and once it forms a paste, you gradually stir in the hot milk, as if you were making béchamel sauce,' she explained. *Béchamel sauce? What the heck was that*? Anyway, I soon learned the technique, although I don't think I was ever brilliant at it, just good enough to get through the drinks rounds. First week's in any new job is hard, but I felt totally inadequate most of the time. Thankfully, Alex was really encouraging and the permanent staff were a pleasure to work with. Who would have imagined that nursing would include teaching me how to make hot milky drinks? That was something I thought I already knew, but obviously not.

Another one of my early student nurse jobs was to help dish out meals at meal times. The porters wheeled a huge, heated metal trolley into the ward at roughly the same time every day. We always knew it was coming by the clattering sound the trolley made. They brought it up from the hospital kitchens, where the food was freshly cooked and prepared. Half an hour before the meal trolley was due, we made sure we put the bed tables in place over the beds so that the men could get at their food. Once the meal trolley arrived, it was all hands on deck – at least, all students' hands on deck! The meals came plated up and covered with a metal lid. The lids, plates, and food were usually hot. Sometimes the plates were too hot if the trolley arrived quickly from the main kitchens. Each plated meal had a card on top of the lid with a patient's name on. It was relatively easy to dish the meals out unless the patient changed his mind and want something else. The latter was not unusual as they chose their meals after breakfast and by the time evening came; they wanted something different. Whilst we tried to accommodate, it was not always possible if there were not enough spare meals. The kitchen staff always added extra trays to the trolley for any new patients who may have been admitted during the day, which gave us a small degree of flexibility.

Once the meals were distributed, we students assisted anyone who needed help with eating or cutting up their food. In those early days, I found it easy to go at the patient's pace, but when the nurse in charge began tutting at how long I was taking, I had to try to speed up. I would have preferred to go at the patient's pace, but we were always so busy. Some patients found the constant shovelling of a fork into their mouths trying, to say the least. I found it hard not to assist patients with eating on autopilot, often thinking of the next thing on my lengthy to-do list, especially when I was new. This was when I had to be more careful not to choke the poor person I was trying to help. Thankfully, I didn't choke anyone, at least not with food; it was much harder not to do so with drinks as the temptation to give too much too fast was ever present.

One morning I was helping a young man coming round after surgery with a drink. When he started to cough and splutter, it frightened me more than him, then I really slowed down. There was no way I wanted Mrs Butcher to ask me to leave because of carelessness.

The toilets at the far end of every Nightingale ward in the opposite corner to the sluice were always freezing as we kept the windows open to reduce odours. The wind gusted right through the ward, often sending papers on the centre table flying. On my first ward and many subsequent ones, the bathrooms housed two enormous, enamelled cast iron baths separated from the toilet area by a thick tiled wall rather than by doors. The baths were very much in demand for patients, not in plaster or traction.

We used a bath lift contraption to sit patients on before wheeling them to the bathroom. The huge metal framed device on wheels contained a toilet-shaped chair. We lowered patients into the bath while they remained seated on it. The first time I used it was to help bath a man called Gerald Blake who had not long had a full leg plaster removed and who was looking forward to his first proper bath in three months.

Like everything in my first week, I found using the contraption more difficult than expected. It took two of us to manage the unwieldy beast – the lift, not Mr Blake – as it was cumbersome and not the safest mode of transport I'd ever seen. Pleased to arrive in the bathroom safely with no major collisions, I turned the wheel that raised him high enough in the air to slide him over the bath. I tried to reassure the patient.

'I'm just going to lower you into the bath now, Mr Blake.'

I tried to sound confident. Now, I had suspended Mr Blake in mid-air over the bath, hanging onto the side handles for dear life. Flo, the third-year student lifted his legs enough to get him in position. I gradually turned the wheel again, lowering him into the ready-filled bath. I didn't want to go too fast. Flo helped Mr Blake to stay seated and not slide off during this manoeuvre.

'I've got your legs, Mr Blake; you try to stay still,' she said, reassuringly. At this point he had wriggled a bit, probably because I had lost control of the wheel for a moment or got too confident, feeling I had the hang of it.

'Slow down a bit,' Flo instructed. Finally, Mr Blake landed at the bottom of the bath and we could all breathe a sigh of relief, particularly me.

The straightforward part was the bathing. Mr Blake managed himself apart from his back, but some patients seemed determined to drown themselves, throwing themselves around. Thankfully, this didn't happen with Mr Blake and my first handling of patient and equipment had gone relatively smoothly. The hard part was yet to come. Turning the wheel to raise the seat with the incumbent patient was a bit more arduous. With a little encouragement from both Mr Blake and Flo, I successfully returned him to safety.

Between the sluice and the toilets was a dayroom with comfy armchairs and a television. The powers that be allowed smoking in hospital dayrooms and ambulatory patients not confined to bed by leg traction would congregate in the day room to smoke and watch their favourite programmes. Back then there were just three channels; BBC1, BBC2 and ATV (which became Central Independence TV in 1982).

The day room was always foggy and unhealthy compared to today's standards, where smoking is no longer allowed in any part of a hospital. I was a smoker in those days, so it didn't bother me too much.

Nightingale wards also had an enclosed balcony leading off one side of the ward. In male orthopaedics, it was on the right. The balconies had glass windows and doors leading outside, with about six beds for recuperating patients who could look out onto a bit of greenery or concrete space. If the ward was high up, they could view the Leicester landscape.

Looking back, I was fortunate with my first ward. It was this Nightingale ward that made me fall in love with nursing and never look back. Happy to be assigned to male orthopaedics, I believed it was going to be good, and it was. I loved it from the moment I started.

I learned early on in my training that if the ward sister was a good one; the ward ran like clockwork and it was a cheerful place to work, no matter how busy. This was one of those wards; Sister Mayfield was always in the background keeping things ticking over and she had the superb Staff Nurse Bingham, who was a great trainer. I learned so much even though it was hard work and I was not supernumerary like students are today.

Senior students often took on the role of teacher/trainer. I was often on shift with Alex, who I'd met on the first day. She was a pretty, freckle-faced girl with dark red hair. We hit it off from day one, although we came from completely different backgrounds. Her family was middle-class, her father was a lawyer and her mother a teacher. My parents were working class, my dad a paint sprayer and my mum an admin assistant. Alex cooked spaghetti Bolognese from scratch, I ate it from a can.

Once I tasted her home cooked Bolognese, I never looked back. Alex lived in the nurses' home and invited me over for dinner after an early shift. The nurses' home building was a relatively new high-rise block close to the hospital. I'd been inside before for drinks with Sue and Grace from my set. Mostly four people shared each flat. It was nothing like the ancient hospital; I liked it, and it was relatively tidy. Alex's flatmates were at work on late shifts. We were having a great chat in the kitchen and she began preparing dinner.

I held on to my jaw to stop it from dropping when I saw her remove long strands of spaghetti from a packet. I had never seen real spaghetti or raw mince. Having been brought up on tinned and processed foods, I must have been – if truth be told – relatively unhealthy. To this day, I remember the meat faggots, made from pork offal, that formed a weekly part of my childhood diet, along with tinned spaghetti and tinned meat pies. I tried hard not to give myself away – it wasn't as if I had never cooked. I had been cooking meals since I was twelve years old, but the only fresh parts in my cooking were potatoes and veggies. Although fresh may not have been the best term, as the veggies were almost always nearing rotten. If there had been a best before date, it would have been long since passed.

When I later looked at the Bolognese sauce remnants on my lily white uniform, I realised that I had probably given myself away. Alex was too polite to notice me trying to work out how to get the spaghetti in my mouth without slurping. I had a lot of learning to do, and it obviously didn't confine itself to the wards.

6

ROUND AND ROUND WE GO

Hospital life comprised rounds, rounds and more rounds. No sooner had I finished one than it was time to start the next. On top of that, we had to get used to the shifts.

Shifts were difficult at first, as my poor body never knew what was coming next. One day I started at the crack of dawn and the next at lunchtime, which wasn't so bad, but sometimes we had to work what we called the *ten day stretch.* This comprised lates and earlies for ten days without a day off in between. The late-early shifts were killers. I finished work at half-past nine in the evening, often going to the pub after work with a few other nurses to unwind and then got up at six o'clock the next morning to get ready for the early shift.

The shift patterns initially were a quarter past seven in the morning to a quarter past five in the afternoon (earlies) and half-past twelve to half-past nine (lates) with one half-hour break and two fifteen minute breaks on the early and two half-hour breaks on the late shift.

We were on our feet all day long and in those early days my feet ached, longing for air. We must have walked miles every day up and down the wards. As well as my feet, my calves ached at the end of every shift; if we had worn pedometers, I would estimate a student nurse walked at least five miles every day.

Nurses' feet are not a pretty sight. They didn't tell me before I started that smelly, sweaty feet would be an occupational hazard. We had to wear nylon tights and tight leather lace-up black shoes. As for the smell of the shoes!

Amazingly, my body adapted, which was a miracle in itself because I was not a morning person at all. I used to put the alarm clock in a saucepan on the opposite side of the room so its incessant ringing would force me to get out of bed to switch it off. Some days, I was so tired; I staggered over to the alarm half asleep, switched it off, and went back to bed and into a deep sleep. At least they saved the night shifts until later in the training.

On the first day, as well as all the washing & toileting mentioned in the previous chapter, I got to do an observations round down one side of the ward. We carried out these rounds, four-hourly on every ward without fail throughout my training and beyond.

'Temperature, pulse and respirations, TPR for short, along with blood pressure measurements, are very important nurses,' explained Mrs Butcher during our first week of training. 'These measurements will alert you to signs of infection, hypothermia, respiratory and cardiac conditions as well as shock, thrombosis and many other conditions, so never underestimate their value.' I must have drifted off during the rest of that lecture, but I remember thinking hypothermia was stretching it as you only got that climbing the Himalayas (little did I know). We had practised on each other during our training sessions and it was one area I felt competent in.

The thermometers contained mercury in the 1970s, as did the sphygmomanometers (blood pressure machines). Mercury is no longer used because of the dangers of the toxic effects from mercury spills. I should be dead now because we were always dropping thermometers on the floor and gathering up the silver bubbles afterwards. On the wall above every patient's bed, a thermometer was housed in a plastic container with pink-coloured disinfectant in the bottom. We used a trolley to do the TPR round with everything else we needed on top. The hinged wooden sphygmomanometers and sterile wipes to clean the thermometer before and after putting it in the patient's mouth were wheeled from bed to bed. The hardest part of the procedure was shaking the thermometer to get the mercury down below thirty-six degrees centigrade. I started training shortly after the switch from using Fahrenheit as the temperature measurement to centigrade. Sometimes the mercury wouldn't budge and the thermometers took a lot of wrist flicking. Until I mastered the art, my rounds took twice as long as the more experienced students. The first round became more complicated when I got to Mr Graham.

'Good morning Mr Graham, I am just going to take your temperature.' No response. Mr Graham was staring at the ceiling. I spoke louder, trying to sound more confident than I felt.

'Don't worry, Nurse, he doesn't speak,' said the man next to him.

'Oh,' I said, not sure what that meant or what to do next. Staff Nurse Bingham was about to pass. 'Staff,' I called, 'I'm doing the round and not sure how to take Mr Graham's temperature.' She took the thermometer from my hand.

'Mr Graham,' she said gently, 'I am just going to take your temperature,' and as she offered the thermometer to his mouth, he opened it and held it perfectly under his tongue. 'It's okay, Nurse, you'll get the hang of this,' she smiled, and walked on. I completed the procedure, also taking his pulse, counting for a full minute, and his respiratory rate. Mrs Butcher had taught us that the latter was best recorded while holding the pulse so as not to alert the patient to the fact that you were counting the respirations.

'Otherwise,' she had explained, 'they might breathe differently.'

I took Mr Graham's blood pressure in much the same way as the temperature. I explained what I would do, and he offered his arm so I could wrap the cuff around it. Mr

Graham, I later found out, had suffered a head injury and although he could hear and understand, the injury left him mute, so he could not engage with those around him.

Every bed on the ward was on wheels, and all the wheels had to face in the same direction. I never remember anyone telling me to do this, although I would think someone did. When you looked down the ward, all the wheels were perfectly aligned. I do not understand how this helped people get better, but in these days of Feng Shui, order might be a perfectly logical reason. I admit to giving a wheel the occasional kick to move it out of line when I was feeling mischievous, much to the annoyance of the Nursing Officer, who would arrive to carry out spot checks. Nursing Officers were the equivalent of matrons from the sixties and had seniority over hospital departments.

We carried out pressure care rounds, commonly known as 'bum' rounds, every two to four hours depending on the dependency of the patient, as many on the orthopaedic ward (young and old) were confined to bed. These rounds included washing and vigorously rubbing the patient's buttocks with soap and water to get the circulation going and prevent pressure sores. It wasn't just bums; we did elbows, shoulders, scapulae and heels as well, and it was the pressure relieving and position changing rather than the rubbing that prevented the sores.

On male orthopaedics, we taught the young men in traction to lift their bottoms and backs clear of the bed every hour using the "Monkey Poles" above their heads to relieve the pressure.

Ward sisters regarded pressure sores, the result of poor nursing care, and woe betide any ward that allowed new sores to develop. Sometimes patients were admitted with sores, and occasionally they developed because of friction from sliding up and down the beds themselves or through degenerative ill health.

Some nurses were a little more vigorous with the rubbing than others and may have unwittingly done more harm than good. I won't comment on whether some may have enjoyed it more than they should or were just plain sadistic.

It amazed me how many different things we applied to bums after the washing, including talcum powder, spirit, creams or oil, depending on where you trained.

If a patient dared to develop a pressure sore, one treatment we used was egg-white and oxygen. We asked the patient to lie on their side to expose the offending area- and then applied egg-white to the wound with a sterile gauze swab. Next, we taped a piece of oxygen tubing to the patient's buttock to keep it in place before switching the oxygen on at a high rate. The theory being that the protein from the egg-white would work with the oxygen supplied directly to the wound to promote wound healing. I'm truly amazed that nobody ever went up in flames considering how close the wards were to the day rooms full of smokers while all this oxygen was flowing.

As mentioned previously, we did regular "bottle" rounds on male orthopaedics and discovered it wasn't always urine in the bottles; sometimes the men would put raspberry drinks in them in an attempt to trick us into thinking it was blood. Sometimes there was blood, of course. We measured the urine and recorded it on an input and output chart, inspected it for colour and tested it once a day. There were no sticks for glucose testing in the 1970s, so we tested urine for glucose in test tubes. It was like being in a science lab except at my school girls weren't allowed to do science. We placed a few drops of urine into a test tube, then added a tablet formulated to turn to the appropriate colour if glucose was present. Glucose testing is much simpler now that there are dipsticks which can test urine for almost everything. We used a different tablet and test tube to test for ketones, and litmus strips to determine the Ph of urine.

~

We mostly did dressing rounds in the afternoons after all the bed making, washing and cleaning had finished and the dust had settled. We cleaned and dressed wounds once a day with some much more frequently, and we did the rounds in twos. There was a "clean" nurse who did the actual wound cleansing and dressing application and a "dirty" nurse who opened all the sterile packs for the clean nurse.

This is not a comment on either of the nurses' personal hygiene or moral habits.

Every nurse has her favourite activity, and mine was removing stitches.

We took dressing regimes seriously, as the last thing that any of us wanted was for a patient to end up with a wound infection or sepsis. We took particular care to clean around the pins (more like huge nails) that went through the patients' legs into the bones, as bone infections were difficult to treat.

I came across countless different types of wound during that first ward experience. Following falls, car and motorcycle accidents, people didn't just break bones but sustained other injuries too. Dressing rounds were probably my favourite chores, and I always enjoyed being the clean nurse once I had developed the skill. We used metal forceps to hold everything, such as sterile cotton wool, gauze and dressings, and this took an element of dexterity. They sent the forceps to a distinct part of the hospital after use for re-sterilisation.

We dressed grazes, wounds that had been stitched, cavities, open wounds, and obviously there was the occasional infected wound.

~

Doctors' rounds took place every day, but when the orthopaedic consultant and his entourage did a twice weekly ward round, we students had to make ourselves scarce. Patients could not use a commode or be wheeled to the toilet while his round was taking place. The consultant was a near-on megalomaniac who met the slightest noise with a glare and a 'tut, tut,' and woe betide any patient who dared ring his buzzer. Sister always had to be on duty; or at least a senior staff nurse – we student nurses had to go to the sluice out of the way.

Some surgeons were and are pompous, but I have also met some who are quite normal and yes, surgeons do sometimes have relationships with theatre sisters and/or scrub nurses. It must be those long hours gazing into each other's eyes over an unconscious patient. I never came across female surgeons having a relationship with a nurse, as there weren't many of the female surgeons about when I started out, but I'm sure it has happened. We're talking about the 1970s, so few hospital staff were open about being gay. Ward nurses and doctors also had relationships, and some got married, although it didn't happen with the frequency that *Casualty* or *Holby City* would have us believe.

The nurses' uniform had a long-standing tradition which stemmed back to Florence Nightingale. Little did she know that the later uniforms would become the slushy, stereotypical object of desire. The "Carry On" films have a lot to answer for.

My first uniform was a plain white cotton-polyester mix, which was see-through, and impractical in terms of colour and design. The uniforms had been given to us during our

PTS and we had been so excited to get them. They supplied us with three dresses, a navy Macintosh which was for outdoor travelling, a navy cape for walking around the hospital grounds, and cardboard hats. I absolutely loved the cape, but as there were no real grounds to wander around at the Leicester Royal, I would have to wait until they based me at the Groby Road Hospital to wear mine. The live-in girls got to wear theirs to cross the road from the nurses' home to the hospital. As I travelled in by bus, it was the Macintosh that I wore, mostly.

They washed uniforms in-house through the laundry, which could be quite tricky when we only had three and worked full time; I lost a beautiful silver cross my cousin had bought me after sending it unwittingly to the laundry in my uniform pocket because we weren't allowed to wear any jewellery other than a single wedding ring. The cross was never returned. The uniform used to ride up as soon as I bent down to do anything and I felt like a granny having to wear a full length under-slip, something I had never worn prior to nurse training. Whilst the white looked smart when new, it was inappropriate when dealing with blood, gore, vomit and all the other bodily fluids that we came into contact with. I was so proud to put it on, and when I walked on to that first ward wearing it, I felt I had arrived. I loved all the pockets, and felt very proud to put my scissors and pens in one of the breast pockets, with my fob watch pinned on the uniform.

We didn't get belts during our first year of training; they

were issued in the second and third years. Throughout my enrolled nurse training, the belt was green, and then navy during my RGN training.

The cardboard hats were equally impractical. Their only use was that they had stripes depicting the type and year of training. First-year students had one stripe, blue for SRN trainees and green for SEN, second-years had two stripes and third-year SRN students, three. There was an art to making up the hats and then attaching them to the hair with grips, but I soon mastered it, although my hat would occasionally hang at half-mast. Amazingly, though, it rarely got knocked off despite all the lifting and lugging of patients we did. Sisters and staff nurses got to wear proper starched frilly material hats, and the staff nurse's hat was gorgeous, with pleats at the back.

Prior to training, they sent us a list of items we had to buy. These included a fob watch which I kept for years, a pocket pen and torch holders, a pen-torch, blunt-ended nurses' scissors and the black leather lace-up shoes. We could not wear make-up, had to keep our fingernails short, no nail polish, and as already mentioned, no jewellery except a wedding ring or stud earrings. Wrist watches were not allowed. They have recently re-introduced most of these procedures into nursing as part of the drive to reduce hospital-acquired infection; along with hand washing, as it had become apparent that some nurses had forgotten how to wash their hands. Doctors, I have to say, were never renowned for washing their hands, except surgeons who were more diligent and, if not, a theatre sister supervised them to make sure they were.

A few doctors seemed to believe bacteria only attached itself to nurses, and that once they got their medical degree, bacteria went around them onto everyone else.

The nurses' buckle was a part of the uniform we were so proud of, as we could only wear this after qualifying. Proud parents often purchased these and then sewed them onto the belt with love to be worn with pride. My mum bought me a silver buckle which fitted that category when I qualified. I still have it tucked away, although I don't wear it these days, mainly because the belt wouldn't fit around my expanded waist, but also because they are no longer required as nurses' uniforms have changed, with many now wearing trousers and tunics.

7

BEDPANS AND WALKING STICKS

The key thing that made male orthopaedics different was that there was a larger proportion of young men than on other wards. Younger men were more likely to break bones through accidents. Many admissions were because of motorbike or vehicle road traffic accidents (RTAs, we called them). Working on an orthopaedic ward should have deterred anyone but the insane from riding motorbikes. Many bikers never made it to the ward as they died at the scene of the accident or on the way to hospital. Some still didn't wear crash helmets, despite it becoming compulsory to wear them in 1973.

At the time I was encountering many of these young men in traction, I was dating a guy called Mike and rode pillion on his BMW motorbike, which I found exhilarating. It was less exhilarating when, after going out with him for several months, he proposed to me while confessing he was already married. I had a principal never to go out with a married man and I was furious with myself for not suspecting the reason we went out so rarely and always went to pubs in the countryside was not because of his love of nature... I was also furious with him for misleading me. The marriage proposal didn't go the way he intended when I told him to get lost (though I might have used slightly stronger language). Thankfully, I never saw him again.

One young man on the ward was just nineteen. He had been riding home late one night when he took a bend too quickly and was thrown off. Unfortunately, in a cruel twist of fate, his back slammed against a bollard, causing it to break. It left him paraplegic, meaning that he was numb from the waist down. This was a high price to pay for one unlucky accident, but it showed just how vulnerable a person was when riding such fast machines. The human body is robust, but cannot withstand that level of impact.

Gary took the diagnosis badly, and although initially he appeared to be coping positively with the wheelchair-confined life, when he left hospital he took unnecessary risks, almost as if he had a death wish. I met him a few years later in outpatients. He had long since left home and was living in a flat where he was self-neglecting, so much so, that he had developed pressure sores. I did my best to encourage him and besides dressing his wounds; I tried to motivate him to get his life back.

'I don't have a life,' he said. 'Girls aren't interested, they just feel sorry for me and I can't feel anything, there is nothing out there for me.' I remembered he had been in a wheelchair basketball team when he first left hospital.

'What about the basketball team?' I suggested.

'I can't play because I keep getting these pressure sores,' he snapped. He couldn't hide the bitterness he felt. He was depressed and needed more support, so I suggested he speak to his GP and try to get help. It saddened me to see that nothing I said was going in. Perhaps he later turned the corner and got his life back together in a more positive way, but who knows.

Many men on the orthopaedic ward were in leg traction, with the leg supported in a metal brace and weights holding the broken bones in place. They suspended these at the end of the bed, and it wasn't long before the rookie nurse would bump into or dislodge the weights, causing the patient to shout some obscenity. Some of them would laugh hysterically because they knew you were new to the game, but others were not so forgiving.

Boyish pranks were common, and the men always took pleasure in winding up the new girls. If it wasn't the constant, 'Hurry up, Nurse, I need a bedpan,' it was 'Nurse, hurry up, I need a bottle (urinal).' One of them once pulled me onto his lap in the wheelchair he was using and then raced up and down the ward doing wheelies and skid turns. Fortunately, Sister was not on the ward.

Bed bathing young men was initially embarrassing, but they were just as embarrassed as I was, except for exhibitionists who would try to get naïve junior nurses to help them with the urinal.

'It's your leg that's broken, not your hands,' I would smile sweetly. I learned how to handle this situation soon after starting on the ward.

Male orthopaedics was always full and always busy, but besides the fun, there was a lot of hard work. Each day would pass by in a blur of activity, but a few personalities stand out.

Sam

One of the first patients who stood out to me was Sam, or should I say, Sam and his father? Sam was twenty-seven and had suffered a head injury from a car accident. Like many people did in the late 1970s, he had been driving without a seatbelt and was propelled through the windscreen. They made seatbelts mandatory for drivers and passengers in 1983. Sam was in the first bed after the Nurses' station.

We kept patients who were the most ill close to the nurses' station, so they were highly visible. We moved them down the ward according to recovery. Dying patients were always nursed in beds near to the nurses' station, too. Sam was semi-conscious during my first few weeks on the ward and fed via intravenous infusion. He needed help with everything at first. His father, John, visited every day and we would chat while I was caring for Sam.

Sam did not understand where he was or who he was

when he came round fully. When I first met him, he had multiple stitches in his head where the surgeon had operated to relieve pressure from the brain because of internal bleeding. Spiky bits of black hair poked through his scalp from where he had been shaved. At first he slept mostly, but after a week he spoke, albeit like a child learning to say their first words. Fortunately, the ward sister allowed student nurses to chat with patients and relatives. I was later to discover that some ward sisters would tell you off for wasting time talking, even to patients.

John, Sam's father, was a divorcée in his late forties, and it wasn't long before he asked me out. In fact, when Sam got better, they both asked me out, which could have got complicated. Relationships between patients and nurses occurred but were against the rules. Some nurses lost their jobs over such infringements if found out. I refused the date offer on both counts but became friends with John and soon discovered he worked as a nightclub DJ. When we were discussing his work while I was caring for Sam, he asked if I wanted to try being a DJ for an occasional session. He had all the musical equipment for parties and clubs, but he didn't like the talking bit. At first I thought he was joking, but when he asked again I accepted on condition he didn't misconstrue this as a date. I was always keen for a new adventure, but more than that, I was struggling to live on my pittance of a salary. Women DJs were almost unheard of, but I thought it couldn't be that hard. I had the gift of the gab, so it was worth a shot, especially as the money for one night was almost a week's wages.

On the prearranged Saturday night, I was already regretting the decision, but couldn't let John down at the last minute. He drove us to a club I had never heard of in the Leicestershire countryside. It was a new venue for John, so he introduced us to the manager and we went backstage. I waited in a dimly lit room while John went to set up the equipment. Finally, he called me onto the stage and I sat behind the microphone and started rattling away. The club was dark apart from the stage where I was and as far as I could see, no-one was dancing. I played some fantastic records from the 60s and 70s, wondering why nobody was dancing. It wasn't going well at all, and the atmosphere felt peculiar. I carried on, regardless.

I could hear a lot of male voices chattering from the dark room, so I knew people were there. Once my eyes became accustomed to the darkness, I realised that the room was full of men, not a woman to be seen. Glad when my time was up, I went backstage and met another woman about to go on. 'They're not very responsive,' I explained. 'I hope you have better luck than I did. What will you be doing?'

'Stripping,' she said. Casually.

My mouth dropped open as finally the penny dropped. *No wonder they didn't dance.* John swore he didn't know it was a strip club, and I saw the funny side later on. There began and ended my career as a DJ.

Sam gradually got better but still couldn't remember

much about his former life. In fact, the sad thing was that he couldn't remember he had a wife, and it was very hard for her. They had been estranged for a while prior to his accident with a trial separation, but she loved him.

She visited regularly at first, but he really couldn't remember who she was, and as they were separated anyway, she decided it was not worth the emotional strain on either of them. She stopped visiting.

Sam left the ward about six weeks later. We kept in touch for a while. John and I remained friends for about a year. He even drove me to the airport when I was flying to Malta to visit Gail and Craig, who had moved from Watton. The RAF stationed Craig in Malta, which was my gain. The RAF left Malta in 1979, so I was lucky to go when I did in 1978, as Gail wanted an update on my training.

Another patient on the orthopaedic ward was Bill, who had been in a car accident, which tragically killed his girlfriend who had been travelling in the passenger seat. He had sustained a broken leg and pelvis, but most of the damage was going on in his head, but he wouldn't talk about it. Alas, accidental deaths were not uncommon, as I have already mentioned, and he wasn't the only one I would come across with survivor guilt.

As a mere novice, I never had the confidence to mention his girlfriend. We were explicitly told during handovers not to. This was in the days before counsellors and I really don't know how he ever came to terms with what had happened. Some days he would be happy and jokey, other days he would be dark and brooding, and sometimes he could be a real pain.

It hurt me one day when he snapped, 'Just go away, Dawn,' for no apparent reason. Now, in retrospect, I understand he was in shock and grieving. On top of that, he had all the guilt mixed in, as the accident had been his error. He needed psychological help, but instead he got a visit from the police. A psychiatrist saw him, but he didn't engage with her, and his needs were way beyond me as a newcomer. I felt for him, though, being of a similar age.

These highs and lows, feelings and dilemmas were ones I either came to accept and deal with or I'd sink. Because I was human, I felt the patients' vulnerabilities. Some nurses and medics advocated not getting emotionally involved. I didn't feel the latter was very helpful to either nurses or patients, but many of the tragic situations a nurse comes across must be dealt with in a way that maintains a level of compassion while not being overwhelmed by them.

Dealing with tragedy

A tragedy happened one morning involving a young man aged twenty-five who had been admitted the day before, with multiple fractures following a car accident. A nurse noticed he had a rash on his chest and he complained of breathlessness. She called the doctor, who was with another patient across the ward. Within minutes, this young man collapsed back on the bed. The "Crash" team tried to resuscitate. Tragically, he didn't make it despite everyone's best efforts, and it later turned out he had a rare complication that could follow bone fractures. He had developed a fat embolism. Events such as this one are extremely rare, and most nurses I have spoken to have never come across anyone with a fat embolism. Pulmonary embolisms that could also be fatal were not as infrequent. When anyone dies suddenly on a ward, particularly one so young, it affects everyone on a shift.

I would somehow learn to laugh and cry as I tried to help people get through some of the hardest times in their lives. All this, while also trying to grow up myself. I was only eighteen and was witnessing traumas that most people may never come across in a lifetime. There were many nights when I cried myself to sleep over the suffering I witnessed. Often, I felt much older than my years.

The adage that laughter is the best medicine was often true. Laughter and jocularity helped diffuse some of the tension. It's too easy to judge health care professionals for doing this, but we cannot always take the weight of a person's world upon ourselves or we would not survive. We were often caring for forty people who all needed to feel that they were the only person the nurse was dealing with that day. Giving of oneself is part of the role, though, and the best nurses can empathise with patients in a way that is unique to the patient without falling apart or being aloof.

The worst kind of nurse is the one who does not feel at all and I had the misfortune to meet a few of those. I have always wondered why such people stay in the job. Granted, it's not always possible to maintain the right balance, and I may have cried my heart out a little too frequently. I also experienced being angry, sad, scared and happy, sometimes all on the same day.

An example of one of the ironic, slightly humorous but still tragic situations happened to me while I was on the orthopaedic ward. It was mid-afternoon, and I was attending a patient next to the entrance to the balcony. I jumped when I heard a massive crash and a loud thump, and rushed out onto the balcony to see what had happened. A man was lying, groaning, on the floor outside. Opening the external doors to see if he was all right, thinking that he must have come from our ward, I heard a commotion above. I looked up and saw that from the ward above, nurses and patients were gawping through the gap of a smashed window. It turned out the man, suffering from schizophrenia, heard a voice that had told him to jump out of the window. He ended up being admitted to our ward with a fractured hip and multiple leg fractures. This was a bit of an extreme way to get admitted. We laughed.

Gropers

Early on, I discovered it was impossible to avoid meeting a groper. The groper always placed a hand where he shouldn't when you tried to lift or move him or, in fact, do anything to him. Men like this took special handling. First one had to incapacitate the hands in some way prior to any procedure. Sometimes we achieved this by getting them to take part in their care where possible and use their hands to assist, thereby keeping them under control. Others had to be more forcefully disengaged without causing them harm. Yet others who didn't get the message had to have a lecture from Sister. I remember one such occasion.

'Now Mr Smith, please keep your hands to yourself and let the nurses do their job.'

Mr Smith denied all accusations.

'Sister, it was an accident,' he said, and then started all over again as soon as Sister's back was turned. Mr Smith certainly did not get a warmed bedpan and, if I'm honest, men like him were just a pain in the neck to be honest.

Jim

Jim was a seventeen-year-old boy who had a rare liver cancer spread from his bones and would never leave the ward. Getting to know Jim was one of the defining moments of my career. While most young women were having fun, I was growing up fast in a world where families had to come to terms with unimaginable grief, and where a young lad would never reach the age of eighteen.

One day, I was behind the curtains with Jim, who had not been told his diagnosis and we were under strict instructions never to mention it. Despite this, I'm sure he knew.

'Dawn,' he said, 'can I ask you something?'

'Yes, of course.' *Please don't ask me about your diagnosis*, I was thinking as I would have to be evasive or I would get the sack.

'Can I touch your breast?' he asked the question in such an innocent, curious sort of way, he might just as well have been asking for a glass of milk. I was pretty sure I'd heard him correctly. I can't remember whether I blushed, but I imagine I did.

'I'm sorry Jim, I can't let you do that,' I said. Amazingly, the unusual request didn't offend me, neither did it shock or flatter; it was a surreal moment. I moved the conversation on as if nothing had happened. This atypical request has stayed with me over the years. Here was a naïve young man who more than likely knew he was going to die, expressing his sexuality in the only way he knew how. That poignant moment still leaves me with a deep sadness. It was a minute in time between a nurse and a patient, but also between a boy and a girl. I sat with him for a little while and talked about other things just to let him know I wasn't angry or upset, and we could still be friends.

I loved that boy who was just two years younger than I was, more than words can express, but it was a compassionate love. I admired how he coped with being in hospital for so long. On reflection, I'm certain he knew that he would not leave the ward alive because he was getting weaker and weaker by the day. He was virtually unable to do anything for himself and needed constant care.

Jim's family visited every day, and one can only imagine the heartbreak they were going through. I watched as they put on brave faces like masks as soon as they entered the ward. They laughed and joked with him while their world was turning upside down. Not enough is said in medical and nursing memoirs about the pain and suffering families and friends go through. There was little support in the 1970s.

Even Mrs Butcher couldn't prepare us for many of the situations we found ourselves in, so we just had to dig deep into our humanity and try to come up with the best response we could. Sometimes we got it right and sometimes we got it horribly wrong.

Injections

I gave my first injection to a patient while on the orthopaedic ward. We had practiced on oranges in training school.

'Orange skin,' lectured Mrs Butcher, 'is the closest thing to human skin.'

We tittered as we did at every opportunity and then practiced. It was difficult to inject an orange, I can tell you, and the needles seemed enormous. In fact, they were enormous. We administered most intramuscular injections through a long, wide-bored needle. We spent hours trying to inject those oranges. Water splashed back, needles bent, and we were lucky if we escaped unscathed.

'Ouch,' yelled Grace as she stabbed herself. 'Crikey, I'm

going to bleed to death,' she complained as the blood poured from her finger. The needles were very sharp, but not *that* sharp. Grace had a tendency to overreact.

'Don't worry,' teased Sue, 'I'll get Nick.' Nick was the latest doctor that Grace had fallen in love with, although she was actually going out with Greg, a medical student.

'He is gorgeous, isn't he?' Grace crowed. Then she forgot all about bleeding to death and treated us to half an hour of her love woes. How was she going to tell Greg that she had met Nick? This surreal monologue continued while the rest of us tried fervently to inject our oranges.

It was bizarre, but each instalment of Grace's love life kept us entertained through thick and thin.

Sue had a long-term boyfriend back home in Manchester, while Charlie and Bette were more interested in their studies. One reason we knew they would go far. I was more interested in my social life than studying, but I loved nursing, and took to it like a duck to water.

Mrs Butcher had persevered with the oranges lesson and explained that needle-stick injuries were an occupational hazard. We were to beware of the risks of acquiring blood-borne infection from contaminated needles.

In order to give my first injection, I was to jab a poor patient who had kindly given permission. I take my hat off to all the brave patients I have met over the years who stoically said,

'They've got to learn somehow, it might as well be on me.'

There was a lot to remember – we gave most of our injections intramuscularly into the gluteus maximus muscle. I trained in the days of: "see one, do one, teach one", that applied to both doctors and nurses, and I knew that once I had given this first injection under supervision, that would be it.

'Now,' I recited Mrs Butcher's instructions over in my head. 'Once you have checked you have the right patient,' *(good point)*, 'break the ampoule, draw up the injection with a needle, discard, then attach a new needle, expel any air, draw an imaginary line dividing the buttock into four, swab the area and give your injection into the upper, outer quadrant to avoid hitting the sciatic nerve,' *(equally good point as this could cause severe damage);* 'make a quick motion with the needle, draw the plunger back to ensure you are not in a blood vessel, and then inject the solution. Withdraw the needle and wipe the area with a swab, ensuring it has stopped bleeding before you leave, then re-sheath...' *(an absolute "no-no," now)* 'the needle and dispose of the syringe, needle and ampoule into a sharps container.'

I did most of the drawing up and drug checking in the treatment room with the staff nurse supervising me. This was perhaps as well because I crushed the first ampoule to smithereens. The second attempt went well, though, and off we went to the bedside with all the medicine drawn up and the syringe placed in a stainless steel kidney dish (so called because of the shape). The patient was helpful and reassuring, an older man who kept smiling and telling me I would be fine. Off he went onto his side, saying,

'Go on, Nurse,'

Staff Nurse said, 'Hurry up, Nurse, I've got loads to do.'

With trembling hands, I picked up the syringe and followed Mrs Butcher's instructions in my head by rote. My stab probably wasn't as confident as it could have been and I think the needle bounced in and out twice, but other than that, sweaty palms and face aside, it went rather well. The staff nurse was pleased and the man kindly said he didn't feel a thing, although I saw him rubbing his behind later when he thought I wasn't looking. I could honestly say, though, that injecting human skin felt nothing like injecting orange peel, but I didn't have the heart to tell Mrs Butcher.

End of the placement

Camaraderie of hospital life was important and working together with other student nurses during my formative years was something special. We had a lot of fun on the wards, went to doctors' mess parties, and the social life we enjoyed was second to none. We worked hard and played hard, as the saying goes.

Alas, my time on male orthopaedics ended all too quickly, and although I was still very new, I had learnt so much during that first placement. There was tremendous excitement a few days before I left when one day, out of the blue, one of my colleagues went to take the mute Mr

Graham his dinner and he said thank you. There was a loud clatter as she dropped the tray on the floor in her excitement. The whole ward was in an uproar as Sister was called and then the doctors. Nobody could disguise the joy they felt that he had regained his speech spontaneously. We were all talking about the miracle for days.

I said a fond goodbye to the staff nurse who had been really helpful, and to Jim, who had not died during my time, which I was glad about. On the day I left, a group of the younger men who had been let loose from traction braved using their walking sticks and walked me off the ward to say goodbye and thanks. It was a friendly gesture, and I appreciated it. I was making it through, and couldn't wait to get on with the rest of my training.

8

EARLY MORNINGS AND LATE NIGHTS

During training, I worked on both male and female medical wards. As a junior nurse, I was told that men were easier to nurse than women because they still tried to maintain an element of manliness and, therefore, were less whiney. I can't say that I noticed any actual difference, and I met brave and tender souls in both sexes.

It was always hard work on the Medical wards. Patients were ill and some of their illnesses were horrendous. Conditions ranged from asthma to cancer and everything in between. There were larger proportions of elderly people on medical wards and because of the nature of the illnesses, and training before the days of "no lifting" the work was both physically and mentally taxing.

It was important to keep patients moving to prevent pressure sores and/or deep vein thrombosis, therefore, our days were filled with shifting people up beds using various lifting techniques, getting them in and out of bed, turning and generally manhandling them.

Patients would call out, 'Hurry up, Nurse, I need to sit up, go to the toilet, use a bedpan, change position,' and so on.

We would then arrive in twos and say, 'Right Mrs ..., up we go.' Before you knew it, we would have one knee on the bed either side of the patient, shoulders under their armpits. They would fly up the bed if they were light, and if they were heavier, they might move two inches. They called this lift the *Australian*. There were other lifts that, like the *Australian,* have mostly been banned from use, but this was a favourite for moving people up beds back in the day.

Lifting people from floor to bed or out of chairs and baths was common. Nurses, like patients, come in all shapes and sizes, and so there would be short size tens like me (wish I was still that size), lifting alongside taller and wider nurses. It's worse for the taller person, as they have further to bend when lifting with someone shorter. Bad backs were more common for them.

The beds were steel-framed with a backrest that pulled out, and that was the sum total of technology available.

Nowadays, the beds go up and down at the push of a button, but in the 1970s, this was not the case. For me, a Shorty, the beds were too high, and for taller nurses they were too low, hence chronic back problems. Back pain was a major reason for sickness. Nurse absences had other causes too, mainly coming under the heading of viral illness. These included late nights, family gatherings and parties.

The first medical ward I worked on was all female and another Nightingale ward. It was busy, and I met some lovely patients.

Janet

Janet was twenty-six-years-old and was admitted with abdominal pain, bleeding and diarrhoea. The diagnosis of Crohn's disease came as a shock to her. This is a condition that develops usually in young people between the ages of fifteen and thirty-five. It's an inflammatory bowel disease, although the inflammation can occur anywhere in the digestive system from the mouth to the anus.

Janet's symptoms were typical of the disease, with crampy abdominal pains, watery diarrhoea and weight loss. She had been frightened she might have cancer, but a barium enema and blood tests confirmed the Crohn's diagnosis. Although relieved that she didn't have cancer, she now had to come to terms with the fact she had a chronic bowel condition with embarrassing symptoms. Janet explained she had been having symptoms of diarrhoea, sometimes up to ten times a day, for about six months. She had stopped going out because she never knew when the pain and diarrhoea would occur. Too embarrassed to go to the doctor, she'd hidden herself away in her one-bedroom flat, making excuses not to go out with friends.

Janet worked in an office and although she tried to hide the need to go to the toilet so often, others had noticed. She had become worried about smells and wind that accompanied the disease and was just about to quit her job when one girl in the office who had befriended her explained she had a cousin with similar symptoms. Thankfully, this friend encouraged her to visit a doctor, and he sent her into the hospital for investigations.

Diagnosis was just the first step in her journey to coping with living with this condition, and she would have to learn to juggle medication to control the diarrhoea, pain relief and courses of steroids for flare-ups. Janet seemed to cope well until, one day, a young man turned up.

'Can you tell me where I can find Janet Ross?' he asked.

I pointed out the bed where Janet was and watched him go down the ward. I saw the look of horror when she saw him and was just about to go and ask him to leave when she burst into tears. He put his arms around her and she cried and cried on his shoulder. Seeing they were now talking, I closed the curtains to give them privacy. Later, when I spoke to Janet, she told me the story.

'I met Jake when I was twenty-three on holiday in Spain. He lives in London. We went out together, seeing each other at weekends and for holidays. Just when all these symptoms started, he took me out to a posh restaurant in Covent Garden and proposed. I was over the moon and said yes, but then I got worse. I thought I had a serious illness. Because of the diarrhoea, I kept putting him off coming to Leicester, and I kept cancelling going to London. The last time he came up here, we had a row. He said I didn't love him anymore and thought I was seeing someone else. I told him we needed to finish, and he stormed off back to London.'

They had both been miserable ever since and would never have seen each other again if he hadn't phoned her mother the day before coming to visit in a last-ditch attempt and asked if Janet had found someone else. Her mother told him the full story. It devastated him that he had not tried to find out what was worrying her, so he took a day off work and travelled to Leicester the next day. Jake became a rock in Janet's recovery, supporting her every step of the way. After we discharged Janet, they got engaged again, and hopefully the relationship succeeded despite her illness.

A few years later, I was at a nightclub in London with one of my flatmates and met a guy called Lance who asked me out. He lived in Sussex, and he invited me to spend a day visiting the sights such as Chichester Cathedral. We were both interested in photography, and I still have some amazing photos from that day out. Lance seemed on edge all day, and I thought this was because he was nervous about our first date. We went back to his flat and then he told me his story. He too had Crohn's disease, diagnosed when he was twenty-two; he was now thirty, but unfortunately his disease didn't improve with medication and he had ended up with surgery and an ileostomy.

An ileostomy brings out a loop of the small intestine

through an opening in the lower abdomen, and it then passes faeces through this opening into a bag. Because the waste doesn't reach the large intestine, it is very runny and offensive smelling. This surgery had obviously devastated Lance, and he thought going out with a nurse would help, but it was obvious that he was very bitter about it and the effect it had on his sexuality.

To be honest, this was all a bit too much for me and probably for him on a first date, and we parted with no plans to see each other again.

It's not unusual for men to ask nurses out because of some hidden agenda. Obviously, for some, due to watching too many "Carry On" movies, but for others, it's like my experience with Lance. What Lance needed was counselling to help him overcome his problems and then to find a girl similar to Janet's Jake. The last thing I wanted after caring for ill people all day was to go home to someone wanting a nurse. Dealing with what life hands out is one thing, but this would have been something else. I liked to pride myself on the fact that if someone asked me out, it was because they liked me or found me attractive, not because of my job.

Enemas

Constipation was a common reason for admission to a medical ward, and the treatment in severe cases was a soap and water enema. Mrs Johnson had been transferred to the ward with constipation in a lot of pain. She was writhing about on the bed. It was time for me to give my first soap and water enema. Off I went to collect all the equipment on a trolley: incontinence sheets, long thick rubber tubing, connectors, a funnel, K-Y Jelly, a jug of tepid water and the container of green soap.

At the bedside, I explained to Mrs Johnson what was going to happen.

'Now Mrs Johnson, don't worry, *we* are just going to give you a "little" enema,' (there was nothing little about it). 'Once the fluid is in, you need to try to hold on to it for as long as possible and you'll feel better in no time.' I was really proud to use the "we" word, not that Mrs Johnson could give a toss.

With Mrs Johnson on her left side, I donned a plastic apron and gloves, looking something like a pathologist out of *Morse*. It was time to proceed. I connected the funnel to one end of the tubing, that I'd already joined with other tubing via plastic connectors. These connections often came apart during this procedure, soaking many a nurse and many a bed. I applied K-Y jelly to the other end of the tubing, which I passed into the rectum, and then I poured the soap and water mixture into the funnel. No sooner was it in than it was out again; spluttering noises were emitted with each passage of greenish-brown coloured water.

Trying to reassure Mrs Johnson and myself that this was just a simple procedure was harder than I thought. When I'd seen others do it, it hadn't had quite the same dramatic effect; some leakage, but not a shower. Staff Nurse Baines soon realised that I was being a little over-cautious with my insertion of the tubing, and it was only half an inch inside the rectum. She guided my hand and helped me to push the tube further in. While there were still some emissions, it was more like a trickle than a torrent. Obviously still a nurse in the making and not totally confident or competent yet.

I'm pleased to say, though, that this is another procedure that is no longer practiced and enemas are now minute in comparison. Compare Mount Everest with an anthill, and you will get the gist.

Just a note on the old incontinence sheets that we used to protect beds from leaks – well, they just didn't. The plastic-backed sheets were disposable and overlaid in what looked like papier mâché. They didn't retain any fluid and would move, tear and disintegrate under patients' bottoms. The bed sheets still had to be washed continually unless we used at least four incontinence sheets on one bed, and even then the liquid would make its way onto the sheet.

The only useful items were the sheets of plastic laid over the central part of the bed where a patient would sit. We then covered these with draw sheets, but even they were not foolproof. The NHS wasted millions of pounds on products that were of little use.

Mrs Brownlee

Mrs Brownlee had bowel cancer, and I got to know her well. She was just thirty-eight-years-old with three young children aged eight, six and four. She was in a bed next to Mrs Blake, a patient with ulcerative colitis who prided herself on being a palm reader. Thankfully, Mrs Brownlee didn't have her palm read. She fought so bravely and I never once found her feeling sorry for herself; we always had a laugh and joke. After they discharged her, we kept in touch for a few years until she finally lost her fight with the dreadful disease and died.

Mrs Blake insisted on reading my palm and told me I would go very far in my career – I moved to London if that counts!

Mrs Bremner

I admitted Mrs Bremner, who had a diagnosis of liver cirrhosis, she was aged sixty-six. A lifetime of drinking had caught up with her and, on admission, she looked at least eighty. Gaunt, with very yellow skin, she looked as if she had been abroad, but not in a healthy way at all. Worry lines covered her face, and she was barely conscious.

The doctor put up an intravenous infusion, and they had given her intravenous diazepam to reduce the drink tremors. She had been transferred to us mid-afternoon on a very busy "on take" day, when we took emergencies from the

Accident and Emergency department and transfers from the Intensive Care Unit.

'Hello Mrs Bremner, my name is Nurse Brookes.' During admission, I was supposed to have a chat with the patient about the ward, how they were feeling, then take a medical and social history. Everything had to be written down before finishing with a full set of observations, checking the drip, making sure they had all the relevant charts and making them comfortable.

I had drawn the curtains around to ensure we had the customary privacy and was trying to get Mrs Bremner to talk, but was getting nowhere, as she was still sleepy from the diazepam. I collated as much information as I could from the notes sent up from casualty and had filled in most of the paperwork when she finally woke up.

'Where am I?'

'You're in the Royal Infirmary; my name is Nurse Brookes.'

'What's your proper name?' she asked.

'Dawn,' I said, 'but don't let Sister hear you call me by my first name or I'll be in trouble.'

'How did I get here?' She spoke with quite a posh accent, and I realised that this surprised me as I held the misconception that all alcoholics were rough people. No idea where I got that idea from; I can't say it was my specialist subject.

'Your sister found you unconscious and called an ambulance,' I answered.

'I bet she did.' She half smiled, and I didn't know whether she was angry or pleased. 'Is there anything to drink around here?' she continued.

'I can get you water, tea or coffee?'

'Flipping heck,' she muttered, then continued, 'How long have I been here?'

'On this ward, about thirty minutes. You were in casualty all night and most of today. Do you mind if I ask you some questions?'

'Ask away,' she said, then fell asleep. I continued with the charts, asked if I could do TPR and BP, to which she grunted consent. I then checked her IV and noted when the next bag change was due. Doctors wrote intravenous fluids up on an IV fluid chart, and we had to work out the rate in drops per minute and manually count how many drops were being released. We needed to check that drips were not going through too fast or too slow, as the plastic clamps were often temperamental. Too fast and the patient would get fluid overload and could end up in serious trouble, with heart failure or worse, if potassium was in the IV fluid. Too slow and the patient would get dehydrated if they were not having other fluids by mouth. They admitted some patients Nil by Mouth and had a sign above the bed to warn us and relatives not to give them food or drink.

I changed hundreds, if not thousands, of drips over the years. Once a drip bag emptied, air could pass into the tubing, making it difficult to put up the next bag. We had to flick air back up the tube until it was all gone, otherwise gravity from the next bag would cause air to enter the veins, which was obviously dangerous. More often than not, blood would flow back through the tubing via the cannula in the arm. This would then clot and the drip would no longer work. If this happened, we had to call a doctor to re-site it, many of whom, being none too pleased about it. We also had to check the entry site as there was a risk of infection or the cannula could move out of the vein and the fluid would enter the surrounding skin. Both scenarios warranted stopping the drip, which had to be re-sited.

I checked the site, and all was well, but on picking up the scrawny, yellow arm I felt sorry for this woman who was more than likely going to die here. I had read her medical history and noted that she had been fit and well until she lost her daughter in a car accident when she was thirty. After that her marriage broke up, and she took to the bottle.

There was little sympathy for alcoholics in the NHS at the time, and a minority of A&E staff were not kind to those admitted.

Trying to punish an alcoholic, sadly, just reinforces their own self belief that they are worthless, which I think just perpetuates an already vicious cycle. I met many alcoholics and drug addicts during my career, and although they can be manipulative and dishonest to feed their habit; a touch of kindness can lead to lifestyle change.

I completed all the relevant charts, noting that Mrs Bremner also had a urinary catheter. In the sluice I found a catheter stand, fixed the catheter on the stand and placed it on the floor, checking it was draining. Six months into training, and I was feeling very skilled. Not so when I first encountered a catheter on male orthopaedics, but that all seemed a long time ago. I was on a late shift the day we admitted Mrs Bremner and before going off duty that night; I went to see if she would like anything.

'No thanks, I think I'll just go to sleep. I feel exhausted,' she said, and I turned to leave. 'Dawn,' she called after me, 'Thank you. I'm sorry you have seen me in this state. I wasn't always like this, you know.'

'I know,' I said and squeezed her hand, blinking back an uninvited tear. 'Goodnight, see you tomorrow.' When I went in the next morning Mrs Bremner had died in the night. Her sister arrived to collect her things; she looked devastated. *What a tragic end to a life,* I thought, and felt utterly helpless, not for the first time since starting nursing.

Group moan & group support

The lates and earlies were catching up with me. It was a tough time, trying to study, working all hours and trying to keep up with my social life, and I wasn't the only one feeling it. One day when I went to meet some of the others in my set for a break, it seemed we were all near breaking point and we were only halfway through our first year.

'I can't take this anymore,' complained Grace. 'I'm so tired all the time and I hate the ward I'm on. Barker is a sadist,' we nicknamed Staff Nurse Baker, Barker as she was renowned for barking out orders. 'Her one aim in life is to make me look small, especially when there are doctors around.'

Knowing how much Grace loved doctors, I could feel her pain. I couldn't remember which one she had on the go at that moment.

'What's she doing to upset you?' I asked. By this time Bette and Sue had joined us and they looked just as cheesed off as we did.

'Sister asked me to pass a nasogastric tube on a patient admitted with a stroke and couldn't swallow. It was my first one,' she managed a smile of excitement, 'but then she sent Barker to supervise. Well, she might as well have sent Jack the Ripper. It couldn't have been more frightening. She hates me. As soon as we went into the treatment room and I started setting up the trolley, she was snarling. "That's not right, Nurse Tanner, you've forgotten the K-Y."' This was used to lubricate the tube to make its passage through the back of the nose, past the larynx into the oesophagus easier.

'I hadn't forgotten. She just wouldn't give me time to set it up before she started criticising. I was going through the list Mrs Butcher had taught us and how we'd set up in PTS, trying to memorise the last one I'd seen Julie, the third year do. But no, Barker, or should I say Jack, wouldn't let me think. She kept tutting and looking at her watch. "At this rate, Nurse the patient will have died of starvation before we get there." I finally got the trolley ready, gave Barker one of my fiercest looks, and marched out of the treatment room to the patient. When I got there, I ignored Barker completely and introduced myself to the patient, explaining what I was going to do and then Barker interrupted: "Good morning, Mrs Askill, I am Staff Nurse Baker and this is Pupil Nurse Tanner. I'm here to supervise the procedure and make sure the trainee nurse does it correctly," she sneered at me. "If you are not happy at any point, please squeeze my hand and I will take over, is that OK?"'

Grace was nearly in tears at this point. 'The patient nodded and then she looked at me sympathetically, even though she was the one who had had a stroke. I wanted to hug her and thank her and determined to get it right, despite Barker. God must have heard my prayer because at this point Sister Mason came in and told Barker she needed to do the medicine round, and that she would supervise. The entire atmosphere changed and Sister introduced herself – even Mrs Askill looked more relaxed.' Grace was laughing now and coming out of her morose state. The caffeine was kicking in.

'Well, what was it like?' we all chanted in unison as none of us had carried out this procedure on an actual patient yet.

'It went really well. Mrs Askill was brilliant at not getting too tense and, after the second attempt, it was in the stomach. It was so exciting. I aspirated with a syringe like they had taught us and squirted a small amount of the contents on blue litmus paper, and it turned pink so I knew it was in the stomach. Sister was delighted and told the patient how good I was to which she nodded, and then I could give her the first feed. Adrian came up to me afterwards and said I was a star.'

Now I remembered. Adrian was the latest flame, a senior medical student in his last year.

'I'm so jealous,' Sue sighed, and then frowned, looking as if she might burst into tears. This was so unusual that we all looked at her.

'What's the matter?' asked Bette.

'Graham finished with me last night. He said it was too difficult with us being apart and that he had met someone else. The worst thing was, I only had enough change to hear this before my money ran out and so didn't even get to finish the conversation. I thought we were so happy, I thought we would marry.' At this point, the tears flowed and we could see from her swollen eyes this wasn't the first time she had cried. The news stunned us. They had seemed the perfect couple; they had met at school and been dating since they were sixteen. Sue hadn't even looked at another guy since starting training and had gone home to Manchester whenever she could, although it was difficult with shifts, and Graham was at Manchester University studying History.

'I can't believe it!' said Bette, 'what a b..........'

'I know how you feel,' Grace sympathised. She had been through more than enough breakups already, although mainly of her own doing. 'There's a doctor's mess party on Saturday night and you are coming, my friend.' She continued, as if this would solve all ills and mend the broken heart we were witnessing.

'I think we should all go just for the sake of getting a drink and forgetting about work for a bit; we don't have to go looking for men.' I shot a warning glance over at Grace.

'That's true, we don't. We will just have some girl fun and a few drinks – that should help. We're back in school on Monday so that will be great and I can celebrate never having to see Barker again.'

'Maybe,' said Sue. 'I was wondering whether to go home and have this out face to face, but if he's met someone else, I guess there's not much point. I don't want him to see me like this, anyway. Or my parents.' My heart went out to her; she looked so sad. I had never experienced heartbreak in my relationships as I had always done the breaking up. I mulled that unbidden thought over for a moment, feeling guilty about the hearts I had probably broken, but it didn't pay to dwell, so I got up.

'Better get back to the ward. See you Saturday; I'll come to yours to get ready if that's all right?'

'Of course it is. Why don't you sleep over, save you getting a taxi or worse still, walking?' Bette replied. They knew I was a terror for walking home late at night after the buses had stopped running, and they worried someone would attack me one night. Sometimes I worried too, but I'd rather walk home than not go out, and I didn't have money for taxi fares. It was easier when I moved out of home and lived nearer to Charles Frears. I did always run up my street after walking home via the main roads; the worst bit was walking past Fosse Park, and I always crossed over to the other side of the road in case anyone was lurking, but thankfully no-one ever was.

They held the mess party in the downstairs rooms of the doctors' halls of residence. Music blared as we arrived. *Dancing Queen* by Abba greeted us as we walked into the room, and I immediately felt like dancing. Grace spotted Adrian and disappeared in a flash.

'So much for a girl's night out.' Bette groaned. Sue still looked out of sorts, which was hardly surprising. We helped ourselves to a drink from the makeshift bar. Booze was always free at these parties. The doctors had more money than we did and stocked up the bar before the party started. I held a glass of white wine in my hand and could see Sue was getting close to tears as she noticed people pairing up.

'Come on,' I said, 'let's dance.' By now Elvis Presley's *Way Down* was playing. I put my drink on a table and we found some space and danced around our handbags. Sue was drinking Bacardi and Coke, the drink popularised in the 1970s from people holidaying in Spain. It wasn't long before she was looking a lot better. Well, maybe worse for wear was more like it, but at least she was smiling. Bette was also getting merry and had attracted the attention of a houseman I recognised from orthopaedics.

I refused all offers to dance, otherwise I knew Sue would end up in tears, and I decided to be disciplined unless she accepted an offer. I knew that was unlikely unless she was out of her head, which was not an impossibility with the way she was downing the Bacardi. Sue wasn't really a drinker, and a few hours and many drinks later, she was rambling.

'I loved him. How could he do this to me? I hate him. I need to find a phone box and tell him how much I hate him.' She staggered off with me in tow.

'No, that's not a good idea,' I said. 'Anyway, he won't be home, it's Saturday night and he will be ....,' blast, I shouldn't have said that.

'You mean he'll be out with a slut.' I didn't think that was fair to the new girlfriend, but I wasn't going to argue.

'Well, he might have gone home to see his parents,' I said weakly.

'Yeah sure, I'll ring him there then; he needs to be told what a despicable pig he is.' That's about as strong as it got with Sue. Just then Bette joined us and, realising I was in a fix, intervened.

'Come on, let's do the bump.' This was a popular dance of the 1970s involving swaying or jumping and bumping hips to the beat of the music; during the dance, girls would dance together or with boys. The locomotion was still popular then as well, and the evening ended at around one o'clock in the morning with this dance. By this time, Sue could barely walk, so we agreed to split a taxi. Grace suddenly appeared from nowhere and we made our way home. Sue was still rambling about making phone calls, but she wouldn't have been able to dial a number, so we just agreed with her. Grace was pretty far gone as well, although thankfully, she and Adrian hadn't fallen out.

‘I think I’m in love,’ she said, but Bette and I shut her up before she waxed lyrical and upset Sue even more.

‘It was a great time tonight,’ said Sue.

Yeah, great, I thought, as I had spent the whole evening playing nursemaid. Having behaved like Mother Teresa for the whole evening, I felt tired. We got to the flat and Sue promptly threw up all over their lounge.

9

CRAWLY THINGS

When Mr Jarvis was admitted to the ward, I was the admitting nurse. He was eighty years old and had been found on the floor at home.

Shortly after he arrived, I went to assess him. It was clear from his dishevelled condition that he was in a state and had not washed for a very long time. Black dirt was ingrained into the wrinkles on his face, and the skin of his arms and chest was dry and filthy. His face was round, with protruding eyes that didn't seem to fit and could have belonged to someone else. The matted grey hair covering his head could have been mistaken for being black, except for recent growth showing its true colour. Scales of dry skin covered his scalp, with telltale dandruff mixed in with the dirt on the top of his head. Even his eyebrows were flaked with scale. His fingernails were excessively long and caked with dirt. His clothes were, quite frankly, ready for incineration.

A stale, mouldy smell surrounded him. Once I had cautiously removed his jacket, shirt, and vest and deposited them into a plastic bag, I decided a hospital gown was the most appropriate attire at this time. He would need a bath as soon as I finished the assessment.

Mr Jarvis had been to casualty before arriving on the ward where they had excluded any broken bones. I suspected he hadn't spent very long there, unsurprisingly. There was no immediate evidence of fleas or head lice, so I helped him take his trousers off and noticed he had grimy crepe bandages covering both of his lower legs.

'Did you put these bandages on yourself, Mr Jarvis?' I asked.

'Yes, Nurse. I look after myself, you see.'

A matter of opinion, but it wasn't time to nit-pick. 'Do you know when you last changed them?'

'Can't say I remember, Nurse. I expect it was a while ago.'

I helped him into a gown to protect his dignity before explaining I was going to get a dressing trolley. 'I need to remove those bandages and see what's underneath,' I explained, grimacing inwardly. I was more experienced now and could make these decisions for myself.

I called one of my colleagues, another first year called Natalie, to assist, and we returned to Mr Jarvis to begin the excavation of what lay beneath the ragged bandages. As I started removing them, holding my breath at the same time, I detected movement underneath. At first I thought this was my imagination, but the more bandage I unwrapped, the more movement I saw. Finally, I revealed what was underneath. Both Natalie and I took two steps back, aghast, and stared at the sight in front of us. Hundreds of huge maggots were busily wriggling around on the wounds.

Natalie had already left, way too quickly, in my opinion, leaving me to take a big gulp. I smiled at Mr Jarvis,

'I need to fetch something. I'll be back in a minute.'

Feeling quite sick, I withdrew to a safe distance and called for Sister Garfield, noticing Natalie was nowhere to be seen.

Sister came and looked, behaving as if the sight was an everyday occurrence. I guess she had seen it all before. She took it in her stride.

'Mr Jarvis, you appear to have some visitors on your legs – maggots, I believe.' Mr Jarvis' eyes protruded even further, reminding me of Gollum from *Lord of the Rings*.

'I thought there was some nibbling going on down there, Sister.'

Sister turned to me, 'Note how clean the wounds are, Nurse Brookes. The maggots have eaten all the slough (pronounced sluff, meaning dead tissue) away.' Slough was difficult to get rid of usually. 'Now just wash them off and make sure they are all removed and disposed of. I don't want any loose on the ward. Then clean the wounds with hydrogen peroxide and dress them with eusol and paraffin-soaked gauze.'

Why me? Where was Natalie? 'Yes, Sister.' I sighed. In later years, sterile maggots would become part of wound debriding for some patients and are now bred in sterile conditions solely for this purpose on a farm in Wales.

Hydrogen peroxide, eusol and paraffin, however, would be condemned for being too caustic and damaging wound beds. They are no longer used in wound treatment.

This was one of life's little ironies, although we don't breed maggots ourselves, thankfully.

Mr Jarvis recovered after lots of washing and feeding. His leg ulcers also improved, and we sent him home spick and span, although I doubt he stayed that way for long.

On the same ward, I met Mrs Rafferty, a Gypsy (nowadays referred to as travellers). Mrs Rafferty was admitted with a breast lump that had been found during a routine examination by a GP who visited the Gypsy camp to encourage people to register with his surgery.

This was quite innovative in its day, as for many years travellers received poor healthcare as their lifestyle made it difficult to register with GP practices. They also held a general mistrust for authority.

Mrs Rafferty was tiny, even compared to me. I think she was about four feet, ten inches tall and very thin. Her clothes had seen better days, although they appeared clean. I handed her a nightdress to change into and explained I would be back to take some observations and ask some questions before the doctor examined her.

When I returned, she seemed even smaller, buried in the one-size-fits-all hospital nightdress with the large split at the back. I never understood the sense of the gaps, except they were designed to make toileting easier. We gave hospital nightdresses to men and women. They were a source of amusement when patients forgot to hold them together at the back, leaving exposed buttocks for all to see.

'I just need to check your temperature, pulse, and blood pressure. Would you mind sitting on the bed?' I explained.

She jumped up on the bed like a spritely youth. As I reached to get the new thermometer from the wall behind the bed, something in my peripheral vision distracted me. Sheepishly looking in that direction, I noticed a movement in her hair. I tried not to gasp and resisted the urge to jump back. An irresistible itchiness came over my own head immediately. I excused myself for a minute and went to fetch Sister Garfield for the second time in the space of a few weeks.

'My, my, Nurse, we are having quite a month aren't we?' she chuckled. Sister was again not at all fazed by the turn of events, although she didn't get quite as close as she had to Mr Jarvis. 'Mrs Rafferty, have you noticed your head itching?' she asked.

'Well, now you mention it, I have been a bit scratchy recently. Is there a problem?'

'I'll just take a quick look.' Sister had a very quick look indeed, briefly parting the hair. 'Oh yes, I see the problem.

You have some unwanted visitors. Would you be okay with Nurse applying some treatment in the bathroom?'

'That would be grand,' replied Mrs Rafferty.

No, it wouldn't, I thought, but having been treated in the past by my mum when the nit nurse found nits at school, it was something I felt able to do. Not with my usual enthusiasm, I might add.

I bought some head lice shampoo on the way home and treated myself as soon as I got through the door and thankfully didn't get any visitors myself.

10

DON'T GET OLD, NURSE

For my geriatric placement, the powers that be sent me to the Leicester General Hospital. It was tricky getting there by bus, and if I was on an early shift on a Sunday morning, I had to walk. This meant leaving an hour and a half before a shift. It was torture for a nineteen-year-old craving a lie in.

The memory of one cold Sunday morning trek across the streets of Leicester stands out in my mind. I dragged myself out of bed at five-thirty, having gone to bed at midnight. I quickly and quietly washed and dressed so as not to wake my mum or brother (I was still living at home at the time). Whispering to myself not to make a noise, I slipped out of the front door, closing it as gently as I could. It was still dark and freezing outside. Frost covered the pavements and the roads, and the cold air shocked my lungs into a coughing fit. The streets were silent; I didn't even meet a paperboy. As I walked, the bracing, ice-cold air woke me from of my sleepy state. Early morning light gradually forced its way through the darkness while I trudged along, hugging my coat and scarf close to my body. By the time I walked onto the ward an hour and a half later, daylight had won, and a bright winter's day followed.

I was still coughing and hacking when I got to work, not helped by the three cigarettes I'd smoked on the way in; I hadn't given up the habit yet. There was no time to recover from the walk. It was action stations as soon as I arrived. Being busy was perhaps as well, as the canteen didn't open that early on a Sunday morning. In fact, nothing opened that early on a Sunday apart from hospital wards.

The charge nurse was an Italian hunk. Attractive wasn't the word, but boy, did he know it. He was both charming and a flirt. It was easy to see why he had become a nurse, and it wasn't for the money. He had a well-deserved reputation for being a ladies' man, and it was difficult not to fall for his charm. In fact, I did fall for his charm and had a brief relationship with him. Brief liaisons were all he went in for, as I also discovered later he was another married man who neglected to wear a wedding ring. I wasn't an angel either, though, as I had a boyfriend at the time. I don't think I got the best out of my geriatric experience because it was rather distracting falling for the man in charge.

Geriatric wards were not pleasant places for patients to be in. Most of them were either in bed or sat out in chairs by their beds. It made me sad seeing most of these people (many of them war veterans), needing help with eating, cutting up food, drinking and most other things. Photos on their bedside tables reminded me that they had been young once and had lived active lives just like me and my friends. Most had loved ones who cared about them and wanted them to get better and go home.

Many of the patients were incontinent, and some were confused, either because of an acute illness or from dementia. Geriatric wards were also what we called "heavy", as we were constantly lifting people and moving them up and down beds, in and out of chairs, on and off commodes, bedpans and such like.

As well as being physically demanding, it was also psychologically draining. It was an absolute tragedy seeing so many sick old people all in one place. One recurring theme that ingrained itself in my psyche from the geriatric ward was that almost every patient I helped would say, 'Don't get old, Nurse,' as if I had a choice in the matter. It was said jovially, though often with a hint of sadness.

As I have got older myself, I understand the meaning behind the sentence, which was often said with a faraway look in the eyes. Many of the patients would talk about when they were young. Nurses who are impatient might miss that this is because patients want to remember being able-bodied and youthful. For those who take the time to listen, every person has an interesting and unique story to tell.

A harsh lesson

Mr Broadley was a seventy-eight-year-old gentleman who had been admitted to the ward following a fall. He was a quiet man, who kept himself to himself and had always looked uncomfortable with being on a ward full of other people. He didn't give away much at all and it was difficult to get to know him.

One day, I was on an early shift, following a late the night before. I was rushing around helping people cut up food or eat their meals. It had been yet another heavy and busy shift, and I was really looking forward to my lunch break. I was clearing away lunch trays, feeling tired and hungry. I got to Mr Broadley and found he hadn't touched his dinner. He was a patient who could feed himself, so I found myself being a bit short with him.

'Come on Mr Broadley, eat your dinner.'

He looked at me with faraway eyes and said, 'I'm not very hungry.'

'Well, you need to eat to get your strength up. I'll leave you with it for a bit longer.'

I don't understand why I felt slightly irritated with the poor man who just wasn't feeling hungry. Because he was so private, we hadn't built up any real rapport that might help me detect anything was amiss. It might also explain my impatience, or perhaps I was just feeling irritable because I was dog tired. I left him to it and rushed off to finish all the other trays and went off the ward for lunch.

When I returned from my lunch break, they had pulled the curtains around Mr Broadley's bed. There was a hush on the ward and I sensed immediately what had happened. They had found him dead in his chair an hour after our conversation, fork still in his hand. It absolutely gutted me. Not because he had died, as many patients died, and a quick death was often a blessing in disguise. It gutted me because the last words he had heard from another person on this earth was a rebuke over not eating his dinner. This, and the remorse I felt at being mildly annoyed with him.

No kind last words, no compassion or empathy, just 'eat your dinner' and then this quiet man exited the world.

The guilt I felt over that incident was tremendous and went deep. If only I could have turned the clock back, I would have asked him how he was feeling, whether he had any pain, squeezed his hand, anything but 'eat your dinner'.

The encounter with Mr Broadley was another reminder that nursing was no ordinary job. If I had worked in an office and got irritated with someone, there would usually be time to patch it up or get over it. But in nursing, particularly geriatrics, death was common and what I said and how I treated people mattered.

Later that afternoon, when his family came to see the body, I could barely look them in the eye. As she left before the porters came to collect the body his daughter looked at me with tears in her eyes, and said.

'Please look after him. I know he's just another patient to

you, but he's my dad.' As if I hadn't felt bad enough before. I felt fifty times worse. Was she a mind-reader?

I assured her I would treat her father with dignity and respect, which I did. After he had left the ward, I went to the toilet and cried my eyes out. It felt like I was the worst nurse in the world, and it took me quite a while to get over that one.

I would love to say I have never been irritated with a patient since, but I'm human and have all the frailties that go with it. I do the best I can in a stressful, emotionally demanding and ever-changing job.

Learning from Mrs Renshaw

Mrs Renshaw was a ninety-year-old who had been admitted via the medical ward suffering with breathing difficulties. Her breathlessness was related to congestive cardiac failure, and she needed a brief spell of convalescence.

She was breathless after a few feet of walking and a little forgetful, but other than that, she was amazing. The physiotherapist tried to get her to use a walking frame, but as soon as she was out of sight, Mrs Renshaw would trot down the ward with no walking aids, only stopping because of breathlessness.

'Mrs Renshaw,' I protested one day. 'You know you're supposed to walk with the Zimmer frame. What will the Physio say?'

'She can say what she likes,' Mrs Renshaw replied with a

twinkle in her eye. 'It won't fit in my house and I'll be going home soon. I don't enjoy being here with all these old people.'

'Really? You know most of them are younger than you?'

'Humph, I'm still the youngest here because I feel young. I looked after my mother and my aunt until they died, but there's no-one to look after me so I will look after myself.' There was some logic to her argument, but she looked very frail. I wondered if she would manage when she got home, being so out of puff most of the time. I feared she might not be able to look after herself for very much longer. She had a steely determination that kept her going, though.

'I was a teacher, you know, Nurse, and I ruled my classes with a rod of iron.'

'Why don't I find that difficult to believe?' I chuckled.

'I think this ward is sloppy, and it comes from the top.' She inclined her head towards our Romeo charge nurse. 'He needs to get a grip and tighten the reins,' she continued.

'What do you mean?' I asked. We were both watching him flirting with a staff nurse who had come to the ward to borrow equipment. I knew exactly what she meant.

'Look at him, he can't keep his eyes off the ladies. He is so gallant, but the staff under him are too familiar by far and that leads to ill-discipline, which leads to shoddiness. Look under that bed, Nurse; dust. You wouldn't get that if he was good at his job.'

With that, she trotted off down the ward, having drawn my attention away from her lack of use of the Zimmer frame. I smiled after her, shaking my head at being duped by a ninety-year-old.

I kept an eye out for "shoddiness" on the ward after that, but other than a few bits of dust and the wheels not all pointing in the right direction, the care was very good. The patients who could respond seemed thrilled with our rather dishy Italian, especially when he flirted with them as well.

Doctors' parties

In contrast to the death and dying of geriatrics, the social life at the General Hospital was first class; the junior doctors organised plenty of parties.

Whenever there was a doctors' mess party, open invitations went out to all nurses, surprise, surprise. Mess party was an apt term, as they usually were very messy afterwards. Doctors letting their hair down was not always a pretty sight. No different to university antics really, and as most of the doctors were fresh out of university, it wasn't unexpected. There was always an abundance of alcohol, a few nurses looking for their ideal husband but most just out to have a good time with doctors looking for their ideal one-night stand.

There was a pecking order between doctors and nurses, which complicated matters. There was also the inequality between men and women in those days. Enrolled nurses were at the bottom of this pecking order. I can't say it was something I noticed early on, but it became more apparent when I was doing my registered nurse training later on. I would hear comments about enrolled nurses then that I had never heard as an enrolled nurse.

It was no wonder some SENs had a chip on their shoulder.

The doctors' mess parties were great for a laugh. I was always careful not to drink too much, having witnessed some of my friends making complete idiots of themselves. I was happy to make an idiot of myself, just not in front of work colleagues. Some of the junior doctors had embarrassing moments to overcome when next meeting them on the ward.

11

THE FINAL GESTURE

Encountering death is inevitable as a nurse, and I came across dying patients regularly. In the 1970s, death and dying nearly always took place in hospital.

The trend came in with the medicalisation of everything to do with health in the 1960s and 70s. It also coincided to some extent with the breakup of the extended family. As people moved further and further away from their roots – yours truly, being an example of this – people didn't have the same support networks in place. With no-one to care for them when they became ill, they had no option but to go into hospital.

I'm not a sociologist, so I don't pretend to comment from that point of view, but in my experience, the breakup of the extended family is one of the most likely explanations for death moving from homes to hospitals. Alongside that, hospitals actively encouraged the practice. However, hospitals were not equipped to deal with death and dying and patients did not always have a "good death".

Pain management was unsophisticated, and I frequently felt inadequate and anguished when faced with the suffering of some patients. I heard debates from time to time about whether doctors should be given the right to put an end to their suffering, a debate that remains to this day. I never came across anyone actually crossing this line myself. Newspapers confirm illegal euthanasia took place in rare cases and was dealt with by the courts.

It amazed me the strength and resilience many people showed when faced with insufferable pain, along with the knowledge that they were dying.

Diamorphine injections offered some relief, although sometimes the effect was too much, and a patient could not communicate their wishes with loved ones.

I remember sitting with an elderly man who was dying and who was in a lot of pain, but he gritted his teeth and refused to cry out. I held his hand until a family member arrived, and she told me he had been a mine clearer during the war.

'He was brave in life and he'll be brave in death, Nurse.' she said.

I couldn't help blinking away tears as I left her with him, and was more determined than ever to maintain high standards despite the 'Hurry up, Nurse' mentality of hospital life.

None of the issues associated with treatment were

deliberate. It was mainly because of the knowledge base at the time and the inadequate staffing levels on hospital wards. I can honestly say, though, that no patient who we knew was dying died alone. Senior staff always allocated a member of staff to sit with a dying person if a relative or friend could not visit.

Staff would rally round to cover the work so that a person could have a dignified death, something I hope still happens in hospitals today.

The hospital chaplain, or a priest or vicar from a patient's parish, would usually visit to perform the last rites when a patient was near to death. We were trained to ask a patient about their religion on admission, and that spiritual needs should be addressed in the same way as physical ones. Where possible, we met these needs, and there was usually a hospital chapel available if patients wanted to attend a Sunday Service. Most patients would declare themselves Church of England or Roman Catholic, whether or not they were practising. Ministers from other religions were on a list held by the hospital reception and called in when needed.

Hospices sprang up in the late 1980s. The hospice movement and many cancer charities worked hard to ensure adequate pain relief, alongside recognition and acknowledgement of when a patient was dying. Palliative care is much improved, and although end-of-life care for people with non-cancer diagnoses lagged behind for many years. There has been a push in recent years to rectify this. More people now end their lives at home, in hospices or on specialised wards. Hospital nurses still see a fair number of deaths as that last-minute panic to call an ambulance is sometimes inevitable.

Laying a patient out was a procedure carried out when a patient died on a ward, and doing this was a part of the training. I saw it as the last kind gesture we could offer to a patient following death.

The inevitable day for me came when a female patient had died and we had to get the body ready to go to the mortuary after the family had left. I went behind the curtain with a third-year student nurse, called Josie, who was going to teach me how to carry out the procedure.

Mrs Hadley was lying on her back with mouth and eyes open, but there was that deathly stillness and pallor. This pallor changes quickly to mottled blue, particularly when handling the patient.

It has been reassuring to me over the years to note that what makes up life, the soul, if you have faith, departs at death. The light in the eyes disappears and to me, what is left is a shell, as the person who was is now gone. This was one of the first impressions I was left with on seeing a dead body.

The tutors had taught me in class what to do, but as always, it was not quite as easy on an actual person. They had taught us to speak to the patient as if they were alive, which took a bit of practice, as it felt daft at first. Later on, speaking with a dead person as if they were alive came as easy as breathing. With some nurses, you're lucky if they speak to you when you're alive, let alone when you're dead! They also taught us to speak to unconscious patients, as no-one knew whether they might hear.

We had washed the front of Mrs Hadley's body when I pulled her towards me so that Josie could wash her back. I spoke to her as I'd been instructed.

'Mrs Hadley, I'm just going to turn you towards me so that Nurse Blount can wash your back.' In doing so, Mrs Hadley let out an enormous groan, and I jumped out of my skin, letting her go. Josie laughed, with tears running down her face.

What no-one had told me was that on moving a body, the air that is still in the stomach can sometimes be expelled when moving a recently deceased patient. This can make a groaning noise, as had happened to me. I eventually saw the funny side, and we continued, albeit cautiously, on my part. I paid great attention to Mrs Hadley in case she was still alive, as I had read about people being buried alive, but I think my imagination was getting the better of me. Sadly, she was dead.

Laying out a patient involved a full wash followed by plugging the back passage with cotton wool, which I always hated doing. It seemed undignified, but it stopped any leakage of faecal matter. We placed any false teeth in the mouth, which was then closed by bandaging from the chin to the head and tying a bow at the top of the head. That was another procedure I really didn't like. I tied a label to the big toe for identification. We then dressed Mrs Hadley in a white plastic shroud and placed her flat on her back. We finally wrapped the body in a sheet. Once finished, we called for the hospital porters to come and collect the body to take to the hospital morgue.

We closed all the curtains on the ward so that other patients would not see the awful metal morgue trolley. Of course, the patients all knew what was going on, although there was a conspiracy of silence. The rattling sound of the trolley breaking the silence was all that could be heard. They did everything else in hushed tones until the body had left the ward and normality resumed.

'Goodbye Mrs Hadley,' I said, and shortly afterwards, the noise and hustle and bustle of ward life returned.

Josie and I finally stripped the bed, cleaned it and made it up, ready for the next occupant waiting in the wings.

12

FUN AND GAMES

Nursing was a serious business most of the time, but we also had fun and games when we could. Not only did the antics keep us going through tough times, they cheered the patients, some of whom had wicked senses of humour. During my time on a medical ward, I learned about "a long stand".

If a new student nurse came across as a bit of a know-it-all, a senior nurse would send her or him to a neighbouring ward to ask for *a long stand*. After arriving on the ward, the student would ask whoever was in charge for the long stand. The nurse in charge would tell said nurse to wait there.

After about ten minutes, the student would think the staff had forgotten her. They would then ask another member of staff for the said stand and would be told to wait.

After about thirty minutes, the nurse in charge would return and tell the student to go back to their ward.

'But I haven't got the long stand,' they would protest.

The nurse in charge would reply, laughing, 'You have had *a long stand*.'

Finally, the student nurse would realise we had tricked them and hopefully return to her ward red in the face and with a little more humility.

Personally, I never experienced anyone being sent for a long stand, but I am assured it was common practice once upon a time. It could be one of those myths that exists in hospital folklore. Maybe I was always humble – I don't think! The nursing auxiliaries swore these things really happened.

Some know-it-all nurses who were not familiar with anatomy were sent to a nearby ward or to the medical room to find a Fallopian Tube, which of course only existed within the female body, but it was fun if a nurse fell for this one; most didn't.

Another funny story I heard from a nursing auxiliary was that a student nurse was asked to take a commode to a patient who was on bed rest, which the nurse duly did. Shortly afterwards, the patient's head could be seen looking over the curtains. The nurse had placed the commode on the bed and sat the patient on it thinking as he was on bed rest, she shouldn't get him out of bed.

There are many such hilarious stories, and I'm sure that

some of them are true and some not so true, but they make for interesting chats on night duty.

Coming under fire

Some ward sisters were helpful, and some were just plain obnoxious. I had an experience with one of the latter while working on a medical ward. Sister Makin had a reputation for being a horror to student nurses. I had been on the ward for a week when a doctor wanted to perform a lumbar puncture on a patient.

Sister called to me, 'Nurse Brookes, set up a trolley for a lumbar puncture.'

'I have never set up a trolley for a lumbar puncture, Sister,' I replied.

'WELL LEARN!' she shouted and stormed off up the ward.

You didn't dare argue. I went into the treatment room and found a trolley. My hands were trembling, and I felt panic tearing through my body. I just stared hopelessly at the multitudes of cupboards, wondering what on earth to do next. Almost in tears, I was saved when Claire, the staff nurse, came in.

Claire was from Burnley. 'What's up, love?'

I explained what had happened and she could see how upset I was. She showed me how to set up the trolley.

Soon afterwards, I heard her telling Sister Makin, 'You

shouldn't have done that to the student, you know. That were right bad that were.'

Claire and I were firm friends for several years following that incident. She lived in the nurses' home at the hospital, and we would often share a bottle of wine after a late shift and chat until late into the night. Her boyfriend was a hippy looking teacher who shared a house with eccentric friends. Claire spent her days off at his. I got to know him well, and they later married, although I think she still had to share with his rather eccentric housemates for a time, even after they got married.

As well as wine, Claire and I shared the same birthday, although she was a few years older than me. We lost touch a few years after I moved to London to do further training. I have fond memories of our friendship and am ever grateful to her for rescuing me from the dreaded Sister Makin. I avoided the Rottweiler sister like the plague for the rest of my stint on that ward.

After qualifying, I worked on the ward next door and Claire, by that time, was the ward sister herself as the ogre had moved on. We would meet for lunch to share stories, compare notes and laugh about the lumbar puncture episode.

Reminiscing

One Nursing Auxiliary had me in stitches when she told me about the time she was nursing during the war. She had been out for the day on leave, but had missed her last bus back to the hospital. She telephoned Matron to let her know she would be late. This meant she was going to be in trouble when she got back the next day, but she had no choice.

On arriving back at the hospital, Matron called her into the office.

Worried she was in for a blasting, she said, 'I'm sorry I missed the bus, Matron. I ran all the way to the bus stop but couldn't get there in time.'

'That's not why you're here, Miss Graham. I want to know why you were yelling at me down the phone.'

'Oh.' Finally, the penny dropped. It had been the first time she had ever used a telephone, and as she was fourteen miles away, she thought she needed to make up the distance and had shouted at the top of her voice to Matron, who had been almost deafened on the other end of the line.

We loved hearing this story, imagining the scene and imagining poor Matron with the phone in her hand. She explained the dilemma to Matron who saw the funny side, reprimanded her for not getting back on time, and let her go. I expect the matron chuckled afterwards.

James

James was one of the few male nurses I met. He was a third-year student nurse with a great sense of humour. We became good friends. He was a ladies' man and went out with quite a few nurses during his training.

I was never sure what the girls saw in James, as he had a severe case of acne and the accompanying nystagmus caused his eyes to flicker in different directions. Having said that, beauty is only skin deep and he was fun to be with. In his spare time, James worked as a nightclub DJ and, unlike my pitiful experience at the strip club, he was good at it. I expect it helped keep him out of debt and gave him enough money to afford to wine and dine his many girlfriends.

Our friendship fizzled out after a holiday in the former Yugoslavia when I got to know him better. One of my best friends was a Great Ormond Street student nurse called Brenda. GOS nurses, as we called them, did a combined child and adult training course, and she was doing her adult training in Leicester. I was good friends with a physicist called Robert, and the four of us took the holiday. This was long before civil war split the country.

Robert and James shared a room, and Brenda and I another. The resort was in a beautiful part of Yugoslavia called Rovinj, on the Adriatic coast, and opposite Venice. We were excited as there was much to see and do, except that when Brenda and I got up on the first morning, James was at the bar, and there he stayed for the rest of the holiday. He thought we were incredibly boring because we didn't want to drink all day, and we couldn't believe what little interest he had in exploring the country. We spent most of the holiday separate from him.

Nude sunbathing in Rovinj was an eye opener. We couldn't believe how many people walked around in the noddy. It was entertaining to watch men playing badminton on the beach with no clothes on, and very difficult to keep one's eyes on the shuttlecock!

Robert was good fun and shared our interests. We hired a speedboat where Robert enjoyed frightening us to death, driving at high speed. We also took the ferry over to Venice for the day; James joined us for that and stayed relatively sober. Don't get me wrong, we enjoyed our fair share of drinking too, just not all day, every day!

It was one of those holidays where you realise who you are compatible with and who you are not, and when we got home at the end of the holiday, James and I parted ways. Some people are friends for life and some are friends for a season, it would seem.

Christmas on the Wards

Wards could be fun at Christmas time, as we tried to keep beds empty and let patients go home to enjoy the festive season with their loved ones. In an effort to cheer up the poor patients who had to spend the holiday season in hospital, we got the doctor to dress up as a patient. We strapped drips and drains to him, then waited to see how long it took before Sister noticed.

Brian, the SHO, had agreed to be a patient, and was lying in bed under the sheets pretending to be writhing in agony. Sister Blunkett was just about to pull the sheets back and find out what was happening when his emergency bleep went off. Brian leapt out of bed, unstrapped himself and tore off down the ward, much to the surprise and consternation of Sister, who gawped after him. We were doubled up with laughter, as were the patients on the ward. Brian reappeared on the ward later and smiled at Sister, apologising for his undignified exit. She smiled in return and explained she had left the bed for him to clean, which brought him, and us, back down to earth.

13

WHAT'S WRONG WITH DECAFFEINATED COFFEE?

Miss Wright had been admitted to the ward during the night with appendicitis and had undergone surgery in the early hours of the morning. Before starting work, we always took a handover from the nurse in charge of the previous shift. On this occasion, the night staff nurse got to Miss Wright.

'Felicity Wright, admitted last night with appendicitis. Had appendicectomy at three o'clock this morning. Came back to the ward at five o'clock. Had one pain-killing injection in the theatre. She's a barrister.' Having said this, the staff nurse rolled her eyes to the sky to lots of sniggering. 'MISS Felicity Wright,' she continued in a dramatic tone, 'has also requested a side room for which she is paying privately!'

Now all the staff were rolling their eyes.

‘She can have sips of water for now and later in the day she can have full fluids and light diet.’

The handover moved on to other patients on the ward.

The issue was that of the patient paying for a side room because this meant she could afford to be different. To me, it was no issue at all. Having worked on a few forty-bedded Nightingale wards by now, if I could have afforded a side room, I would have taken it. I’m sure most of the nurses at that particular handover would have done, too.

Most nurses who were unfortunate enough to require hospital admission automatically qualified for a side room. It was a professional courtesy, so there was an element of hypocrisy here.

The barrister bit struck a chord for some too; this meant well-educated and to some extent powerful. Nowadays, nurses would ensure that she got the best care to make sure they didn’t get sued as we live in a much more litigious climate.

Whilst I understood the class barrier thing from both sides, it was never a big thing. As far as I was concerned, I would be friends with anyone who wanted to be friendly. As a nurse, I was there to do a job and one patient deserved the same attention as another. Obviously, I liked some patients more than others, but I would like to think they could never tell the difference. That was a daily challenge.

Sometimes being in a side room had its disadvantages. It was easy to be ignored or forgotten with all the commotion going on the ward. Miss Wright obviously had this experience, as she hobbled out of her room, clutching her side. I saw her and asked what she wanted.

'Please may I have a cup of decaffeinated coffee?' she spoke with an upper crust English accent.

I had never heard such a posh accent. Patients in nearby beds also started doing the eye-rolling thing, gawping at her, so I thought it would be best to assist her back to her room.

'I'll get you one,' I said, wondering where on earth I could find decaffeinated coffee. Remember, this was the 1970s; it was not a common request.

'Oh thank you,' she replied. I was trying to ignore the guffaws following us back to her room.

Hospital wards were boring for patients once they started feeling a little better, and so this sort of thing was just what a few of the more mischievous patients were looking for.

'While you're at it Nurse, could you get me a decaffeinated coffee as well?' Mrs Froome bellowed in her Leicester accent, trying to make it sound posh.

'I'd like decaffeinated pee,' shouted Mrs Rawlings,

'And I'd like a gin and tonic,' Miss Jones added.

Felicity looked back, bemused, while I glared at the mischief makers. The other nurses were sniggering, and even Sister was finding it difficult not to smile.

'Hurry up Nurse, my chauffeur will be here soon to take me home,' cried Mrs Smith, who was being discharged that day. I could see this was getting out of hand.

'Come on, Miss Wright. Let's get you back to bed,' I said,

hurrying the poor woman, still clutching her side along the final few steps of her journey. I was also trying to work out how I could fulfil the request for decaffeinated coffee. There weren't any shops nearby, not that Sister would have let me off the ward, anyway. Tremendous relief poured through me when we got to her room and Felicity said, 'There's a jar of decaffeinated coffee in my locker, Nurse.'

I could still hear laughter coming from the ward when I went to the kitchen to make the coffee, although the cheery conversation had moved on to stories about Mrs Rawlings' nephew, who worked as a nightclub bouncer.

I checked the instructions on the coffee jar, because I wasn't sure if decaffeinated was made in the same way as normal coffee, and was relieved to find it was. I was adept at coffee making, consuming huge amounts to keep me going when there was no time to eat. I took the coffee into the side room and spent the next few days looking after Felicity, as none of the other nurses would go near her. On her last day, she came onto the ward to find me and gave me a card.

'Nurse Brookes,' she said, 'I have been watching you. You will go to the very top of your profession.' With that, she turned and left the ward with her head held high.

For a humble second-year student nurse, this seemed unlikely, but it was kind of her to say so.

The other nurses did the rolling-eyes thing again, and I turned to them, exasperated, and asked, 'What's wrong with decaffeinated coffee?'

They laughed, and we all went on to the next job on our lists.

14

JERRY, MY ROCK

Nurses, like everyone, have people that are important to them, and these people often provide the support needed at the end of a hard shift. They also have to put up with the unsociable hours, which often interferes with the ability to make plans. Jerry was one of those people.

I met Jerry at the start of my second year while having a meal with my friends Jackie and Bill. After going out for a drink at the Corn Exchange in the marketplace, we often stopped off for a meal on the way home at an Indian restaurant on High Street.

It was a busy Thursday night, and the waiting staff showed us to a table containing a rowdy rugby crowd. I was sitting next to one player, and we started talking. He was tall at around six foot, had dark black hair and brown eyes, and was also handsome. I noticed a bit of a beer belly, and a beard and moustache that I didn't normally go for, but he seemed a good sort. He introduced himself as Jerry and apologised for his rowdy mates. I noticed he wasn't smoking, but he didn't seem to mind that we did (I gave up a few years later). By the end of the meal, he had asked me out.

Jerry became a long-term boyfriend (long-term for me anyway) and we made up a foursome with Jackie and Bill for the whole of my second year and beyond.

A short time after meeting Jerry, I moved into my beloved bedsit on Holmfield Road, opposite the school of nursing. Jerry was a regular visitor at weekends.

My bedsit was close to where Bill's flat was on Uppingham Road. Jerry lived in Oadby, which was a few miles north. He was a significant support throughout the rest of my training.

Jerry was a carpenter working for a building firm and earned a reasonable salary, so we went out a fair bit. I was slightly less overdrawn while going out with Jerry. We often played tennis together and chatted for hours, although he was relatively quiet for a rugby-playing carpenter. He was basically a kind young man with a good upbringing who was always polite. Spending time with him was a pleasant interlude and respite from the wards.

The only fly in the ointment was that Bill got on Jerry's nerves as he was the complete opposite, being loud and a bragger. Jerry put up with Bill, my shifts, and didn't complain too much when I worked most weekends. He even put up with me working nights.

The best fortnight we had together was on a camping

holiday in northern France. I had never been camping before, but it was fun.

Jerry had booked us on a hovercraft to Boulogne, and unusually, there was a heatwave. Jerry looked like a packhorse, carrying a huge rucksack containing our clothes and a tent. We walked for miles, and I got sunburnt which was the only downside.

We took a train to Paris for the day but saw little of the sights before having to get a train back to Boulogne. After that holiday, Jerry became more serious, and I was getting itchy feet. I knew the day would come when I'd have to tell him I wasn't as serious about him as he was about me, but selfishly, I enjoyed the comfort of him being there.

Despite the shifts, we had a good social life during that second year of training, sometimes to the point of madness. One night Jerry, Jackie and Bill were sitting in the Corn Exchange when we came up with one of those moments-of-madness ideas. I was on an early late that weekend so had finished at five-fifteen and wasn't due to go into work until twelve-thirty the next day, which was a Sunday.

Bill suggested we drive to Skegness, a mere sixty miles away, to go for a paddle in the sea. It was November, and the sea was not uppermost in my mind, but I went along with it. The four of us bundled into Jerry's car, and off we went. Jerry was good at sticking to drink-driving limits, and as far as I remember, had done so on this occasion.

We arrived at the seaside town at two o'clock in the morning. I was feeling a lot more sober and less enthusiastic than before we started the journey. Jerry parked the car next to the beach.

We ran onto the beach, more to keep ourselves warm than through excitement, and I began a fairly cautious paddle. Before long, the cold woke us up again, and I was the first one to be thrown into the sea, which of course meant that we all ended up in the freezing cold North Sea. This was all very well, but we didn't have any change of clothes with us, and more importantly, no towels. Once the laughing stopped, the cold set in.

We were frozen, wet and not a little hungry. It was now five o'clock on a Sunday morning, and back in 1978, nowhere stayed open during the night. Sunday was still a day of rest for most people, so there was absolutely no chance of warming up anywhere or finding food. Even worse, I had to be at work later that day. My enthusiasm waned rapidly, and I suggested we go home.

The journey home was less animated than the one going, and we were all shivering. Poor Jerry's car was soaked through from four wet human beings, and despite the heating being on full blast all the way home, we were barely dry when we finally made it.

We got back at around eight o'clock, as the lack of motorways and Jerry's shivering made the journey rather slow. We had breakfast at my place. The others soon felt better as they were all heading home for a long sleep.

I decided it wasn't worth trying to sleep before going to work and went in for half-past twelve. The rest of the day was a haze. While the other three were tucked up in bed I worked through to nine thirty in the evening and then had an hour's journey to get home. I definitely slept well that night after being up for over forty hours, and would like to say I learned my lesson about not burning the candle at both ends, but I didn't.

As I said before, Jerry was my biggest support throughout the final year of training and I don't think I could have got through it without him.

15

BAFFLED AND BEMUSED

I had given up smoking not long before starting a psychiatric placement. I thought I was doing really well, but there were many occasions during this tenure when I was tempted to start again.

It was often the case that psychiatric hospitals were on the outskirts of cities, and the one I worked at was just outside a village fourteen miles from where I lived.

I had recently passed my driving test, and my dad had bought me my first car, a Mini. It was an ancient jet black Mini with a "B" registration. I was thrilled when my dad proudly presented it to me and handed me the keys. The only thing was, I had only just passed my driving test, and I was going to have to drive over a hundred miles on my own in a car on a motorway for the first time because I was visiting a friend in London.

I found my way onto the M1 and was driving in the

inside lane. After fifty miles, I could barely believe it when I noticed smoke coming from the engine. I pulled over onto the hard shoulder, with no idea what to do. I hadn't even thought about joining a breakdown service prior to collecting the car. My saviour came in the form of a man in a van who pulled in after seeing my dilemma. He opened the bonnet as I didn't know where the latch was and showed me that the smoke was pouring from the radiator.

'Radiator's dry, love,' he said. 'We'll let it cool off for a bit and then I'll tow you to the next service station.' My knight in shining armour did just this and even showed me how to fill the radiator with water. Thankfully, the radiator hadn't burst, but he poured in some liquid that would fix any small cracks, just in case. 'You've got an oil leak as well. You'll need to get the gasket checked when you get home.' I'd had enough of foreign languages for one day but nodded, anyway. I never told my dad that his gift had turned out to be a wreck.

The stories of my relationship with that car, which stayed on the road for about a year, could be the subject of its own book. Whenever I drove it, smoke came in through the dashboard, much to the alarm of any friends who braved the passenger seat.

'Don't worry, I'll open the window,' I would say. Many of my friends wouldn't even get in. The passenger door didn't open, and any person courageous enough to join me had to climb in through the driver's door.

That car managed to get me to and from the psychiatric hospital for the whole placement. How, I'll never know.

The grounds of the hospital were beautiful, with a long, winding driveway up to the principal building. A pristine green lawn flanked by flower beds stood in the centre with an abundance of trees on either side. It was a wildlife haven.

I was allocated to an acute psychiatric ward, although there were some long-stay patients in the ward.

Some patients were admitted compulsorily under what is commonly known as "a Section". A Section was and is part of the Mental Health Act that enables the authorities to admit people to hospital against their will, either for their own or for the public's safety.

Many such patients manifest psychotic behaviour and have little or no insight into their condition, usually refusing treatment and not taking medication.

For a general nurse, working on a psychiatric ward was frightening, and for me it was going to be testing from day one.

The first problem I had was that as a rookie nurse, I found it difficult to differentiate patients from staff, especially as some patients introduced themselves as doctors or nurses. Psychiatric nurses appeared to be a different breed of nurse, and they and the patients blended into one when looking at it from the outside. It was also made more difficult because they didn't wear a uniform. Of course, it made sense because uniforms create barriers that hinder effective communication on equal terms. But it didn't help me, and I stuck out like a sore thumb as I had to wear my student nurse's uniform.

I noticed a large sitting room with a TV and stereo. For obvious reasons, this was not like any ward I had been on at all, so I was in an unfamiliar environment from the outset.

There was an activities room with a large table tennis table that dominated the space. There were tables and chairs with chess and other board games available, and some residents sat painting.

The communal area was like Smoky Joe's café and reminded me of a pub, but not in a good way. A thick smog hung in the air, filling my lungs with the second-hand nicotine I had recently given up.

It seemed to me that every patient and every member of staff smoked, which was really not helping my cause. I realised from the outset that this was going to be tough.

As I said, I stuck out. It was impossible not to. Obviously, I had no clue what I was doing, and I probably spent the placement looking permanently bemused. That's because I *was* permanently bemused.

There was little in the way of routine on the ward apart from medicine rounds, although these too were performed in a rather haphazard way, and it always amazed me how patients got the correct medicines if they did.

There were therapy sessions and meal times. For the rest of the time, there was no 'Hurry up, Nurse,' at all. The pace was slow and sometimes dull, but that was only because I didn't have enough psychiatric knowledge and was out of my depth.

The idea was to communicate with patients rather than rush around carrying out tasks, and whilst I agreed with the ethos, it was difficult to slow myself down, having been on the treadmill of general nursing for a while. I had always spent time with patients and got to know them as much as I could within the constraints of hospital life, but this was very different. I was a fish out of water.

Mrs Jacobs

Mrs Jacobs was one of the first people I met, an elderly lady of seventy-six-years. She was a long stay patient, having been in the hospital for the best part of thirty years. Mrs Jacobs was on the acute ward as the other long-stay wards had become full and she had been safe enough to move.

A short, obese woman with deep wrinkles carved into a round, pale face. On reflection, I'm sure she had a curved nose, looking like a witch caricature. Mrs Jacobs looked terrifying enough, but she made this worse because she always wore black. The colour added a deathly air to her being. She reminded me of Miss Haversham from Charles Dickens, *Great Expectations.* Any minute I expected her to set herself alight.

One day I was going on duty and she was sitting out on the veranda in front of the ward, in the pouring rain. I should have known better than to try to bring sense into her world.

'Come on in from the rain, Mrs Jacobs, you'll get wet out here.'

She snarled in a deep voice, 'GOD TOLD ME TO SIT HERE.' Naively I thought a little gentle persuasion would help and so I tried to gently take her arm. Next thing I knew she flew out of the chair like an eighteen-year-old, grabbed me by the arms and inches from my face yelled, 'GOD TOLD ME TO SIT HERE!' This time I believed her, and thanking God she hadn't thumped me, I sheepishly went onto the ward to see what else awaited me that day. Of course, I didn't mention my uncomfortable encounter with Mrs Jacobs on the way in.

The shifts in psychiatry were a long twelve hours, made longer by the slower pace of life and my inadequacy. I spent most days chatting with patients or attending therapy sessions. Some days I went home feeling I had not had one conversation that didn't come under the heading of bizarre, either with staff or patients. Mainly this *was* because I hadn't had a conversation that wasn't peculiar.

Nowadays, students have mentors when on a placement, so they know who to ask if they have any questions, and the mentor helps them settle in. Sadly, there was no such luxury during my psychiatric placement. I never knew who I would work with from one day to the next and although the staff were nice enough, they weren't much interested in student general nurses.

Some of the psychiatric nurses felt that general nurses were just not on the same wavelength, which, of course, was true. I was never on the same wavelength, and no-one stands out as particularly helpful. Some nurses just aren't cut out for psychiatry. I'm one of them. I tried to make the best of my time and studied to understand some of the conditions patients presented with.

Pete

Pete was nineteen and suffering from manic depression. He would have mood swings from extremes of high to low and back again, and he was apparently going through a depressive stage when we met.

Our conversations were therefore monosyllabic and morose. The psychiatric nurse had instructed me to motivate him into talking about cheerful things. I asked.

'Tell me about your happy memories.'

He began telling me about an auspicious time when his family was all together, and I thought I was doing great. Soon he was on to the family arguments, the divorce and his illness, and before long we were back to the lows.

He was a lovely looking young boy, average height, a bit on the slim side, hazel eyes and long black hair. He wore black, which seemed to be standard attire, particularly in the depressive stages of mental illness.

I got to know Pete well, and it transpired that he was a Christian, but didn't feel that he was doing very well at this, as they sometimes frowned upon mental illness in his church. We talked about his faith a lot and this always brightened him up. Often by the end of the day he was feeling more positive, but more often than not, by the next morning, we had to start over again.

Pete went for electroconvulsive therapy (ECT, electric shock treatment) and came back in a worse state than before. They never convinced me about this rather barbaric treatment, despite being assured by the psychiatric nurses that it worked.

I got into trouble with the ward sister for refusing to accompany and observe ECT. Having been called into her office to explain myself, I tried to argue that one should be allowed to be a conscientious objector to it, as it was not a proven treatment. I told her it seemed like an extreme last resort, which should have been reserved for the likes of William the Conqueror rather than twentieth century nursing. The sister was having none of this and said I was lucky I was a general nurse or I would be out on my ear. I won the battle, but clearly not the war.

There was pandemonium one day when Pete went missing; staff were sent out to look for him. They had informed his parents in case he arrived home. The psychiatric nurses were searching the village and the pubs (any excuse) but for once I felt confident I knew this patient better than they did, and as I was surplus to requirements, they let me join the search.

I walked through the beautiful grounds that, in another

world would have been so peaceful, and around the driveway to the hospital Chapel. There was Pete, sitting in a pew, head bowed, praying. After waiting for him to move, I told him that the entire world was searching for him, as he was not supposed to leave the ward unsupervised. I asked him how he had managed to get out as the ward was a "lock up".

'I just walked out with one of the visitors,' he smiled. He looked brighter, and it was from there he turned the corner. His demeanour changed along with his clothing colour – at least he went into greys and blues rather than blacks. We went happily back to the ward, and I thought maybe I could enjoy psychiatry after all.

Henrietta

Henrietta was another patient with depression who was in her mid-fifties. She was average height, overweight, with thick grey hair. She was a talented artist and when she was recovering, painted beautiful scenic watercolours.

Henrietta was nearing the time for discharge as she had made excellent progress in the therapy sessions and was conversing normally. By that, I mean her speech contained pitch variation rather than being monotone. She displayed the latter during the depressed stage of her illness.

I went into the ward one morning and found Henrietta looking dishevelled, scruffy and dressed in dark brown. She showed me the paintings she had been working on. These paintings were of various unrecognisable creatures with evil eyes eating harmless animals such as pet dogs, and they were as dark as dark could be.

'That's what's inside me,' she stated, and even I knew we were back to square one. It was disheartening. At least with Henrietta, it was clear from her paintings what was going on inside her head; it was not always as clear as this.

16

JONATHAN LIVINGSTON SEAGULL

The ward staff held therapy sessions every morning for groups of patients, with a psychiatrist, a psychiatric nurse, and a therapist facilitating them. I attended quite a few of the meetings as an observer. They were aimed at encouraging the patients to communicate and share their problems with each other.

In the timeless tradition of human gatherings, group therapy could be chaotic with one patient dominating proceedings, or with everyone sitting in (uncomfortable for me at least) silence, hoping someone else would speak. The psychiatric professionals were at ease with the silence and so I felt this must be productive in some way. For me, though, I was sitting on my hands to stop myself from nudging someone, inwardly willing one of them to say something.

Towards the end of one particularly long, silent session a

patient called Gerald muttered in a barely audible voice, 'I feel very low.'

We waited to see what words of wisdom the psychiatrist was going to offer for an inordinately long time. The psychiatrist, Dr Jason, looked like he was in a daze. The therapist's feet were shuffling and other staff members were also looking at him to see what he was going to say. He usually offered leadership and guidance. After a long time, the psychiatric nurse looked at Gerald, who was looking at the floor, and then at Dr Jason.

'Gerald has said he is feeling very low, Doctor.'

Dr Jason was unresponsive, but finally said, 'Very good, same time tomorrow then.' He got up to leave, muttering on his way out, 'Oh yes, good session, see you all tomorrow.'

Off he went, leaving everyone staring after him in disbelief. We were all dismissed, and the therapist stayed behind to speak to Gerald. We didn't see Dr Jason the next day as he went off sick with depression, would you believe?

Dr Bradley led the sessions for the next few weeks. They were a lot more lively and engaging, and I found I quite enjoyed them. Looking back, I don't know how on earth we didn't recognise the signs of depression in Dr Jason, but I think we just forgot that doctors and nurses are human, too, and susceptible to the same illnesses and weaknesses that happen to patients. We become so good at acting and putting on the professional persona that we sometimes neglect ourselves to our own detriment.

I have frequently witnessed nurses and doctors over the

years needing help but finding it very difficult to acknowledge their own frailty. I think we gain the misconception that because we are in the caring profession and people look to us for help that we must always be the perfect support to everyone else, sometimes forgetting to care for ourselves.

Julie

One day, someone asked me to monitor Julie, a teenager with anorexia. Julie was eighteen years old and had suffered from anorexia since she was fourteen when, for no obvious reason, she began believing she was fat. Initially, she had hidden it from her parents, who felt that she was going through a teenage phase, but it became increasingly obvious that she was unwell when she lost masses of weight and her parents started hearing her vomiting in the bathroom after being encouraged to eat.

Doctors had excluded any physical cause for the anorexia, and Julie had been just over five stone on admission to the ward under a Section. Her health was deteriorating so rapidly she was at risk of starvation.

She had improved slightly and was now six stone, but still very thin and wasted, looking rather like a skeleton on legs. Julie had light brown, curly hair and freckles and would have been attractive at a normal weight, but she still insisted she was overweight and that we were making her look obese. During therapy sessions, Julie was always quiet, but one day she said that she felt fat.

'What makes you think that?' asked Dr Bradley.

'My best friend,' she said.

'Did your best friend say you were fat?' asked the therapist.

'The girls at school called her fatty,' Julie said, and finally there was something to work on with Julie. The mood in the therapy session became upbeat. It transpired that Julie's best friend was overweight and had been teased at school. While her best friend had found it upsetting, she had not taken it too seriously, whereas Julie had developed a fear of bullying by proxy.

On this particular day, I had been told to observe her and make sure that after eating; she didn't go and throw up anywhere. Dutifully, I chatted to Julie and stayed with her most of the day. At some point, though, I must have been distracted, and she gave me the slip – no point applying to MI5 then!

I checked the ward and soon deduced she would most probably be in the toilets getting rid of her dinner. I was right. On entering the toilet, I saw her wiping vomit from her face. She was furious at being caught out, or maybe she was hungry having just thrown up her dinner, because, in a lightning flash, she grabbed my hand and duly bit my wrist before marching out.

Julie had taken me completely by surprise; the wound hurt from where the bite had broken through the skin. I had human teeth marks on my wrist for weeks and was lucky the wound didn't get infected. Stupidly, I didn't report it, and didn't get a tetanus injection, but lucky for me, I was okay. The experience only confirmed what I already knew; I really didn't like psychiatry.

I should have reported the incident, but nobody had told me to, and I should have had a tetanus shot and a gamma globulin shot. Human bites are actually serious and prone to infection because of the multitudes of bacteria living in the mouth.

Nurses were at times prone to injuries from patients, usually, though from the confused or those suffering from dementia. I gave Julie a wide berth after that incident and was always on my guard if she came anywhere near me. She was a smiling tiger.

Emily

Emily was in her early thirties, a lady with schizophrenia who was allocated to share a room with Mrs Jacobs. They seemed to get on very well together as they could have rather strange conversations between themselves without either of them getting upset because they didn't listen to each other.

Emily was pretty, with long, dark brown hair and big blue eyes. She had been a loner as a child; she told me and moved between jobs. On returning to her home from one of these jobs, she had become suspicious of her family. She felt they were plotting against her and that she was in danger.

Emily changed the wiring in various plugs around the house, stopped eating, and barricaded herself in her room, becoming aggressive towards her family. They admitted her to the ward under Section 25 of the Mental Health Act.

When I first met Emily, she appeared bewildered and would giggle inappropriately. She was convinced that creatures were coming out of her food and skin. Once she had settled in, I went and sat with her. She looked frightened and her eyes kept darting about as if she was seeing something or someone that I couldn't see. Eventually she said, 'What do you want to know?'

'My name is Dawn; what's yours?' was all I could think of to say.

She smiled and giggled. 'I'm a dancer, just come back from Thailand.'

'That must have been great.' This was good, I thought, she is at least having a conversation.

'They were all evil; I used to dance out of time to the music.'

'Why did you do that?'

'Because they were evil. They're evil in here too.' And so the conversation continued. She would jump from one subject to another, making me think I had missed something. Her thoughts were all jumbled up, coming out in spates intermingled with long silences, in which she would stare into space as if to go somewhere else. I thought how awful it must be for her, suspicious of everybody. Most of the time Emily appeared emotionless, but sometimes she would display anger at being in hospital against her will, and said she wanted to go home. Much of the time, she would accuse people of trying to poison her, and she became neurotic.

One evening, she tried to run away from the ward, walking off in the middle of a conversation. I caught up with her and asked her to come back. She refused, and a male nurse came to offer support. What followed was a scuffle, and the male nurse and another nurse escorted her firmly back to the ward. Although the nurses handled Emily as they had been trained to, I felt ill. I had never had to force anyone to stay on a ward against their will and it didn't sit at all comfortably with me, except, perhaps, in the case of Phil.

Phil

Phil was a recent admission. He was tall and slim with lovely blond hair and sky-blue eyes. He was seventeen and told everyone he was Jonathan Livingston Seagull. *Jonathan Livingston Seagull* is a story about a seagull who believed there was more to life than being with ordinary seagulls, so he is transported to a much higher plane, and sent back to tell other seagulls about this better place. Thereafter follows a seagull rebellion, with many young seagulls following Jonathan. Phil believed he was on a better plane and tried to get people to follow him.

Phil's plane, however, was a psychotic state caused by

LSD. He was definitely in another world. Phil felt that we should allow him to fly free. He had tried to fly off a roof once but broke an ankle in the process, scuppering his attempt to escape to another world. Phil wanted to get away from the ordinary seagulls (us) as he believed we were hindering his freedom.

Sometimes Phil's world was pleasant, and he could be charming. At other times, it was terrifying. He could change from laughing and joking one minute to throwing furniture or anything else he could get his hands on, the next. I was to witness this darker side of him one day when I came on shift.

Phil was sitting in a chair in the lounge when suddenly, for no apparent reason, he stood up, marched across the room, picked up an armchair, and threw it at a wall. Fortunately, the chair didn't hit anyone. I was still enthralled by his apparent strength as bedlam then ensued.

Our now manic patient jumped through a window in a dividing door, leaving shattered glass in his wake. He began throwing missiles at everyone passing. Staff were ducking the missiles while trying to isolate Phil and move other patients to safety. The ward turned into carnage in a matter of minutes.

To make matters worse, Phil was winding up all the very vulnerable patients, and the scene was becoming more chaotic by the minute. It was one of the most frightening experiences I ever had as a nurse. I was scared of him; I have to admit, and was delighted, I didn't have to deal with him in this state. He was uncontrollable; imagine someone like this out in public.

After about forty-five minutes, when he had run out of missiles and been cleverly herded into a corner by staff, four psychiatric nurses finally extracted him from the communal area. He was locked in a room with nothing but a mattress on the floor and given a sedative injection. Funnily enough, having had a major crisis of conscience a few days before over the Emily situation, I had no problem with Phil's incarceration. I was just relieved that no one was seriously injured. Phil had cut himself with glass from the window, and one nurse had sustained a cut lip from a missile.

Psychiatric nurses went up in my estimation that day. They somehow maintained an element of calm (calm being relative here), protected other patients and handled Phil firmly, but with no anger or too much evidence of stress, although there obviously was some swearing. Sometimes, with Phil on the ward, it reminded me of the film *One Flew over the Cuckoo's Nest*.

After the Phil situation settled, I realised that Emily had also been detained by force because she was in hospital under a Section. There was a duty of care to keep her there until the Section ran out. Eventually, Emily responded to medication and became less suspicious. When her Section ran out, the review panel decided they could no longer keep her in under a Section, but they advised her to stay in as a voluntary patient.

Confused last day

On my last day on the ward, oh happy day... I went to say goodbye to Emily, who was due to go home the following week.

'I just want to tell you a secret; come here,' she said conspiratorially. Feeling honoured she wanted to share something with me, I leaned over so she could whisper in my ear.

'I have been in Mrs Jacobs' body,' she said, and then giggled.

Still some work to be done then, I thought, and was glad to leave the psychiatric ward behind. Definitely not cut out to be a psychiatric nurse, was my conclusion. Thankfully, some nurses are.

17

TREADMILL NURSE

Surgical wards had a faster turnover than medical wards, and the ages were more mixed. It was on the surgical ward that I first heard terms such as "the appendix in bed eight," "the gallbladder in bed twelve," and so on. To this day, I still hear some nurses and doctors refer to patients as "the leg ulcers," or "the ulcerative colitis," rather than Mr so and so with the leg ulcers or Mrs Jenkins who has ulcerative colitis.

I realised time was precious, and we didn't want to go all around the houses to get to the point, but I always felt this was going a bit too far. How would a doctor like to be called *the moustache*, or a nurse, *the forty-inch breast* (wish that were me), or even worse, *the nose*? I don't think so. They often called me *the student,* so I had some understanding of how demeaning these terms can be. Every student reading this book will understand that last one. I must admit, we did sometimes nickname certain doctors and nurses. There was *the beast*, *the crab*, *gobby* and so on.

Silence: surgeon on the ward

As I mentioned earlier in this book when referring to orthopaedic consultants who were surgeons; surgeons could be a different breed. They were skilful in operating, but the bedside manner was often lacking.

Consultant surgeons usually arrived on the ward surrounded by an entourage of white coats. They always asked for Sister, who wasn't hard to find to be fair, as she would be on high "ward round" alert. Then the ward round would begin. I was never sure if they were all sporty, but they walked and talked at a rate of knots that us mere mortals found difficult to follow.

Some consultant surgeons loved showing off. Mr Barnes was one such case in point. The poor senior house officer (second from the bottom in junior doctor terms) told him what they had admitted they patient with. For example, pain in the groin, and then tell Mr Barnes what they had done so far. A nice surgeon would coax a diagnosis out of the SHO, but not so Mr Barnes, and many others like him. He barked questions at the SHO while belittling every answer. He did all this either to impress the patient and sometimes Sister, or for some sadistic reason only known to himself. Mr Barnes would then reassure the patients he was in charge and the one looking after them, making out he was surrounded by imbeciles. Sometimes he was, if I'm going to be really honest.

Finally, he would conclude a consultation by muttering something under his breath like: 'Let's remove half the bowel. That should do the trick.' The SHO would be bright red in the face by this time and the medical students would smirk, appreciating it wasn't them being belittled for a change. The poor patient would stare, bemused, after the entourage already halfway down the ward, surrounding the next person. Mr Barnes was an excellent surgeon, but brilliance often comes with caveats.

Behind the Curtains

One thing about hospital wards that was always a mystery to me was the curtains surrounding beds. Obviously, they served a purpose in relation to visual privacy, but on a surgical ward round, the nurse was lucky if she got them closed before the company was moving to the next bed.

I felt sometimes consultants deliberately waited for the curtains to be closed before they marched back through them. The nurse had to move like greased lightning to open them and then close the next lot before the doctors moved on again. It was funny to watch if you weren't the nurse doing the curtains.

As I said, the curtains offered some visual privacy so that the doctor could examine the patient and all the medical students could take their turn examining the patient. If the patient had little pain prior to the round, they would certainly have plenty after five pairs of hands had prodded them thoroughly.

In terms of confidentiality, though, curtains offered no protection. Every patient would know what was happening to the patient next to them by the end of the round, which was perhaps as well, as it often needed them to interpret what the doctors had said.

The entourage often left the other patients and nurses trying to explain to the patient what the surgeon had said, that's if we had picked it up ourselves. Junior doctors might try to explain, but their knowledge was as limited, if not more so, than ours. Thankfully, Sister would do a daily round of patients herself and explain everything.

On a more serious note, there were major issues around confidentiality on hospital wards. Nightingale wards with their high ceilings helped dissipate some noise, and the space between the beds was larger than it is now.

Routine

Routine was everything on a surgical ward. There were admission and discharge procedures and everything in-between.

'Hurry up, Nurse, take this tube out. Hurry up, Nurse, I need a bedpan. Hurry up, Nurse, this patient needs to go to theatre, X-ray, Timbuktu,' and so on.

There was always some procedure to be carried out.

During the ward round, the surgeon would give his instructions, 'Take it out, Nurse,' referring to the removal of stitches, clips, wound drains, catheters, drips (intravenous infusions) and nasogastric tubes, to mention just a few. We wrote everything down and we'd go through the list afterwards and either share the work out amongst ourselves or hand it on to nurses on the next shift.

Besides this, duties included checking drips were running properly and to time; dress wounds; put in catheters and nasogastric tubes. If we weren't putting tubes in, we were removing them. Parenteral nutrition was then in its infancy, and we were responsible for setting it up and much more besides.

Theatre Prep

When preparing a person for theatre they had to have a bath, having been nil by mouth for an inordinately unnecessary length of time. We shaved the operating site prior to surgery and finally gave the patient an operating gown to put on.

In the 1970s a man would shave men's genital areas where required and women, women's. If a male nurse was not available, the doctor (male or female) would do the male shave, otherwise Sister (who was clearly gender neutral) would do it. The rules were sometimes hard to understand.

Similarly, female nurses were not allowed to catheterise

men, nor men, women, although male and female doctors could do both.

Once ready for theatre, a nurse accompanied the patient to the anaesthetic room until they had been given the anaesthetic. Surgical nursing was rewarding in many ways. People would often be admitted in pain and eventually leave the ward happy – assuming the right part had been removed, that is. I have fortunately not been involved when the wrong kidney or leg has been removed, but I've read the newspapers like everyone else.

Always Learning

I was taught a humbling lesson from one patient when working on that surgical ward. It was, yet again, one of those days where everyone was rushed off their feet; there didn't seem to be any let up, and I was tired. Some days we worked so hard, rushing from here to there and back again. I would feel like I had run a marathon, and my legs cried out for rest. This was one of those days. Mr Graham called for a commode which I duly took to him as he was just post-surgery. I went to collect the commode and tried to dash off.

'Could I have a bowl of water?' he said. I must have looked confused because he then snapped, 'I am sure, Nurse, that when you have used the toilet, you wash your hands afterwards.' Feeling ashamed of myself, I apologised, taking him a bowl of water after I had disposed of the commode. I never again forgot to give a patient the opportunity to wash their hands after using a commode, bedpan, or urinal. Thank you, Mr Graham.

Empathy

Sometimes, because the wards were always so busy, one would forget the person underneath the hospital gown. Ward turnover was high, and occasionally a reality check was required.

One night I'd been on a busy late shift and it was almost time to go home. This was when I noticed Diana, a sixteen-year-old girl, on a trolley with a porter at one end. She was about to be whisked off to theatre with the night shift student nurse, Geraldine. Geraldine was looking through her list of *to-do's* for the night and hadn't noticed Diana trembling. I was dead on my feet and longing to go home, but I couldn't just walk away.

I knew exactly how Geraldine was feeling. She needed to memorise everything on that list before midnight. It was a must before the night sister appeared, and there was no way she was going to notice Diana.

'Hey, Gerr, I'll take Diana to theatre if you like? It's near the changing rooms.'

'Would you? Oh thanks Dawn, I owe you one.'

I took Diana's hand.

'Nervous?' I asked. She nodded and fought back tears. 'Hey, don't worry, I'll be with you. Nothing bad's going to happen. You'll have a lovely sleep and then the worst of this pain will be gone, just a bit sore for a few days, that's all. The anaesthetist on tonight is fantastic looking.' She managed a smile and off we went. I held her hand and chatted to her all the way. She didn't let go of my hand until she was fast asleep.

'Thanks,' she said as she drifted off. That was a reminder of what the job was all about; helping people at their most vulnerable times when all the guards are down. Who would have known that what I said in my very first interview would turn out to be so true? What a privilege and an honour it was to be a nurse, I thought. Somehow I felt reinvigorated.

18

TESTED

During nurse training, we had to take and pass four supervised practical assessments prior to finals. These included:

- A medical assessment – bed bath
- A sterile procedure assessment – any dressing or procedure requiring use of an aseptic technique
- A medicines round assessment – a full medicines round
- A management assessment – managing the ward for a shift

The dreaded surgical assessment day arrived. This was my sterile procedure assessment, and Sister Rowntree was coming from the School of Nursing to assess and supervise me.

I chose a suture removal for this, and had asked one of the patients, Mrs Flowers, permission to remove her stitches for my assessment. I explained a Tutor would be there to make sure I did it properly.

'That's fine by *me,* duck,' she had said in full Leicester twang.

I arrived on shift early to prepare myself and remind Mrs Flowers.

'Don't worry, you'll pass.' She tried to reassure me. I kept looking around for Sister Rowntree, who was due any minute. I felt the inevitable butterflies in my stomach.

I had met with my classmate, Sue, before going on shift. She had passed her assessment the week before, Bette was doing hers the following week. Charlie and Grace had passed theirs in their previous placement.

This was my second assessment as the first had been a bed bath in my first year. Sister was leaving me alone today; understanding I'd be nervous and therefore useless until the assessment was out of the way. She had also given me a lighter workload. Finally, I heard the footsteps above all the din of the ward. The unmistakeable clop, clop, clop of high heels on marble sent me into a tizzy.

Clinical tutors and night sisters were the only staff who got away with wearing heels in hospital. I think night sisters wore them deliberately so they wouldn't catch us doing anything we shouldn't! I went to meet her.

'Good afternoon, Nurse Brookes,' Sister Rowntree said.

No smile; the tutors rarely smiled before or during an assessment, even if they were nice.

'Good afternoon, Sister,' I replied.

'Let's get on with it then. Who are we seeing today?'

'Mrs Flowers, a sixty-year-old lady who had a laparotomy and division of adhesions ten days ago, Sister. Her stitches are due out today and she's given consent for me to remove them.' Strictly speaking, patients were not supposed to be prepped prior to an assessment, but we all did it, choosing patients unlikely to cause us any additional trauma to that of being watched.

I walked towards the treatment room with Sister in tow. Here, I had to wash my hands correctly before setting up the dressing trolley. I cleaned the trolley with a sterile antiseptic wipe starting at the top, making sure I cleaned the legs and then the bottom shelf before ending at the bottom where the wheels joined the legs. I then had to wash my hands again before placing the equipment on the trolley.

I placed an unopened dressing pack along with the extras needed on the bottom shelf. Extras included an orange solution called Cetrimide. Cetrimide was an antiseptic for cleaning the wound. I added a stitch cutter. Once ready, I pushed the trolley towards the patient, making sure I only touched the legs below the top shelf.

Katy joined us at this point, another second year, who was to be my "dirty nurse". My hands were shaking already. This was going to be a long procedure. Mrs Flowers was beaming when we arrived at the bedside. Patients were always helpful when nurses were doing assessments and often did their best to make sure we passed. They would have kept smiling and thanking us even if we totally botched it, which some nurses did.

'Good afternoon Mrs Flowers, I'm Nurse Brookes. This is Sister Rowntree who will observe me today, and this is Nurse Jackson. We are going to take your stitches out today; is that all right?' Thankfully, during the prep, I had explained to Mrs Flowers that I would have to introduce myself, despite her already knowing who I was. Otherwise, she would have looked at me as if I was the one who should be in the bed!

'Hello, Nurses, hello, Sister,' she beamed, 'Thank you, Nurse, I'm sure you'll be as gentle as you always are,' she continued with a wink. Sister smiled slightly, knowing exactly what the patient was up to, but pleased, nevertheless. The Clinical Tutors could immediately tell if we had a good rapport with patients, and would be worried if it was lacking.

'I'm just going to pull the curtains,' I said. After this, Nurse Jenkins explained to Mrs Flowers that she would need to fold back the covers and expose her abdomen while keeping her top covered by her nightdress and her bottom half covered by bedding. I continued, 'Nurse Jenkins and I will now wash our hands.'

Once back from hand washing, Katy took the dressing pack and peeled it open, allowing the sterile pack to drop on the top shelf of the trolley with none of the unsterile bits touching it. This was an art. Too close and the outer packaging would touch and too far and the sterile pack could end up anywhere.

I carefully took the corners of the dressing pack and peeled it open. The first thing I had to do was attach a paper bag to the side of the trolley for the waste. I then had to take the sterile sheet off the top of the pack and place it below the wound without touching the patient in the process. We didn't wear gloves for these procedures. I then picked up the stainless steel forceps, one in each hand, and carefully set out the contents of the dressing pack neatly.

After exposing the gallipot (small stainless steel bowl), I asked Katy to pour in the Cetrimide. Again, with care, she peeled open the plastic sachet and poured the contents into the pot. She then peeled open the cover for the suture cutter and dropped it onto my sterile field.

The suture cutter had a curved blade. Katy then removed the old dressing covering the wound and placed it in the bag. We now considered her unclean, so if I needed any extras, she would have to wash her hands again. The entire process only took a few minutes, as we were so used to it. Sister watched intently for any slip-ups, but thankfully none so far.

I looked at the wound to make sure it had healed and that the stitches were ready to come out, counting them out loud. I already knew from the records that there were twenty-one stitches, but had to be sure. The most common skin sutures were black catgut.

'Right Mrs Flowers, I am just going to give the wound a clean and then I'll remove the stitches,' I said.

'Go ahead, Nurse.' Even she was looking nervous now. After cleaning the wound, I placed a piece of sterile gauze on the sterile sheet below the wound so I could place the stitches on top. I then took the stitch cutter in my right hand.

My hands were trembling a little; I took hold of one of the loose ends of the first stitch with the forceps in my left hand while slipping the blade underneath. The idea was to cut close to the skin to ensure none of the stitch that had been exposed to the air would pass through the inside of the patient when it was removed, reducing the risk of infection. Thankfully, the first one came out with ease and didn't stick. There was always a bit of a tug as the forceps pulled the stitch taut for cutting, but Mrs Flowers pretended not to notice.

'Didn't feel a thing, Nurse,' she smiled. Smiling back with trembling hands, I removed the other twenty stitches. I counted them out loud before discarding them in the bag, removing alternate stitches to start with. Once sure the wound was not looking like it would open up anywhere, I removed the rest.

Only two were stuck and needed a little more pulling. At that point, I could feel the sweat building up and my face flushing, but once they were out, I could breathe again.

'There we are, Mrs Flowers, all done,' I said as I folded away the remnants and put everything in the rubbish bag apart from the gallipot and the forceps; I would send these for sterilising.

'Thank you, Nurse. What a great Nurse you are.' Mrs Flowers smiled at Sister who smiled back. My job wasn't quite finished. We had to return to the treatment room, dispose of the waste and clean the trolley. Finally, after washing my hands, I turned to Sister. She smiled at last.

'Well done, Nurse Brookes, you passed.' She filled out some paperwork and left the ward. The first thing I had to do was to let Mrs Flowers know. You would think she had passed. She was so overjoyed. Nursing really could be a magnificent job at times. I floated through the rest of that shift.

19

THE BIG 'C'

All wards had their share of sadness. This included when a patient came back from theatre having been opened up only for the surgeon to find that a cancer was inoperable, and would close up without removing anything.

Mr Trainer

Mr Trainer was one such patient on the receiving end of an open-and-closed laparotomy. He always tried to put on a brave face while his family visited. Mr Trainer often cried when they left. He was the first person I ever discussed dying with in any depth. He asked questions to which there were no answers. Such as what does it feel like to die? He didn't expect replies, but it helped him to speak about how he felt.

Mr Trainer decided not to tell his children about the big

'C' diagnosis, as he put it. He didn't want them 'fussing' over him, and he and his wife kept his cancer a secret for many months before he became so ill he had to tell them.

He was finally admitted to hospital for one last time. His wife later told me he died with family around his bed and with as much dignity as he could muster, but had been in a lot of pain.

Secret diagnosis

In the late 1970s, it was common practice for a relative to be told the diagnosis of cancer before the patient. Relatives would often hide the diagnosis from the patient.

Such situations created an incredible strain on relationships and a moral dilemma for those of us involved in caring for patients. It never felt right that a dying patient couldn't put their house in order, and I'm glad it's different now.

Mastectomy

I came across many women who had to have a breast or breasts removed (mastectomy). Sometimes this was a minefield and a steep learning curve in the art of communication. Some women didn't seem to mind at all and were just happy to have the offending article removed; some would even joke about being lopsided.

Others were more distraught about removal of a breast

(sometimes two breasts) than about the diagnosis of cancer. Some surgeons were hasty in delivering the news to a woman that she should have a mastectomy, and with their communication skills being a little suspect, some of them added to a woman's trauma.

The altered body image and sense of loss that some women went through was awful for them and, where relevant, their partners, with many feeling that they could no longer be "a woman".

Every woman's reaction to a mastectomy was unique. It didn't seem to bear any relation to age or background, nor to whether or not they had a partner, and so one couldn't identify which women were going to take it badly.

The clues often surfaced when it came time to remove the dressing post operatively. This was the first opportunity for a woman to see herself without a breast, and many of them found it too much to bear. They taught us not to push women to look, but to offer them the choice, and gauge their reaction. It was never easy; firstly they had to look at a lengthy wound with extensive bruising and a truckload of stitches. Besides this, there was often a tube drain or sometimes a corrugated drain poking out. Then, if they hadn't passed out or looked away, they had to imagine that part of the body without a wound.

As I mentioned, some found it easier to deal with than others. Some of the reactions would also depend on their husband or partner. Many men found it as difficult as the women.

Breasts were and still are symbolic of womanhood. They form a part of a woman's sexuality and many men found it too much. Some of them offered reassurance to their wives or partners, but then refused to look at the wound. These reactions didn't inspire confidence, and in many ways, the psychological impact affected both sides of a relationship. Men felt guilty that they were feeling a sense of loss when the alternative (cancer and death) was so much worse and they tried to hide their feelings.

Many women felt their sex life would suffer, and some didn't care, while some men felt the same way. As nurses we did the best we could with the time we had, allowing each woman to decide in her own time when it was right for her to look at their body without the breast/s, and help prepare them for what they would see.

The vast majority discovered their imagination was worse than the reality and that it was nowhere near as bad as they had envisaged, but a very few found the opposite.

Those who didn't adjust were referred for counselling and psychiatry to assist with the change. In the late 1970s and early 1980s, breast implants weren't widely available and a padded bra or a false external breast was the best that could be bought, mostly not on the NHS.

Miss Henshaw

Miss Henshaw was a forty-nine-year-old lawyer. She had noticed a lump in her breast while bathing and ignored it at first, hoping it would go away. After a week or two when it didn't go away, she described how she became obsessional about it, checking it all the time to see if it was growing while hoping she was imagining its presence. Finally, she told her sister, who insisted she see the doctor. By this time, she feared the worst, but hoped the doctor would tell her she was fine.

The GP told her he needed to refer her to the hospital to be checked out. This was before routine mammograms, although she would have been too young anyway, and as there was no family history of breast cancer, she would not have been eligible for early mammography.

The consultant confirmed her worst fears twelve weeks after she had first noticed the lump. She was told she had breast cancer.

I met her on the day of her admission. She was due for surgery the next morning and a total mastectomy was planned. Miss Henshaw was personable and openly spoke about the dreaded cancer. I was taking her history when she suddenly blurted out, rather ironically, 'I've just finished paying the mortgage. I paid extra because I wanted to be debt free.'

It wasn't difficult to understand where she was coming from. Miss Henshaw was asking the time old question that, I have noticed, people often ask when the rat race stops momentarily and they face the reality of their mortality.

'What is the point of it all?' She was an intelligent woman and breast cancer survival rates at the time weren't great. Chemotherapy was still in its infancy, and radiotherapy was usually the post-operative treatment option because often the cancer had spread by the time of diagnosis.

Miss Henshaw came through surgery and coped well with the loss of her breast. The surgeon was optimistic that he had got most of the cancer, only time would tell. I admired her enormously for the dignity and bravery she showed for the entire time she was on the ward. She would chat to other patients, help some of the older ones with their drinks and pass them things that were out of reach, while all the time she was coming to terms with the dreaded big 'C' diagnosis. Added to that was the loss of a breast and the fact that the next few years for her would be a walking time bomb.

Her faith in God helped her; she was openly religious and kept a Bible on her bedside table. Although she acknowledged her fear, she portrayed a sense of peace and calm.

I never saw her again after she left the ward and I don't know whether she lived a short or a long life, but I don't think I have ever met anybody so ready to meet their maker as Miss Henshaw.

20

BREAKING POINT

There was a television series filmed between 1975 and 1983 called *Angels*. I used to watch it and loved the title (obviously) but sometimes I was certainly no angel.

One Saturday morning I came on shift feeling exhausted. It was a boiling hot day, and the ward was heaving. I was getting fed up with shift work, trying to have a social life, and the constant demands of the job. It was taking its toll.

I was feeling down in the dumps, wishing I was doing some other job in some other place, and feeling very sorry for myself. Every day presented itself with some new tragedy for some poor, unsuspecting person or family.

The ward I was working on was as busy as ever, and I managed to put on my "nurse" mask and start my tasks as cheerfully as I could. I was never a person to bring problems into work. Not that I really had any problems apart from wanting to be away from work for a while, sleep for twenty-four hours and soak my tired, aching feet for as long as possible.

Everything was a struggle that day and I was irrational, suddenly resenting the fact that I couldn't grow my fingernails, wear jewellery or nail varnish and that my feet were enclosed in ugly, flat leather shoes. My friends and boyfriend were going to a barbecue that afternoon without me - 'Again,' he had moaned that morning. I was twenty going on sixty that day, feeling so much older than my years despite patients always saying, 'You don't look old enough to be a nurse.'

Well, I felt old enough. Maybe I should have thrown a "sicky" like some nurses did occasionally, but I reasoned I wouldn't have been able to go out, anyway. No, there was nothing to do but to get on with it.

The morning went fairly smoothly. Sister Blunkett was in a good mood, although we were short-staffed as two people had gone off sick. I wondered if they had felt like me when they woke that morning. We got on with the jobs without too much interruption. One of the pleasant things about weekends was that there was no routine surgery, and most of the patients were recovering post-operatively. We had been on call the night before, so most of the emergency operations had been done during the night, and as the ward was now full, we couldn't take any more new patients.

If I thought I was tired, I was spritely compared to David, the SHO, who had obviously been up for most of the night.

The difference was that he believed it was his right to be grumpy and to punish everyone because he hadn't been to bed. In fairness to him, it wasn't unusual for a junior doctor to work for seventy-two hours or more with little or no sleep, being called out in the night to prescribe medicines, re-site drips, assist in theatre, or clerk in new patients.

By the end of the morning, I was feeling more like my normal self and having gone around the ward cheering up the patients I had cheered myself up in the process. Sister sent David off to get some sleep, remarking that he should also take a wash, shave and personality transplant before he came back to her ward. He had sheepishly agreed. By the time I came back from lunch, I loved my job again and floated through the afternoon bantering with patients and other nurses. *Perhaps I'm becoming a manic-depressive*, I thought. The real reason I cheered up was when I noticed the weather taking a turn for the worse. A barbecue in the rain didn't seem that big an attraction after all. I even smiled at the thought of Jerry eating soggy burgers not very angelic, but no longer at breaking point.

21

PROLAPSE?

One weekend, an incident occurred which remains ingrained in my memory forever.

We were on call and told that a teenage girl was being admitted with a vaginal prolapse. This was unusual. I was on duty with the junior ward sister, Sister Davies, who was like Marjorie from *The Good Life* in mannerism and Mrs Bucket from *Keeping up Appearances* in personality. Sister Davies was always immaculate and the only sister I had worked with who had long fingernails, always wore nail polish and plastered her face with makeup.

She never did a stroke of work, hence the fingernails. Even paperwork was beneath her, and she always had a mirror to hand in case her lipstick needed touching up. We were her minions, and we knew our place.

On this particular day, the paramedics arrived with the young girl. They explained they had applied a support truss to hold the prolapse in place and given her pethidine for pain. I accompanied the reluctant Sister to admit the girl to the ward. Sister Davies removed the bedclothes, and what followed caused her to go up in my estimation enormously.

'THIS GIRL IS HAVING A BABY!' she yelled, glaring at the paramedics while ringing the emergency bell. I have to say she was the only calm person during the ensuing chaos.

'Get me some Syntometrine from the paediatric ward,' she called to me. By that time, other people were arriving, and I was pleased to get away, not having a clue what to do.

I left Sister Davies who was in full control. 'You get a dressing pack and some gloves, and you bleep the paediatrician,' she instructed the paramedics.

Mrs Butcher had always taught us to walk swiftly in an emergency. She instructed us, 'Never run.' Well, that advice went right out of the window as I ran to the paediatric ward, rehearsing the name of the drug I had never heard of all the way.

Finally, I arrived and asked for the Syntometrine. I didn't know what it was until later when I learned that we give it in the third stage of labour to help the uterus contract and reduce the risk of postpartum haemorrhage.

When I got back to the ward, the baby had been delivered and rushed to the special care baby unit at a different hospital. Sister was with the young girl, who was obviously upset. She administered the drug I had brought and delivered the placenta, inspecting it for completeness before sending it to the maternity unit at the main hospital for disposal. Unfortunately, the ordeal had a tragic outcome; the baby died within a few hours of transfer. The poor girl denied concealing the pregnancy, saying that she had continued to have periods throughout and just thought she was gaining weight. Her parents were devastated.

The paramedics had asked all the right questions regarding pregnancy, although on reflection they would probably realise that a vaginal prolapse in a teenager is almost unheard of, whereas pregnancy was more common. The doctors believed the outcome would most likely have been the same wherever she had been delivered, as the newborn was too premature to have survived the trauma of the girl's labour.

The heroine of the day was Sister Davies, who later said to me, 'Every nurse should know how to deliver a baby.' She had been a midwife in a previous life. No surprise then that a few years later I did my midwifery training.

22

ALL THINGS GREAT AND SMALL

Children's wards were frightening for general nurses, as things were so very different. Apart from the obvious fact that children were so much smaller and there were little things called babies, the routines were also different.

Most adult wards had similar routines, which took some getting used to at first, but once mastered, the schedules were similar. Arrive on shift, have handover, get on with it: make beds, help patients wash, dress, shave (men obviously), sit out, go back to bed, bum rounds, dressing rounds, drip rounds, drinks rounds, catheter rounds, rounds, rounds, rounds... but on paediatrics this was not the case.

This change of everyday routine was a bit like psychiatry, but nothing like psychiatry, I didn't get bitten for one thing! There were no standard rounds, but there was a relaxed atmosphere, and I could play with kids. Okay, so there were feeding regimes for babies and medicine rounds. Trying to bottle feed sick babies could take up to an hour, and there were nappy changes, but babies went at different times so they couldn't be confined to "nappy rounds". Nursery nurses mainly kept the toddlers entertained.

Some children had drips up, but they went through machines that alarmed when empty so didn't need quite the same amount of observation.

Aprons were an absolute necessity, especially as, you remember, we wore white uniforms – one bit of baby sick and we would have been changing all day long. Unfortunately, babies didn't always remember to puke on the apron. Our shoulders weren't protected, so gowns also came in handy. If a baby had pyloric stenosis, there was no protection, as the projectile vomit could catch you on the other side of the room.

Diarrhoea in babies was a common reason for admission and nappy changing posed real challenges for the novice. No sooner had I washed a sufferer's bottom than more brown (or yellow) stuff poured away and I had to start over. Nappy changing could take ages, and the staff nurses would laugh when they saw my face scrunched up in concentration while a baby screamed its head off.

I felt an empathy with every mother on the planet. Until I did midwifery, though all babies looked alike and while I could coo, coo with the best of them, they were not my cup of tea. Far too much wailing and pooing for my liking, but the poor little ones were ill and couldn't exactly let us know how they felt in measured tones.

The paediatric wards housed a mixture of medical and surgical cases.

There were cubicles for children and babies with infectious diseases such as diarrhoea and vomiting, and these children were barrier-nursed. Each cubicle had a trolley outside with fresh gowns, masks and gloves, and we washed hands before donning oneself in the garb.

I often tried to imagine myself as a baby or very young child in a strange cot in a cubicle looking for mummy and in comes an apparition of light blue, with the only visible thing being the eyes. Bearing in mind, different people have different eyes, some very scary. No wonder there was a lot of crying from inside the cubicles.

Babies sometimes just wanted a cuddle, but nurses didn't really have the time to go through the rigmarole of all that washing and changing to oblige, so it was always a great relief when parents were around.

Some parents, like some nurses, were better than others at their job, and sometimes I reluctantly handed a baby over to what I may have considered a terrible parent. There has always been a fine line between poor parenting and abuse (more senior staff dealt with the latter), but I just wished some parents would leave off child-bearing.

The ward sisters and qualified staff on children's wards were, without exception, wonderful human beings. There must be a reason one becomes a paediatric nurse or a psychiatric nurse, and I have huge respect for nurses of every specialism.

Children's wards were cheerful places once you got used to not being watched and not being told off for talking to patients. I was still young, although I felt a lot older, so I could still remember how to play. They even allowed us to call each other by our first names, and the children did so too.

Paediatric medication was an absolute mystery. We measured injections in micrograms rather than milligrams, and at 0.1ml and other such oddities. Most oral medication came in liquid form, which complicated the calculations until we got the hang of it. Fortunately, we were well supervised, and the calculations got easier with time.

Nights at Christmas

Sister Chang was a lovely ward sister, who I worked with on a paediatric ward. I was near the end of my training and on night duty on Christmas Eve. Her parting words after handover were, 'Remember, we are not on call, so do not accept any new admissions.'

It was a quiet night, so we decided to fill all the cubicles with dolls and put up drips and various other bits of equipment, just to complicate things. We also filled some of the beds on the ward that Sister wouldn't examine closely first thing in the morning. She arrived on duty early and flung the doors open, storming past all the cubicles with trolleys outside on to the ward.

'I thought I said no admissions!' Her voice shrilled with displeasure.

'I'm really sorry, Sister, the other paediatric ward was full and the Nursing Officer said we had to accept all the extras, there's a bug going round,' I lied.

We sat down for handover and she looked glum. It had ruined her Christmas Day. I managed to get through the handover without laughing and finally said, 'The baby in cubicle two is very ill and has strict barrier nursing in place. The doctor requested quarter-hourly obs.'

'QUARTER-HOURLY OBS!' Sister Chang was now at the end of her tether.

'Sorry, Sister, I hope the day gets better. Happy Christmas,' I replied and left the ward.

We pretended to go off duty but once outside; we peeped through the window and watched her wash and scrub her hands, put on overshoes, gown, mask and gloves and enter the cubicle. We heard a yelp, and she came chasing after us down the corridor, laughing her head off and shouting, 'I'll kill you!' She took it all in good spirit, and fortunately let us go home to bed rather than tidy up the ward after all the mess we'd made.

I left the children's ward after Christmas to go back to school, as we used to say when we were classroom-based for our two weeks at the end of a placement.

Paediatrics was fun, but I was definitely an adult nurse,

and left certain I wouldn't be doing paediatric nursing anytime soon. Much later, I did a spell on a Special Care Baby Unit (SCBU) as part of midwifery training, but this would never be a career option either. Delivering babies, well, that's a different kettle of fish altogether.

23

CASUALTY

It goes without saying that Accident and Emergency Units (A&E) was where the action was, but it could also be a high stress, adrenaline-pumping job.

There were disproportionately more male nurses on the A&E unit than in other areas of nursing. There was also the occasional superiority syndrome. Despite all this, I liked the work and even considered working in A&E after finishing training, mainly because of a fantastic sister.

Television programmes like *Holby City* and *Casualty* have glamorised A&E departments.

'Hello Nurse Brookes, could you help me bring this patient back to life, and by the way, what are you doing for dinner tonight?' they were not. Doctors did occasionally fight amongst themselves, mainly when someone's ego got in the way.

There was also one rare doctor who wanted to have

relationships with anyone within a three-metre radius, but most of the doctors certainly didn't fall into that category and when they did, they weren't exclusive to emergency departments.

Some nurses working in A&E didn't go in for building relationships with patients in the same way that ward nurses did. In fact, some rarely looked a patient in the eyes. Most of the emergency nurses were, out of necessity, interested in the diagnosis, providing quick and efficient treatment and moving patients on to a ward or discharging them home.

I learnt a lot of things during the emergency placement. We weren't allowed to do things like stitch as students but we could undertake many other procedures, including applying or removing Plaster of Paris (POP) casts under supervision.

I spent most of my time working in the "dressings" area, which tended to be more routine and less intense than the acute emergency room. Here, I was allowed to do things rather than just watch.

Patients came to A&E with a multitude of ailments, from cuts and bruises, to fractures and heart attacks. They could be any age, from babies to older people. Weekends were always busy following nights out, sports and DIY activities. In winter, we admitted people with respiratory conditions from flare-ups of chronic bronchitis, and heart disease often secondary to illnesses like influenza.

Burns

We treated patients suffering burns with surprising frequency during the summer months. Men mostly, who had never cooked in their lives, would take to the barbecue preparing food, which often ended up matching the colour of the charcoal they were burning.

When the barbecue didn't light fast enough for them, they would squirt flammable liquid on to the coals, sometimes resulting in a burst of flames that took them by surprise, and caused flame burns.

I had a strange liking for dressing burns; not sure what that says about me, but I did. Opinions on blister management changes frequently, but we used to remove blisters and then apply paraffin gauze. It's ironic that we placed something flammable over a burn to protect it, I know. This was the least-adhering wound dressing available at the time, although it stuck once dried out. Another commonly applied wound and burn covering was the wonderful N/A dressing, again non-adherent, and afterwards there were the outer layers of dressings and bandages to apply. We applied everything with great care because surface burns were more painful than deep burns, although the latter were more severe.

Hells Angel breaks loose

One Saturday night, I was working a late shift in A&E when an unconscious Hells Angel was carried in by his friends. They didn't know what was wrong with him. They told us he had just collapsed for no reason. The doctor put up a drip, and I had just applied a blood pressure cuff when he woke up.

'Where the f...? What the f...!' he was shouting. You get the message, I'll spare you the expletives. Suddenly, monitors and drips were flying around the place. A doctor came rushing in and tried to help me calm him down. I was five foot one and seven and a half stone; this man was six foot something and huge. It was no contest – he was up off the trolley, dragging everything behind him. The drip stand fell over as he thrashed his arms around. The heart monitor crashed to the floor after he punched it hard.

All the time I was trying to maintain a sense of calm, speaking to him and explaining where he was. Finally, the doctor called in the Hells Angel friends (the patient's, not the doctor's), who picked him up and put him back on the trolley. They managed to stop him demolishing anything else.

It's amazing what one will try to do when in a uniform trying to help people. I have been in many similar situations at work that I would have just run away from if I was on the street, but wearing the nurse's uniform came with a responsibility to always try to assist a person, no matter how badly they behaved.

The man's friends confessed to the doctor that the maniac on the trolley had been drinking heavily before passing out, unconscious. The doctor was not amused and told them to sit with him until he had slept it off. We moved on to the next person, albeit a bit shaken and with few bruises ourselves. The doctor got a black eye for his trouble, and I got a bruised arm and a grazed knee from something hitting me.

One man ruined the monitors that night, thousands of pounds' worth of equipment trashed in less than five minutes. The patient didn't care who he hit, and although his friends apologised profusely, he never did.

Dodging fists

A few days after the Hells Angel incident, I was taking the blood pressure of a harmless elderly person when a fist flew out and hit me in the mouth before I knew what was happening. *Great, now I look like I've been in a fight*, I thought. I didn't always wear body armour to work.

Obviously, when patients were known to be aggressive because of dementia or confusion, it was easier to take precautions, but more often than not, these attacks came out of the blue.

Comparing notes with Sue, Bette, Grace & Charlie

towards the end of our training, we had all had moments like these.

'Mr Brown ran straight into my shins with his wheelchair and it left me with a massive bruise,' Bette explained. 'Poor man thought he was escaping from the Japanese because he kept shouting about Nips.'

'I was removing a dressing from Mrs Bloom's abdomen post-op and she suddenly hit out with a punch. Thankfully, I moved quickly and ended up with a slight bruise to my arm,' Charlie shared.

'My worst one,' said Sue, 'was just after I started on the psychiatric ward. I was speaking to this patient who was very nice. He was sharing some of his life experiences with me when this woman pulled my hair from behind and head butted me. It came right out of the blue and I ended up with three stitches in my head.'

'You win,' I said.

'For me, it was when Mrs Watson came round after being unconscious and I went to reassure her and tell her where she was,' Grace said. 'Then, before I knew it, she was out of the bed and I was on the floor with her on top of me. The other staff rescued me just in time. I was mentally scarred rather than physically and I've always been a bit wary since then.'

'Mine has to be the bite.' I said.

Reminiscences like this were helpful, as at least we could laugh about the situations we had been in, and it was somehow reassuring to know that we were not the only ones. Patients were also violent to other patients at times, and it required a lot of supervision when there were several patients with dementia in the same place, as they sometimes needed protection from each other.

Bully Brutus

The ward sister in A&E was a young woman who was an outstanding teacher. She always had time for student nurses and tried to make sure we got the best out of the placement. One member of staff was the exact opposite. This staff nurse was particularly arrogant and had the attitude of a Rottweiler. We called her Brutus. Whenever Brutus was on duty, we students groaned, especially if we were attached to her area. Many a student nurse ended up in tears when working on shift with her. I was determined not to let it happen to me.

It was hard to report staff during training, as it was more likely to kickback on the person who reported it. They would be seen as a snitch and disloyal. There was more of a "cover up" culture back then, and although the good sisters ran a tight ship and kept bullying to a minimum, there were some wards where the bullying came from the top.

My turn to work with Brutus over a few shifts came. It was hard not to cry (or punch her) as she spent most of the shift belittling everything I did. It was much better if it was busy because I could ignore her and get on with my work. What really got to us was how she spoke to patients. She was cold and uncaring. None of us could work out why she had chosen to nurse for a career. We thought that she was probably deluded and imagined she was a prison warden rather than a nurse. After that, we called her Screw.

There were a few people like that during my training. Bullies, basically, who chose to make the lives of the weak and vulnerable as miserable as possible, and for far too many years, the NHS tolerated them.

We came up with an idea for the next government reform in the 1970s that would include rounding up the malingerers and bullies in the NHS and bringing back National Service just for them. Fortunately, though, there were far more caring people in the profession than not, and most of us tried to do the best we could within the constraints of being part of an ever-changing political football game.

A cry for help

One tragedy about working in the emergency department was seeing people coming in after taking an overdose. The reasons for overdoses were many and varied. The drug of choice was often paracetamol because of its availability. Quite a few young people came in, having taken a paracetamol overdose. What they didn't realise was that paracetamol overdose could cause irreparable damage to the liver. The long-term effects of severe liver disease and premature death would occur sometime in the future. You might think this was the least of their worries if they wanted to die anyway, but many people who overdosed were using it as a cry for help rather than really wanting to die. Some obviously wanted to die; many of them succeeded.

I can't speak for all A&E nurses, but a few of the A&E nurses I met didn't tolerate self-harm very well; these nurses didn't sympathise with people who abused alcohol, drugs or people who attempted suicide. Some even used the stomach pumps a little too roughly on over one occasion, and many patients recalled their treatment in A&E as a horrible experience.

Maybe some nurses thought that by being rough or rude they were teaching the person a lesson, and that this would prevent them behaving in this way again. However, most people who self-harmed already believed they deserved to be punished, and the treatment in many general hospitals just reaffirmed this mistaken belief. Whilst I understood that A&E was busy, and it was, I could never agree with the opinion that those who a minority of nurses termed "genuine" cases deserved priority over "time-wasters" who self-harmed. I would argue that until we've walked in another person's shoes, all human beings deserve to be cared for with compassion and respect.

One benefit of being admitted to hospital following an overdose (other than having one's life saved) was that the patients got to see a psychiatrist, albeit for a fairly routine interview. They followed some of these up. Stomach pumping was not a pleasant experience and I'm sure that most people who underwent it once would think twice before going back for more.

Crash

We had our share of tragedies in A&E. One situation I always hated was when patients were brought in following a cardiac arrest and we failed to resuscitate them. It was all too common a scene.

If you were looking on from the outside, you would see a stressful but efficient scene as everyone took their place trying to bring a person back from the dead.

Sometimes it was successful, but more often than not, it wasn't. Most people died because of the delay in defibrillation, which is why there is now a concerted effort to get as many defibrillators into the community as possible.

A&E was always depressing after losing someone in this way and we would sulk about, not wanting to talk about it but feeling it all the same. We needed debriefs, but we never got them. Neither were we allowed to sulk for long, as there was always the next job to be done. 'Hurry up, Nurse,' was never far from our ears.

There was no point becoming hardened to these horrible facts of life, but equally nurses and doctors had to learn to deal with the emotions they felt and experienced every day of their working lives, so don't blame us if we occasionally miss the mark. Most of us are human, too.

One evening I was on a late shift when a fifty-year-old man was brought in looking very ill, to say the least. He was obviously in shock, even I could see it. His clothes were soaking wet and covered in sand. It was reported he had fallen into a pit of some sort. Controlled panic stations began, and the doctor put a drip up, and we set about pumping plasma products into him to try to get his blood pressure up.

I was told to cut his clothes off and started close to where the big blood stain was so that we could assess the damage underneath. I cut off the shirt and then had to grab hold of the trolley to avoid passing out when I saw that his left arm was completely severed from the shoulder.

'Right!' the doctor cried. 'Get this man ready for theatre.'

I feel sick, I thought, as thankfully they pushed me out of the way while the more experienced nurses got him ready. I went off shift with flashbacks of that horrendous injury. They stayed with me for days. Even now I feel queasy remembering the scene.

Unfortunately, the man had been lying in the wet for too long before they found him, and the surgeon could not reconnect the arm back to the shoulder again.

My A&E placement ended soon after this event, and I concluded perhaps I was not cut out to be an A&E nurse after all.

24

NIGHT NURSE

If ever there was ever a challenge to a student nurse's stickability and determination to finish training, it was night duty. Not only was it physically taxing, because the body objected to being up all night (except when partying), but it was also tough mentally for two reasons: night sisters and nursing auxiliaries. I'm not getting at nursing auxiliaries. It has nothing to do with snobbery or power. It was the spooky stories they scared us poor students half to death with and which had us looking behind us every time we walked up a ward or down a corridor. Hospital corridors and ward sluices are the scariest places to be in the middle of the night. I will explain more soon, but let's start with night sisters.

Every night, the night sister on duty would do at least one round of the wards. Senior students were often in charge of a ward at night, but either a sister or a qualified nurse would come over to do the medicine rounds with us.

When the night sister came onto the ward, usually between midnight and one o'clock in the morning, she would expect to be escorted around the ward and told every patient's name, age, diagnosis and any current treatment. There were usually forty patients on the ward and it didn't matter whether it was your first night or last, you just had to know. Excuses were not acceptable.

The first night on was always the worst. I always paid extra attention at handover, writing down all the details, and then, while trying to deal with patients, drug rounds and other jobs, I repeated every patient's name, trying to remember what was wrong with them. Once rehearsed, it felt better. The best way I found was to learn them in a clockwise direction by rote, because woe betide me or any of us if we didn't know all this by the time Sister arrived.

The first time I had to do this was the stuff of nightmares. We had finished all our duties and were sitting at the nurses' station at the entrance to the ward. The auxiliaries and junior students were chatting and having fun (in whispers of course), and I was reciting names and diagnoses in my head, dreading the ward round in case I forgot anything.

Someone had informed me we weren't allowed to use notes or torches during the round. Even though the names of patients were on the bed frame at the foot of the bed, they couldn't be seen clearly in the dark. I had practised trying to see them once the lights were out, but it was difficult to do without being obvious, so I kept this back as a last resort. Any night sister would be on the lookout for this and pick up on it immediately. I was just starting to relax and join in with the whispered conversations, thinking maybe Sister was going to give us a miss that night, when I heard the swing doors open at the outer entrance to the ward, followed by high heels on a marble floor. Everybody stiffened and started reading through patient notes. As Sister walked onto the ward, we all stood, as this was the required response.

'Good morning,' she said (it was half-past one), and she smiled. I knew I would like her from that moment as sisters rarely smiled.

'Good morning, Sister,' we replied (I defy the Waltons to have done any better).

'You're okay, it's Sister Robertson, she's nice,' whispered the Tanya, the auxiliary, and I felt myself relaxing just a little.

'Right, Nurse Brookes, shall we do the round?' And off she went to the first bed.

'Yes, Sister,' I muttered as I hurried after her. It started off quite well. I introduced the sleeping patient and told her about the diagnosis and treatment plan, and then we moved on to the next bed. This was all going fine until a patient on the other side of the ward called out.

'Nurse!' I wasn't sure whether I was allowed to go over or not. My colleagues must have been hiding because they were nowhere to be seen. Sister Robertson recognised my dilemma and crossed the ward ahead of me. I overtook her just in time to read the patient's name off the end of the bed, as we were now well out of order.

'Hello Mr Jones. This is Sister Robertson.' He glanced sheepishly at Sister, who smiled back. 'What can I do for you?' I asked, hoping and praying that it wasn't anything too complicated.

'Would you mind moving my pillows for me? I can't seem to get comfortable and I'm frightened to move in case any of these tubes fall out.' I could have kissed him. He had a catheter, an infusion and a wound drain so I could understand his quandary and I was only too pleased to make him comfortable, as this was something I could manage. 'Thank you, Sister,' he said as we left to go back to the other side of the ward.

You're welcome, I thought. In fairness, Sister had helped. When we crossed the ward again, I had totally lost my place.

'Right, Nurse Brookes, that was Mr Frew who has had a repair of a ruptured inguinal hernia, wasn't it?' she prompted kindly. I not only liked her now; I loved her. One day I was going to be a kind night sister and all trainees would adore me. This experience also showed me that, contrary to popular opinion, sisters listened to the information imparted to them during the ward round, but how she remembered it was beyond me. The rest of the round went well, and I only forgot two patient names out of forty. Not bad for a first night.

'Well done, Nurse Brookes. Bleep me if you need me,' she said, as she left the ward.

Phew, I could breathe at last and my heart stopped pounding in my chest. For the first time that night, I felt relaxed, and despite buzzers going off continually, I was floating on air again. I had passed another trial and was no longer a fledgling, for that night, at least.

Night duty always brought its share of deaths, often taking place at around four o'clock in the morning, so we regularly walked the wards to make sure patients were all right. If they didn't appear to be breathing, we took a closer look. No one was going to be found dead on my watch if I could help prevent it. This habit that was hard to get rid of.

Years later, I was babysitting for a friend. When she arrived home, I reported that her ten-year-old son was fine and still breathing. I had checked on him regularly. She looked a little taken aback.

'Do many children die when you're babysitting?' she laughed nervously.

'Old habits die hard,' I smiled, before hurriedly explaining about nursing and night duty, just in case she thought I needed psychiatric help or worse.

Ghost stories

Most nights followed a familiar pattern if we weren't on take for emergencies. Once the patients had been bedded down, medicines had been administered and the night sister had been, we would sit at the nurses' station while patients slept.

This was when the auxiliaries came into their own. On one occasion, we had just settled down, some of us having whispered conversations while others studied. Janet, the auxiliary, suddenly hissed, 'Did you hear that?'

'What?' I replied.

'It's old Smithy again.'

'Who's old Smithy?'

'She used to be the ward sister here. She died about thirty years ago and now she walks around the hospital every night.'

Nervously, I laughed, expressing disbelief, but by the time the conversation ended and the buzzer went off with a patient needing a bedpan, I was less confident. I ran in and out of the empty sluice faster than an Olympic sprinter. I never heard or saw any ghosts, but this didn't make the stories any less frightening for a young and impressionable student nurse, which of course encouraged the story-tellers all the more.

Once the ghost stories were exhausted, our conversation turned to more upbeat things like boyfriends, music, books, anything else that would help keep us awake.

Thankfully, the buzzers sounded frequently and there were Kardex's to be written, drips to be checked, catheter bags to empty and observations to be done. Sometimes the ward was on-take for emergencies and would be a hive of activity throughout the night, much to the dismay of patients trying to sleep.

Trying to sleep

I used to meet up with friends from my set and others I'd got to know in the canteen for breaks. Somehow, it became natural to have a bite to eat in the middle of the night. It was hard to keep the imagination under control on the journey, often subconsciously hearing footsteps on my way. The ghost stories played mind games with me during the long walks along those huge, empty corridors. I was always relieved if I met someone on the way (not a ghost of course) so that I could forget about the scary stories.

Sleeping during the day after a night shift was a real challenge. The world is just not geared up to daytime slumber. During my night duty stints, I was living in my wonderful top floor bedsit across the road from the Charles Frears School of Nursing. Most people in the house didn't work.

The large house had been converted into bedsits with one on the ground floor, two on the first, and my room on the second floor in the attic. Adam, who lived on the first floor, was a Marxist who took his political stance seriously. He didn't work, so he had a lot of time to study his beliefs, and was always looking for a political argument. His equally Marxist girlfriend often stayed with him.

One day, I was fast asleep after a long and busy night

shift when someone banging at my door woke me. I dragged myself out of bed, feeling groggy. I opened up. There was a rather stressed looking Adam.

'I'M NOT A HOMOSEXUAL!'

Shaking my head and rubbing sleep out of my eyes, wondering if I'd entered some parallel universe, I tried to focus.

'I'm not homosexual,' he whimpered.

'I never said you were.' *What the heck was this all about?*

He was inside my room before I was fully awake and cried for several minutes. I made us both a strong coffee. Finally, with coffee in hand, he told me what had happened.

'I was out in the park and this bloke came and tried it on with me. He said I was homosexual. I'm not,' he protested. The next thing I knew, he was pulling me into his arms, trying to kiss me. I pushed him away, waking up rapidly.

'Adam. Stop. You don't need to prove anything to me. Drink your coffee then give your girlfriend a ring.'

'Okay,' he muttered, and like a spoiled child, he left with his head down as quickly as he had come. I stared at the door, dumbfounded. Needless to say, I couldn't get back to sleep and went into work tired that night.

There was another guy in his forties who lived in the ground floor bedsit. It amazed me how many women went in and out of his room. I wasn't sure what he was up to, but I didn't trust him an inch and nicknamed him Casanova.

The house was not the easiest place to live in when trying to sleep during the day at the best of times. With

Marxist meetings on the floor below and Casanova always hanging around waiting for the next female prey to enter his den, I had to have my wits about me.

Apart from the downsides, I loved my bedsit in the roof. It had two single beds, so I could have friends stay over. I even learned to cook a decent meal on the little Baby Belling cooker that came with the territory. I deliberately didn't buy a television, having grown up in a house where it was on constantly. I was pleased to be without one. Music was my passion, and I spent a fortune on my first Panasonic music centre, which had a radio, record player and cassette player. Cassettes were becoming more popular in the late 1970s, but records were still very much a part of the music scene. I had nearly all of Elvis Presley's LPs and was always playing music. When I wasn't working or out with friends, I would stay up half the night reading or painting. Oil painting became a favourite pastime in those bedsit days.

Many nurses took sleeping tablets to help them sleep during the day after working on nights, and after a couple of nights, I could understand why. Crash, bang. Doors slammed shut all day long. Car engines appeared to rev louder and human voices were incredibly irritating when trying to sleep, not to mention the sun.

'Why does the sun shine so brightly when I'm on nights but it pours with rain when I'm off?' I whined at Jerry. He smiled and put his arm around me, knowing I wasn't looking for an answer. I would walk through the door after an eleven hour night shift, climb into bed and fall asleep almost immediately. I then woke up after what felt like eight hours sleep only to discover, when I looked at the clock, it was midday. I had slept for three hours. I'd spend the rest of the day tossing and turning, trying to drown out house and street noises.

Daylight and all the other things that go on during a normal day would finally win the sleep battle and I often gave up by mid-afternoon. By the time I was due back on shift, I was ready for bed. Many a time, I asked myself if I really wanted to keep putting my body through this permanent assault course.

We worked eight nights on and four off. Although the four off seemed like a lot, they passed all too quickly. The first day off was recovery day, and I slept, setting the alarm to wake me at lunchtime so I would sleep that night. Of course, this would be the day when I could have slept a full eight hours, but no, I had to drag my tired body out of bed. The fourth day off, I would try to have an afternoon nap before going onto nights again. Night duty was tough.

I usually met up with Jerry and friends before going on a night shift. I couldn't drink alcohol, so had to sit in the pub supping lemonade. During the first few nights, when I felt like Mother Teresa through my enforced detox, I waxed lyrical about self-denial. I brayed about job satisfaction that nursing brought and how I was going to change the world.

The novelty wore off on around day four when I moaned like a toddler!

Jerry and I often played tennis before I went onto night duty, and the adrenaline surge from the exercise often helped me feel better for the first few hours.

I didn't switch meal times around, and ate dinner before going on shift, often a kebab or takeaway. I would have breakfast before going to sleep in the morning.

The hospital canteen was open during the night and as I mentioned previously, I would brave the corridors, ghosts and all, in order to get a middle-of-the-night snack, a cup of coffee and a cigarette, my on-off relationship with smoking was back on. It was always fun to meet up with my friends and fellow students in the middle of the night. We would share experiences and a joke or two.

Grace and Sue were on nights at the same time as I was. Grace had fallen in love with yet another doctor. This time it was for real, she argued, again. Sue and I had lost count of how many true loves there had been before that. Of course, a month later we were picking up the pieces of her broken heart again, as the doctor concerned had moved on.

Grumpy doctor on the ward

Many doctors hated being called out of bed in the middle of the night to re-site an intravenous cannula. Most of us did our best not to call them. I learned quickly that if I was going to be shouted at by anyone other than a ward sister, it would be from a tired and overworked junior houseman in the early hours, but sometimes it couldn't be helped.

Doctor Brian had been on the ward until one o'clock, catching up with his jobs from the round of the morning. There was also a list of jobs for him to do in the ward book. The jobs mainly comprised prescribing pain killers' intravenous fluids for patients, plus re-siting any cannula that had come out or stopped working. Finally, he went to bed. And can't have been gone more than an hour before one of the junior students let me know that a patient's drip had stopped working. I went to check and tried a few of the tried and tested ways to get it going but couldn't, so I knew I had to call Dr Brian.

'Blast, he's not going to be happy,' I said to Carly, the other student. *Understatement of the year, as it turned out.* I phoned switchboard and asked if they could bleep Dr Brian. Thirty minutes later and no phone call. It was now around three o'clock. I called switchboard again.

'Could you bleep Dr Brian please?'

'Has he not called yet?' asked the operator.

'No.' I replied.

'Okay, I'll try again,' he said wearily.

About ten minutes later, the ward phone went. 'What is it?' snapped an exhausted voice.

'Sorry Doctor, Mrs James's drip has stopped running.'

'Why didn't you tell me when I was up there?' he snarled and slammed the phone down before I could tell him that it had been running at that time he was on the ward.

Four o'clock came and still no sign of Dr Brian, I daren't ring him again, so regrettably, I had to let the night sister know. This night sister was old school and Dr Brian was not going to like a call from her. Sister Kennedy marched onto the ward, clearly pleased she had someone to tell off from the spring in her step. She snatched up the telephone.

'Bleep Dr Brian,' she commanded and then slammed the phone down and waited. I wanted to tell her to shush or she'd wake the patients, but that would have been suicide. The phone rang a minute later. 'Dr Brian, this patient has now been waiting two-and-a-half hours for you to get your lazy body out of bed. Make sure you are here within the next five minutes or I will call Mr Hoskins.'

With that, she slammed the phone down again. This was turning into a phone slamming competition, and I knew who the winner was going to be. Mr Hoskins was a brilliant but formidable surgeon who no-one would want to cross. Personally, I wouldn't want to cross Sister Kennedy either. Five minutes later, Dr Brian appeared on the ward. He looked his young age, terrified and sheepish.

'Sorry Sister, I didn't get to bed until really late.'

'Don't give me your excuses Doctor, go and apologise to the patient and while you're at it, replace that drip.'

'Yes, Sister,' he muttered, before obediently following the junior student to the patient's bedside, where he replaced the drip.

Sister Kennedy seemed in no hurry to go, much to my

dismay. She smelled blood and was enjoying herself too much.

I wouldn't have minded, but she had already ruined my night by making me do the whole round anti-clockwise earlier, which had thrown me out of synch. Some of the meaner sisters, well aware that we learned the patient's names and diagnoses clockwise, would belligerently start on the right. This meant trying to remember backwards, which was nigh on impossible on the first night and they knew it. She had huffed and puffed all the way through the ward round complaining about my tardiness. Her parting shot to me had been, 'Next time, pay more attention to your patients, Nurse.' I'd have given anything not to call her back up to the ward that night but patients came first.

Finally, Dr Brian finished re-siting the drip. It must have been difficult because he had been gone for ages. When he came back, his red eyes looked incredibly sore and tired. I felt sorry for him even though he had shouted at me.

He was about to leave when Sister said, 'You are wanted on Ward 18, Doctor.'

Off he stumbled with a tremendous sigh.

Sister was almost floating by now, sadist that she was. 'Goodnight, Nurse Brookes,' she chirped as she left the ward.

We all stared after her, hardly able to believe how much she had enjoyed adding to the young doctor's plight. Although, as student nurses, we got it from every side, so I didn't feel sorry for him for too long.

25

FINALS

At last, we were in for our final nursing school block. Our set had reduced to thirty. Just as Mrs Butcher had predicted, eleven of the group had left and they encouraged five to leave who had failed assessments along the way. My circle of friends were all still there, I'm pleased to say, and we were all really excited to be approaching the last hurdle.

We had passed our practical assessments and coursework, which included written Case Studies, now all we had to do was pass a two-hour exam.

Taking a multiple choice examination might sound easy, but it really wasn't. I still have the revision books we used for practise and when I work through them, I still don't know answers to some of the questions. The problem for us was that the questions could be about anything. They contained a mixture of anatomy, physiology, or questions relating to any illness. The exam was hard.

When I did my RGN training a couple of years later, I had to pass all the practicals again with an extra one. I also had to submit more case studies and sit yet another one of these multiple-choice exams. On top of that, there was a three hour written exam. Was I a glutton for punishment?

Everything moved a little too quickly as our two years came to an end. We sat finals and then were back on the wards until the results came out. Once the results were out, there was a rush and a flurry of job applications while working on the wards until our contracts ran out.

We were never in school again, so there was no huge celebration or get together. In fact, unless we met up at work, we didn't know who had passed and who had failed, which probably wasn't such a bad thing.

We held a bit of a party during our last block in school, but it wasn't that good because most of us were either revising or making sure we had passed everything we needed to in order to take the exam. The top and bottom of it was that I never really got to celebrate with my friends, and we parted ways without much ceremony. It remains one of my biggest regrets. For two years, we had supported each other through thick and thin, and then it all fizzled into nothing in a matter of days. Not everyone who had come to Leicester to train stayed, so it was a bit of an anti-climax, apart from the joy of qualifying.

Jerry was around, of course, as we were still going out together at that point, but we split up soon afterwards. Sadly, I wasn't ready for the commitment he wanted and I realised I was being unfair keeping him dangling when he was so obviously the marrying kind. The inevitable time came for me to let him go, which he took quite hard.

I just felt I was too young to settle down. If there had been anyone, I would have married back then. It was definitely the long-suffering Jerry, and I hope he is now happily married with oodles of children and grandchildren.

Although passing finals was incredibly exciting, it was a mixed blessing. My Great Ormond Street friends moved back to London soon after I qualified.

Having said that, I was too busy to worry about it too much because of the need to find a job, and obviously there were a lot of students in the same boat.

After we got our pass letter, we had to pay and complete registration with the then English National Board for Nursing and Midwifery before gaining the State Enrolled Nurse certificate. We had a final few weeks of work placement to complete while waiting for the registration to come through.

I asked Mrs Butcher at the end of my training if I should go on and do my Registered Nurse training.

'I'm not sure you would cope with the academic aspect,' she said, 'but you go and prove me wrong,' she finished with a twinkle in her eye. I often wonder if she meant what she said. Granted, I was slow to start with, academically, as I was lazy in terms of studying, but did she really think I wouldn't be able to cope? Prove her wrong, I did. Becoming an RGN, a midwife, gaining a degree, then a Master's degree and a few Postgraduate diplomas along the way!

26

QUALIFIED AT LAST

My first job as a qualified nurse was on Ward B at the Groby Road Hospital in Leicester. Ward B was a medical and infectious disease ward. The ward sister was a dragon with a reputation for being impossible to work with. *Just my luck,* I thought.

For some reason, only enrolled nurses were employed to work on the ward and no students were allowed. I was one of three SENs who worked with or opposite Sister's shifts. The blocks were called A, B, and C and formed were three stand-alone wards: each block was a single storey with twelve beds. Block B was next to Block C, where my staff nurse friend, who'd rescued me from the other ogre sister over the lumbar puncture incident, was now the ward sister. We often met for lunch and drinks after work. They had originally designated the wards, TB wards. Groby Road

Hospital was not popular with local residents, some of whom remembered it as the old workhouse.

Sister's office was immediately opposite the entrance at the centre of the ward. There was a treatment room and then six cubicles on either side of the main office with glass partitions, meaning Sister could see all twelve cubicles from her office.

The ward had a kitchen, bathroom, and the usual sluice room on the opposite side of the building. The linen cupboard was the only place where we could hide to chat without being observed from the office.

After working on the ward for a few weeks, I realised that Sister's bark was worse than her bite. She didn't do small talk, but she had a heart of gold underneath the abrupt exterior. My friend Margo and I nicknamed her "Special" because she was one in a million whatever way you looked at it.

Special ruled with a rod of iron, but was loyal to her staff and incredibly protective. I think we were the only family she had. She always spoke in clipped tones and called me Nurse, even when I was at home.

The phone rang at eight o'clock one Sunday morning. I was due to work a late shift and had been out late the night before, so was fast asleep.

'Hello,' I mumbled, still half asleep.

'You can come in an hour later today, Nurse.' The phone went dead. I was totally confused. Who the heck was that? Then I realised it was *Special*. I turned over and went back to sleep. Another time, a friend was staying over after a late night out. The phone rang early. Becky answered.

'Is Nurse Brookes there?'

'Who? Oh yes.' She handed me the phone, unimpressed at being woken up so early. It was *Special* again, telling me I could go in half an hour later that day. I apologised to my hungover friend.

'Is she mad?' she asked.

'No, just eccentric,' I replied.

Although Block B was small compared to the Nightingale wards, it was still busy. A lot of patients had to be barrier-nursed because of the nature of their infectious diseases. We were the only specialised ward in Leicester.

One of the first patients I admitted was a young man with typhoid. I had never come across anyone with typhoid before and it was not at all pleasant. Mr Baker had recently been to India and soon after returning, he began having sweating episodes and felt weak and lethargic. They admitted him to us with severe bloody diarrhoea. He had a temperature of forty degrees centigrade. Initially, stool and blood samples were sent to the laboratory, and we aimed the primary treatment at bringing his temperature down, which involved tepid sponging.

I remember looking at this very young man, who had obviously lost a lot of weight. He was skeletal with long, black hair and a beard and moustache. He was very ill and could barely lift himself out of bed to use a commode. It must have been frightening for him, as we confined him to the room and barrier-nursed him. He was only allowed one visitor each day, and so his parents and his boyfriend took turns to visit. They too had to learn how to put on a gown, mask, and gloves before entering his cubicle. Once the diagnosis was made, he was treated with antibiotics and gradually improved, being discharged a month later. It was always rewarding to see patients go home; but it wasn't to be so for Mr G.

Mr G was a homeless twenty-seven-year-old who was admitted after being found unable to walk in a local park. He had a severe cough and was bringing up a lot of sputum from his chest; it was an unpleasant blood-stained green. Shortly after admission, the doctor sent him for a chest X-ray. The X-ray arrived. *Special* called us into her office.

'Nurses, look at this chest X-ray; you will never see another one like this in the whole of your career.' The X-ray was fascinating. I was no expert, but I could see that instead of the normal dark areas of lungs where air should have been present, these lungs were full of thick white patches, like cottage cheese.

'What is it, Sister?' I asked.

'The worst case of tuberculosis you will ever see, Nurse,' *Special* replied.

'Can it be treated?' *He is so young*, I was thinking.

'We can try, but I don't think so.' At that point, the Senior Houseman walked in.

'Here's the drug chart, Sister, let's get started.' Dr Jerome looked at our worried faces. 'He'll be up and around in no time.' He smiled. *Special* glared at him.

The next day, I was on duty when I saw Mr G collapse back on his bed. I rushed into his room; he wasn't breathing, and the pulse was fading fast. I called for my colleague to dial the "Crash" team and when his pulse disappeared, I began resuscitation. Bedlam ensued as doctors arrived, but the sad outcome was that we could not bring him round. The doctor declared him dead an hour after all our efforts. Mr G had no known relatives, they had arranged a state-funded burial. He would be interned in what we referred to as a pauper's grave; an unmarked grave funded by the Council. My colleague and I wanted to go to his funeral, but she was too frightened to ask permission, so I knocked at *Special's* door.

'Yes, Nurse.'

'Sister, I was wondering if Nurse Froome and I could go to Mr G's funeral.' I stammered.

'Why?' Special asked.

'Because he'll be all alone with no-one who cares about him, and we don't think they should bury anyone like that.'

'You may go,' Special replied, and I think I saw a note of genuine pride in her eyes on recognising that her nurses cared. *Special* was wonderful to me after that day and became like a distant aunt, never friendly, but in her way she let me into her life. We kept in touch for years after I left the ward. *Special* was also nicer to my friend after that too;

previously, she had given her a hard time because she was relatively new to the ward.

Special was incredibly experienced; she knew the chances of that young man surviving were slim, and her prediction was absolutely right. I never saw a chest X-ray like that one again, even when I worked in a specialist chest hospital and saw many cases of TB; there was never another like that one, thankfully.

There were many other patients I met and cared for on the ward with various chest conditions, but it will always be Mr G, I remember. I left the ward after about six months when I secured a place on a cardio-thoracic course at the London Chest Hospital. I was sad to leave Leicester and my mum again, although she had got used to me living away, and I was sad to leave *Special*. My next adventure, though, was about to begin. I packed my bags, said goodbye to my beloved bedsit, and boarded the train to London. This time I was going to be living in a Nurses' Home.

THE END

London, 1980. When they encounter a screaming girl and cockroaches in the kitchen, a group of young nurses' know they are in for challenging days ahead!

Draughty windows, radiators that won't turn off, and food that goes missing in the night. Will these nurses' from all over the United Kingdom manage the stresses and strains of working in a specialist hospital?

Follow Dawn Brookes to London's East End for another exciting insight into a time when cancer chemotherapy was in its infancy and pioneering heart surgery was becoming commonplace.

Hurry up Nurse 2: London Calling

Meet the lovable charming Mr Robinson who sees potential in this party-loving young woman, and the energetic Mrs Chang who keeps the nurses' on their toes. You'll love getting to know the novice nurses. Then there's the night porter who enjoys a late-night chat and of course the patients' who touch all their lives. If you liked the first book in this series, you will love this one.

ACKNOWLEDGMENTS

It took several years to complete this book, and I give thanks to my friends Sue Dundon and Ruth Lonsdale for encouraging me in this endeavour. This version has been fully rewritten and revised.

When I left school, nursing never entered my head until I made friends with a person in Norfolk who made the suggestion. I give heartfelt thanks to Gail for this. I hope that I have made a good go of it and that you are pleased with yourself and with me. I am also ever grateful to patients I have cared for both then and now; without you, I wouldn't have had the pleasure of working in the NHS for the best part of thirty-nine years.

HURRY UP NURSE 2

LONDON CALLING

Dawn Brookes

Oakwood Publishing
www.dawnbrookespublishing.com

DAWN BROOKES

HURRY UP NURSE 2: LONDON CALLING COPYRIGHT

This book is a work of non-fiction based on the author's experiences. In order to protect privacy, names, identifying factors, dialogue and details have been changed or reconstructed.

Published by DAWN BROOKES PUBLISHING
www.dawnbrookespublishing.com

Cover Design by Dawn Brookes

PREFACE

This second book contains a collection of memories from my experiences of a training course in London's East End. The recollections take place from 1980 to 1982 prior to my RGN training in 1982, which is covered in *Hurry up Nurse 3: More adventures in the life of a student nurse.*

The procedures and practices outlined throughout this book are a true recollection of my memories. I have tried to recreate events, localities and conversations from memory and from notes taken during the two-year period. I have changed the names of individuals and places to protect confidentiality of patients and the anonymity of others. I have also mixed up identifying characteristics to further protect anonymity. I have changed details relating to the timing of incidents and places and wards where they occurred, along with the order of training in some instances.

Moving to London in 1980 proved to be one of the

defining moments of my life, both professionally and personally. I made lifelong friends, met during my time at the London Chest Hospital, and two wonderful tutors supported me to go on and further develop my career.

In 1980, cancer chemotherapy was in its infancy, but coronary heart surgery was becoming routine. Tuberculosis was on the rise again, despite new treatments. I hope this memoir will give you with an insight into life in one of London's pioneering hospitals. London in the early 1980s was a fabulous place to live, as many new and innovative treatments were being developed.

1

LONDON CALLING

I took one last look at my beloved bedsit in Leicester, partly to check I had left nothing behind, and partly to say goodbye. It seemed silly being attached to a one-room bedsit, but I had spent two very happy years living there and was feeling irrationally attached to it at that moment.

Finally, I sighed, whispered farewell, and looked at my rather large suitcase containing all my worldly possessions. It was an old brown suitcase that my mum had given me the week before when I had gone to say goodbye. A solid suitcase with two fastening clasps made of metal, a case that was of a type common in the 1970s. My mum had looked a little forlorn as I left, and I tried to make as light of it as possible, promising I would take care of myself and that I would visit when I could. London was only one hundred miles from Leicester but it may have been John o' Groats, as far as my mum was concerned.

'Don't worry mam, I'll be fine and I will write and let you know how I'm doing.' Mum was doing her best not to show the sadness she was feeling and smiled as I left, but I knew she would cry when she went back inside the house.

It didn't pay to dwell on these morose thoughts though, and so I locked the bedsit door and dragged the suitcase down the stairs, sneaking past Casanova's flat on the ground floor and stepping outside into the fresh air. Casanova was a man in his mid-forties who constantly had women going in and out of his room at all times of day and night.

It was a bitterly cold Sunday morning in October 1980. I realised I wasn't dressed for the weather, as I had on a pair of light trousers and my favourite beige jacket; I immediately felt the icy wind blowing through my jacket and light silk blouse. *Oh well, too late now*, I thought, as all my clothes were in the suitcase and there was no way I was going to try opening it again after sitting on it that morning to make the clasps fasten. It had ended up being a battle of wills between me and the suitcase: I had finished up lying on it and getting it into a judo hold before finally getting one clasp to click into place. That had been followed by another monumental effort to get the other one closed. After shutting the front door leading into the house of bedsits that had been my home, I left my suitcase on the doorstep and popped down the road to post my keys through the landlord's door like he had asked me to.

I realised when walking back up the road how quiet it was on a Sunday morning and gazed across the road to the

Charles Frears School of Nursing. The magnificent Tudor building where I had trained, and felt another sense of nostalgia. I arrived back at the house and half-carried, half-dragged the suitcase up the road to the bus stop. Thankfully, my bedsit had been fairly close to the main London Road, and I crossed over with relative ease, as there was hardly any traffic around. By the time I got to the bus stop, I was feeling a lot warmer because of the weight of my suitcase. For the first time that morning, I felt excited about the adventure ahead of me and couldn't wait to get to London.

Finally, the bus came, just as I was about to cool down again, and I arrived at Leicester train station in plenty of time to catch a train. I had left early, knowing that Sunday buses were few and far between. There were a few more people around by the time I got to the station, and I bought a one-way ticket to London. I had about an hour to kill before my train would arrive, and I bought a cup of coffee. The train station was freezing and there was nowhere warm to sit, so I sat trying to think warm thoughts. One of my friends had always said that if you thought of a lovely warm coal fire when it was cold that you would feel warm. I wrapped my hands around the plastic cup of coffee, which was lukewarm due to the cold, and tried this tactic unsuccessfully.

August 1980

I had applied for the cardio-thoracic nursing course I

was about to embark on just a few months earlier and was accepted on the same day as the interview, much to my surprise. I had been a bit late applying in the August after my friend, who was training at Great Ormond Street, had spotted the advert in the Nursing Times. Brenda and I had met while she was doing her adult placement in Leicester during the previous year and we had become great friends. I missed her when she went back to London and she had missed me too, it seemed, as she was constantly on the lookout for jobs that might interest me.

I thought back to the interview, which had taken place on a much warmer day than this one on a weekday rather than a weekend.

I had taken the train to London on my day off from the Groby Road Hospital, where I had been working since qualifying. On that day, I had left at around eight o'clock in the morning despite my interview time being at two o'clock in the afternoon. I knew it would take time to find my way to the hospital by Underground tube train, and I had planned to have a closer look around the area before attending the interview. I was disappointed that Brenda could not get the day off, but she was on an early and we had agreed to meet in Holborn later that afternoon. The tube hadn't been difficult to negotiate, and I had sauntered along, arriving at Bethnal Green tube station at around midday. I asked someone in the street for directions to the London Chest Hospital. It was only about a five-minute walk from the tube station. On turning onto Bonner Road, the hospital was the first building I saw. It was set back on a corner, with a surrounding metal fencing inserted into a dwarfed wall. The hospital itself, though large, was tiny compared to the Leicester Royal Infirmary where I'd trained. It was a similar size to Groby Road Hospital, but more compact, as Groby Road was spread out over a large area of land; however, this one had a pleasant look to it. The surrounding streets left a lot to be desired though, and the area looked generally run down.

I had walked around for quite a while before realising it was nearly time for my interview, and then I braved the walk through the hospital gates. The entrance comprised two ancient and foreboding oak-wood doors that were closed shut. I opened one of the big, heavy doors and walked in – almost fell in, actually! The door had opened with a lot more ease than I imagined it would. I gathered myself together, hoping no one had noticed my clumsy entrance, straightened up and approached the hospital reception desk, which was just inside. The receptionist was on the telephone and I waited while she put calls through to various wards. The smartly dressed woman with long brown hair looked at me, smiling. 'Yes?' she enquired.

'I'm here for an interview.' She smiled again.

'Name?' *Obviously, she saved her longer conversations for the telephone.*

'Dawn Brookes.'

Finding my name on a list in front of her, she ticked the pad before looking up again. 'Take a seat.' She nodded toward a bench on the opposite side of the corridor. I obediently sat down. The woman, who had been economical with her words but not unfriendly, picked up the phone again, and heard my name mentioned. I had arrived ten minutes early. I couldn't see much of the hospital from where I sat, just a long, marble corridor, heading in both directions. It appeared to run the length of the hospital. There was the usual of hustle and bustle, phones ringing, voices everywhere, some laughing, and some shouting. I worked out it was visiting time, because of the people dressed in outdoor clothes milling around. Some of them stopped at the reception desk to ask the way to a ward. I was feeling nervous tension. Even though I hadn't got my heart set on the job, the prospect of being interviewed was still nerve-wracking. I heard my name mentioned; it was the receptionist.

'Miss Brookes! Left along the corridor, past the stairs, then it's the second door on the left. There's a sign on the door saying: Senior Nursing Officer.'

'Thank you.' I got up and walked along the corridor, finding the door, but once there, I didn't know whether I should knock or wait outside. I was staring at the door like an idiot when it opened and a kindly, Caribbean-looking lady wearing a navy blue uniform opened it.

'We were beginning to think you had got lost,' she said, beaming. I knew I would like her immediately. 'Come in,' she continued. She wore a starched, frilly hat and for a moment it fixated me, but then I pulled myself together.

I noticed three other people in the room. 'This is Miss Bale, senior nursing officer, Mr Robinson, tutor, and Mrs Chang, tutor. I am Mrs Lumumba, nursing officer. Sit down, Nurse Brookes.'

They asked for my certificates and qualifications, and I handed over my enrolled nurse certificate confirming that I was a real nurse, and my school certificates for what they were worth. I had a few CSEs, one O level and not much else. CSE stood for Certificate of Secondary Education and a Grade 1 was equivalent to an O level, Grade C. Many secondary schools in England, Wales and Northern Ireland only allowed study for CSE subjects to pupils, although some offered O level subjects to the more academically able. CSEs meant pupils did at least leave school with nationally recognised qualifications. Both of these examinations were replaced by GCSEs in 1988. Mr Robinson raised a quizzical eyebrow on inspecting the school certificates. I couldn't remember a lot about the interview except for two questions. The first came from Mr Robinson. 'You don't appear to have many school qualifications; why is that?'

I was a bit taken aback and felt my face flush while I wracked my brains for an answer. Eventually, I went for the honest option, explaining that I had found school difficult and had experienced some problems at home. They seemed to accept this. Mr Robinson smiled. He was dressed in a dark grey suit, wore black-framed glasses and had thin grey hair; he appeared to be in his sixties. I noticed a lovely twinkle in his eye when he smiled.

The next question came from the nursing officer who had invited me in, Mrs Lumumba. 'Tell me a story that shows me how you can deal with stress. It doesn't have to be work-related.'

Where were these questions coming from? I looked up to see their expectant eyes boring into me. Although the question put me on the spot, I told them how I had been interviewed for the Samaritans a year before and had been asked what I would do if presented with a flasher. A flasher referred to a person (usually male) who exposed themselves in front of others. I told them I had answered, 'I would say: never mind, perhaps it will grow.' At this, they all laughed freely, and I felt relaxed for the first time since entering the room. That answer was going to make or break me, but I couldn't think of anything else at the time.

There had also been the customary, 'Why do you want to work here, Nurse Brookes?' question of course, and I had practiced my answer on the train.

'I am really interested in cardio-thoracic nursing, having worked on a medical ward for the past ten months.' As per my first entry into nursing, when asked this question the reality was quite different to the answer I gave at interview. The actual answer should have been, *because my friend has been nagging me to move to London for ages*, but of course, I would never say that. The interview ended, and they explained that the course was due to start in October, and I was a bit late applying for this year. They told me to sit outside, which I duly did, except there were no chairs, so I stood! After about twenty minutes, they called me back in. They were all smiling.

'Congratulations,' said Miss Bale, 'you have been accepted. You can start in October this year as we have had someone pull out. We will put a letter in the post.' I was stunned. I hadn't expected to be told on the day and I certainly hadn't expected to be moving to London a couple of months later, assuming I was applying for the following year. *How was I going to tell my mum and how was I going to tell Special?* Special was the ward sister I worked for on a medical and infectious disease ward. I had nicknamed her *Special* because underneath a formidable exterior, I had discovered that she really was quite special. Obviously, I never called her *Special* to her face, but I'd become fond of her and although she would never say as much, the feeling was reciprocated. I wouldn't go so far as to say we were like family – she was a bit like the maiden aunt in David Copperfield. I admired her.

I floated out of the hospital and made my way back to the tube station. Later that day, Brenda and I celebrated. She was delighted that it would all be happening so soon. I ended up getting a late train back to Leicester as I was working the next day.

I had received the promised letter in the post the following week. The offer explained they had accepted me for a twelve-month, fully funded course in cardio-thoracic nursing and told me the salary (the usual pittance) – and there was some mention of a London Weighting Allowance, which meant nothing to me. I later discovered the London Weighting Allowance was an extra amount paid to people of certain professions (usually in the public sector but not exclusively), who were employed in London because of the higher costs incurred from living there. They instructed me to report to the London Chest Hospital, main reception, on a certain Sunday in October 1980, and they would provide me with a room in the nurses' home. Enclosed was a health questionnaire for me to complete and return in the post. The letter also informed me a doctor would examine me during the first week of training.

October 1980

So, here I was at the station in Leicester at the start of my journey. The train was on time and the journey to London, King's Cross, took about two and a half hours. It should have been much shorter, but Sunday trains were always slower, the guard who came to check my ticket informed me.

'When will we arrive in London?' I asked.

'Twelve-thirty, duck. Train stops at every station today – its Sunday, duck.'

He must have been from Leicester, as the customary "duck" was native slang to the area. When the train finally arrived in London, I realised I was hungry: I remembered I hadn't had breakfast, because I'd had no food left in the house and even if I had I wouldn't have been able to eat with a combination of excitement and nervousness of that morning. I hadn't eaten on the train because food was too expensive on trains and I was nearly broke already, even though I had been paid in September. Travel, cigarettes, and parties had taken most of my salary, and I had spent almost all of my remaining money on the train fare. October was going to be difficult in terms of money, but at least I would have a roof over my head. Payment for that would come out of my salary, which would be paid in arrears. I could go into my overdraft if necessary, but that had become more and more common recently. I might have to do some agency work around my new job, I thought.

I heaved my suitcase off the train and realised I was at the far end of the platform; it seemed to take an eternity to get to the ticket barrier, as I had to keep stopping to put the case down and then starting again. I finally made it, and the man took my ticket from me. I dragged the suitcase across the station and arrived at the tube sign. The steps down to the Underground had been a lot easier on my interview day when I hadn't had the heavy burden that I was carrying today. *Never mind,* I thought, *almost there.* I bought a tube ticket and descended the last bit of the way on a wooden stepped escalator. The Underground was busy but not crowded; I could hear a variety of languages as tourists were present, even on a chilly day in October. There was a busker playing the guitar and singing as I walked towards the platform I was heading for. I smiled at him, but he didn't smile back as I didn't give him any money! I looked at his cap laid on the ground and thought to myself that there wasn't much money in it. If there had been, I might have been tempted to ask him for a loan. The Underground platform was quite busy, as King's Cross was a mainline station from the north and the midlands into London.

Finally, a tube train arrived, and I dragged the suitcase onto it. I was exhausted by now and my stomach was rumbling. I had fallen out with my suitcase and kicked it in place as I sat down, but the kick hurt me more than it hurt the suitcase. The train became less and less busy as it headed towards the East End of London. By the time I arrived at Bethnal Green tube station, there were only three passengers left in the carriage. I had wondered whether I might meet anyone else moving into the nurses' home, but didn't see anyone fighting with luggage.

I got off the train at Bethnal Green and saw to my dismay that the escalator wasn't working. I had to drag that wretched case up hundreds of steps to get out into the daylight. By the time I got to the top, I was wondering if my worldly goods were worth this effort, but decided that they were. I thought I should have left my books behind, as they were probably weighing me down. I had left my cherished Panasonic music centre with my mum and had said I would collect it, along with my records, at the first opportunity.

The last part of the journey seemed to take the longest. I was hungry and thirsty, and my right arm felt like it was going to drop off. In fact, both arms were aching, as I had been swapping hands every few minutes. I mainly dragged the suitcase along the pavement now, making a lot of noise as I made my way through the streets to the hospital, but I was past caring. I turned onto Bonner Road and saw the welcome gates to the hospital. With a sudden burst of energy, I made my way to the front entrance and then cursed as I saw the steps up to the front doors. They had, of course, been there on the day of my interview, but I hadn't been tired that day. I sat on the bottom step for a few minutes and smoked a cigarette. Later, in 1983, I gave up smoking. Feeling reinvigorated, I dragged the case up the steps and pushed open one of the big brown doors. *Hello world, I have arrived.*

On entering the hospital, I showed my letter to the receptionist, a man this time.

'Hello love, you need to go down the corridor, past the stairs and you'll see doors on the right that take you out into a courtyard. Go straight across the yard and the door to the nurses' home will be right in front of you.' He smiled, then looked at a list in front of him. 'You're on the first floor, right at the top of the stairs, end room on the left, and your name will be on the door.'

2

NURSES' HOME

I found my room at one end of the corridor on the first floor and pushed the door open. The key was in the door, and there was the label with my name on it on the outside. I was disappointed, as the room was tiny compared to my bedsit. As I opened the door, it hit the bedside locker, and I looked to the right to see a single bed. At the foot of the bed was a small wardrobe. Against the left-hand wall was a small chest of drawers with three drawers, and there was a sink in the far (well, not that far) left-hand corner of the room. The room looked out onto the courtyard and the hospital rear side, and there was scaffolding to the right of the courtyard, which was to remain in place for the entire time I lived there.

I sat on the bed, exhausted, and there was a knock on the door, which I had left open. Before I had the chance to reply, in came a very tall, slim girl with dark curly hair. 'Hello,' she said, 'are you starting the course tomorrow?' I detected the Welsh lilted accent immediately.

'Yes, I am, are you?'

'Thank God for that. I've been here all day and haven't seen a soul. My name's Fran, I'm from Swansea.'

'Hi, I'm Dawn, from Leicester. What time did you get here then?'

'My dad dropped me off at ten o'clock. He took me out to lunch and then he had to get back.' *Lunch and a lift*, I thought. *Lucky you*.

'I've been travelling most of the day,' I replied. 'Trains are really slow on Sundays and this case weighs a tonne.'

'Do you want a coffee? I've got some welsh cake my mum made too if you would like some,' she offered, and I knew I would like her from that moment on. I nodded enthusiastically. 'I'll be back in a jiffy,' she said, and turned and went away as quickly as she had arrived. The very welcome coffee and cake arrived a short time later, and we both lit up cigarettes and shared our stories. Fran had trained in Swansea and never lived away from home before, but she said she was up for the challenge.

'I think my parents were beginning to think I would never leave,' she laughed. 'Hints have been dropping for the past two years, but now I think they will miss me. They wanted me to marry a boy who lived down the road, not move to London.' Fran was pleasant company after my long journey.

After a while, we heard lots of noise and fresh voices as

other people arrived. Fran showed me the kitchen that was about halfway along the corridor on the opposite side of my room. It was a good size, with lots of cupboards, a fridge, and a cooker with four gas rings and an oven. There was a kettle and a toaster that both looked like they had seen better days. The bathroom was next to the kitchen and there was a single bath; the toilet was next door to the bathroom. I counted twenty rooms on the floor, and there must have been the same number on the ground floor and second floor. A palace it was not.

A short time later, three other girls had congregated in my room along with Fran. There was May, a vicar's daughter from Bournemouth, Jen from Stornoway (I had no idea where that was) and Blanche, a black girl from Leicester whose parents had brought her down. *If only I had known her before*, I thought. We were soon laughing and joking and sharing life stories, and we became firm friends from that day forward.

It took a while to get used to Jen's thick Scottish accent, but we mastered it soon enough. Stornoway, she explained, was the chief town on the Isle of Lewis in the Outer Hebrides. I was no wiser, but have since discovered it is a long way north. It was nice to meet someone smaller than me in Jen; she was four foot eleven inches tall, and I was five foot nothing (half inch actually, but I rounded it up or down). She had mousy brown hair, similar to mine, although hers was short and mine was shoulder-length. May was medium height with darker brown, shoulder-length, straight hair and a posh accent, and Blanche was medium height, chubby but not fat, and had a really open and kind face with dark brown eyes and medium frizzy black hair. Blanche was Afro-Caribbean.

'How did you get here?' I asked Jen once I realised Stornoway was on an island.

'I flew over to Glasgow yesterday and stayed overnight with a cousin, then I got a train to London, but I had three changes before arriving in London. I got a taxi from King's Cross to the nurses' home.' *Blimey,* I thought, *and there was I feeling hard done by*. I related the story of my journey, but it didn't have quite the same impact after hearing about Jen's. May had been driven up by her father and she was looking forward to life outside of a vicarage. She laughed. Blanche was the only one with a steady boyfriend, who lived in Leicester, and she had every intention of moving back there as soon as she had finished the course, as she was already missing him.

By the time we heard people coming off the wards following their shifts, we had already gelled into what would become a close group of girls. Fran was the oldest at twenty-three, May was almost twenty-three, Blanche was twenty-two and Jen and I were the babies at twenty-one. At around six o'clock, we decided to unpack and agreed to meet up and go over to the hospital canteen and find some food. I unpacked my suitcase and was just about to close it when I noticed something at the bottom; it was a letter from my mum with two ten-pound notes inside. I was ecstatic; that was a lot of money for me, and maybe I wouldn't have to starve all month after all.

We had found the canteen in the hospital basement and eaten well, as hospital food was relatively cheap, and I think we were all feeling much better as a result. Jen was looking like she might fall asleep at the dining room table.

'Come on, girls, I think it's time to call it a night. We need to be in class at nine o'clock in the morning.' May put into words what we were all thinking, so we headed back to our rooms to get ready for the following day. Some of them still had to unpack.

I sat down on the bed for a while; there was no chair, so it was the bed or the floor. I looked at my writing pad, thinking that I should write a letter home to my mum. She didn't have a telephone, so the only way to keep in touch was to write, and I also wanted to thank her for the twenty pounds which had saved my life. I would miss out telling her that last bit though as I didn't want her to worry; I knew she didn't have much money herself, so would never cadge from her. Just as I picked up the writing pad, I heard screaming coming from down the corridor. I opened my door and saw a commotion up near the kitchen, so I went to see what was going on. There was a fair-haired girl standing there, screaming her head off, and a few people had gathered round.

'What on earth's the matter?' I asked.

She just stood there trembling in the corridor. 'In there.' She pointed towards the kitchen. Fran had come out of her room by now, as had May. We looked into the kitchen but couldn't see anything.

'Turn the light off,' the trembling girl said.

Obediently, I did what she said and tried to calm her down.

'There, it's off,' I said, beginning to think I had moved into a psychiatric home.

'Now turn it back on.' I did so and as I did, I saw about ten enormous cockroaches crossing the floor before scuttling underneath the kitchen units. We all stepped back, startled, though none of us had quite as dramatic a reaction as the screaming girl.

'That's all we need,' said Fran, who shared that her Nan had a farm in Wales and they were forever invading the kitchen there. At that moment, someone popped their head out of a room down the corridor.

'Would you lot keep it down, I'm on an early in the morning,' she said, and then closed the door.

'Come on,' said Fran, 'you look like you need a nice cup of tea.' She took the trembling girl by the arm and steered her towards her room. May and I followed.

We discovered that trembling, screaming girl was called Flora and was also one of our set. I had mixed feelings about having a hysterical girl in the group. She had arrived later than the rest of us, as her train had been delayed. Flora was from Hull, and her journey had been rather eventful. First, her dad was going to give her a lift, but he was a vascular surgeon and he had been called into work in the middle of the night, so her mum took her to the train station where she bought her a first-class train ticket. *As well for some,* I thought. She had to change trains somewhere along the way and the second train didn't have a first class carriage – *poor thing;* I thought. This train stopped in the middle of nowhere for an hour and nobody knew what was going on. There were very few railway announcements back then, and even if there were, you couldn't understand what was being said, and they never told you what was going on. You were lucky if you got: 'This train has been delayed.' The guards were never anywhere to be seen if something was wrong. Finally, the train got moving again, but Flora had lost her seat to someone who took it when she went to find out what was happening. Flora had to stand for an hour before arriving in London. She hadn't wanted to brave the Underground, so she had made her way to the street and was about to get into a taxi when someone nudged her out of the way and jumped in. Poor Flora was by now terrified of London and waited for a while before another taxi pulled up and brought her to the hospital. She had just found her room and the kitchen, and was going to make herself a bedtime milky drink when the invasion of the cockroaches occurred. It was obvious to the rest of us that Flora was going to need looking after, or she wouldn't survive a week away from her cloistered upbringing.

Once we had all had a cup of tea, Flora finally calmed down. I had thought about joking with her that cockroaches were poisonous, but decided she'd experienced enough traumas for one night. Meanwhile, Fran was in Welsh mothering mode.

'Don't you worry, they're filthy creatures, but they are more scared of you than you are of them. I'll ask someone if they can get rid of them tomorrow.' May and I looked at her cynically, but she gave us both a warning glance, so we nodded knowledgeably.

'Yes, I'm sure someone will re-home them,' May smiled, and I nearly laughed, but for another warning shot from Fran.

'Do you think so?' asked Flora.

'Oh yes,' I said. 'No doubt about it. Anyway, I think I'm going to go to bed now – see you in the morning.' May and I left, and when we saw Fran escorting Flora to her room like a mother hen, we knew we would all be in good hands as long as Fran was around. I also made a mental note not to be the first in the kitchen at night!

I thought it perhaps as well that Flora didn't know the history of our new home, or she may never have moved here. My dad had revelled in telling me stories about the place, taking far too much pleasure in relating the more frightening parts of its history. Bethnal Green, in the East End of London, appeared to have had a dubious past. Probably no more so than any other area in the East End, but its associations with the Kray twins and Jack the Ripper made it rather notorious. We discovered that many locals in the surrounding pubs were quite proud of its fame, albeit from less than desirable celebrities. The Kray twins were gang members who were infamously responsible for a London underworld of crime and violence. Other members of the family were also criminals, and they had lived in Bethnal Green in their early years, a couple of miles away from the hospital. Almost every pub we went into was reputed to have had the twins drink there, so I'm not sure whether I ever drank in one they had truly frequented. It may well have been true, as Bethnal Green has a long history of boxing and the Krays were boxers in their early years. There were often gangland feuds across the East End because of the Kray twins' operations. The Krays had long been imprisoned by the time of my move. For many years Bethnal Green was a poor area, and Jack the Ripper reputedly operated towards the western edge of the area and into Whitechapel.

There were also philanthropists operating in and around Bethnal Green. The Quakers and bankers, for instance, who originally brought the dream of a hospital for people with tuberculosis to life. They were responsible for the building of the London Chest Hospital. Quakers still meet on Old Ford Road, which was the road I walked along whenever I took a tube into London. There was also a Bethnal Green Medical Mission that had been established to help the poor.

Finally, I got back to the room that was going to be my home, with thoughts of cockroaches and criminals whirring round in my mind. It was boiling in there, despite the cold outside. I noticed there was a radiator under the window but there was no way of switching it off, so despite the freezing cold outside, I pulled the top sash window down halfway and crawled into bed. At least there was bedding, because I didn't have any of my own. The white, starched sheets were uncomfortable, and as I fell asleep, I wondered if they doubled up as hospital sheets – I hoped not, but suspected they might.

3

SCHOOL AGAIN!

Crash, bang! I awoke with a start, wondering where on earth I was, and then I remembered. It seemed the girls starting on the early shift weren't too concerned about waking anyone up as they banged around and slammed doors, or maybe they were getting their own back from the night before. The girl in the room next to me must have been on an early, as I could hear her crashing around in her room and the taps running. Every time someone turned on a hot tap, the pipes gave off clanging noises, which eventually turned into a high-pitched whine. This was going to take some getting used to, I thought to myself.

I was freezing cold and wondered why, but remembered I had left the window open and it was howling a gale outside. The net curtains were blowing around in the room, and a picture I had put on the windowsill was now on the floor. I looked at the clock: six o'clock! I had never been a morning person, so I dragged myself out of bed, closed the window and went back to sleep, waking again at eight o'clock when my alarm went off. Despite being used to sharing a bathroom and toilet from my bedsit days, this was different. Every time I went down the corridor to the toilet, it was locked. When I was getting near to bursting point, I decided to go up to the next floor and found the one up there unoccupied. There were three floors to this nurses' home, which was one of three residences. There was a residence for specialist trained staff and one for the doctors who were on call; we were in Residence 2 which was for course trainees. We were all qualified nurses but were training for a specialism, so it was back to being a student for a year.

I decided a strip wash was going to have to do it, and then a cup of coffee. I did at least have a jar of coffee which I had brought with me, but no milk. Fran had said the night before that I could use hers, which she had clearly labelled and put into the fridge – as if that was going to make a difference. I would soon learn that labels meant nothing in a nurses' home, and if you wanted to keep any food for cooking, it was best kept in your own room. Things had a habit of walking in the night, and despite the rude messages stuck to the fridge and cupboards, no-one took any notice. There wasn't a lot of room for storage space anyway, as the shabby cupboards were pretty full and some people had even put their names on the doors. The fridge was large but antiquated, and it certainly wouldn't have passed the CFC emissions tests of today. In fact, it was probably this one fridge alone that was responsible for a large proportion of global warming! The bacteria that grew inside it could also have filled a pathology laboratory for biology students who wanted to practise growing stuff in their Petri dishes.

I met Fran and the others downstairs, as we had arranged to congregate at the entrance and go over to the classroom together on our first day. The classrooms were on the ground floor of another residence – the one where permanent staff lived. As we entered, we met the other girls who were going to be in our set. There were ten of us in total.

Mrs Chang entered the room; a bundle of energy, small, rotund and always smiling. She spoke as fast as she moved, and I liked her from the off. She was nothing like the serious but kindly Mrs Butcher who had been my tutor in Leicester. Mrs Chang had moved to England from Malaysia in 1970 to find work. She was in her early thirties and had married a Malaysian man who she had met whilst working at St. Thomas' hospital in London. She had become a nursing tutor in 1977, the same year I had started my initial nurse training. They set the classroom out with tables rather than desks, and we all found seats. Mrs Chang began by introducing herself and then, after she had called out our names from a register, she asked us to introduce ourselves and say where we had come from.

Six of us had already met, so we were eager to meet the rest of the group. Chloe introduced herself as being from

London and explained that she lived in a flat not too far away in Bethnal Green. She was originally from the West Indies, but her family had moved to England when she was four years old, and she had moved to London to do her general training in 1977. She had studied at Bart's (St. Bartholomew's) hospital for her training and continued there after qualifying. Supindra had been born in England and was still living at home with her family, who were from India; she had worked at The London Hospital in Whitechapel before starting the course. Margaret was from Margate in Kent, and she had moved into the nurses' home, although we hadn't met her the day before. She said that she had arrived in the evening, and had heard the screaming episode while she was unpacking, but hadn't come out to investigate because she had been a little scared of the noise. Fran and I looked at Flora, who blushed. Kath introduced herself as being from Bristol, but told us she had moved to London a year before and was living with her boyfriend in Hackney.

I could tell immediately that we were going to gel as a group. The only one we didn't get to know quite as well was Kath, but the rest of us became good friends and often socialised together. Kath joined in and was great fun during class and on the wards, but she had a life outside of the hospital.

'Now we have all introduced ourselves, let's get started,' began Mrs Chang. 'As you are aware, the course you are embarking upon is the Joint Board of Clinical Nursing

Studies (JBCNS) 162 – cardio-thoracic nursing. It will last twelve months, and you will gain a multitude of experience in this hospital.'

Mrs Chang continued in this vein for a while, explaining that there were two main wards on the second floor of the hospital, as well as an intensive care unit for cardiac surgery. The wards on the second floor were named Riviere, which was a medical ward specialising in tuberculosis, and Hilton, which was also a medical ward. On the first floor of the hospital were two surgical theatres, a high dependency chest unit for people post-lung surgery, a surgical ward called Lister, and the coronary care unit. The ground floor of the hospital housed the outpatients department and a cardiac catheter laboratory, as well as all the administrative offices, including those of the nursing officers. In the basement were the canteen, the main kitchens, the mortuary and post-mortem room.

'You will rotate through all of these wards (thankfully not the mortuary) and units on both days and nights,' – groan – 'but you will have to go over to the Brompton Hospital for your paediatric experience as we don't see children at this hospital.' Double groan, scary, I thought. Mrs Chang then moved on to explain how the course was to be assessed, and we were all delighted to know that there would be no final exams but that we would undergo continual assessment. Actually, this involved a lot of hard work, but not having a final exam was a bonus. The continual assessment would involve tests once a month; two case studies, one cardiac and one medical; and successfully passing all ward placements. Besides this, we had some practical skills to pass, including giving intravenous drugs. The latter was one of several extended roles for nurses, previously undertaken by doctors, that were gradually introduced from the late 1970s onwards.

The scaffolding outside my room, I learned, was to be a hospital extension where another ward and theatre would be added, but they did not complete this until after I left the hospital a few years later.

'On this course you will cover respiratory disease, including in-depth anatomy and physiology as well as surgical techniques; and cardiac disease in the same manner.' Mrs Chang obviously loved teaching. She was so enthusiastic. For the first time in my life, I realised that learning could be fun. There was no formality with Mrs Chang, and – a first for me – we were allowed to call each other by our first names. We did respectfully call her Mrs Chang, but she never made us call her Sister Chang. 'We have recently started to treat lung cancer with cytotoxic drugs (cancer chemotherapy was in its early stages) and we are very excited about this.' Mrs Chang explained that after a coffee break we were to go to the outpatients department to see Dr Caplin for a medical examination.

Dr Caplin was a chest consultant at the London Chest Hospital and specialised in tuberculosis. He was an incredibly intelligent man with a social conscience. Apparently, he had been born in the East End after his

Jewish parents had fled persecution in Poland during the First World War. He remained committed to the people of the East End throughout his life, and even founded a refuge for homeless people with tuberculosis (TB). Dr Caplin was sixty-three when I met him and had started to specialise in lung cancer and chronic bronchitis. He insisted on meeting all the new trainees and ensuring that we would not become victims to tuberculosis, which, although declining, would make resurgence in the East End of London in later years. Dr Caplin earned an OBE in 1983 and had a ward named after him at the London Chest Hospital, which I left in 1982. Sadly, he developed dementia in his later life and died in 2011. I knew nothing of all this when I waited outside his room to see this widely renowned man; to me, he was just another physician.

'Nurse Brookes.' The nurse called me in.

'Good morning, Nurse,' Dr Caplin looked at me.

'Good morning, Doctor.'

'Have you ever been in contact with TB?'

'Yes Doctor, there was a patient on my last ward who died of the condition.' He raised his brow quizzically, and I could see he was genuinely interested.

'Really? What happened?' I explained about the homeless man I had cared for, and about Special (I didn't call her that) telling me I would never see a chest X-ray like that for the rest of my career. He was even more interested now, and obviously impressed with my previous ward sister.

'Describe the X-ray, Nurse.' I could see the nurse in the

room looking at her watch and knew the others would be queuing up outside, but Dr Caplin didn't seem in a hurry, so I described what I had seen. I explained how both lungs on the X-ray had looked like they were full of caseated cheese. He was suitably impressed by now.

'I have certainly seen such X-rays in my time but not recently, so Sister Froome may be right, let's hope you never do see another X-ray like that one – okay Nurse, we had better examine you.'

After listening to my chest and heart, checking my blood pressure and pulse, he looked for the BCG mark on my left arm.

'Sorry Nurse, it's not visible; we are going to need to give you a tine test.' I had been given a BCG, following a negative heaf test at school, and had declared this on my health form before being accepted, but if the scar was not visible, Dr Caplin would not take any chances.

The heaf test and tine test are multi-puncture tests where four to six needles coated with tuberculin bacilli are pressed onto the skin of the forearm. The heaf test would be read between two and seven days, but the tine test could be read within forty-eight to seventy-two hours and was favoured by Dr Caplin. In the USA, the Mantoux test is used and the tine test is not recommended. The heaf test is now discontinued as a test.

Growing up in England in the 1960s, they gave all children a BCG vaccine to protect against tuberculosis, if showing a negative heaf or tine test in between the ages of ten and fourteen years. In my school, they gave us it at fourteen years of age, and I remember having both the heaf test and then the subsequent BCG (Bacillus Calmette–Guérin) vaccine. The vaccine stopped being given routinely in 2005 in the UK. I didn't mind having the tine test, as I too would rather not have developed TB, and it was no more than a scratch. Thankfully, mine was positive a few days later, meaning that I did not have to have a repeat BCG. Even more thankfully, I never developed TB either. As I was leaving, Dr Caplin asked, 'Where did you work before, Nurse?' and he wrote the ward and hospital name down. I suspected he wanted to look at that X-ray, and Special would be hearing from him.

After our medicals, we had lunch in the canteen and then went back to the classroom. Three of us had needed a tine test, and we had fun looking for each other's BCG scars before Mrs Chang joined us.

That afternoon, we began our studies, starting with the respiratory system. Mrs Chang explained that most of our teaching would be provided by herself, as our classroom tutor, and Mr Robinson, the kind man I had met at interview. The consultants would also do some teaching, as would their registrars. Registrars were doctors who had worked as junior hospital doctors and had chosen to specialise in an area such as surgery, cardiology or medicine. A lot of our learning would take place on the job, but I was used to that. We had this initial week's block training and then we would have a day a week in class, with a couple of extra blocks towards the end of the course. This was like original training, but much more needed to be crammed in this time. The assessments would take the form of written classroom tests, case studies and ward reports.

Unlike Mrs Butcher, who had assured us of dropouts and failures, Mrs Chang promised us we would all complete the course and that although it would be hard work, we would be very happy at the London Chest Hospital. She was right on both counts. To be fair to Mrs Butcher, the dropout rates in general nurse training are much higher than those for specialist courses, and the numbers starting training are much greater, too.

That first week we were immersed in lectures each day, and Mrs Chang made our learning fun, although it was delivered in great depth. We had to learn physiology from the cellular level, particularly if we were to understand what occurs in chronic bronchitis and emphysema. These were the conditions we were to learn first, along with asthma, and we had to understand the physiological changes within the lungs so that we could understand the treatments. At that time, there were only two types of inhaler available to treat asthma and these contained salbutamol and beclomethasone. We could also give salbutamol via nebulised oxygen, which was a frequent treatment for acute attacks that resulted in patients being hospitalised. Salbutamol tablets were commonly given to people with asthma, as were aminophylline injections. We rarely use the latter in current practice and there are a multitude of inhalers on the market now.

I already knew about nebulisers because we had used them on my previous ward. A salbutamol solution was inserted into a chamber attached to an oxygen mask – we then turned on the oxygen and this forced the solution to be dispersed as a spray, which meant the inhalation provided greater relief. The relief was probably more because the patient received the correct dose of salbutamol; since because of difficulties in mastering the technique (particularly when the patients struggled to breathe in the first place), most patients hardly got any salbutamol from the inhalers.

As we got used to our daily routine and living in the nurses' home, we started to explore the local area. As previously mentioned, Bethnal Green was not the most salubrious of places. The houses opposite the hospital were, like the hospital, Victorian buildings, and they had grand steps leading up to their entrances. The majority of these had been converted into flats and were not usually lived in by families. Historically, they had probably housed quite wealthy people with servants.

The London Chest Hospital site formed a triangle on a plot of land with sides leading onto three streets. We accessed the main entrance through the gates on the corner of Bonner Road. As mentioned previously, the Quakers had built the hospital in the 1850s for people with tuberculosis (then known as consumption), because there was nothing available to treat patients with the condition in the East End of London. Diagnosed patients were not allowed into ordinary hospitals for fear of spreading the disease. Coincidentally, the architect chosen to design the hospital had originated from Leicester, like me, so I was obviously destined to work there. The hospital had quite a large lawn area to the front. They added balconies to the wards in the early 1900s. Prince Albert had laid the foundation stone when building had begun. They did not name it The London Chest Hospital until 1923, having had two other names prior to that. The hospital had suffered bomb damage during the Second World War, when the chapel and the nurses' home were destroyed, as well as one of the wards. Thankfully, no-one died, although some patients and a nurse were injured. During a second bombing raid, the pathology laboratory was also destroyed, along with historical records and specimens. It became an NHS Hospital when the NHS was founded in 1948 after World War II. The London Chest Hospital was one of the first hospitals to undertake coronary artery bypass surgery in the 1960s.

During that first week, they gave us our uniforms. I loved it; there was a green dress because I was still an enrolled nurse. They made the dress of much thicker cotton than the one I had worn in Leicester, but the best was yet to come. We got to wear starched white aprons, just like I had seen in magazines of nurses from the past. Now I felt like a proper nurse. Not only were we given aprons, but they also gave us starched white hats – I felt I was in nursing heaven. These uniforms were so much smarter than the ones worn in Leicester. I couldn't wait to get on the wards. In addition to this, they gave us five uniforms each, one for every day of the week; no more fighting with laundry to try to get uniforms washed in time as I had been forced to do frequently while working in Leicester, where we were only given three uniforms. In Leicester, I'd sometimes had to wear a uniform two days running, which wasn't pleasant, as usually there was some blood or other unsightly stain from a previous shift. We had also worn cardboard hats in Leicester, but I had better not get started on that one. These starched linen hats were beautiful in comparison. We were all happy with the uniforms, although some were not quite as enthusiastic. Jen said her uniform in Stornoway was far superior. Jen was homesick so everything in Stornoway was far superior at this point, but she soon settled as we found the local pubs and clubs and explored London.

One of the first places my friends and I discovered on that second night was the local pub, called The Bonner. It was actually The Bishop Bonner, but it was known locally as The Bonner and that was the name that stuck. The Bonner stood alone on a street with derelict houses. I believe that Chas & Dave used to sing there regularly, but if they did, it was before my time. There was often live entertainment though, both during the week and at weekends. We found the pub after school on that first day and would go there twice a week until we explored further afield. It was a busy pub and all the locals used it. We stood out as it was obvious we were not local, but the people were friendly and were used to staff from the hospital popping in for a pint – or a half in our cases.

I was delighted to discover Victoria Park on my second day of living in London: an enormous park that our nurses' home backed onto. We could go out of the back gates and be there in minutes. That park would become my refuge, and I would spend hours and hours in the summer months walking and reading there.

The first weekend in London, Jen, Fran, Blanche, May, Margaret, Flora, and I decided to go to the cinema in Leicester Square. I don't remember what film we saw that weekend – I think it was pretty boring actually – but I remember going to see the second Star Wars film later that year. After we had been to the cinema, we found a nightclub called the Empire in Leicester Square and agreed to go dancing. It cost a fortune to get in, and although I was twenty-one, I was age checked (you only had to be eighteen to get in, but I always looked younger than I was). I hated this, as it happened to me a lot in those days, but of course I am thrilled now that I look so much younger than my years.

We had a great time, drank too much, and shared a taxi back to the hospital at three o'clock in the morning, as the tube trains had stopped running. As I fell into bed that night, I realised I couldn't live like this if I wanted to stay solvent, and decided to join an agency as soon as possible to earn some extra cash.

One thing stood out to me following that night out, and that was having our handbags searched when entering public places. The IRA was very active during the 1970s and 1980s and London was a prime target, hence the need for these searches. They became noticeable when going out to the theatre, a concert, and to places like Wimbledon, where I went later on in my training.

That Sunday I hardly saw anything of my friends, as I think we all felt pretty lousy. I woke up with a splitting headache but managed to sleep through all the early shift workers getting ready and the door-slamming. The nurses' home was relatively quiet, as some people had gone home for the weekend and others were working. Once I had drunk three cups of coffee and eaten some toast (someone else's bread), I told myself that I must get some food basics in and return all the 'borrowed' food I had eaten that week. I decided to go and explore Victoria Park. It was a bright but cold winter's day and I felt pretty happy, looking back on my first week in London. So far, so good. I had met some lovely people and Mrs Chang was dynamite in the classroom, making lectures far from boring. She held my attention almost all the time, which was a first in my life. I have to thank her for the love of studying and learning that I have developed throughout the years since then.

I followed the path into the park, and after about ten minutes, came to a lake. I walked away from the path and closer to the lake area until I found a secluded spot and noticed a large rock by the shoreline where I found a comfortable position to sit and watch the water and the sky; I sat there for quite some time. It would have been easy to stay longer, but the cold was starting to bite and I realised I needed to walk some more to warm up. That spot became my refuge during my first year at the hospital, and I called it "my rock". I would frequently visit my rock and spend hours thinking and contemplating life there; I would also take books in the warmer weather and go there to read when I wasn't working or at the end of an early shift.

My rock met three of my needs. The first was that I had a love for water and so the lake enabled me to relax, particularly if work had been stressful. The second was my need to think. I was still very young, but found that I was a deep thinker and would mull over many things in my mind. The third was my love of reading; I had always loved books and preferred reading to any other activity, although dancing and parties came a close second. My rock and I would meet each other, and that solitary place in that busy park offered me solace on many occasions.

4

SPIT IT OUT!

Although I was a qualified nurse, this hospital was a specialist centre, and caring for the patients who were admitted was not at all simple. The medical conditions were complex, and I was a new girl once again. Starting a new job was always daunting, but having had a week of specialist lectures, I realised that this one was going to be quite demanding in terms of both stamina and knowledge. The only textbooks I had, if you could call them that, were my revision books and my Baillières Nurses' Dictionary, which every nurse who trained in the 1970s had a copy of. I still have this dog-eared dictionary – it had a front page on which you could put the start and end date of your nursing training, and I must have been feeling conscientious as I fully completed it. It remains a treasured possession.

Thankfully, Mrs Chang gave us a lot of handouts (the paper variety) as I didn't have any spare cash for books; not that there were that many specialist books for nurses back then, though there were plenty for doctors. Come to think of it, there were hardly any nurse memoirs written back then either; the only one I had come across was Monica Dickens' *One Pair of Feet* (still a favourite) and she hadn't exactly been a career nurse, as she had moved on to do many different jobs. There were, of course, biographies of Florence Nightingale, but reading about the Crimean war didn't appeal to me, although I have since read a few biographies about our Flo, as she is known in the profession.

The shifts at the London Chest Hospital were like those I had worked previously. The early was 07.30 am to 4.30 pm, the late was 12.30 pm to 9.30 pm and nights were 9 pm to 07.45 am. I had looked at my timetable and seen that my nights would start in the following February, then decided it would be best not to look too far ahead as I had enough to learn in the present.

The second morning after starting on my first ward, I bumped into Fran when leaving the bathroom. I was not a morning person and didn't like undue conversation, especially not at 6 am. I had hardly slept, looking at the clock every hour, as I hadn't wanted to sleep in. Fran was just the opposite; she loved mornings and looked immaculate. Her hair was well groomed, and she had a wonderfully upright posture, which is something I have never been able to achieve.

'I'm so excited,' she said with a smile. 'First day on CCU.' (Short for coronary care unit.) 'I went to the ward yesterday to introduce myself and they all seemed friendly.' *Why hadn't I thought to do that before my first shift yesterday?*

'That's great, can't wait to hear about it later,' I mumbled, as I walked back to my room. I felt a little better once I had dressed in my uniform. At least I only had to walk across the courtyard and up two flights of stairs to get to work, rather than take two buses like I had done previously. That cheered me as I ate a slice of toast, finished my coffee, and smoked a cigarette before making my way over. Blanche was going to be working on the same ward as me, but she was starting the next day. They had given her the Monday and Tuesday as days off. I was off later in the week, but we would work together at the weekend.

My first ward was one of the medical wards, Riviere. I'm uncertain where the name came from, but it seemed a bit of an odd one for a hospital ward. The ward was for people with respiratory problems and also housed patients with tuberculosis. The wards were not Nightingale wards, such as those I had been used to in Leicester. We accessed them up two flights of cantilever stairs (I loved those stairs) with metal railings. Once you got to the second floor, there were two huge archways that separated them, Riviere to the left and Hilton to the right.

There were statues carved into the archways all around the hospital. There was even a statuette of Jesus over the main entrance to the hospital. 'This must have been what had attracted the God squad,' I used to joke to my friends. My friends and I had heard that there was a group of

Christians working at the hospital, collectively known as the God squad – more on that later in a later chapter. In reality, it was not uncommon for Victorian buildings to have statues carved into pillars, and the architect (from Leicester) had previously designed churches.

The wards were divided up into bays, with a day room on each floor. There were small toilets in the centre for patients who were too ill to get to the main bathrooms at either end. The ward kitchens were also in the centre of each floor. There was a Sister's office at the far end of each ward and this is where we would have handovers.

A senior nurse gave the handover on one shift to the nurses coming onto the next shift. There were usually three handovers on any given day. The staff working on an early shift were given a handover from the nurse in charge of the night shift. Staff on the late were given a handover by the nurse in charge of the early, and then the night staff got a handover from the nurse in charge of the late shift. Every patient would be discussed, along with any important information such as when drips were due, what medications had been changed, how often 'obs' were required, any changes in their condition, any new results and diagnoses, visitors they had seen, what mood they were in and so on. We would dutifully write everything down on scraps of paper and refer to these throughout our shift. At the end of a handover, the nurse in charge would allocate us our work and then we would disperse. The two nurses in charge would stay and chat for a bit longer, probably sharing the latest gossip while we got on with the work.

There are many things that stood out to me when I first started working at the London Chest Hospital. The first was that there were no student nurses, just post-qualified nurses like myself undertaking specialist training. We inevitably became the students, although not to quite the same extent as during general training. Mostly, we were treated with a little more respect, although there were still a few dragons who felt it was their right to tread us underfoot like unwanted ants.

There were, of course, nursing auxiliaries, who, as always, were the backbone of the hospital wards. They could make or break a ward, and they often knew quite a lot more than people gave them credit for. After all, some of them had worked at the hospital long before many of the trained staff; even the ward sisters were relatively new to the hospital. There were no Specials at this hospital. Special was a sister who had worked on the same ward for most of her career, but London hospitals tended to have a more fluid workforce. Often this was because of the costs of living in the big city, which even back then was expensive compared to the rest of the country. This became apparent as I discovered that most of the trained staff lived in hospital accommodation or rented flats in the East End of London.

The next thing that stands out in my memory is the sputum rounds. I had noticed the sputum pots at the bedsides on my first day. Sputum, as eloquently defined in my Baillières Nurses' Dictionary, is:

'Excess of secretions from the air passages. It consists chiefly of mucus and saliva, but in diseased conditions of the air-passages it may be purulent, blood-stained, frothy, and contain many bacteria.'

The dictionary follows this definition with a warning:

"Sputum should always be regarded as highly infectious and should be expectorated wherever possible into disposable containers and incinerated."

Many patients ignored that latter part as they insisted on swallowing the sputum. In lectures, we had learned all about the multitude of things that could be discovered from sputum. That may be the case, I thought, but unfortunately there were no students to delegate the daily checking of sputum to, so they left this to the trainees, much to our displeasure. It was something I never got used to; it didn't matter how many times I carried out this routine, my stomach would always retch. I think that particular job was responsible for my lifelong stomach problems.

As we were working in a chest hospital and the two wards on the second floor were designated chest (respiratory) wards, in strict obedience to my revered dictionary, every patient had a sputum pot on a locker at the side of their bed. These were white plastic containers not dissimilar to those that used to be used in fish and chip shops, hence my dislike of mushy peas in a pot. They had lids, and the patient's name was written on the lid along with the date, since they had to be changed every morning and replaced with new ones. Early shifts therefore involved lifting the lid and examining the sputum as well as estimating the amount.

'When you check sputum,' Mrs Chang had taught us – I would have preferred that to be an 'if,' – 'you are looking at colour, consistency and amount. The colour will tell you if there are signs of infection; you also need to check for blood, and if blood is present, you need to assess the colour, type and consistency of that too.'

I remember there had been lots of cries of 'yuck!' from that class. We had learned that clear sputum meant no infection but large volumes of clear, frothy sputum might indicate pulmonary oedema, where there was fluid in the lungs as a result of heart disease. Yellow sputum was typical of chronic bronchitis and emphysema, while green sputum was usually a sign of infection or chronic infection in patients with bronchiectasis or cystic fibrosis. Blood in the sputum could be from pneumonia, lung cancer, tuberculosis or pulmonary embolism. I would come across patients with all of these conditions and more at some stage during the next year.

'I'm not sure I will be able to examine sputum Mrs Chang. Can we opt out?' Blanche had asked. Mrs Chang had laughed, thinking that Blanche was joking, but most of us were feeling much the same. It was one thing collecting the occasional sputum sample to send off to the laboratory; it was quite another to examine the stuff in detail.

'I will tell the patients it's best for them to swallow it,' whispered Jen.

'You wouldn't!' exclaimed Fran. Jen smiled in response and we weren't sure whether or not she was kidding. Fran was about to say something else when Flora piped up.

'Oh, I'm not worried about it at all.' Flora surprised us with this flippant comment after the cockroach fiasco of the night before. Jen looked at her disbelievingly.

'My cousin has cystic fibrosis,' she explained, which made us all nod understandingly. I resisted the temptation to suggest that some sputum might look like mashed cockroaches, but giggled to myself at the thought.

Graham was the first person I met with a diagnosis of cystic fibrosis, which was a condition I had not come across before – mainly because specialist hospitals saw patients with the condition such as this one. Graham was sixteen years old and a regular in-patient to one of the wards, with frequent infections. He had blond hair and blue eyes, was around five feet five inches tall and apart from being very thin, pale and barrel-chested, he could have been an ordinary sixteen-year-old. Cystic fibrosis was, and still is (albeit with a much better prognosis), a life-limiting condition that babies are born with. The condition is not always obvious at birth and there is now a screening programme to detect it in newborns. Most patients with the condition would die in their teens or early twenties and never reach adulthood. Nowadays, people can survive well into their forties, and this is likely to improve even more in the future.

Cystic fibrosis cannot be caught, as it is a genetic disorder. The gene is carried by the parents, and when two people who carry the gene marry, there is a one in four chance that a child will be born with the condition, and a two in four chance of a child being a carrier of the defective gene. The condition mainly affects the lungs, causing thick mucus and sputum, which has to be expectorated frequently to limit the number of chest infections a person suffers. It also affects the digestive system, meaning that the patient has to take enzyme supplements to help with digestion. Men with cystic fibrosis are also infertile, which has become more of an issue in recent years as people with it now live longer. Men with healthy sperm can now father children through the aid of fertility clinics. Women with the condition can usually have children, although some may need fertility treatment.

By the time I met Graham, he understood better than I did how to manage and treat his condition. Every morning he and another boy called Dave would treat themselves with postural drainage, and then we would give them physiotherapy with the aim of keeping the lungs as clear as possible. Postural drainage involved elevating the bottom part of their bodies so that their chests were lower than their legs, and the use of gravity would help them to cough up the sputum. I met a wonderful, cheery, Chinese physiotherapist called Bart, who taught me this procedure, and the physiotherapy required.

'You need to cup your hands and then tap very quickly from the base of the lungs to the top, like playing the drums.' Bart smiled. I was far too gentle when I started out, but I didn't want to leave these very thin boys with chest bruises to add to their problems. Bart was a patient teacher.

'Nooooo,' he would laugh. 'Show her, Graham.' With that, Graham would tap himself with one hand and was far rougher that I would ever be.

'Okay, let me try again,' I smiled, and gradually, with help from the physiotherapist and patients, I learned the technique, which I remember to this day.

Over the next two years, I got to know Graham and Dave well, as they were frequent visitors to the hospital, both as inpatient and outpatients. Graham sometimes joined us at the local pub when he was undergoing treatment, and I met him for a day out in Hampstead Heath, near to where he lived, the following spring. I don't think I ever saw Graham low in mood, although he had every reason to suffer with mental health problems. He was amazingly well balanced and resigned to living a much shorter life than the majority. I found it difficult to understand how he could be so positive, but he just was. I grew really fond of him and Dave and would have found it very difficult if either of them had died while I was working at the hospital.

Sometimes one or other of them was admitted in a really bad way when they had chest infections. Seeing them struggle to breathe was heart-wrenching. We used to open the windows on the ward to encourage air flow, give them nebulisers, and they would start intravenous antibiotics. The worst time for them was evening and night, as the stickiness in the lungs got worse despite hourly postural drainage and physiotherapy. We would place their beds on wooden blocks to tilt the head down so that the sputum could come up. After a day or two, they would start to improve and we would see them laugh again, and the light would return to their eyes. I knew, and more importantly, they knew, that one day the treatment would no longer work and they would likely die from one of these infections. Neither of the boys had a girlfriend, and they had both missed so much school time that they had left at sixteen.

Graham's mum had given him some home schooling, more out of necessity than desire, and both his parents had done their best to provide him with as normal a life as possible. He regularly played football with his dad, just kicking a ball around really, because he couldn't run. He loved walking, though, as I discovered on my day out with him to Hampstead Heath. Graham also loved nature, once telling me if he hadn't had cystic fibrosis, he would have loved to work with nature, but his illness meant he couldn't get a job, because he would have to take too much time off sick. I was impressed with his knowledge: while we were out, he could identify birds, spiders and beetles, as well as every type of tree. As a city girl, born and bred, I was suitably impressed because I could only just tell a sparrow from a pigeon. I like to think that when he died, his parents scattered his ashes somewhere on his beloved Hampstead Heath.

Evenings and nights were tough times to work as most of the patients with acute respiratory conditions couldn't breathe. Mornings were worse for the patients with chronic bronchitis and emphysema as they tried to clear their lungs of the overnight accumulation of sputum. This leads back to the sputum part of the story, which you may have noticed I had to take a break from.

The first morning I was on sputum duty occurred on my second ward day, which was an early. We had by that time been through the sputum lesson with Mrs Chang, and the ward sister asked me to check the sputum pots. My stomach heaved at the thought, which was not a good start. I had come across small amounts of sputum on the medical and infectious disease ward I had worked on after qualifying, but it was collecting a small sample to send to pathology. This was going to be something entirely different. Funnily enough, Jen, Fran, May, Blanche, Margaret and I had been discussing the sputum issue in my room the previous night, as four of us would be based across the two medical wards. Jen and Fran were working on the coronary care unit, so they didn't have to face this just yet. The others in the group were allocated to the surgical ward.

'I hate sputum,' I had complained. 'I'm not sure I will be able to check the pots without pulling a face.'

'You'll be fine,' Fran said. 'Don't think about it while you're doing it, pretend its something else.'

'Like what?' Jen laughed, and the conversation had deteriorated from there, none of it very helpful to me.

Here goes, I thought, and was greatly relieved to see that the nursing auxiliary was exchanging the used pots for new ones. At that moment, Staff Nurse Trenton came up behind me.

'Does that mean I don't need to check them?' I asked hopefully.

'Yes,' replied the staff nurse, 'Kate is a very experienced auxiliary; she will ask you if she's unsure, but we decided to let you get used to the ward before dropping you in it.' I was going to love this hospital – no such luxury would have occurred as a student nurse.

'Thanks,' I smiled.

'That's okay. Come on, let's do the 'obs' round.' I followed her to the treatment room where we collected equipment, greatly relieved even though it was only a temporary let off. I would indeed have to get used to pots full of sputum and would have to train my stomach to behave. Once I gained the ability to assess and estimate amounts of sputum, it was much easier, as I could take a cursory glance and immediately notice if there was anything untoward. If not, the lid went back on faster than I could blink an eye and I would move on to the next one.

'Obs' rounds, or observations rounds, I was more familiar with. These involved checking temperature, pulse, respirations and blood pressure, and were carried out four- to six-hourly depending on the patient's condition.

There was a bit more to the rounds in this specialist hospital than in my previous experience, particularly in relation to respirations. Many patients with chronic respiratory conditions have faster than normal respiratory and pulse rates, and we had to learn what was normal for a particular patient and what was normal for the condition that they had. This was important, otherwise I would have been forever calling doctors to check up on patients who were actually stable.

Besides this, patients with such conditions had different levels of breathing, using different muscles, and again, it was hard to judge what was serious and what was normal for that patient. Some patients also developed different-shaped chests because of a chronic lung condition. What I thought was going to be a simple 'obs' round turned out to be a real learning experience, and I felt inadequate again, like a new girl starting from the beginning, which in some ways was correct. I was half wishing that I had started with the sputum round, but realised that was just plain silly. The round went something like this.

'Staff,' I called.

'Don't worry,' she replied. 'That's a barrel.'

'That's a pigeon.'

'That's a funnel, oh, and that's kyphoscoliosis.'

We'll have a lot to discuss in the pub tonight, I thought.

I had to call the staff nurse over at least four more times during that first round because, even though I could check the charts and see what the previous respiratory and pulse rates were, I was not always clear that the pattern of breathing I was seeing was normal for the patient. We kept observations charts on clipboards at the foot of the bed so that they were instantly accessible to nurses and doctors (and nosey visitors). These included charts for TPR and BP, fluid, drugs (medicines), and sometimes additional ones such as IV charts for those having intravenous infusions or intravenous antibiotics.

'Don't worry nurse, Mr Hickson always breathes that way, he is using his accessory muscles to assist due to emphysema,' Staff Nurse had reassured me. Mr Hickson was leaning forward with his elbows on a table, using his shoulders to assist with breathing. This is quite common in patients with emphysema, although we now call the condition chronic obstructive airways disease, or COPD for short. Mr Hickson smiled at me.

'Not to worry Nurse, I'll tell you if I get worse.'

If you get any worse, I thought, *you will be dead.* The poor man looked dreadful but was obviously used to breathing with this level of difficulty when in hospital. He looked like he needed more oxygen, as he was blue in the face.

'Should I turn the oxygen up, Staff?' I asked.

'No, he's a retainer.' I looked quizzical, and she realised I hadn't got a clue what she was talking about.

‘He retains carbon dioxide, so if you turn the oxygen up it can cause metabolic acidosis.’ Again, I looked stupefied. *Where was Mrs Chang when I needed her?* ‘He could die,’ she said – ah, now that I understood. Though I thought a little more study was going to be necessary. Throughout that first week, they bombarded me with respiratory jargon, most of which I did not understand. Medical jargon would fill volumes of books all by itself. The terminology alone was confusing, without the additional acronyms and made-up words.

In my early training, we had often used mnemonics to learn anatomy such as when we had to learn the twelve cranial nerves. The only thing was that after a while, we could remember the phrase and the names but could not always the order of the nerves – it was better than nothing though. The mnemonic for cranial nerves was *‘On Old Olympus Towering Top A Fox And Gibbon Vaulted And Hopped.’* Difficulty arose because there were so many beginning with ‘O’ and ‘A’. It was a matter of repetition and we had great fun with this, and many others. Some mnemonics would be too rude to mention.

Going back to Mr Hickson, doctors would check his blood gases each day to measure the levels of oxygen and carbon dioxide in his blood as well as the PH. This was before the days of pulse oximeters, which are now used in all hospitals, and there are miniature versions for use in the community. These devices, often referred to as sats monitors, measure the oxygen saturation, and they just clip on to the end of a finger. Blood gases may still be required, though when oxygen saturation is low. Blood gases can now be tested from a capillary blood sample through a small nick to the ear, but can also involve the same procedure as used in 1980, where an arterial blood sample is taken. The first time I witnessed the procedure, it seemed barbaric, but Mr Hickson didn't seem to mind it at all and said it wasn't painful unless the doctor missed the artery.

'Nurse, I need to check blood gases on Mr Hickson; can you assist?' Dr Graham was a white South African doctor who always spoke in short, clipped tones. I didn't take to him at all, which was unusual, as I always tried to get on with everyone. There was something about his manners that I didn't like; he always gave off an air of superiority although he was a junior doctor. Many doctors had a superior attitude, but there he had an air that was totally unpleasant. He was a tall man with curly, light brown hair that looked as though it had been permed. His whole demeanour was condescending, and he was racist. I only discovered this later in the year when he wouldn't allow Blanche to accompany him to carry out a procedure. He said he was too busy, but I realised it was because she was black. I had met people who were racist before but never one who was so obnoxious to work with. I was more angry than Blanche over the issue, but she shrugged her shoulders and said it was his South African upbringing, as apartheid was still prevalent in that country. He was pretty horrible to all of us female nurses too, so I don't think his prejudice was just restricted to colour. *I dread to think what he'd be like as a consultant*, I thought, as I followed him and closed the curtains around Mr Hickson's bed.

'Hold the wrist, Nurse,' he commanded. *Talk about stating the obvious,* I thought, as I did as instructed and smiled at Mr Hickson. I had to hold the arm out so that the wrist was exposed, as he would insert the needle into the radial artery where the radial pulse could be felt. He inserted the needle at a ninety-degree angle, and it fascinated me to see that the colour of the blood was so bright compared to that of venous blood, which I was much more used to seeing. I realised it would be pointless to ask the doctor questions, as he was clearly disinterested. At the end of the procedure, Dr Graham took the sample and just walked off without a word. I applied pressure to the insertion mark.

'Full of the joys of spring, that one,' said Mr Hickson, as he put his oxygen mask back on. I smiled at him but said nothing as I didn't want to let on that I thought the same thing. Professional courtesy was everything back then, and even if we detested a doctor or a colleague, we tried not to be negative in front of patients. At times, I am sure this was misguided.

'Let's see if the bleeding has stopped,' I said, and removed the swab I had been pressing. It had stopped, and I applied some tape over a clean cotton wool swab that I had placed over the needle mark. 'There, good as new,' I said. 'Do you need anything?' I asked before leaving him.

'Just a fresh pair of lungs, Nurse,' he smiled, but there

was a faraway look in his eyes as he said it. *If only I could,* I thought sadly, as I smiled and walked away.

As an addendum to this part of my story, I have met and worked with many doctors, nurses and other health professionals from South Africa, and none of them have been like Dr Graham. Thankfully, he was a one off.

5

CLASS DOWN

One downside to being a nurse, particularly in the early days, is that when you move hospitals or wards, you come across new bugs. This often meant that shortly after starting a new job, and particularly in the winter months, our immune systems were bombarded with new strains of viruses and bacteria that we hadn't formed a resistance to. This was particularly true after starting at the London Chest Hospital, and obviously those of us on the respiratory wards where patients were coughing all day long were susceptible. It was in January 1981 when we all started to go down with one thing or another, mostly respiratory illnesses. Those working on the cardiac wards didn't escape though, because we met up for a class once a week, and also most of us were in and out of each other's rooms and socialising at night.

Jen was first to go down with a cold that spread to her chest, and she ended up with a chest infection. Of course, this brought out the 'fresh air of Stornoway' nostalgia. Jen had actually trained in Glasgow, but she was a Stornoway girl through and through. She was off sick and Fran, Blanche, May, Margaret, Flora, and I took turns to make sure she was fed and watered. Flora did this with a little less gusto than the rest of us, saying that she was of a weak constitution and that her parents had told her to stay away from bugs – *working in a chest hospital – oh yes, as if that was going to happen*. I made a mental note to self that Flora's parents were probably living in a parallel universe along with their daughter.

Fran, Margaret and May were the next to go down with heavy colds. They soldiered on for a few days, but then May developed an ear infection and Fran and Margaret, chest infections. Now there were three of us left in the nurses' home to do the nursing after shifts, although Jen soon joined us as she recovered. Flora was forever finding excuses as to why she couldn't take her turn, and I was sorely tempted to drop some cockroaches into her room. A few days later Blanche went down, as did the rest of the girls in our set, even those that lived out. Thankfully, Fran and May recovered and helped, while Flora spent most of the time in her room.

'I'm going to kill that girl,' moaned Jen. 'Even when she did look after me, she was in and out like a hare. One day she even wore a mask! Can you believe that?' *Yes, I could believe it.*

'Never mind,' I said. 'Almost everyone has had it now and they've nearly all finished their antibiotics, so we can get back to normal soon.'

It was quite tiring, working shifts and then playing nursemaid to one's friends in-between, but we all looked out for each other. Well, most of us did, anyway. I was quietly congratulating myself on my robust constitution when I developed a rip-roaring headache while on a late shift just before my days off. That night my temperature rose, and I went down with the dreaded heavy cold. It wasn't the cold that was the problem; all of us developed secondary bacterial infections – probably because of the amount of bacteria floating around in the hospital wards. I was no different; a few days after developing the cold, I had terrible pain over my cheekbones and knew it had gone to my sinuses. My temperature was climbing and the pain in my face got worse and worse. Now the girls were looking after me, apart from Flora, who had taken to her room completely now after her shifts.

A few days later, after forcing myself into work with a red face and worsening pain, I had to make the customary trip to the GP in Bethnal Green. He prescribed antibiotics and signed me off sick for a week. That was in the days before they granted us permission to sign ourselves off sick for seven days. The antibiotics did nothing, and the pain got worse. Mrs Chang decided it was time to send me to occupational health. The doctor I saw examined my face, pressing on my sinuses, and said that he would send me over to the Ear, Nose & Throat (ENT) hospital. A phone call later and I was on a bus over to the hospital with Brenda in tow, as she had come over to visit me that day. The beauty of living in London was that there were teaching hospitals everywhere, all keen to get their hands on patients to practise on, which may or may not have been a good thing.

We traipsed across London on buses and arrived at the ENT hospital, which was called The Royal National Throat, Nose, and Ear Hospital. The doctor at the London Chest knew a doctor at the ENT hospital and so he had arranged for me to be seen that day. The hospital was on Gray's Inn Road, King's Cross, and it tempted me to get on a train and go home. I was sure my mum could put some Vicks on my chest and all would be well again, just like when I was a child. With a sigh, I followed Brenda into the hospital. We arrived at the Outpatient Department and I showed my letter from the doctor to the receptionist. The department was heaving with people. I was still feeling dreadful and my face was boiling just above my cheekbones where my facial sinuses were. After about half an hour, a nurse called my name.

'Follow me,' she instructed, and I did so. She led me into a room where a doctor sat; he read the letter I had brought along and told me I would need my sinuses drained.

Really? Is that necessary? I shouted at him in my imagination – in reality I replied, 'Ok, Doctor.'

He then took two very long, wooden sticks (orange sticks – I have always wondered why they are called that) about the length of barbecue skewers, but thicker. I think they were probably about six inches long, really. They had cotton wool wrapped around them about one inch in length at one end. The doctor dipped these sticks into a pot of thick yellow/orange stuff (paste actually) and asked me to tilt my head back. *Oh no, what's he going to do with those things?* I thought. The next thing I knew, he inserted one of them up my left nostril and punched it through the membrane at the back of my nose. I was trying really hard not to pass out, thinking they would assume I was a typical nurse baby if I did. He then did the same thing with the other nostril, inserting the second stick until I had two of these things sticking out of my nose. I was feeling light-headed by now.

'There you are,' he said. 'That's done, we just need to give them time to numb you and then you will need to come back for the drainage.'

You have got to be kidding me! Just when I thought it was all over. On the way back to the waiting room, I asked the nurse, 'What was that yellow stuff?'

'Cocaine,' she said. 'Didn't you know?'

No, I b........ didn't, I thought. 'No.' I replied.

'You were ever so brave; most people faint,' she said as she left me in the waiting room. *Great – now she tells me. I could have allowed myself to pass out after all.* What I must have looked like, sitting there with these two skewers hanging out of my nose, I don't know. Brenda was chatting away, but I wasn't feeling much like talking. I had my head in my hands, feeling very sorry for myself. To cheer myself up, I explained in graphic detail what had just happened. I was pleased to see that Brenda looked a bit pale too when I related this, but saw that other patients were looking frightened, so I spared them and changed the subject.

Finally, the nurse called me again. I took a quick look at the exit and wondered about doing a runner – King's Cross Station was looking very inviting right now. Having second thoughts because of my nasal appendages, I turned and followed the nurse sheepishly back to the torture chamber, where Robert the Bruce was waiting gleefully. Was it the cocaine, or did I really see manacles and chains in there?

'Sit down and put your head back, and we'll get on with it,' instructed Robert the Bruce. *This can't be happening,* I thought, as I saw him pick up what looked like a chisel. In fact, it was a bone chisel. He removed the orange sticks, which were now orange because of cocaine staining – *give me back my cocaine,* I thought as he inserted said chisel into my right nostril. While the nurse held the back of my head, he applied incredible pressure and I could hear and feel the bones crushing as he forced the chisel through the bone to allow entrance into the sinus cavity. Finally, he had broken enough bone, and he sat back looking a little breathless himself after his exertion. Thankfully, the cocaine had done its job and there was no real pain during the procedure.

'Ok,' said Robert. 'We will now drain the sinuses.' *Might as well,* I thought. He inserted a fine rubber tube through the nose and into the cavity. I was thinking like a nurse now and developed a bit more interest in the procedure. Next, he poured water into the cavity through the tubing until the most horrendous-smelling gunge came pouring back out. Yellow and green foul-smelling pus mixed with water and blood filled the bowl the nurse held. This procedure was repeated three times until he seemed satisfied he had got the worst of the infection out. Both Robert and I looked exhausted by the time he had finished.

'Right, you now need to take these antibiotics for two weeks and you'll be as right as rain,' he said, giving me a bottle containing metronidazole.

Where's the cocaine? I thought. I was quite pleased Brenda had come with me because I felt peculiar on the bus on the way back and my nose was pouring with blood, which it continued to do for a couple of days afterwards. Brenda insisted I come and stay at her place for the weekend as she was off, and I was grateful to do so. Thankfully, I was in much less pain once the pain in the back of my nose had gone, as Robert the Bruce's torture had released the pressure. The antibiotics took effect, and I was back at work on the Monday. I had bragging rights for a few weeks that I had definitely had the worst infection, although I think some of them thought I was exaggerating. Trust me, I'm not.

The one person who didn't pick up the virus at all was Flora, of course. I think even Fran would have liked her to have picked up something. Once we were all feeling well again, we were a lot more forgiving and more accepting of Flora's delicate constitution.

Mrs Chang was delighted to have us all back in the classroom on Wednesdays so that we could continue with our studies. Friends had collected handouts for any of us that had missed lectures and we occasionally had group revision sessions either in the nurses' home or at Chloe's, whose flat was a short walk away. Those of us who had taken sick time would need to make it up, either by using holidays or tagging time on at the end of the course, because we needed a one hundred percent attendance record to pass.

I only had one other malady during the year and that was toothache. I woke up one Saturday night, a few weeks after the sinusitis episode, with agonising pain in my tooth that paracetamol couldn't touch. I tried everything, including a hot water bottle, and Fran gave me some cloves the next morning, but they didn't help either. Thankfully, I wasn't on duty on the Sunday. May came over to my room at lunchtime and said she had asked on the ward, and discovered there was a dental hospital open seven days a week. *Another hospital full of eager students*. I sighed, but I was desperate, and nothing could beat the Robert the Bruce episode. The hospital was in Leicester Square, and Fran came with me because she had a day off. We took the Underground tube from Bethnal Green and found the hospital.

I had been to Leicester Square a couple of times nightclubbing, but had never seen the dental hospital before. Someone must have blinkered me because the building, which is now a hotel, was huge. The only time I'd had a tooth extraction was as a child when dentists were still putting patients to sleep with gas for extractions. I remember being very sick afterwards and was telling Fran about it. We shared dental experiences for a while, but thankfully I was seen quite quickly. A dental student introduced himself and said he would pull the tooth for me. I was pleased that he was at least supervised by a trained dentist. Having said that, I would have let anyone pull the tooth out at this point, as the pain was excruciating. They sent me for a dental X-ray first, and they agreed the tooth should come out – perhaps as well or I would have pulled it out myself.

The student was a bit clumsy, and I smiled as I recalled giving my first injection. I think this was probably his first extraction. He had a minor accident and squirted local anaesthetic from the syringe into the back of my throat before finding the right place. After three different injections, during which he was over-generous with the anaesthetic (the numbness to my face was still spreading after he had pulled the tooth out), he managed to remove the tooth on the third attempt. The dentist supervising him was a saint compared to consultants, who would have annihilated the poor young man by now and taken over. At one point, I wished the dentist wasn't as patient and would take over. Once finished, totally numb down the whole of the right side of my face and unable to move my tongue, I found Fran in the waiting room. I would have smiled, but my mouth wouldn't move. I couldn't thank the dentist, but grunted and nodded to say I was alright, and with that we left the building.

As we were in Leicester Square, Fran decided we should walk over to Trafalgar Square, which wasn't too far away, and feed the pigeons. All I wanted to do was sleep, but as she had wasted hours of her day off accompanying me to the dental hospital, I didn't feel I could refuse. We walked, and she talked, as I was still numb. I started to get some tingling feeling to parts of my face after we had fed hundreds of pigeons. Trafalgar Square was always packed with tourists, and people from every nationality would buy bags of birdseed to feed the birds, who were totally fearless. The only thing one had to be careful of was to steer clear of any flying overhead so that you didn't get bird poop on your head. I relaxed as the tiredness wore off, and I got a second wind, and even started to enjoy myself. It was lovely to be pain free. Eventually, Fran had satisfied her need to feed pigeons, and she suggested we head back to the hospital.

Feeding the pigeons at Trafalgar Square was a tradition enjoyed by thousands and immortalised in the film *Mary Poppins*, but they have banned birdseed sellers since 2001 and the London authorities made it a criminal offence to feed them in 2003. There are many pigeon deterrents in use, and hawks have been used to drive them away. The reasoning behind the new rules was that the poop was damaging Nelson's column. Whilst I have every respect for our famous landmarks, I think it's sad that tourists and children can no longer have this experience.

When we got back to the nurses' home that day, and the feeling in my face came back hours later, I was able to eat a light meal and have a wonderful night's sleep before going on a late shift the next day.

6

THE GOD SQUAD

Shortly after arriving at the hospital, we were all advised to avoid what people termed as the hospital "God squad". Apparently, there were some members of staff who were overtly Christian, and we referred to them to as the God squad or Bible bashers. If anyone ever told me to avoid people for any reason, then that was one sure way to ensure that I did the opposite. I was still young and had an enquiring mind and basically didn't have a problem with what others believed.

I would often hear people say that they would not discuss politics or religion, but I felt this was small-minded and I would discuss both. In fact, I would discuss anything. I had spent many years reading fiction in my childhood and my school reports had always commented on this, recommending that 'Dawn should read more non-fiction.'

Well, teachers, I thought, *you would be very proud because since leaving school I have definitely enlarged my reading repertoire.* Part of this was down to my friend, Jill, who had recommended nursing to me in the first place. She was a fan of Erich von Däniken, who believed that the visions in the book of Ezekiel in the Bible were those of aliens who had visited the earth in a spaceship thousands of years ago. The von Däniken books were interesting, but left me wondering why the aliens had never returned. I also read many other books about many things. I had tried to read the Bible as a child but found it too difficult, and my knowledge of it was limited to knowing the names of the Gospels and the Christmas story.

One of my best friends at school had been a Catholic, and I had once attended mass with her, but giggled all the way through, as they held it in Latin. My friend said she would never take me again as I had embarrassed her. The God squad comprised two ward sisters, some staff nurses and a couple of hospital porters. Martin, one of the porters, was the first one I came across. The hospital was quite small, so we came across the same people again and again. Martin had long, light brown hair down to his shoulders, and I first noticed him sitting in the hospital canteen reading his Bible. He always sat alone, mainly because people avoided him because he was a bit over the top. He was a good-looking young man in his early twenties. I arrived at the canteen for lunch one day and it was really busy, so as Martin was sitting at a table for four, I joined him. 'Hi,' I said, as I sat down and put my food on the table. 'I'm Dawn.'

'Martin,' he replied, and put his Bible down on the table.

'Good book?' I asked.

'THE Good Book, Dawn,' he replied.

'Where do you come from?' I tried a different tack.

'I was born in London. I live in Hackney.'

'I'm new here; how long have you worked here?'

'About six months. I did a maths degree at Oxford but realised that God wanted me to be a hospital porter, and so I am following His calling.'

'He's not very ambitious then!' I tried humour.

'Jesus was a carpenter, Dawn, and he was born in a stable.'

Sounds like my upbringing, I thought, but decided that this very serious young man would not respond to humour. 'Do you like being a porter?' I continued.

'Yes. I get to pray for people all day and tell them about God.' *No wonder they avoid you,* I thought, but managed to get a few sentences in before he moved the conversation back to his being a Christian. His form of religion, I decided, was probably a bit too much for me too, and whilst I would have been interested in having a conversation about his beliefs, it was all a bit too intense for my liking. I was beginning to understand why some people preferred to avoid discussing religion – not that this had been a discussion. I saw Jen come into the canteen, but as she was about to do a detour around to my table, she saw Martin and turned away. Thankfully, he got up to go back to work, so Jen joined me.

'There were no seats,' I laughed.

'I'd rather sit in the park,' she responded. 'I said hello to him one day, and he replied, "Hello, Jesus loves you,"' she continued, rolling her eyes. 'Even May avoids him and her dad's a vicar!'

'He seems harmless enough; intense though,' I said, and then we started talking about life on the wards. I told her about the South African Houseman, Dr Graham, and how I found him unpleasant and ignorant.

'There are some weird people working in this hospital,' she said. 'Have you met Mrs Lumumba?'

'Not since my interview; she was on the panel. Why?'

'I'm sure I saw her coming out of her office drunk the other night. She was swaying all over the place and she was still in uniform.'

'Really? Maybe she was off duty but not changed out of uniform.'

'Maybe, but I don't think so.' This was a small hospital, and I soon came to realise that gossip spread like wildfire around the place. Some of the gossip was true and some far from true. We ended the conversation and went back to our respective wards to see what awaited us there.

I had been in London for about four weeks before Brenda and I had the same weekend off. We had arranged that I would stay the weekend with her in her flat in Holborn, next to Russell Square tube station. It was a room rather than a flat, I discovered, but about three times the size of mine. There was only a single bed, but she had a sleeping bag for me to sleep in on the floor. The building was owned by Great Ormond Street Hospital (GOS) and so the GOS students got to live there. Brenda was now nearing the end of her third year. As her course was a combined adult (SRN) and children (RSCN) course, she had to do four years. Her uniform was a beautiful pink and white striped dress, and she also wore a white, starched apron like we did at LCH, but her hat was a frilly one whereas mine was plain. We were thrilled to see each other again, and we had lots to catch up on, so I knew we were in for two late nights before I returned to the nurses' home on Sunday.

Brenda cooked her favourite dish, which was chicken casserole with jacket potatoes. I think it was the only thing she ever cooked because I can't remember any other culinary delights. Not that mine would have been any better, as I lived on takeaways unless I was really poor, and then I would cook spaghetti with tinned tomatoes and grate cheese on top, which was my go-to meal in those days.

'How's it going then?' Brenda asked.

'Loving it.' This was our first opportunity to have a proper talk, as we worked a fair way away from each other and our shift patterns meant we spoke little. It was also hard to communicate by telephone as we only had a public telephone in the main hospital and calls had to come through reception – and although there was a phone in the main building where Brenda lived, it was often engaged.

'Mrs Chang, our tutor, is brilliant: she makes classes really interesting, and the hospital is so friendly. The girls in the nurses' home are all nice and I have got to know the ones in my set really well.' I paused for breath and as Brenda didn't reply I continued, 'Guess what, we also have a hospital God squad.'

'Really? How do you know?'

'It's one of the first things I learned after moving into the nurses' home: avoid the God squad, I was told. I have only met one of them so far, a porter called Martin.'

'What's he like?'

'Strange, to be honest. Every time you see him, he mentions God or Jesus; he doesn't seem to be able to have a normal conversation. I saw him in the grounds the other day. "Hello Martin," I said, "nice day." "My Father made it," he replied. "Thank him for me," I said. "Why don't you thank him, Dawn?" And that's how every conversation goes. I wouldn't mind having a discussion with him, but he doesn't seem to be on the same planet.'

'I'm a backslidden Christian,' Brenda remarked. I must have looked astonished – I had met none of this type of born-again Christian before and now I seemed to be surrounded by them. 'Don't look so surprised. I met a group of girls when I first moved to London and they were into religion, so I went along. They took me to a Billy Graham concert.'

Is he a pop star I haven't heard of? I must be out of touch, I thought.

'Who's Billy Graham?' I asked.

'He's a famous American evangelist.'

Not that famous, I thought, *and what's an evangelist?* – Obviously religious speak was like hospital speak, with its own lingo. 'Anyway, I stopped going to church when I moved to Leicester and haven't been since.' *Hope that wasn't my influence,* I thought. I suddenly had guilt pangs, but realised I had met Brenda when she had been in Leicester for about six months, so could breathe a sigh of relief.

'Well, if you go back, don't get like Martin, because he is a bit too heavenly minded if you ask me.'

'I won't,' she promised, and then we moved on to hearing about the sick children she had been looking after recently at GOS. Now she was more senior, they gave her a lot of responsibility, and when she described all the tubes and things that she dealt with, I had to imagine the ones I used in micro-fashion. After a late night exchanging hospital stories, we finally fell asleep.

The next day, Brenda introduced me to a fantastic pancake house close to where she lived. I had never seen pancakes like it. The menu comprised nothing but pancakes; there were sweet ones and savoury ones, topped with everything you could think of. The plates were enormous, three times the size of a standard dinner plate. I ordered my favourite, which was plain old pancake with lemon and sugar, while Brenda was a little more adventurous and ordered a pancake with berries and maple syrup. The pancakes were relatively cheap for London and I felt pretty full after eating. The pancake restaurant was still there a few years ago when I visited London, so hopefully it continues to turn out huge pancakes for every taste.

After lunch, we got the tube into central London and Oxford Street. I fell in love with Oxford Street straight away. I think we went into every shop, including Selfridges and many of the smaller stores. Brenda bought quite a few clothes, but although I had finally been paid, I was wary of spending my money on Oxford Street, as I knew it wouldn't go far. Brenda was okay because her family was well off and supplemented her income, but I had to live on what I earned, plus my overdraft facility, so had to rein myself in sometimes. An early lesson I'd learned was that money didn't go very far in London. I chose to spend my money on drink and dancing in those early days until I discovered the theatre and classical music later on. I also had to buy food, and there were no large discounted supermarkets around every corner in 1980.

That night we went to Soho, where food was relatively cheap, for a Chinese meal. The area was a bit shoddy, and it was packed with restaurants of all sizes. Bright neon lights shone from many of the buildings, and they absolutely fascinated me. We ate in a small, budget restaurant that was packed with people even in early November. They brought the meals to us, or should I say threw them at us, as service wasn't their forte. They gave us chopsticks, and I had great fun trying to eat rice with them. Brenda was quite good at this, as she had lived in London for much longer than me and had been out quite a bit. The rice was served in a small bowl and the other dishes were on small plates. The idea was to add small amounts of the food to the rice and eat it with chopsticks, holding the bowl in one hand close to your mouth. There were quite a few Chinese people eating in the restaurant and they were shovelling the food into their mouths at a great pace. The waiter who had thrown the food on the table showed me how to hold my chopsticks, and I got the hang of picking up bits of meat, but the rice thing was beyond me. After the meal, Brenda ordered Jasmine tea, which came in a large pot and was poured into tiny cups. I had never had Jasmine tea but liked it immediately, and from then on, ended a Chinese meal if taken to a restaurant with this drink.

The thing I grew to love about central London was the constant buzz of activity and the fact that there was always something going on. People were always out, day and night. It wasn't like that in the East End where I lived; life there was more akin to what I had been used to in Leicester. But because it was so easy to get into the West End, activity was never far away. How could one not fall in love with this city? Even with the constant threat of the IRA, it didn't stop us from enjoying ourselves. We had to learn to be observant though, and make sure that no-one left unattended bags or luggage anywhere. It was a habit that most people living in London developed and many people checked under their cars before getting in them, as car bombs were a common form of attack.

Brenda was loving being back in London, but she missed

her family. They had moved to Ireland, as her dad worked for Waterford Glass in the very south of the country. She was close to her family and talked about them a lot. I had met her mum when she had visited Brenda in Leicester while she was on her adult placement there. She was a larger-than-life woman who insisted on hugging me the first time we met, which was a bit awkward as I didn't come from a demonstrative family.

The rare weekends off with Brenda were fun, and we explored London together, visiting the Natural History Museum and the Victoria and Albert Museum. I liked museums but there had only been two in Leicester, which I had visited ad infinitum. Jury Wall Museum was my favourite because it had the remnants of Roman walls and baths in the grounds. The contents inside were interesting too, but I had seen them so many times, they had lost their interest. The museum was on the way into town from where I lived as a child, and I spent many summer days walking around and checking out the exhibits. I think I also went for something to do and somewhere warm to go when it was raining; plus it was free entertainment, and I never had any money. Leicester was a big city and had quite a few activities, but there was no comparison to London.

Brenda was also lucky in that she lived near to central London and everything was within a reasonable distance, which made visiting her even more exciting.

7

CONSUMPTION

Tuberculosis had once been called consumption, and the term can be found in novels by Charles Dickens. Charles Dickens himself had praised the work of the London Chest Hospital for providing care for people of the East End of London.

We nursed people with tuberculosis in bays in the early 1980s. Prior to that, there had been male and female wards for them, and balconies where they could be nursed in the fresh air. There were no longer large numbers of patients with tuberculosis needing inpatient treatment that there had been in the past, but the condition was always ready to rear its ugly head whenever it could. Dr Caplin or one of his team saw many patients with the condition in the outpatients' department. I was told that the tubercle bacillus, (the bacteria called mycobacterium tuberculosis and the prime culprit responsible for tuberculosis), rose into the air for 48 hours before falling to the ground, hence the high ceilings in most tuberculosis hospitals and the need for fresh air. Interestingly, although I don't think they knew this at the time of the construction of the hospital, there were vents near to the ceilings that extracted air, which turned out to be an unwitting bonus to the design of the building.

The land next to Victoria Park in Bethnal Green had been acquired because of its large plot, and balconies were added onto the wards in the early 1900s to enable patients with TB to recuperate in the fresh air. Tuberculosis had been decreasing in the three decades prior to my working at the hospital, mainly due to antibiotic treatment, and that is why the hospital had moved on to treat other respiratory conditions and heart conditions in the 1960s. By the time I worked there in 1980, it had become part of a special health authority called the National Chest & Heart Hospitals, which also included the Brompton and Frimley Hospitals.

The fundamental problem with tuberculosis, I discovered, was getting the patients to adhere to the treatment regime, which involved taking three different antibiotics for six to nine months. Many patients stopped taking their treatment and developed antibiotic-resistant strains of the disease. In fact, it was in the 1980s that TB began to rise again due to drug-resistant strains, just when people were talking about the disease being eradicated. Health professionals may have taken their eye off the ball because of the emergence of HIV and AIDS in the early 1980s.

We mainly found TB among the homeless and the Asian population at that time. The condition had long been associated with poverty and overcrowding, hence its ability to thrive in Victorian Britain and why it was common in the East End of London. It would spread rapidly due to people coughing and sneezing. Interestingly, there were widespread public health campaigns in the early 1900s encouraging people to cough in handkerchiefs, similar to recent public health campaigns to stop the spread of influenza. Unfortunately, they did not have disposable tissues to throw away back then, so it may not have been as effective, but it had to be better than coughing into the air. Hand-washing facilities in Victorian Britain were pretty scarce too. Symptoms included bloody sputum, cough, night sweats and weight loss. Patients would often appear at the hospital looking like they had come straight out of a concentration camp.

When patients presented with classic signs of TB, they were admitted to the ward for sputum samples and chest X-rays for diagnosis, but as it took weeks for the laboratory to grow the bacillus, they began the treatment regime before confirmation of the diagnosis. This was the ideal time for us to explain the importance of sticking to the treatment, and to explain the dangers of stopping before the treatment had cured them. One of the doctors had given us our TB lectures and instilled into us the importance of spending a lot of time with patients explaining the treatment. The treatment regimes had dramatically decreased in length of time. Treatment had been for two years in the early days of using antibiotics. They then reduced this to eighteen months, then to nine months, and finally to six months. This was because of developments in medicine and new antibiotics, but it was still a long time for many people (particularly the homeless) to stick to taking multiple medications. The beauty of working in London, and at a specialist hospital, was that we were at the forefront of medical advances and would become familiar with new treatments before they were rolled out across the country.

Many patients were still taking a treatment termed 'triple' therapy, which was given for eighteen-months, but the new treatment regime included just two drugs (although this later became three again, but different drugs). The early triple therapy included streptomycin, isoniazid and ethambutol. Ethambutol had replaced a powder called para-aminosalicylic acid, or PAS for short, and shortened the course of treatment from two years to eighteen months.

The new triple therapy treatment regime that I would become familiar with included isoniazid, rifampicin and pyrazinamide (PZA), and this soon shortened the length of treatment again to nine months and then six months. Prior to the discovery of penicillin, about half of people with TB died of the disease.

Brian had been admitted after being found in Victoria Park, barely able to stand. His cough was typical of the disease, as was the sputum he coughed up. He was as skinny as a rake; I could count his ribs without touching him, and he looked much older than his thirty-seven years. Sputum samples had been sent away and his chest X-ray showed a consolidation of his lungs that was typical of tuberculosis.

'Right, Nurse,' Dr Mackintosh had looked at me. 'Let's get the treatment started. Can you explain to Mr Durham what is going on.'

It was a statement, rather than a request.

'Yes, Doctor. Come with me, Mr Durham.'

'Call me Brian,' he said. We walked over to the treatment room where I was going to give him his first dose of the drugs and explain the six-month course of antibiotic treatment.

'Right Brian, you will need to take three tablets a day, as TB is treated with what we call triple therapy, which means three different antibiotics. We have found this to be the best way to cure the disease, but only if you complete the course. One antibiotic on its own does not work as the bugs get used to it and start to fight it.'

I showed him the tablets, explaining that these treatments would need to be taken every day in the morning. 'The most important thing you will need to remember, Brian, is that even when you start to feel better, the disease will not have gone, and if you stop taking the medication before the end of the course, the TB will come back. Not only will it come back, but these tablets may no longer work or be able to kill the bacteria. Do you understand?' I asked.

'I think so,' he replied, 'but that's a long time, Nurse. I'm forgetful, particularly when I've had a drink.' I knew they had found him in Victoria Park and that he was homeless. Many homeless people had drink problems.

'Brian, you're still young, and TB is a horrible disease which can make you feel terrible, as you have already discovered. People die of it.' I waited for this to sink in. 'So you are going to need to remember, no matter what else happens. Dr Macintosh has arranged for you to go to a hostel for a while after you leave here and they will help you to get into a routine as well.'

'Yeah, maybe, but I prefer to look after myself.' I knew what that meant; he preferred to drink himself into a stupor. He was already suffering some tremors, and they were not just because of the TB infection.

'Give the hostel a chance; you might even like it,' I smiled. 'Anyway, you don't need to think about that now because you will stay with us for a while yet, while we get the treatment started.'

Many young men like Brian had left home and moved to London thinking that the streets were paved with gold, only to find that they brought their own problems with them. Whatever they were running away from, they were unlikely to find a haven in London's East End, where they were targets for criminals, or where they couldn't find work and ended up on the streets. Try as I might, I got the feeling that

Brian was unlikely to stick to the treatment regime; but I was going to give it my best shot, just in case.

Funnily enough, although I came across many patients suffering from tuberculosis in the two years that I worked at the London Chest Hospital, I never came across one as bad as the young man who had died in Leicester. Special had been absolutely right when she said I would never see a chest X-ray like the one I had seen back in 1979.

Special and I wrote to each other for about five years after I left Groby Road Hospital in Leicester. Her letters were brief and to the point, letting me know what was happening on the ward and how the staff were doing. They were never personal, but I got the feeling I had become family to her. I am not sure whether she had any other family, and she didn't socialise at the hospital. This was not surprising, as she scared most people to death. I'm not sure when we stopped writing. I guess time just took over and life became so busy. It is one of my regrets that we lost touch. I think I last heard from her when she was retiring, and perhaps without the ward stories to recount, there was nothing much else to say. She enjoyed hearing my ward stories for a while and she shared her love of gardening, something a young girl in her twenties was unlikely to enthuse about.

Bart, the physiotherapist, was always around on the chest wards, mainly carrying out chest physiotherapy, although he did some mobility exercises too. His primary task in life, though, was to help patients to clear the gunge from their chests, and as I said before, this was not something he could do alone, so we were all trained in how to carry out chest physiotherapy. Bart was a lovely man, always cheerful; we would hear his cheery voice as he came onto the ward and he brightened up our day. The patients loved him, unless he was battering their chests, that is. He would tell them funny stories in his Chinese accent and make them laugh.

One day, a crowd of us were in the canteen when Bart came in. 'Hi girls,' he called, frowning slightly as he saw Martin sitting in the corner reading his Bible. He came and joined us for lunch. 'How's it going?' he asked.

'I'm knackered,' said Jen. 'I can't sleep, there's always too much noise. I'm not used to it. In Stornoway, all you hear are the birds in the morning. Here it's loud voices, banging and clattering of doors, and loud music.' At this point, she glared over at a girl at another table who was obviously the music culprit. Before she waxed lyrical about the beauties of Stornoway again, May piped in.

'I'm loving the cardiac ward; it's so interesting. I'm sick of hospital food though.'

'I have an idea,' Bart replied. 'Why don't you come over to our flat next week for dinner? My partner's a chef.' Excitedly, we all accepted the invitation and agreed the following Wednesday when we were all on earlies. Bart gave us the address.

The following Wednesday, we all pitched up at Bart's flat and a man about twice the size of Bart opened the door; he had curly brown hair.

‘Hi, I’m Charlie.’ We had assumed Charlie was a girl, and it took us a minute or two to allow it to sink in that Bart was obviously gay, although the term wasn’t used back then; we would have said homosexual. I have to say that Bart was the first openly gay man I had ever met (relatively open at least), and they made a lovely couple. Charlie was indeed a chef, and we were treated to the best meal we had eaten since arriving in London. A month later, Bart looked very glum when I saw him on the ward.

‘Are you okay?’ I asked. He had tears in his eyes.

‘Why don’t you and the others come over for dinner later this week and I’ll tell you.’

Jen, Fran, May and I agreed on an evening when we were all off and we went to Bart’s. Charlie answered the door again, but he too looked glum.

‘Oh dear, they must be splitting up,’ whispered Jen.

We ate another wonderful meal and then Bart broke the news, holding Charlie’s hand as he did so.

‘My father is ill; he is dying.’ We all made sympathetic remarks. ‘As I am the oldest son, it is my responsibility to provide for the family. Its tradition,’ he smiled weakly. ‘There are no government benefits in China and my family will have no money if I don’t return. I have given in my notice and I leave for China in three weeks.’ We all stared, aghast, hardly knowing what to say. Being totally unfamiliar with this type of culture, there was nothing we could say. One thing we realised immediately, though, was that Charlie would not be going with him.

'I couldn't live in China,' Charlie explained, 'and even if I could, Bart's family would never accept me; or us as a couple.' We got that; it was hard enough in this country, but in many parts of the world it was much worse for homosexual men. All we could do was express our sympathy, and it was genuinely meant. We had become so fond of Bart; he was part of the furniture at the London Chest Hospital, and his cheerful demeanour and friendship would be a significant loss.

On the way home, we discussed the evening's turn of events. 'That's really sad,' said May. Even though her vicar's daughter upbringing couldn't quite allow her to embrace the homosexual thing, she genuinely liked the couple.

'What an awful thing to happen. I didn't realise other countries didn't have a benefits system,' responded Jen. We looked at her with incredulity and wondered where she had been all her life – *Stornoway*, of course.

'I will miss Bart,' chimed in Fran. 'He really helps me with the chest physio and he's an outstanding teacher.'

'What an incredibly unselfish thing to do,' I said. I couldn't imagine being that dutiful myself.

Bart did leave, returning to his own country, never to be heard from again, and I don't know what happened to Charlie. We went to his leaving do, which was held at their flat, and although we had plenty to drink, it was a fairly sombre evening. We went home feeling like we had been to a funeral, and I guess, in the grand scheme of things, it was pretty much like that.

Another patient I had met who was suffering from tuberculosis was Mrs Flavin. Mrs Flavin had been sent to us from casualty at the London Hospital not far away after suffering from worsening breathlessness. Her chest X-ray showed pleural effusion, and because she had tuberculosis, the hospital was concerned that the effusion would contain tuberculosis. They were correct in this assumption, as it had indeed contained the bacillus.

A pleural effusion is where fluid enters into the lining of the lungs, and it can be small or large; occasionally, it can occur around both lungs if congestive cardiac failure is the cause. In Mrs Flavin's case, it was around the left lower lung lobe, and because it was causing severe breathlessness, the consultant had ordered a chest drain to be inserted. We had been taught about the procedure in lectures and I had experienced measuring contents of numerous chest drains, but had not seen one inserted. Staff Nurse Blenkinsopp had suggested I assist for the experience. *Why do they feel it's necessary for students to see everything*? I muttered to myself unreasonably.

Dutifully, I had set up the trolley, and I knew I would not like it – never mind that Mrs Flavin would probably like it even less.

'At least she would be less breathless at the end of it; what is in it for me?' I mumbled.

'Experience.' Staff Nurse Blenkinsopp had crept up behind me and heard my mutterings. Sometimes I really thought I was too squeamish for nursing, but I always came back for more. Doctor Reynolds was the registrar who worked on Dr Caplin's team at the time, and he was a born and bred Londoner.

'Right, Nurse, let's get on with it.' *If you insist*, I thought, but turned to Mrs Flavin.

'Right Mrs Flavin, we just need to turn you over onto your right side so that the doctor can put the drain in. It shouldn't take too long and you'll feel much better afterwards.'

I had already closed the curtains around the bed, and I then helped her into position. It was a sterile procedure so Dr Reynolds was gloved up, but because TB was also involved, we were both gloved, gowned, and masked once Mrs Flavin was in position. Dr Reynolds painted the whole of her left side with iodine before doing anything. I passed him the syringe, needle and local anaesthetic solution, and he injected an area between the ribs. Then came the gory bit. I opened a long plastic tube which contained a thick metal spike, like a knitting needle, but much sharper and much thicker.

'Ok, Nurse, support the patient,' instructed Dr Reynolds, and I went around the other side of the bed to support Mrs Makin, holding her hand to reassure her and myself. I was glad she was holding my hand. Thankfully, Dr Reynolds was superb at the procedure; I observed quite a few junior doctors later who were not nearly as adept. It takes quite a bit of force to get the spike through the chest wall, between the ribs and into the pleural cavity. Once he was certain he was in the correct place, he pulled the contraption out, leaving the tubing in place with a clamp over it. The tube was then attached to a pressurised bottle about the size of a large plant pot with water in the bottom, and the clamp was removed. Before long, pus, blood and gore were draining into the bottle, and Mrs Makin was breathing a bit more easily.

'Thank you, Doctor,' the sweating patient and nurse said in unison, me thankful it was over and Mrs Makin thankful she could breathe again. Antibiotics were started, and we sent Mrs Makin for a chest X-ray to make sure the tube was definitely in the right place. We measured the chest drain bottles daily until it was time for their removal. Occasionally, one had to be changed if it became full or lost its suction.

Mrs Makin made a good recovery and continued treatment for the tuberculosis until the disease was cured. I know she was cured because I met her again in outpatients a few months later, and we reminisced about the chest drain episode. Surprisingly, she said she hadn't noticed that I had been squeamish at all – another case for RADA then. For those who don't know, RADA is the Royal Academy of Dramatic Art in London, where budding actors and actresses go to study. Every nurse could also be an actress.

'I thought you had seen it performed a thousand times before, Nurse,' she said. 'I just hope I wasn't squeezing your hand too hard.' *Or I, you,* I thought. 'It'll be nice not to be treated as an outcast anymore.' Mrs Makin remarked, and I realised that patients with TB suffered more than just the physical symptoms of the disease; there was still a lot of fear surrounding the condition.

Infectious diseases do frighten people into somewhat irrational behaviour at times. TB was one of many conditions that people were worried about catching – not surprising when considering its history.

8

MAKING ENDS MEET

I soon realised that either living in London was costing far too much money or I was spending too much. Whatever the cause I was not just broke, I was way more overdrawn than usual. So much so that I received a letter from the bank manager enquiring about my overdraft – in other words telling me to sort my finances out. Receiving a letter from a bank manager at twenty-one is a scary experience, and one that was not to be ignored.

He was absolutely right; I had been going out far too often and living on fast food which should have been free, considering the health problems I was likely to incur in later life, but unfortunately it wasn't. The proximity to the West End of London and all its attractions was too much for me, and that, coupled with going out with the girls to the Bonner a few times a week, had taken its toll on my finances. In addition to this, Brenda lived close to central London and she had much more money than me, and always wanted to go somewhere to eat or to a show. The list of shows I saw in London is way too long to go into but I saw Evita in its early days; Educating Rita; Jesus Christ Superstar and many more besides.

The theatre was a lot cheaper than it is now, but it was still pretty expensive, costing about a quarter of my weekly salary. Then there were the art galleries and museums and *Madame Tussauds*. I was never going to have any money. Thankfully I discovered classical concerts and the opera later, otherwise I would have been in even more debt. Brenda's favourite eating house was the *Hard Rock Cafe* near to Marble Arch. I loved it too, being an Elvis fan, but it wasn't cheap.

The bank manager's letter brought me down to earth – I was not a tourist on permanent holiday, I was a nurse earning a very low income. I also felt bad that I hadn't been home at all since moving to London, but there was no money for train fares on top of my living the high life. No, it had to come to a halt. No more jaunting off into the West End every time I had a day off. I still wanted to go out to the Empire in Leicester Square a couple of times a month though, and Thursday night at the Bierkeller near to Trafalgar Square was definitely not going. The Bierkeller was the highlight of my Thursday evenings when not working – we all sat on benches at really long tables in the cellar of the building. There we drank German lager by the jug-full and joined everyone waving glasses in the air while singing songs all evening at the tops of our voices. They don't do nights out like that anymore.

I decided to join a nursing agency and work my days off and some evenings. I found an agency called London & Provincial Nursing Services and they had offices on Regent Street, so I applied to them for work. They snapped me up, and soon I was being booked in for shifts all over the place. The pay was better than what I got for working at the hospital, as higher hourly pay was the perk that attracted nurses to agency work. My first few shifts were at St. Thomas' hospital.

St. Thomas' or Tommy's as it was known, was set back next to the River Thames, across from the Houses of Parliament. It has been a London landmark for years due to its proximity to Parliament. I was very excited at being able to say I'd worked at Tommy's, which was seen as being really posh, and Tommy's nurses' were well thought of in the profession. The reality though, was that it was just like any other hospital, with scary ward sisters and sick patients. The main difference was that the nurses thought they were a cut above the rest and the patients could be a bit more demanding. I had been booked for a late and an early shift on a surgical ward where they were short staffed. The nurses and many of the patients spoke with posh southern accents. The majority of patients I'd met so far at the London Chest Hospital had cockney or Asian accents.

I felt a bit like a fish out of water as I didn't know anyone, and because I was an agency nurse they were not going to spend time getting to know me; I was there to do all the jobs they didn't want to do. At least it wasn't for the most part emptying bedpans though, because they needed me to do dressings rounds and 'obs' rounds. I found it difficult at first not knowing where anything was, and when I did find the equipment room I had to make multiple trips, because the dressing packs didn't contain everything I was used to. It was also difficult because I didn't know who any of the patients were. I had been given a list of people I needed to see, but it was not in any sort of order. The ward staff were obviously busy and short staffed, hence my presence, and sighed every time I asked them anything. I also stood out to both patients and staff because my uniform was different. I wore the London & Provincial uniform, which made me stick out like a sore thumb.

I was getting to the point where I thought I would never finish anything, when a student nurse came along.

'I've finished my jobs; do you want me to help?' I could have kissed her.

'Yes please; I don't know who is who.' Bryony turned out to be a great help and a good laugh too. She had a good rapport with the patients as well, and made them laugh with her Irish brogue. Bryony attached herself to me for the rest of the shift, which is not surprising as the staff nurse who was on duty was obviously too posh to wash, or do anything else for that matter. She sauntered up and down the ward examining her nails as if admiring a freshly performed manicure, and sighed every time anyone spoke to her.

'That's Snail,' explained Bryony. 'She is always on when it's busy and because she is so slow, it gets ten times busier, as everyone else has to do double the work.' As if to reinforce what Bryony had just told me, Snail slowly turned around and walked back down the ward again, having achieved absolutely nothing.

'Hello Mr Bronson,' Bryony turned to the next patient on our list. 'We are just going to take your stitches out.' We closed the curtains and Mr Bronson entertained us with tales of his family life. It was lovely being back on a surgical ward where people came in, had surgery, and for the most part got better and went home. I realised that I had only been on medical wards so far at the London Chest Hospital. I was yet to move to the cardiac and chest surgery wards. Mr Bronson was an absolute gentleman and couldn't thank us enough as we left to go and change the trolley for the next dressing.

'You've got some nice patients on this ward,' I remarked. In fact, in my experience the majority of patients did their best to be pleasant. There was always the exception to the rule, and for some you couldn't do anything right, but they were not common.

'We have,' Bryony agreed. 'I have met a few awkward ones and some very demanding ones, but for the most part I am enjoying it. The staff can be trying though; Snail is a pain but Sister Proud who you will meet tomorrow is a nightmare. We call her Jaws.' *Oh lovely, just when I thought I had left that type of sister behind in Leicester.* Bryony and I went to break together and she told me how she had moved from a big Irish family farm in Ireland to London.

'At first, I was scared,' she said. 'I wasn't sure how people would be with us Irish, what with the troubles and all, but the girls in my set are lovely. That's perhaps not surprising because we have girls from all over the world, including Australia and Singapore.'

'My set are all from the UK now although some weren't originally,' I said, 'but we do have staff members from all over the world. London is so cosmopolitan isn't it?'

'I had never seen a coloured person until I came over here,' Bryony said. The term "coloured" was not an offensive term in the 1980s, and was in general use as a polite way to refer to people who were black and to people who were Asian.

'Really? I grew up in Leicester, and we have areas that are predominantly populated by Asians and parts that are predominantly populated by Afro-Caribbean people. There's a fantastic area for buying Asian food too. It's not without its tensions though; in fact in Leicester, when I was growing up, there were frequently fights on a Saturday night between black and whites, whites and Asians and black and Asian. I have never understood why people fight over the colour of their skin.'

'We have the Catholic and Protestant thing,' said Bryony, 'and that probably beats the lot.' With that, we decided to talk about nicer things and compare notes of places we had been to in London. Bryony was only eighteen, and had not been to as many places as I had, but she had perhaps explored more of the cultural elements of London. She told me about the Houses of Parliament and the changing of the guard, and I realised, much to my surprise, that I hadn't been to see Buckingham Palace yet. I resolved to do so at the next opportunity, because at least it was free to go and watch the changing of the guard and stand outside the Palace gates. Apart from being an attractive building, I wasn't very interested in going inside the Houses of Parliament though.

It was difficult getting into central London the next day to start the early shift at Tommy's, and I had to wake at the crack of dawn. I then found myself standing sandwiched on a tube train for the whole journey with hardly an inch of space between myself and the next person. So this was the London rush hour that everyone spoke of – I couldn't believe how ignorant people were. No-one stood for elderly people, and men sat on seats while women stood. This was unheard of in my world. Every time the train stopped at a station, more people crammed in. I didn't think it was possible for anyone else to get onto the train, but on they came, elbows first, and somehow they managed. I was fascinated by this early morning activity and looked around, surveying the scene. It was as if everything was happening in a dream. Nobody spoke, nobody looked at each other. Men read newspapers, balancing on briefcases while holding onto an overhead rail, or standing sardined into position by those around them. Women read books or magazines and some carried Walkmans with music tapes inside, with earphones on their heads. Prior to the invention of Walkmans it was not uncommon to see people carrying around Ghetto Blasters, much to the annoyance of the many.

The majority of people on the tube were wearing suits of some description. I had my uniform in a rucksack and was wearing jeans and a bomber jacket, not that anyone noticed. I suddenly realised that I could die on that train and nobody would notice or even care. For the first time since moving to London, I had found something I didn't like. For a moment I imagined my respiratory patients trying to breathe in an environment like this and realised it would be impossible – as it was I was having to breathe shallower than normal due to the close proximity of a rather large man.

I was very much relieved to finally arrive at Westminster tube station and get off the train, except that everyone else got off too and I was carried along with the throng. I wasn't sure I was heading in the right direction, but I realised that even if I had wanted to go another way, it would not be possible. People weren't just walking, either; they were marching, verging on a trot. Hundreds of faceless people marching to who knows where. I was carried along to the escalator and crammed onto that too. Many people were trying to walk up the right-hand side as it was traditional on the Underground to stand to the left if you wanted to be carried up the escalator, allowing room for people to walk up or down on the right. This could be quite amusing at times when people who didn't know this rule, usually tourists, were thrust out of the way by some impatient Londoner. There wasn't a lot of walking going on that morning, due to the delays at the top of the escalator caused by people trying to exit using the ticket barriers.

Once at the top I managed to grab hold of a wall and stand for a minute to get my bearings. I realised I was going where everyone else was so there was nothing for it but to follow – or be dragged along with the crowd. "Follow the crowd" took on a whole new meaning to me that day.

The day didn't get any better, as Jaws was eating student nurses for breakfast; even Bryony made herself scarce. I was told to go and help with the breakfasts, do an 'obs' round and then change the intravenous infusions (IVs) that were due. Snail was on duty as well but didn't seem to go any faster with Jaws on duty than she had the previous day, although she wasn't quite as visible. I was still recovering from the tube journey and so no task could faze me today. I was dreading a repeat of the morning, realising that I would be finishing shift at rush hour, so was delighted when Bryony suggested going to a pub across the river after work.

After that first initiation to the London Underground in rush hour, I did get used to the crush, as I worked many agency shifts in central London. It wasn't long before I too learned to stand on a tube train without holding onto anything and read a book on my way to work for those shifts. *If you can't beat them, join them*. I did always stand for elderly people though, as that was something I couldn't get out of my system. My mum had taught me as a child to always stand for adults (women at least) and the elderly. Some habits, I believed, were worth cherishing, and that was one of them.

I worked agency shifts at a number of London Hospitals, including The Cromwell Hospital in Kensington, which was a brand new private hospital, opened in 1981 where I was later offered a job. The rich and famous were treated at the Cromwell, many of them from overseas, and its state of the art facilities made it a dream to work at. It remains private but has changed hands a few times. The footballer George Best died at the Cromwell long after I had stopped doing any shifts there.

I also worked in some patients' own private residences. I worked regularly at a lady's home in Kensington; she was a frail old woman who didn't really need a nurse, but she felt she did. On the first day I arrived at a large Victorian terrace with the customary multiple steps leading to the door. Think *Upstairs, Downstairs* and you will get the picture. The door was answered by a cook, who showed me upstairs to a large drawing room where a tiny, grey-haired and immaculately dressed lady sat on an enormous settee.

'Hello, Nurse, I am Mrs Bellings. There is a list of jobs for you over there; it is cook's day off and I don't like to be alone,' she continued.

I checked the list and couldn't believe my eyes – I was here for eight hours and all I had to do was check her blood-pressure, pulse and blood sugar (she was a diabetic) and provide her with tea at 11am, lunch at 1pm and tea at 3pm.

Doddle, I thought. I almost felt guilty about being paid for the privilege. Mrs Bellings looked at me. 'I don't want you hanging around up here with me. There is a sitting room for you downstairs.' *Even better*, I thought. Mrs Bellings turned out to be a delightful 80-year-old aristocrat (she was titled) with a razor sharp mind. I think, had Agatha Christie met Mrs Bellings, she would have based *Miss Marple* around her. Her diabetes was well controlled with twice-daily insulin and a carefully crafted diet made by cook. She did like the odd biscuit or two, but I didn't dissuade her from this, her only vice. Her husband had worked in the City of London, that small area where the whole country's financial markets are traded. He had died five years prior to my meeting her and she missed him dreadfully. She wasn't a demanding patient at all; in fact, I used to sometimes try to get her to be demanding.

Mrs Bellings liked tea made in a pot with one ordinary teabag and one Earl Grey mixed in, and she would only drink from china cups with saucers and spoon. I developed a liking for the tea mix and occasionally, when I use a teapot these days, rather than a bag in a mug, I make this mix and smile with fond memories of Mrs Bellings. The other treat she was partial to was a giant mushroom, with butter, baked in the oven.

I worked regularly at Mrs Belling's home throughout my training for three reasons. Firstly, the work was light; secondly, I was able to study around her minimal routine; and thirdly, I liked her. It worked well for both of us.

Sometimes cook would change her day off around my shifts because she knew the old lady liked me.

Thanks to my agency nursing shifts, the bank manager was happier – at least I think he was (he never said) but he stopped writing to me, and I was able to continue to enjoy the treats that London had to offer, albeit in a slightly trimmed fashion.

9

CHUGGING ALONG

The most common form of cancer that I came across at the London Chest Hospital was lung cancer. Mr Robinson had given us our lung cancer lectures over a few weeks.

'Now ladies, I am going to teach you the symptoms of lung cancer in a way that hopefully you will remember.' He then bent over with his arms by his side, and gradually started moving his arms round and round in a rhythmic fashion, pretending to be a train.

Jen nudged me and whispered, 'He's flipped; can happen to anyone, you know.'

I was beginning to agree with her when he started to make chugging noises like a train starting up, which then got faster and faster. After a short while he replaced the chugging noises with a rhythmic recitation of, '*Cough, sputum, dyspnoea, pain, haemoptysis; cough, sputum, dyspnoea, pain, haemoptysis; cough, sputum, dyspnoea, pain, haemoptysis,'* interspersed with, *'loss of weight is often late.'*

I can still see him now standing at the front of the class. Soon we all joined in, and he was right: I have never forgotten that lesson and I doubt any of us ever did. He taught us this in roughly the order that the symptoms develop in lung cancer, with the cough often being the earliest symptom.

Lung cancer was often diagnosed too late, meaning that the prognosis was poor. Treatment was limited back then anyway, although some patients did survive. Each type of lung cancer was determined by its cell type, and all but one was associated with smoking. I remember looking long and hard at my cigarette during break after this lecture, and I tried giving up about three times while working at the London Chest Hospital. The first time I tried to give up was after meeting Brian.

Brian was admitted to the ward for bronchoscopy. Bronchoscopy involved introducing a flexible tube with a light and camera attached to it into the lungs. The doctor, usually a consultant at the time, could then see any suspicious areas in the lung and take a biopsy. This biopsy was sent away for histology testing to look for cancer cells. We were one of the major centres for lung cancer treatment in the East End of London and therefore it was not uncommon to see a disproportionate number of people with the disease. This tended to skew our view a bit, and it was difficult sometimes not to imagine that everyone had lung cancer, which of course they didn't.

Brian was forty-three years old with a wife and two young children, aged ten and seven. He worked in a brewery in south London. He had been a smoker since he was fourteen, and had developed what he called a smoker's cough about a year prior to admission. Six months later he noticed he was coughing up sputum, and more recently he realised he was becoming breathless. He had shrugged it off, telling his wife that he was out of condition, but she insisted he go to the doctor when he started to cough up rusty sputum in the mornings. His chest X-ray had shown a small shadow in his right lung and he was admitted for tests and bronchoscopy. His results came back showing he had oat cell (small cell) carcinoma (cancer) which was one of the worst and most common forms of lung cancer.

Cancer was rarely spoken of with patients initially and it was usually a relative that was told first, but Brian had asked the consultant, Dr Bright, to be honest with him, whatever the results. I was with Dr Bright when he came to see Brian and his wife, Grace, on the ward. Children were not allowed to visit the ward because the risks of them picking up infection were too great. Brian could see by Dr Bright's face that it was not good news.

'I'm sorry Mr Blake, I have bad news for you.'

Dr Bright was better than most doctors I had come across in these situations, who would usually blurt out in clipped tones, 'It's cancer you've got,' or: 'Hard luck, it's cancer,' but Dr Bright allowed his first bit of news to sink in before proceeding.

'You have lung cancer.' Another pause while he allowed the news to sink in. Grace was welling up by this time and there was a deathly silence. I could hear myself breathing.

'Unfortunately, it is not one we can operate on, but we can offer you cytotoxic drugs.' Cancer chemotherapy was in its infancy and sometimes experimental at this time. Patients were rarely given a choice about treatments back then either. They were told what was available and it was generally assumed that they would go along with it, even though they did have to sign consent forms. 'We can start treatment tomorrow. I will see you then.' Dr Bright sighed, shook Brian's hand and then left.

Brian was silent. I could tell he was processing the information and could see the fear in his eyes, but he was trying to comfort Grace. 'Don't worry, I'm in good hands aren't I, Nurse?' He looked at me.

'The best,' I said weakly, remembering the prognosis that Mr Robinson had taught us in class. Months, not years, he had said. Patients rarely asked about prognosis in 1980 as things were just not discussed openly. It was a time when everything was bottled up. It made it a lot easier for us healthcare professionals in many ways but on the other hand it was really difficult. We knew, and usually patients knew, that their end was near, but we didn't talk about it. Some relatives would ask the doctors in private and some would not. Nurses didn't usually give out the bad news in those days either; it was almost always doctors, and most of the time they were not very good at it.

After Grace left the ward that afternoon I noticed that Brian was just staring into space, unable to comprehend that a week ago he was at work and now he was facing his mortality. It was impossible to imagine how he was feeling, but anyone with a bit of empathy could have a good guess. Fear, anger, regret, family, children, why me? I went over and asked him if I could get him anything.

'I need a cigarette. Is it worth stopping now?' he asked. Smoking was not allowed on the wards at the London Chest Hospital but there was a designated smoking area for patients. Thankfully, it was a rhetorical question as I would have wanted to say *no it's not* at that point, but couldn't have said it out loud.

'I think I'll just go for a walk if that's okay?'

'Of course,' I said. 'Do you want company or would you rather be alone?'

'Company please,' he said and after letting the ward sister know where I was going, I followed him off the ward. We got downstairs to the ground floor and went outside onto the front lawn where there were benches. Brian had on his slippers and dressing gown and I was in my short-sleeved uniform. Thankfully it was a warm rather than cold spring day, a bit chilly, but nothing I couldn't manage. We sat on a bench and he got out a cigarette, and just held it in his mouth without lighting it. We sat in silence for a while and then I asked him how he had met his wife.

'I was doing a delivery at a pub in Hackney and I saw this beauty come out with a couple of other girls. She took my breath away and I nearly dropped a barrel on my foot. I was in her way and so she had to look at me. I was just turned thirty and recently split up with my fiancée; she was twenty-five at the time. I smiled at her and said, "Do you come here often?" It was the only line I could think of, and I was dazed. She laughed and said that was original, and before I knew it we were chatting over a barrel of beer. By the end of the conversation I had asked her out and we arranged to meet at that pub the next night. I was smitten. Do you believe in love at first sight?'

No I did not. Lust at first sight maybe, but not love; however I replied, 'I'm sure it happens.'

'It does and it did. From that night on I knew we were made for each other; I had never felt like that with my fiancée. We had drifted along together and started living together without ever discussing it. In fact we never discussed anything, and finally we drifted apart in exactly the same way, without any discussion. With Grace though it was entirely different. I knew I wanted to spend the rest of my life with her.' Realising what he had just said, he welled up and then he looked at me. 'I just thought it would be a lot longer.' I put my arms around him and he cried and cried and cried. I thought he would never stop, but finally he did and then he sat up.

'Sorry,' he said.

'You have nothing to be sorry for,' I managed to say, as I

was beginning to well up now. It started to rain, and we looked at each other – twenty-one year old me and this man whose world had just come crashing down.

'Come on,' I said, 'better get inside.' I stopped myself saying 'before you catch your death'.

It was one of those moments that I look back on and think what a privilege it has been to stand by people at the most vulnerable times in their lives. Even when it is impossible to cure or heal them, the next best thing is to be able provide a strong shoulder to cry on. After that conversation with Brian, I remembered back to my interview at the start of my nursing career and how I had no idea why I wanted to nurse, but when asked the question I had replied that I wanted to provide support people when they were ill, when they were vulnerable. That answer, though contrived at the time, was inspired, because it became the backbone of the reason why I continued to nurse. As was often the case, the strong shoulder wasn't that strong, and when I went off shift that afternoon, I cried alone in my room. I decided to give up smoking immediately, after I had finished the next packet, of course.

Cancer chemotherapy was fairly new to the hospital and was given in clinical rooms. The senior sister, who was one of the God squad, administered chemotherapy and often spoke to people about God. Some of the staff thought this was dreadful, touting religion when people were vulnerable. One such person was Steve.

Steve was doing agency shifts at the hospital when I met

him. He was quite short at five foot six inches, had wavy, long blond hair and lovely blue eyes. He was also an Enrolled Nurse; he had moved up to London from the south of England and was doing agency shifts to supplement his income while working at King's College Hospital full time.

We met when I was working on Hilton Ward, which was the second respiratory ward in the hospital. We hit it off straight away and it wasn't long before we were sort of dating. I say sort of because I was already going out with someone else, a Turkish chap called Mustafa who was probably way too old for me anyway, and I was also trying to avoid an amorous taxi driver who had decided I was the one for him after dropping me off after a night out. Mustafa and I had met in a pub across the river; as soon as my friends and I walked in, he made a beeline for me. By the end of the evening he was asking if he could see me again and we drifted into a fairly platonic (on my part) relationship. On the Sunday before I met Steve, Mustafa had taken me to Petticoat Lane market – an incredible place which was absolutely jam packed. It was also a haven for crime, so I had to keep my handbag close at all times.

Petticoat Lane is a famous market in the East End of London, popular with tourists, and I believe that Alan Sugar started out there as a stall holder. Stalls sold just about everything you could think of, including a lot of stolen goods, and it made Leicester market seem small. The unusual thing back in 1980 was that it opened on a Sunday, as most markets were closed on Sundays.

Mustafa had insisted we have our photo taken with a little monkey on my shoulder. The monkey was similar to the one in the film *Raiders of the Lost Ark*, which I saw a few years later. I was starting to tire of Mustafa as he was a bit too clingy for me, and although I don't think he had marriage in mind given that his family would want him to marry a Muslim, he certainly had other things in mind. It had been a convenience relationship and I had decided on that Sunday that I would not be available in the future.

There was a marvellous night receptionist/porter called John who used to keep my admirers at bay, as sometimes I found it difficult to turn down dates. John would ask me who I was happy to see and then tell anyone else I was working or out, and he would also shield me from telephone calls. John and my friends used to laugh at the predicaments I got myself into, and there were some tricky moments when more than one guy would turn up at reception at the same time. I am ever grateful to John, who became a good friend and who taught me that it was ok to say NO. Men would get over it, he told me. John, himself was engaged to a lovely girl called Laura and I had met her at their engagement party in the spring.

Steve and I seemed to be getting along really well, and he was certainly the most interesting man I had met since moving to London, although he was a bit moody. He could be really interesting and we would have deep conversations, but he could also be quite negative. He basically had a chip on his shoulder and felt that he was owed a living because life had given him a hard time. From what I could tell, the only hard time he had was that he had to work. His parents were well off, but his father had made it clear to him that he should make his own way in life before being given any handouts – he resented his father for this and so had become a nurse because he thought his father would disapprove. In actual fact, his father thought it was a good thing to do and that he would learn some discipline. Needless to say, once Steve got onto this subject he became very pouty. I can't say I had a lot of sympathy as my upbringing had been far harder than his (not that we were comparing), and I never felt that the world owed me a living. It's odd how different people can be, but I still liked Steve very much until one day when I was going back on shift after a lunch break, and met him on the stairs.

'THAT WOMAN,' he shouted, 'is preaching to people who are terminally ill; she should be sacked.'

I knew straight away he must be talking about Sister Blair, the senior sister from one of the wards who administered cancer chemotherapy. I was a bit tired.

'So what?'

'It shouldn't be allowed; these people are weak and vulnerable and she's taking advantage.'

I could see his point in one respect but then again, I could see hers; what if she was right? 'I'm sure they can make up their own minds,' I said, starting to get slightly irritated with him. I was more irritated with him shouting at me about something that had nothing to do with me, even though I knew it was because he was frustrated and he couldn't shout at her. On top of that he was a confirmed atheist, and had really taken a dislike to the God squad from the word go. He was one of those people who hated anything to do with religion, not in a normal way but in a very aggressive and unreasonable way.

'They shouldn't have to listen to that crap when they are dying,' he continued in a very loud voice that was starting to draw attention to us; and now people thought we were having a row.

'I don't see how telling people that God loves them when they are dying can be so wrong,' I replied. 'Anyway, can we talk about this later, I need to get back to work.'

'Arrogant cow,' I heard him mutter loudly as he walked off, and I hoped he wasn't referring to me.

That was the last I saw of Steve; he never did any more shifts at the London Chest Hospital. I was a bit sad because I liked him but boy was he volatile. I have no idea why I defended Sister Blair, who I didn't even like that much as she was a bit too much like Martin, a bit too intense for me. Having seen many people near to death who would ask about life after death, and actually wanted to talk about spiritual things to which I never had the right answer, I thought that maybe she was just fulfilling a need rather than imposing her views. Steve was overreacting to hearsay, I thought, although I would never know, and nurses could indeed be sacked now for proselytising to patients. I couldn't understand why Steve was so angry, but for some people, religion is an absolute taboo subject whereas others will gladly discuss the matter. I wondered if I had reacted differently, whether Steve and I would have developed a deeper relationship, but then if he could fly off the handle over something I was not responsible for; what would he be like if it were something I had done?

I am not sure what Sister Blair said to patients but none of them ever complained about her to me. Some would laugh and call her the nun and others would actually want to know more and request a visit from a clergyman. We did have people of other religions in the hospital, in particular Muslims and Hindus, but I don't think she overtly tried to convert them.

When administering cytotoxic drugs, Sister Blair would wear theatre-type clothing and a big rubber apron, a bit like those worn by pathologists. She would also wear double gloves, a face mask, a hat and goggles. This was all to protect herself from exposure to these very toxic drugs. She was quite small, like me, and the gear she had to wear used to drown her. It was a wonder that this diminutive woman could talk about anything under all of the coverings she had to wear.

In some cases cancer chemotherapy was given as well as radiotherapy and/or surgery. Chemotherapy could be given before or after either of those treatments, but not at the same time. Although I was not able to administer the chemotherapy I did have to care for the patients on the wards, and so needed to understand the treatment and the side effects.

A group of us had got together over a meal with Mrs Chang at Chloe's flat one night. Chloe had invited us all but only seven of us could make it, and as Mrs Chang was coming we asked if it could include some revision – we were all feeling like our heads might explode with all the information we were trying to take in. In addition to this we still had to do our shifts and ward work – not to mention my agency work and night life. A few of the others were doing some extra shifts at the hospital on their days off to earn extra money. I was trying to avoid this as I didn't feel I had enough experience yet; some of the others had worked on intensive care before starting at LCH, so they could do shifts in the cardiac ICU.

Mrs Chang always managed to cheer us up no matter how tired we were feeling, and Chloe's cooking helped – not to mention the wine. Once we had washed up and drunk enough wine Mrs Chang explained to us the importance of observations after chemotherapy. Jen had wanted to know why people lost their hair and May had questioned whether the treatment was any good at all, while I wanted to know why a patient had to wait weeks before being given a second lot. Surely it was better to blast the cancer. Mrs Chang was patient with us.

'The reason for any of the side effects, including hair falling out, is that the treatment hits good cells as well as bad. Tumour cells divide more rapidly than normal cells so it does attack them mostly, but there are cells in the body, such as hair cells and those helping to fight infection, that are affected because they also divide rapidly. That is why there is a decreased resistance to infection and why people's hair falling out is a common side effect. As treatments get better and more research is carried out I'm sure they will become more cancer-specific, but for now we have what we have.'

'That brings me on to my point,' said May. 'What is the point of having a treatment that nearly kills people? Wouldn't it be better to leave well alone?' I did think that May had a point; I had seen well looking patients come onto the ward for treatment. A few days later they were vomiting everywhere, had terrible diarrhoea, developed infections as their white cell count was lowered, and some bled from any orifice, not to mention the hair falling out.

'While we have a treatment, albeit still fairly rudimentary, and it offers hope, we cannot deny people the option. For some it will cure them and for others it will prolong their life,' replied Mrs Chang. She sighed. 'It is better to have a little hope than none at all, and treatments are improving all the time. New drugs are being developed and one day there will be a cure, of this I am sure.'

Mrs Chang was ever the optimist and ahead of her time in many ways. There are cures for many cancers now, and new advances in the treatments over the years have most certainly improved people's chances.

'Some people,' continued Mrs Chang, 'may well decide

that enough is enough; and I know that for lung cancer things aren't great at present, although they are improving, but it is up to the patient, not us. If we have a treatment we offer it, explaining the risks and benefits, and then it is up to them whether they decide to take the risk.'

'I still think sometimes the doctors are just experimenting,' May retorted. 'What's the point of an extra few months?'

'It might be during those extra few months that a cure is discovered,' said Mrs Chang. *Now that was a good point*. 'Or it may just give people time to sort family matters out: attend a wedding; see a birthday. Also, some people will always live longer than we think they will and many have surprised us all.' She was right there – I had recently met a seventy-year-old patient called Mr Young who had been told ten years ago that he had six months to live.

'I wasn't going to let that whipper-snapper of a doctor tell me when I was going to die,' Mr Young had confided. 'What made him think because he had been to medical school that he could determine when someone would move off this mortal coil? No, Nurse. Your time's up when your time's up, and that's what I told him.' Mr Young certainly did seem to be a medical miracle. He was riddled with cancer but he just kept on going. A positive mental attitude certainly did seem to help people to live longer. I have met people who should have lived for years, who died within a short space of time after being given a cancer diagnosis, and people like Mr

Young who lived far longer than anyone ever thought they would.

My thoughts were interrupted and I re-joined the conversation just as Chloe was putting the kettle on. 'So why can't we mega-blast the cancer then?' I asked.

'Well, that is what happens, mainly because although the patient has intermittent treatment, the doses of the drugs are high. They tried it with a single drug to see if there would be fewer side effects, and there were, but the cancer cells developed a resistance to the drug. The best treatment at the present is to give a high-dose combination of drugs intermittently, because resistance takes a long time to develop, and side effects are less because the bone marrow is given time to recover before the next treatment.' We all looked suitably impressed, even more convinced than ever that Mrs Chang went to sleep reading textbooks.

'Does your husband work away a lot?' Fran asked, putting into words what we all thought. Mrs Chang laughed good-humouredly but didn't answer the question. We loved our little Malaysian tutor; she was so bubbly and so unlike most of the horrible ward sisters from our student days. Mrs Chang never frowned, although her energy was exhausting sometimes. Perhaps it was as well for her husband if she did go to bed with a textbook, as who could keep up with her?

We ended the evening with coffee and cake and were all very happy. Chloe's flat wasn't far from the hospital and it was easy enough for us to walk back to the nurses' home afterwards. Mrs Chang's husband came to collect her in his car and we all tried to see what this man looked like. He appeared Chinese was all we could see in the dark, as he drove away with our lively teacher.

When we got back to the hospital, I joined John behind reception for one of our late night photography chatting sessions. We were both keen photographers, although he was much better at it than me, but we would discuss all sorts of things that would help us to improve our skills. He always had the latest photography magazines too, and we would discuss the latest techniques. I had a Chinon single lens reflex (SLR) camera, which was a Dixons Stores own make, and I had been planning to take some black and white photos around the rougher parts of the East End on my next day off. John gave me plenty of advice about how to get the best shots. Before I knew it we were talking into the early hours, which often happened when John and I got to speaking about photography. I finally decided it was time to call it a day, or should I say a night, and headed back to my room in the nurses' home. As I lay on my bed that night, I thought how great it was to live in London and work at the LCH, in spite of the poky little room, the scaffolding outside and the cockroaches.

Mr Robinson's train demonstration popped into my mind, and I smiled as I drifted off to sleep that night.

10

CABBAGES

As well as its respiratory specialism, the hospital was renowned for coronary artery bypass surgery. Because we rotated around the hospital we all worked a stint on the surgical ward, which was mainly for people recovering from open heart surgery. Jen and May had really enjoyed their stint on the ward and now it was my turn. I would be joined by Fran and Flora for this placement. We hadn't yet worked on the intensive care unit where people went immediately following the surgery, but we had each done a shift in theatre to witness it. This was mandatory for all of us so there was no way out. Amazingly, I hadn't wanted to miss out on this one because it would be so interesting, and not many nurses would ever have the experience.

My turn came one Tuesday morning, and I had been warned by my colleagues that I could be standing for 4-6 hours depending on how the surgery went. Thankfully, Fran and I went in together, and we were not expected to do anything apart from stay out of the way and keep quiet, while observing. The surgeons were used to trainees being in theatre and they did not pay us any attention. There were two surgeons, one to remove veins from one of the patient's legs and one to perform the heart surgery. There was also a registrar who assisted the heart surgeon and a junior doctor to assist with anything else and to learn. There were two scrub nurses and two huge surgical trolleys, one for each of the surgeons. The bypass equipment was quite bulky too, and took up space on one side of the theatre bed. In addition to all of these people there were two anaesthetists, one to ensure the patient was anaesthetised throughout and one to keep a check on the bypass equipment. Then there were a few nurses who were there to provide any additional equipment that the doctors or scrub nurses may need. The theatre was pretty packed and there was not much room for Fran and I to position ourselves so that we could watch the procedure.

'Ooh, isn't this exciting?' whispered Fran.

'It would be more exciting if I could see,' I replied. Fran had the advantage of an extra seven inches on me as she was five foot eight whereas I was five foot one. The patient had been brought in by the anaesthetist and everyone had gathered around the bed in their green theatre gowns, masks, gloves etc. It wasn't long before the patient was covered in green sterile sheets and I couldn't see a thing through the sea of green. I spotted a stool on the other side of the theatre and decided to go for it while everyone was busy setting up.

'I'm going to get that stool,' I whispered to Fran, and I started to slowly move around the edge of the theatre, making sure I didn't touch anyone who was wearing a sterile gown. The stool was almost in my grasp when one of the theatre nurses went for it at the same time as me – our heads cracked and we both yelled. Everyone turned to see what the noise was.

'Ssshhh,' hissed the theatre sister.

It was hard to tell who was who as you could only see eyes, but then I noticed that the heart surgeon's eyes wrinkled in laughter. He then put out his left hand and said, 'scalpel,' and carried on. With attention moving back to the real action, I whispered an apology to the theatre nurse and made my way back, minus the stool, to Fran, who was laughing behind her mask. I was rubbing my head and noticed the theatre nurse doing the same.

'That hurt,' I muttered.

'Never mind,' said Fran, who was now watching the surgery. The stool was still in place over the other side, as neither I nor the theatre nurse had picked it up. I decided against a second attempt, particularly as the surgeon was now opening up the chest – or I assumed he was because I couldn't see. I was getting bored because I was just standing there and all I could see was the sea of green theatre cloth. I couldn't even watch the surgeon removing the vein from the leg, as he was on the opposite side to me.

‘What’s happening?’ I whispered to Fran.

‘Mr Brown is just about to open up the sternum.’

I saw him pick up a saw, and as the noise of it started to ring through the theatre I took my chance. In a move that James Bond would have been proud of, I was round the other side of the theatre, returning with stool in hand without anyone noticing. With my prized possession in hand the sawing stopped; I was now as tall as Fran and could see what was happening. I saw the surgeon insert the cannulas that were attached to the bypass machine. Blood was then transported via various tubes, filters and a gas exchanger for the next hour, leaving the heart almost empty of blood, allowing the surgeon to perform the bypass. The heart was stopped by reducing its temperature.

I was fascinated as I watched the skill of the surgeon; as he cut the vein that had been removed from the leg into three, he stretched each one out and inspected them like choosing a prime steak. Once he had chosen the best bits he applied the grafts to the affected blood vessels supplying the heart. When the surgery was complete, the heart was restarted and the bypass machine removed. In this instance the patient’s heart went back into a normal rhythm straight away.

I hadn’t realised while the procedure was taking place how much tension there was in the room, as everyone was on high alert in case anything went wrong. Once the bypass was discontinued, the surgeons, sister and anaesthetist started to chat about golf and Wimbledon, which had just started. It was the summer of 1981.

'Do you think McEnroe will beat Borg this year?' asked the anaesthetist, while the surgeons were busily pulling the patient's sternum back together. McEnroe had lost to Borg in the final the previous year.

'No, I think Borg will win.'

'You cannot be serious,' replied the anaesthetist, mimicking McEnroe's pouty expression and swan song of the time. Everyone in the theatre laughed, and conversation continued in this vein until the surgery was finished. The patient was then transferred to Intensive Care, where he would be ventilated for twenty-four hours or so following surgery. The surgery had taken six hours, and as I stepped down from the stool, I realised how tense the muscles in my legs, neck and shoulders had been from concentrating.

'I'm starving,' Fran complained.

'Come on, let's go and get something to eat.'

Our shift was effectively finished, as we had been in theatre for an hour before surgery and an hour after helping with the clear up. We hadn't had a drink or anything to eat since we started at eight o'clock that morning. We made our way to the canteen as there was nearly always food there. There were some leftovers from lunches but very little choice, so we opted for sausages and chips.

'That was fascinating, wasn't it,' Fran remarked.

'It was once I could see.' We both laughed, remembering

the head clashing incident. 'I've got a lump on my head, feel here.' Fran felt my forehead.

'You have as well, lucky you didn't get a black eye.' We both laughed again. Caffeine and food were starting to revive our energies after what had been a long day in theatre.

'I couldn't do that every day.'

'Me neither; you'd end up with varicose veins, standing in one place all the time.'

'I would never remember what instrument to give him. Did you notice how he just held his hand out sometimes and sister placed the right instrument in his hand without him even asking?' I said.

'I guess she's seen so many of the same operations, she could probably do one in an emergency,' remarked Fran.

'I'm going to Wimbledon on Saturday.' I changed the subject.

'Really? I don't really like tennis to be honest. Who are you going with?'

'Cally.' I replied, and Fran frowned. Cally was one of the God squad.

'You be careful.'

'It's not an infectious disease,' I laughed. 'We haven't got tickets, but Cally says if you go early enough and queue you can get ground tickets.'

That is what happened, and I remember having a great day out on a lovely, sunny June day in 1981. We queued for around three hours, had our bags searched and then saw

Stan Smith play in the doubles and also John McEnroe. Stan Smith did get through to the doubles final that year but lost to McEnroe and his partner. McEnroe also beat Borg in the singles final. Cally was nice; she was definitely a born-again Christian but not as intense about it as the others in the hospital. We had sensible discussions as I was interested in the whole thing. I was impressed by the way she lived her life, but felt deep down she needed to get out more. Time would tell whether I was right.

I made two new friends while working on Lister ward. Holly was from Buckinghamshire, an overweight, lively girl with long, dark hair. She was doing the SRN/RN version of the training which was identical to ours. Holly spoke with a posh accent, as did Tina. Tina was also doing the SRN version of the training and originated from the north of England. I got on really well with Holly and Tina but they didn't really get on with each other, so I had to go out with them separately when we socialised.

Tina had a car, which was a rarity in London, so we could go out a bit further afield in the East End. We often went to a pub across the river from where I lived in the nurses' home. Tina lived in a flat not too far away. One night Tina dropped me off back at the hospital, and I was just getting out of the car when Mrs Lumumba came flying out of the front entrance of the hospital, almost falling down the steps.

She started waving her arms in the air like Shirley Bassey, but the arm-waving lacked the Shirley aplomb.

'Nurse Bates,' she shouted. 'I'm your nursing officer – TAKE ME HOME!' With that, she flew down the steps and got into Tina's car. Tina looked horrified. I was laughing my head off, without letting Mrs Lumumba see me, of course. Tina scowled at me and drove off. She later related that it had taken a while for Mrs Lumumba to remember her address, and even when she did, she didn't know the directions. Poor Tina – she was totally unimpressed at being commanded by a drunken nursing officer to provide a taxi service. I remembered the conversation with Jen of a few months before, and had to admit that Mrs Lumumba certainly liked a drink. She did have her uniform on but I had no idea whether she was on duty or not, and I didn't ask. I think she may have had a drink problem, but it was more than likely confined to the end of her shifts, as there was never a smell of alcohol when she came onto the wards, and she always behaved appropriately.

Tina was not happy when I saw her the next day, fuming at the audacity of the woman she had been made to drive around London for ages, looking for an address in an area that she didn't know. I didn't say much because I was secretly fond of Mrs Lumumba for giving me the opportunity to move to London, and found the whole thing amusing – but then I was not the one who had been accosted in the hospital forecourt so I could afford to laugh.

Many patients who came to the London Chest Hospital for heart surgery were local NHS patients, but quite a few came from abroad, paying privately for surgery. Wealthy

Indian and Pakistani men were treated and operated on. It wasn't just foreigners who paid privately; we also had wealthy businessmen from the UK who were treated privately. This was not unusual in the NHS, where consultants would undertake private work in addition to their NHS duties. I'm not quite sure where all the money went other than in consultants' pockets, as none of it came into the hands of other NHS staff, who provided the majority of the care. One such wealthy businessman was being cared for on Lister and I was checking his 'obs'.

'Do you like cocktails?' he asked.

'I like most drinks,' I replied. He reached over into his bedside locker.

'Here,' he said, and handed me a ticket. 'I was given a ticket to a business cocktail-tasting party taking place in Bow, but as you can see I won't be able to attend,' he smiled.

'Ok, thanks,' I said, and put it in my pocket. It could hardly be considered a bribe, since it was a free cocktail party. I looked at the ticket when I got off the late shift that night, and realised it was for the next day, at 5 o'clock in the afternoon. Formal wear, it said on the ticket, and business people only. I wasn't going to be put off going to a cocktail-tasting party on a minor technicality, and I decided to go. Sadly, it was for one person only so I couldn't take any of my friends. The next day I put on my interview clothes, as these were the only decent clothes I had. A beige, brown-speckled skirt and a light brown blouse. It was a warm day so I didn't need a jacket, and I walked along to the venue with the aid of a map and a few stops to ask directions.

I arrived at a small hotel and entered confidently, seeing the sign for the cocktail-tasting event in the foyer. I followed the sign and handed my ticket to the person on the desk. Fortunately, there were lots of people entering at the same time so they didn't really look at me, otherwise they would have noticed that I was the youngest person in the room.

The room was lined with tables in a U shape and a rectangle of tables in the centre, meaning that there were tables to the left and the right as I started along the route. The cocktails were laid out in cocktail glasses, about a third full, which was perhaps as well. I was doing nicely, and was on my fourth taster when a man in a business suit sidled up beside me.

'What business are you in?' He looked at me sceptically. I put on my posh voice and replied that I was in computers – hoping that he knew nothing about computers because I certainly didn't. We still hand-wrote everything, including our case studies, and the only computers I knew were cardiac monitors and the like. I continued along my way, trying to ignore him, but he was determined.

'What type of computers?' he asked. 'You look very young.'

'Yes, people who develop computers are very young. It's my father's business.' I was astonished at how easily I was able to fabricate stories. I think that one I did inherit from my dad. 'To be honest, I like to forget about them when I'm out. What business are you in?' I tried a different tack. It worked because he was now in his element.

'I'm a banker.' Yawn, yawn, I was still off bankers with the letter from my bank manager fresh in my mind. He started talking about investments, stocks and financial markets. I think he might have even given me a few share tips, but I wasn't listening. I was flying around the room drinking cocktails, while he was following me, continuing in full flow. *Was he never going to tire of his own voice?* Twenty cocktails later (I think), I thought it was time to leave and said goodbye to my banker shadow, who was still singing the praises of financial markets. *Really, he needed the cocktails more than me.*

'Nice to meet you,' he finally said. 'Whoever you are.' I knew he hadn't believed my story and I can't say that was surprising as I had always looked even younger than my now twenty-two years, but I didn't really care. At least I was out of the door and I had enjoyed my outing. It would have been a bit nicer if I could have taken more notice of what I was drinking, but it had been a pleasant experience. I'm not quite sure how I managed to walk back to the nurses' home that night, but I had certainly had an interesting diversion. I made a mental note for the future to always have a story at the ready, and eat before ever attending such an event again. Alas, no-one has ever provided a free cocktail-tasting ticket since.

Mr Williams was admitted to Lister ward for cardiac catheterisation with a view to surgery. He had been suffering from angina as a result of coronary artery disease for four years. His angina had worsened and he was also very breathless. When I first met him, he was really overweight for his relatively short stature of five foot six inches. He seemed much older than his sixty-six years.

I could tell he was really anxious on admission, and his mobility was poor; he was brought to the ward in a wheelchair.

'Hello Mr Williams, I am Nurse Brookes,' I introduced myself. 'That is Mr Fogherty in the bed next to yours, and on the other side is Mr Jones; across the other side of the bay are Mr Black and Mr Fox.' All of the patients smiled at him apart from Mr Black, who was not a friendly man.

'Don't worry,' said Mr Fogherty in his thick Irish accent. 'The nurses are nice and the food's not half bad.' He winked at me. Mr Williams attempted a smile. His wife had accompanied him to the ward.

'I'll close the curtains and leave you to get into your pyjamas.'

'Thank you, Nurse,' his wife smiled; she had told me that she would stay with him for a while and help him get settled in, because he was such an anxious man. She was used to doing most things for him at home, including wheeling him around in a chair they had purchased. After he had changed into his pyjamas I returned, armed with the nursing care notes that I needed to complete in order to admit him to the ward. He was quite breathless, though some of this was due to his anxiety and once he felt more at ease the breathlessness improved. I wrote in his notes that he would need reassurance. I was looking at his medical notes while I admitted him, and one of the doctors had written that he was a 'whiner'.

The days of doctors writing rude remarks in patients' medical records was almost at an end, but not quite. Medical notes were confidential, and some doctors felt it gave them the right to say what they liked about patients. It wasn't unusual to see patients referred to as 'fat' or worse – ignorant; paranoid (when they were just worried); time-wasters and all sorts of other things. Sometimes they could be regionally insulting, using the letters N.F. in front of the initial letter of a town or area – translated as 'Normal for...'. Not all doctors did this, and hospital doctors were often the mild offenders compared to GPs who could be downright rude – even in their admission letters, which would sour the minds of ward staff towards a person. Sometimes what they wrote had truth in it, and sometimes it was just their interpretation. Doctors' letters to each other both from and to the hospital could begin with words such as:

'This very nice young woman'

'This neurotic woman'

'This obnoxious man'

'This fat, lazy man'

'This charming gentleman' and so on. These judgemental remarks said more about the doctor than they did about the patient, because the vast majority of doctors rarely strayed away from the polite and professional, keeping their letters and records objective. Nurses, too, could and would write derogatory remarks in their records, but this was less common, as most ward sisters and matrons would come down on them like a ton of bricks.

I checked Mr Williams' observations and they were normal, apart from a faster than usual respiratory rate. I realised that he would not be able to breathe with the standard two pillows, and went to fetch him three more so that he could be well propped up when in bed. I asked Mr Williams about his medical history.

'Mainly this angina, Nurse; I did have an appendix out when I were a youngster,' he informed me. 'The only other time I was in hospital was when I broke my ankle playing football in my twenties.' It was hard to imagine Mr Williams ever being my age, but of course he would have been. I often found it sobering when meeting patients to imagine that they, like me, were once youngsters, and that they all had lives outside of the hospital wards. I found it did me, and them, good to ask about their lives in most cases.

'What did you do for a living?'

'I were a plasterer until five years ago. I had to give up when this angina started up.'

'Are you from around here?' I continued.

'I was born in Southend and have lived there all my life except during the war. I'm a home-loving man really; met the wife at a party when I were twenty-three. It took me most of the night to pluck up courage to ask her to dance, and then I trod on her toes for the rest of the night.' Mrs

Williams obviously didn't mind as she agreed to marry him when he proposed. 'We were married in June 1938,' he said proudly. 'The next year we declared war on Germany and I was drafted for military service.' Most men between the ages of eighteen and forty-one were drafted.

'Where did you go?' I asked. The men in the surrounding beds were all sitting up listening now as they were all war veterans too, apart from Mr Black, who had a heart murmur and had been refused entry, which hadn't helped his attitude any.

'I was signed on for the navy and worked in the engine rooms of a submarine; I was also taught to fire torpedoes.'

'I was RAF, flew spitfires,' chipped in Mr Fox.

'Were you really? I was RAF, air traffic control.' Mr Jones joined in the conversation. Before long, they were all reminiscing about their wartime escapades and reminding themselves how lucky they were to have returned intact. Mr Fogherty had been in the army and had been stationed in Singapore for a while.

Mr Williams had returned from the war to be reunited with his wife, and they had two boys who were now both married with children of their own. He was delighted to have two grandsons and a granddaughter, and he had spoilt them rotten prior to his condition worsening. He said he found it difficult now because they wore him out, but he still loved seeing them.

The next morning Mr Williams was taken to the cardiac catheterisation lab for coronary angiography. This procedure involved inserting catheters into a vein and an artery, then a dye was inserted and the coronary arteries were filmed on a screen by a specialised camera. The outcome for Mr Williams was that he had severe blockages to his coronary arteries. He was seen by the consultant, who explained the problem and offered him surgery. Mr Williams agreed to the operation, and returned home with an appointment for surgery in the following February. He seemed much happier on discharge.

'I feel like something can be done now,' he explained. 'Before it was like being in a dark tunnel with no end in sight, whereas now I have hope. The doctor said that my symptoms will be a lot better after surgery and that I could live a normal life.' His eyes lit up as he told me this and I realised again how easy it was to judge people when they were vulnerable. Many patients with chronic illnesses suffer depression and anxiety as a result of their symptoms and the debilitation they cause, and while some are able to remain positive, not everyone can. It was lovely seeing him so happy, and he even said he was going to try to lose some weight before surgery as the doctor had advised him to. He had already given up smoking just before admission, and this would help his symptoms too.

On the same day that Mr Williams had gone for his angiogram, Mr Fogherty had gone to theatre for coronary artery bypass grafts – known as CABG and pronounced cabbage. I had found it really confusing when I first started working at the hospital and people kept talking about patients and cabbages.

'We had three cabbages today,' remarked Fran.

'That's a lot of cabbages – why?' I had asked. Fran had looked at me a bit strangely. 'Because they needed surgery.'

'What has surgery got to do with cabbages?' Suddenly Fran, Jen and Blanche realised we were on different wavelengths and they burst out laughing.

'Cabbage, coronary artery bypass grafts, Dawn – CABG,' laughed Jen.

How was I supposed to know? Silly hospital acronyms. I had joined in the laughter once I got the joke. Everything is easy when you know. It wouldn't be the first time I mixed up acronyms – it's a bit like singing the wrong song lyrics for years and then realising.

Mr Fogherty lived in London's East End, where he moved for work following the war. He had worked in the building trade for many years until he developed angina in his sixties. In spite of the damage to his coronary arteries he continued to smoke, which was not uncommon, much to the despair of cardiac surgeons. It was at this time that I began to question my own hypocrisy – advising people to stop smoking while I continued to smoke myself never sat comfortably with me. As I said previously, I attempted to stop smoking myself on at least three occasions but didn't manage to last longer than a couple of months.

Mr Fogherty was married to his childhood sweetheart and

they had four children, two boys and two girls. One son was a teacher, the other was a plumber, and his daughters were married with children. One daughter was a social worker who had moved to Leeds some ten years previously; the other was a part-time shop assistant and mother who lived in Guildford. The family remained close, and met up at least once a month. There were eight grandchildren. I had got to know Mr Fogherty quite well since he had been admitted for surgery.

Two days prior to surgery, he was visited by the anaesthetist, who examined him and prescribed his pre-medication. On the day of surgery he was given valium 20mg orally at six o'clock in the morning and then intra-muscular omnopon and scopolamine at seven o'clock. He was also given intramuscular antibiotics that would continue for ten days. I had shaved Mr Fogherty's chest and leg the day before and explained to him that he needed a pubic shave. 'I can do that myself, Nurse.'

'You might not be able to see properly but don't worry Mr Fogherty, Nurse Brown will do that for you.' Alan Brown was an Australian male nurse who had recently joined the hospital, working on a twelve month visa. Mr Fogherty looked relieved; it would have been embarrassing for him to have a pubic shave from a snippet of a girl, as he used to call me. Alan also assisted him with the iodine baths that were part of the pre-operative regime for two nights prior to the operation and on the morning of surgery. I had given him two glycerine suppositories the night before surgery to ensure his bowels were empty. So many procedures had become routine to me over the past few years. It was hard to imagine that innocent young eighteen-year-old who had first started nursing four years before and at twenty-two, I had seen and witnessed so many things that most people may not witness in a lifetime. For the most part I counted it a privilege to be a nurse, although sometimes I wished I didn't have to see so much illness, heartache and death.

Thankfully, when one of us was down because of some trauma we had witnessed, the others would help us through it. On that particular morning when Mr Fogherty was in surgery, Mr Fox called me over, saying he felt unwell. He was pale and clammy, and I was about to call the doctor when he collapsed back on the bed.

'ARREST' I shouted, while feeling for a pulse and checking for breath all at the same time, and one of the nurses ran to fetch the resuscitation trolley while I removed the pillows and commenced cardiac massage. I asked one of the patients to pull the curtains.

In every hospital at the time there was a special cardiac arrest telephone number which was dialled, and then all the on-call doctors would get an arrest bleep, which was usually a rapid, continuous bleep. They would get to the nearest telephone to find out where the arrest was and then come running. This whole process happened in minutes, which I was grateful for because cardiac massage drained energy fast and was stressful. Alan was on duty, and he brought in the resuscitation trolley and applied a face mask with a bag attached to it to administer breaths to the patient when cardiac massage paused. After a few minutes the first doctor arrived and then an anaesthetist; they took over the resuscitation and then shouted their instructions. They would shout for various drugs used to assist with restarting the heart and set up the defibrillator. Resuscitation techniques have improved dramatically over recent years, and defibrillation is given much faster as this is usually what saves lives. I had grown attached to Mr Fox, a gentle seventy-year-old man who was due to go for surgery the next day, but at that time I was working on adrenaline. As the team continued to try to bring this man around though, the adrenaline wore off and I realised that they were not going to succeed.

During cardiac resuscitation there is a moment when realisation sets in that it is not going to be successful, and a hush replaces the frantic activity. Usually resuscitation was attempted for at least an hour, but when that moment comes it is horrible. The doctors and nurses exchange glances and then the doctor will usually shake his/her head and all the work will stop. The doctors then look at their watches, agree time of death and walk away back to rounds or clinics. The nurses are left with a chaotic mess and a dead patient. Alan and I looked at each other and then slowly started clearing away the mess. I looked at Mr Fox with tears in my eyes.

'I'm sorry that we couldn't help you, Fred.' It was the first time I had called him by his first name. I held his hand for a moment, which by now had turned cold. Fighting back tears, I helped Alan clear up the resuscitation trolley and tidy up the bed. The nurse in charge had called his family and they were on their way to the hospital, not knowing yet that he had died. Alan and I also had to re-stock and re-check the resuscitation trolley, accounting for all the drugs that had been used so they could be replaced, and double check everything. As we emerged from behind the curtains Mr Black called, 'I've been waiting for my painkillers for an hour, Nurse, and my bed hasn't been made this morning.'

'Bl...y wait,' Alan muttered under his breath.

'I'll bring them in a minute, Mr Black,' I replied, uttering the same sentiment under my breath. 'Your bed will be made when there is time.'

As soon as we had finished checking the trolley, bells were ringing and the nurse in charge called 'Hurry up, Nurse. The lunchtime medicines need to be given out now. We are running behind.'

'Oh dear,' I turned to Alan. 'How could Mr Fox have been so inconsiderate? Did he not realise there were beds to be made and medicines rounds due?' I chanted sarcastically. Alan smiled grimly. We understood that a death on the ward affected some more than others, and we continued with our jobs.

Mr Fogherty returned to the ward two days after surgery, and he was so relieved to be back his euphoria spread to the other patients. It was the lift we all needed after the death of Mr Fox. Mr Fogherty was a new man; although he had post-operative pain he was ecstatic at being given a new lease of life. Mrs Fogherty was also ecstatic, and this pleased him too.

Post-operative care included four-hourly 'obs', chest physiotherapy three times a day and deep breathing exercises. He also had steam inhalations four times a day. These were given through a white pot called a Nelson's inhaler – named after the doctor who designed it. Boiling water was poured into the container and then a cork stopper put in place. The cork had a hole in it to allow tubing to be placed inside so that the patient could inhale through this. There was a spout to allow the steam to escape and reduce the risk of burns.

A chest X-ray revealed that he had developed collapse in the bases of his lungs following surgery.

'He'll need the Bird, Nurse,' the doctor said to me.

The Bird was a machine that provided assistance to patients to expand their lungs via a process called intermittent positive pressure ventilation. It was quite common for patients to develop lung base collapse, because they found it difficult to breathe deeply due to the pain from surgery. The Bird, if given four times a day, would push a mixture of air and oxygen into the lungs and expand them. I explained the process to Mr Fogherty.

'The physio will show you how to use the machine,' I told him.

'I don't mind, Nurse, I'll do anything to get better,' he smiled.

'That's good,' I said, 'because you will be mobilising from

tomorrow. Time to get you moving again,' I laughed. The next morning I helped him walk to the bathroom and got him a chair to sit on at the wash basin.

'It is so long since I've been able to walk very far,' he confided. 'I have been an invalid with the wife doing everything for me.' After his wash I wheeled him in a chair to the dressing room and took off his dressings. Both the leg and the chest wound were healing nicely.

'There's just a small bit of oozing at the bottom of the chest wound,' I told him. 'I'll put a dressing on that but the rest we can leave open now.' I also helped him to put on a white anti-embolism stocking, which took a lot of heaving and pulling on my part. He would need to wear the stocking for three months, I told him.

'Good job my mates won't see it,' he laughed. It was lovely watching Mr Fogherty become a new man every day – he was his old self again, said his wife. The only time he was reluctant to move was around the fifth day after surgery, when all the bruising came out. Once he knew this was normal, though, he soldiered on, and by the end of ten days he was ready for discharge. His lungs were back to normal, his stitches were all out and the antibiotics finished. He opted to go for convalescence, and was discharged to Frimley Park Hospital. I was absolutely ecstatic to see him leave the hospital in a far better state than before. The surgeon had not really considered him a good candidate for the operation but he was as pleased as everyone that it had been a success. Mr Fogherty would no longer be a cardiac cripple, and he left the hospital full of hope.

I had learned more lessons again as a nurse, and gone from an extreme low following the death of Mr Fox to euphoria following the transformation of Mr Fogherty. The highs and lows were something that I never totally got used to; I didn't like the emotional swings, as they didn't suit my personality. Nursing was always going to be emotionally challenging though, but it was at times like this that I knew why I loved the job.

11

THE SMELLY SHOES EPISODE

The second medical ward I worked on later in the year was called Hilton. This is where I got to meet my friend and member of the God squad. Sister Wright was in her late twenties, average height with dark brown hair tied up in a ponytail. Cally was a quiet, almost shy, unassuming woman who went about her work in a professional manner. I didn't get to know her well initially, but by the end of my placement we had become good friends, along with a staff nurse trainee called Lottie, short for Charlotte. Lottie was also a church goer, although she didn't call herself a born-again Christian; she had been brought up in the Church of England and was an Anglican. I was still quite ignorant in my understanding of all of this as I thought in terms of Catholic and Protestant, and was only just discovering that there were all sorts of denominations relating to Christianity. It was all very confusing for an agnostic.

Whilst working on Hilton ward I met Miss Smith, a thirty-eight year old lady who was admitted to the ward for chest investigations. I was the admitting nurse, and on taking her history I discovered that she worked as a private secretary to a bank manager. I was tempted to relate my story of letters from the bank manager, but decided against this. Miss Smith was single, and stated she was happy to be so as she enjoyed work and travelling. She had travelled quite a lot, visiting many countries including the USA, Barbados, Australia, Israel and Mexico. She had two older brothers who were married, and her parents were elderly but well. Miss Smith was a non-smoker and her only problem prior to this admission was that she had suffered from chronic sinusitis since the age of twenty.

Miss Smith said she had suffered from a chronic, dry cough for about ten years. Her GP had told her that this was due to the sinusitis and had advised her to have antrum washouts, which she had refused. Again, I resisted the temptation to relate my recent experience of antrum washouts, and my meeting with Robert the Bruce.

About two weeks prior to admission she had developed a persistent cough with what we in the profession term purulent (lots of) sputum. Her GP referred her to us for investigations. From the outset, Miss Smith made it clear she was not happy about being admitted to hospital, but I think it was more out of fear than for any other reason. After all, she hadn't met Robert the Bruce.

After filling out most of the paperwork, I checked her

temperature, pulse, respirations and blood-pressure. We were still using mercury-filled thermometers and sphygmomanometers. A sphygmomanometer, or 'sphyg' as we called them, was used to check blood-pressure. They came encased in a hinged, rectangular wooden box. When the lid was opened you could see the mercury-containing measure attached to the lid. An arm cuff was placed around the upper arm of the patient and then, whilst inflating the rubber cuff by squeezing on a hand-held rubber ball, we had to use the other hand to apply the stethoscope over the brachial artery in the mid-arm. This procedure had taken many attempts to learn when I was first training in Leicester, and we had practised on each other until we got it right. It was the dexterity required that had been difficult to master. The other thing we had to learn was to resist the temptation to over-inflate the arm cuff, as it could be painful and patients would complain. Not that we minded when we practised on each other in the classroom.

Anyway, with the skill long since mastered I discovered that Miss Smith's blood-pressure was normal. Her temperature was raised slightly, so she would have four-hourly TPR taken, but daily BP. Her parents had come down from Manchester and were staying in a London hotel not too far away.

After the doctor had examined her and requested blood tests, he also requested that four sputum samples be taken; three to be checked for infection and one to be checked for cancer cells. I gave her four small, sterile sputum pots and explained that she needed to cough the phlegm (as she called it) from her chest into the pots. Miss Smith was also sent for a chest X-ray. This showed a patchy shadow in the left lower lobe of her lung, and the doctor decided that it was suggestive of bronchiectasis. He then arranged for her to have a bronchograph the next day.

I had never seen a bronchography before, and so was encouraged to go with Miss Smith. *I really thought that it would be alright not to see everything*, but Florence would have turned in her grave at my cowardice, so I tried to sound enthusiastic. I was beginning to think that specialist nursing wasn't for me as I progressed through the course and got more and more involved with specialist treatments and tests.

I was still recovering from assisting Doctor Reynolds with the chest drain episode, even though some time had passed since then.

The doctor had explained to Miss Smith what the procedure would entail, and she had taken it all in her stride, unlike me, who was going to have another sleepless night wondering if I would pass out.

The next morning I did manage to turn up. I had considered throwing a sicky, but Jen had told me not to be such a baby. We were in the Bonner the night before.

'It's a simple, straightforward procedure,' she had said. 'I've watched a few times now – it's nothing that Sweeney Todd couldn't have done.'

Yes, that was really helpful.

'Thanks for that Jen. Anyway I've decided to write up

Miss Smith for my chest case study if she gives me the go ahead, so that should help me be a bit more objective.'

'That's the spirit,' chipped in May. 'In for a penny, in for a pound; speaking of which, it's your round.' We were in the Bonner, whispering in hushed tones so no-one would hear us. Not that you could hear anything over the juke box and the nattering – you certainly couldn't see very far through the cigarette haze. I slept reasonably well after a few glasses of lager, and woke in the morning with a new determination.

Miss Smith had fasted from midnight, and the night staff had given her the obligatory white theatre gown to put on with nothing underneath. An hour before she was due to go to the X-ray department where the procedure was being carried out, she was given a pre-med of omnopon and scopolamine. The pre-med was given to keep a patient calm before or during a procedure. It's a shame there weren't pre-meds for nurses. I gave Miss Smith a theatre hat to cover her hair, which she duly applied.

I walked alongside the trolley, which the porter pushed into the X-ray department where the bronchograph was going to be performed. Miss Smith had had two days of intensive physiotherapy prior to the procedure, to make sure the lungs were as clear of secretions as possible. Doctor Reynolds was going to be performing the procedure, and he explained again to Miss Smith what this entailed.

'We will put a bit of local anaesthetic into the skin in front of the throat first, and then inject deeper into the throat to numb the area inside. Once that is done we will insert a slightly wider needle so that we can insert a plastic catheter into the airway (trachea).'

Note that when a doctor or nurse says that something is 'little' or 'slightly wider', always read 'large' and 'much wider'.

Miss Smith tolerated the procedure well, and actually, apart from the thought of someone injecting anything into my throat, which gave me the heebie-jeebies, so did I. Afterwards the catheter was inserted and an X-ray was carried out to ensure that it was in the right place – good idea. Finally, a contrast medium was passed into the lungs and radiographs were taken while tilting and rolling the patient into various positions. While the catheter was in place it prevented Miss Smith from speaking. She was therefore asked to raise a hand if she was in pain. Once the films were taken, the catheter was removed and a small dressing applied over the area.

The results of the tests did in fact show that Miss Smith had bronchiectasis, where there is an abnormal widening of the bronchi which then becomes a reservoir for secretions and multiple infections. This accumulation causes further widening, and the small sacs in the lungs become baggy and enlarge. The disease in Miss Smith's case was secondary to the chronic sinusitis that she had suffered, but it was confined to the left lower zone, which made her an ideal candidate for surgery.

Dr Reynolds explained the diagnosis, as he was the respiratory consultant.

'You have two options,' he explained.

That's a rarity, I thought, *giving the patient options.*

'You can be taught how to perform your own chest physiotherapy and postural drainage. You would need to take a small dose of antibiotic every day to try to prevent infections, and we can treat future infections with antibiotics at a higher dose. The alternative is that you can have the lower lobe of your left lung removed, which is likely to result in a full cure, and you will be able to live a normal life afterwards.' Dr Reynolds and I were shocked that she chose option one, but she obviously had a fear of surgery, as she had previously refused antrum washouts for her sinusitis. Respecting her decision, Dr Reynolds explained that as long as she took the prophylactic antibiotics and carried out the physiotherapy for the rest of her life she could go on living normally.

'Are you sure?' I asked her later.

'Yes, for now. I just can't face the thought of major surgery at my age, but if I can manage the condition myself, I would much rather be in control of my own destiny.' She had a point, and she was an intelligent and determined woman who would likely manage the condition very well. She learned the physiotherapy techniques really well and the physiotherapist was happy that she had mastered them. Miss Smith went home with a very positive attitude and was started on tetracycline 500mg twice daily, which was the prophylactic dose that was effective at the time. Dr Reynolds said he would see her regularly in the first year to ensure that she was coping physically and mentally, and the surgery option was kept open for her if at any time in the future she changed her mind.

Miss Smith had a very supportive family, and she taught me a valuable lesson at the time. For me, the choice would have been to get rid of the disease and take the surgery, but not everyone feels that way and, while there were two choices available, it was right for the consultant to outline them both.

I realised I hadn't been out for a while; work had been piling up and I had been writing the two case studies that were a course requirement. Brenda suggested that we go out to the Empire on Saturday night, and as I was working an early followed by a late, I agreed. We met in Leicester Square and went for a drink first. It was therapeutic to be out dancing again and experiencing some normality, as I sometimes felt I lost perspective when surrounded by sick people all of the time. It was also good to hear about her work at Great Ormond Street children's hospital and the kids she came across. We laughed at the stories of the antics the staff got up to on the ward in order to cheer the children up. There weren't too many antics on the wards at LCH because people were too ill, but we did play tricks on each other at times.

That night, I got a taxi home at around three o'clock in the morning, and after a very quick chat with John I headed back to the nurses' home. I was feeling bright and a bit mischievous. On entering the nurses' home I noticed all the shoes outside of the rooms. We always kept our smelly working shoes outside our rooms in the corridor, because the rooms were small and the stink of sweaty feet was very unpleasant. I had the sudden urge to play a prank and decided to swap all the shoes around, even moving some upstairs. After about an hour, I had moved virtually every pair of shoes on all three floors and, pleased with my work, I went to my room. It was now around five o'clock and I drifted off to sleep immediately.

I was awoken an hour or so later by shouts and exclamations as those getting up for the early shift were stomping up and down looking for their shoes. I could hear raised voices and anger and soon everyone was up, with people frantically trying to find their shoes before going on shift. I was really tired and just wanted to go to sleep, but the racket was too much. Eventually I opened my door, and I could see furious faces all down the corridor. I was feeling a bit guilty now, and also a bit scared that if I owned up I might be lynched. Thankfully I had moved my shoes the night before too, so that I wouldn't be a suspect. *It's always good to have clarity of mind when committing a crime,* I had thought. The only difference was that I knew where mine were.

'Can you believe what some idiot has done?' shouted May.

'What?' I said.

'Some prat has swapped all the shoes around. Of all the selfish, idiotic things to do....' She was marching up and down frantically trying to find hers – she was obviously on an early.

'If I get my hands on the b..... fool that did this – they'll know about it!' shouted Jen from the other end of the corridor.

I could see that some people had found theirs and were heading off to work. 'I think I'll find mine later,' I murmured, and went back to bed. I couldn't help smiling at my handiwork in spite of myself. This was one prank I was never going to own up to though, and I never did. To any former friends and colleagues reading this, I'm sorry; it seemed funny at the time. I did get a little retribution later though as I couldn't get back to sleep and ended up going on shift with a splitting headache – reciprocity.

12

FLAT TIME

Brenda had been going on at me for a while to think about a flat share with her and two of her Great Ormond Street buddies. I had met Sharon and Lynne a few times, and we had been out for meals together when I had stayed with Brenda. Sharon was quite posh, the daughter of someone very high up in the Royal Air Force, and Lynne was equally posh and quite unassuming.

I had been living in the nurses' home for almost a year and was soon to be finishing my course, so I needed to move anyway as new students would move into the home I was in. I agreed to join them and we started flat hunting. It wasn't long before we found a first floor flat in a large Victorian semi-detached house in Stoke Newington, north London. The area was populated largely by Jewish people, with the majority of men sporting long beards with long sideburns and wearing black clothing along with rather large black hats. The flat we decided to rent was owned by a Jewish man who lived around the corner.

After living in the nurses' home this flat seemed huge. It had a large kitchen and bathroom, and an enormous lounge. The only downside was that we would need to share bedrooms, but these, too, were huge. We agreed to take on the flat, which was furnished, and would move in a few weeks later. The room that Brenda and I shared was the biggest, and both rooms had twin beds. We all figured that as we worked shifts and were often away (at least, they were often away) that we would manage.

The flat situation worked very well and was quite timely, because we were all qualifying in the near future. Some of my gang were going to be staying on at LCH, although some were moving back home, Flora included. I worked out that I could get a bus from the end of the road to Bethnal Green and so would be able to travel to work by bus and wouldn't need to get a tube. The tube station was a half-hour's walk away, whereas the bus stop was just five minutes down the road. It wouldn't be as easy as walking across a courtyard though.

There were two sisters living in the ground floor flat, and we later discovered that they often had parties, which they invited us to. Sharon spent a lot of time with her fiancé, although there was a little catastrophe when she went on holiday to the Cayman Islands without him and had a fling with a rich man from England who was living on the island. On her return she was convinced she had fallen in love with this man and broke off her engagement, planning to move to the Cayman Islands as soon as she could. Everything about Sharon was very dramatic – she didn't do ordinary at all. Once she got back to work and realised that she really did love her fiancé, the wedding was all back on; Lynne and I took a train to Wallingford in Oxfordshire a year later and witnessed what we had come to term as the Royal wedding. True to form she and her new husband drove away in an open top Bentley. I had been rather amused when we stopped off at Sharon's home once to find there was a cook and housekeeper, she was obviously used to a more privileged lifestyle than the average nurse.

We spent the winter of 1981-1982 in the flat and one night, after it had snowed, I awoke in the morning to see melted water dripping down the electric light pedestal in the bedroom. Lynne and I were the only ones there so we agreed to go and tell the landlord. It was a Saturday, and the landlord wouldn't answer the door, as they observed the Sabbath to the exclusion of all else. In the end we posted a note through the door, but we didn't see anything of him until the Sunday, and even then nothing was done about the leaking roof for about a month.

One night I was going onto night duty and was waiting at the bus stop when a guy bumped into me. A short time later we got onto the bus, and when I went to take my purse from my pocket I realised it was gone. I walked up to the man, who had also blatantly got on the bus, and asked for my purse back. He just gave me a load of verbal abuse, and I was too scared to do anything more. I felt terrible; I had no bus fare. The bus conductor had seen what had happened and didn't ask me for any fare, which was a great relief. I think that episode put me off living in Stoke Newington. I went onto shift that night feeling quite shaken and violated. I couldn't believe that anyone would steal like that, but obviously people did so. I realised it could have been worse, and that at least I was not harmed. I didn't carry bank cards in my purse to work so he would only have stolen a couple of pounds. It was still my hard-earned money though, and it was not an easy incident to forget.

Lynne met a boyfriend while she was living in the flat, and it became obvious that they were starting to go steady and that she was thinking about moving in with him. Brenda appeared to be going through some sort of personality change, and became moody and a bit hostile, which made her difficult to live with. The forces of nature were at work that would split up our little home after about six months, and everyone would decide to go their separate ways. It was all a bit like the breaking up of the fellowship in the *Fellowship of the Ring*. Sharon and husband moved to Oxfordshire after she was married and I stayed with them for a short time when I later moved to Reading.

We had some really good times in the flat, and because it was quite large it was great for entertaining; we had lots of dinner parties for friends from both hospitals. Also, it was nice because friends from Leicester could visit, which had been a bit tricky when living in the nurses' home. I think my mum was pleased I was no longer living in the East End of London, although she wouldn't have been so happy if I had shared the bus stop episode.

I had met Robert, a physicist, while working at the London Chest Hospital, a nice man who had not long moved to London himself. He offered to cook dinner for us and came to the flat one evening to make moussaka. I have to say he was a good cook and became a good friend; some time later he joined Brenda and I on a holiday to the former Yugoslavia, where we stayed in a place called Rovinj. We were also joined by a male nurse friend of mine from Leicester, who preferred drinking to tourism. I later introduced Robert to Cally and they ended up getting married.

One night when Cally came round for a meal I shocked her, not to mention myself, when I said I would join her for church one Sunday. I think she nearly fell off her chair, as she had been asking for about six months. I had grown increasingly inquisitive and impressed with the way she conducted herself and lived her life. I was also aware that when being confronted with so much illness and death I frequently felt totally inadequate.

I had recently had a very traumatic experience while working on the high dependency chest unit. This was an eight-bedded unit where patients were looked after following chest surgery. Mrs Frampton was a sixty-year-old lady who had returned from surgery following the removal of a lung. She was doing really well, although still needing a lot of care. Her husband had visited one afternoon and asked how she was, and I had explained how she had coped well with surgery and was stable. He left the hospital at around five o'clock, and one of the doctors came in to change the tubing attached to a central venous pressure line. While he was doing this, Mrs Frampton took a deep breath and collapsed, going into respiratory arrest. We had tried in vain to resuscitate her, but unfortunately did not succeed. I remember vividly her husband being called back into the hospital and, with tears in his eyes, saying to me, 'But you told me she would be alright.'

I felt terrible, not for the first time, and cried myself to sleep that night.

Cally seemed so certain that there was life after death, and she had challenged my lifestyle on a number of occasions. I didn't understand the God thing really, but wanted to see if there was anything to it.

I did go with her to the church she attended in Mile End, and I thought they were all bonkers. There was lots I didn't understand, but I had to admit that they all seemed very happy, and not a drink in sight. As this book is about my nursing career, I will cut a long story short. I was sitting on my rock a few weeks later, and as I looked out upon the water and up at the sky, I felt like I was experiencing the wonder of creation for the first time. I prayed a very raw and amateurish prayer, having never prayed in my life apart from in school assemblies, and I felt different – and, in fact, was different. Obviously my friends had been right to be worried about Christianity being a contagious disease. I won't go into any more detail about this subject here, but I did get a lot of stick from my friends, and my dad was furious. I think he would have reacted better if I had said I had become a prostitute. My mum was alright with it just as long as I hadn't joined a sect that took away all my money. *What money?*

13

UP, UP AND AWAY

During our final few weeks in training we had taken our last tests and all successfully passed. We had also passed all of our practicals and case studies, so we were feeling very pleased with ourselves. Fran was staying on at LCH to work on the coronary care unit. Jen was staying on for six months to consolidate her learning and then would head back up to Scotland.

We all attended Blanche's wedding in Leicester on the final weekend of the course, and saw that she and Jeremy were absolutely made for each other. It also gave me a chance to see my family, who I had neglected somewhat during my time in London, and to reassure my mum that I was alright. Blanche looked beautiful, and was married in a lively Pentecostal church, showing me once again that the world was raining Christians.

I was offered a job on the cardio-thoracic surgical ward at the Cromwell hospital, which would pay more money because it was a private hospital. I was going to take it, but Miss Bale called me into her office. I had written a letter of notice and thought that she was calling me in to say goodbye.

'Sit down,' she said sharply, and then she scowled at me. I had never seen her angry. 'I could shoot you as soon as look at you,' she continued.

'What have I done?' I asked, astonished by her anger.

She picked up my letter. 'This.' She held it up like a poisoned chalice. 'How could you? We gave you a chance, when no-one else would have. We took you without the qualifications you needed for the course, and this is how you repay us all.' She was quite pink in the face now. 'I will keep this letter for one week young lady.' Miss Bale sat down in her chair looking quite exhausted with all the activity. I realised I was dismissed and left the room.

At first I was angry, but the more I thought about it, the more I realised she was right. They had given me the opportunity, and I had gained all the benefits of the specialist experience. No-one had ever challenged me like this before, but I realised that the least I could do was offer my fully trained skills to the hospital that gave me those skills. I swallowed my pride, said goodbye to the pay rise and backed down, withdrawing my notice. Miss Bale was over the moon, as were Mrs Lumumba, Mr Robinson and Mrs Chang.

'It's not as if you don't like working here is it?' May asked. She had taken a job on the ICU.

'No, I love the hospital, it was only the pay rise and the attraction of living in the West End; but I guess I would have spent too much money anyway.'

We had met up in the Bonner for a last drink before some of the girls left.

'Well I can't wait to get back home,' Flora said. 'Although I will miss you all when I leave here.'

'You won't miss the cockroaches?' Fran teased.

'I do have a bone to pick with you about that,' Flora continued. 'You never did ask anyone to get rid of them, did you?' We all laughed, including Flora.

'Well I won't miss you if I get sick,' Jen said to Flora. The evening continued with good-natured banter. Some of the girls were moving into the qualified staff nurses' home, and others had found flats like me and were living elsewhere.

I ended up taking a job on one of the medical wards, but I did extra shifts around the hospital to keep up my skills. Mr Robinson and Mrs Chang collared me towards the end of the course.

'Dawn,' Mr Robinson smiled. 'Mrs Chang and I both think you should do your SRN training. You will get bored with life as an enrolled nurse, because you are sister material, and that can never happen if you don't do your SRN.'

'Do you think I would get accepted without the

educational qualifications?' I asked, remembering Mrs Butcher and my first interview.

'There are a few hospitals that offer the training via entrance exam still,' Mrs Chang replied.

'I have drawn up a list of the hospitals that do.' Mr Robinson handed me a piece of paper. I could have cried. This kindly man and woman both believed in me and were going out of their way to help me. They had no obligation to do this, but I am forever grateful that they did.

I took the piece of paper, and saw that there were about six hospitals offering a two year shortened course for enrolled nurses via entrance exam. They were all out of London, which I wasn't so keen about, but I could always come back, I thought. I applied to three in the south of England, and the first one to respond was Reading in Berkshire. Mr Robinson arranged for me to go and sit the entrance exam at St. George's Hospital in Tooting, as he used to be a tutor there. I did a bit of studying, as I knew from the first time I had sat a similar exam in Leicester that it was IQ-based, with maths and English questions. I was surprised at how nervous I was about it when the day came, but I had now set my heart on doing my SRN training. I needn't have worried; I passed with flying colours. Mr Robinson told me I got 96% and I was thrilled.

I went for my interview at the Royal Berkshire Hospital in January 1982, and was offered a place for the September cohort. I was pleased about this because I could give at least six months work back to LCH after Miss Bale's lecture. Mr

Robinson was over the moon, and gave me his old textbooks for when I started. They were too old, but it was a kind gesture from a lovely man.

Tina and I were chatting on the hospital bench in the front gardens of the hospital, as our courses had finished more or less at the same time. I was telling her how pleased I was about getting in to do my SRN (RGN) training, and she suggested a trip to Asia before I started the course saying she had always wanted to travel. It was a timely suggestion, because at that time the government was allowing nurses to cash in their superannuation payments, and I knew that I could pay for such a trip if I did this. We had a short discussion and I agreed. We decided to take a three month trip, leaving in June 1982 and returning at the end of August, as I was due to start training at the beginning of September.

Quite a lot happened in my personal life during the three months prior to the Asia trip. My flatmates were going their separate ways, with Sharon getting married, Lynne moving in with her boyfriend and Brenda deciding she was moving back into the nurses' home. I managed to find a room with a girl from my new-found church, so wasn't homeless. My brother got married at some point and didn't invite me to the wedding, which was disappointing. I think he had forgotten he had a sister due to my rare trips home. On the positive side, I discovered the Royal Albert Hall, the Royal Festival Hall and All Souls Church in the West End. I developed a real love for classical music. I also went to various concerts, and saw Cliff Richard, Chris De Burgh and the Moody Blues.

I continued to enjoy my work at the London Chest Hospital and I was relieved to discover that Miss Bale approved of my leaving to do my RGN training; she even accepted the Asia trip as an acceptable part of growing up. These did not constitute mutiny, whereas leaving her NHS hospital to work in a private hospital did.

Tina and I planned our trip, deciding to start in Singapore, travel up through Malaysia to Thailand and Burma, and then across to Sri Lanka, India, Nepal and Pakistan. Alan had written to an Australian mate in Singapore and arranged for us to go and stay with him and his girlfriend on the first leg of our trip. Tina had told one of her patients about the planned vacation, and as he was from Karachi in Pakistan he offered to put us up when we got there. The rest of the journey we would have to play by ear – staying at guest houses and such like. We found a bucket shop (travel agent) on Regent Street, and went to buy our plane tickets. The only tickets we bought were an outward flight to Singapore, an open ticket to take us from Bangkok to Sri Lanka and a return from Karachi to London, which would be our final destination. The man in the bucket shop gave us the name of his brother, who lived in New Delhi, and suggested we call on him when we got there.

About eight weeks before we were due to fly to Singapore I went to the doctors' for multiple vaccinations. I had been given a typhoid and cholera vaccine, and then gone onto a night shift on the intensive care unit.

Intensive care units are totally different to any other hospital wards because, although there is a patient underneath all of the machinery and tubes, it is the machinery and tubes that are the main focus of attention. The reason for this is that the patient's condition is monitored through the checking of the various contraptions that are inserted and applied. The intensive care unit at the London Chest Hospital had single rooms where patients were ventilated post cardiac surgery. The ventilators in use were pretty basic Brompton-Manley ventilators that had a concertina bellow, which thudded with every breath given to the patient. On this particular night, following my vaccination, I felt myself developing a temperature. My arm swelled up and I was feeling pretty lousy. I could feel myself falling asleep, but thankfully the rhythmic thud, thud of the ventilator and the need to do various checks every fifteen minutes kept me going through the night. There was a cardiac arrest in one of the other rooms that created a commotion in the early hours, and in that case, the resuscitation was successful. Morning came, after what seemed to be an eternal night, and the patient and I had both survived. I was very glad to get to bed that morning after taking a couple of paracetamol tablets.

My final few months of work flew by, and before I knew it, Tina and I were on our way to Heathrow airport, saying goodbye to the London Chest Hospital. I knew that when I returned, another chapter of my life would begin in Reading. I had gone out with those of my friends who still remained before leaving, and had arranged to return to London for a few days after the Asia trip before finding somewhere to live in Berkshire, as there was to be no accommodation for me. Sharon and her husband were living about twelve miles away from Reading in Wallingford, and offered to put me up until I found somewhere closer. That was all I knew as I sat in the Heathrow lounge with Tina, excited about what lay ahead.

We boarded a Pakistani International Airlines jet and were up, up and away.

HURRY UP NURSE 3

MORE ADVENTURES IN THE LIFE OF A STUDENT NURSE

Dawn Brookes

Oakwood Publishing
www.dawnbrookespublishing.com

DAWN BROOKES

HURRY UP NURSE 3 COPYRIGHT

This book is a work of non-fiction based on the author's experiences. In order to protect privacy, names, identifying factors, dialogue and details have been changed or reconstructed.

Published by OAKWOOD PUBLISHING
www.dawnbrookespublishing.com

Cover Design by Dawn Brookes

PREFACE

This is the third and final account of my years as a trainee nurse. I initially trained as a state enrolled nurse (SEN), meaning that it took me a lot longer to get to the stage where I was a registered general nurse (RGN). Had I known how long it would take, I would probably have opted for going straight into RGN training when the tutors realised from my first entrance exam that I had the ability to do this. On reflection, I'm pleased I didn't realise this, though, as I may well have stayed in Leicester for the rest of my career and missed out on London days that count among my favourite and happiest times.

With hindsight, I'm pleased my trainee years went the way they did and that I moved to the south of England, where I lived for the best part of thirty years, made many friends and trained as a cardio-thoracic specialist nurse, a RGN, a midwife and a district nurse, gaining two degrees along the way.

This book focuses on the details of a two-year conversion course I completed in a town in the south of England from 1982–1984, and my experiences of that course and the people I met. My enrolled nurse training and a little of my RGN training are covered in Book 1 of this series, *Hurry up Nurse: Memoirs of nurse training in the 1970s*. My cardio-thoracic course and how I managed to get an RGN training place is covered in Book 2, *Hurry up Nurse 2: London calling*.

Life as a trainee nurse before Project 2000 was gruelling, but also thrilling and fulfilling and I wouldn't have had it any other way. I'm grateful to friends, colleagues and patients who made the journey count among some of the best years of my life.

Dawn Brookes

THE PLIGHT OF A FIRST YEAR

Poem Sue Dundon

This poem was written by a friend and fellow nurse. It describes the lot of a junior nurse.

I am a first-year student nurse
And I'm being socialised,
I have to work and work and work
Without it being realised.

The auxiliary is very helpful,
She tells me what to do.
She is very friendly with sister
And I hope I will be too.

But I'm not in sister's good books,

I gave a thirsty man a cup of tea.
I only found out later
He was fasting for an IVP.

The school of nursing didn't tell me
How hard I would have to work.
They tell you how to do some things,
But on the ward it doesn't work.

The whole of my set do get on very well
We go through heaven and hell,
We take our moans and groans back to the
    nurses' home,
But we have lots of fun as well.

The home sister is a dragon
She won't give me a pass to go out,
But when I'm ill she's an absolute angel,
Of that there can be no doubt.

The medical staff don't talk to me
They make me like a wee moose.
When the Consultant comes to do his round
I disappear to the sluice.

Oh how I wish I was a third year
I might have better things to do,
I might even be able to talk to patients

Without getting myself in a stew.

The staff are always watching me
To make sure I'm working hard,
But I hope things will be different
When I'm eventually in charge.

Sue Dundon

1

ANOTHER HOSPITAL, ANOTHER TOWN

What on earth was I doing pitching up at yet another school of nursing to take yet another course? Not only that, I had landed in yet another town. I had been nursing for five years, but here I was, doing all these things once more.

'Why should I train again?' I asked.

My Irish friends laughed at me. 'To be sure, to be sure!' they joked.

It was the first day of my shortened two-year training course to become an RGN at last. The course was referred to as a conversion as nurses converted from being enrolled nurses to registered nurses.

I woke early, grabbed a coffee, a slice of bread and butter, and left my new place of residence to see what life had in store for me over the next few years. It was a cold but bright

September morning as I revved up the engine of my Suzuki 125 to ride to the hospital. I knew the way following a recce the day before. The roads were busy with traffic as it would be a rush hour – 9am – start, but thankfully I could skirt around most of the traffic on my newly acquired motorbike.

Once I arrived at the hospital, I parked up under a bike shed next to the school of nursing. *Surely they won't mind a motorbike being next to the row of bicycles?* I didn't have time to find out, instead heading towards the school of nursing building block in the hospital grounds.

Crowds of giggly girls milled around inside, and although I was only twenty-three myself, they seemed much younger. Either that or I felt older than my years. I was joining a set of second-year students for the shortened RGN training course. The school of nursing was relatively small, although not as small as the prefabricated unit I'd come to know and love at the London Chest Hospital – I sighed. How I missed London!

The main foyer area led into a larger hall with seats scattered about around small coffee tables. The walls had been plastered with magnolia coloured paint and were adorned with notice boards; no pictures, just notices and signs. The reception – if you could call it that – was manned by a woman in her fifties who looked like she'd dropped straight in from a library. Speaking of which, the library on the first floor of the building seemed to extend to places there just wasn't room for – a bit like Mary Poppins' bag! In reality, it stretched over a bridge leading to the doctors' boardrooms.

The racket from the excitable girls rang through the air. Their greetings, hugs and kisses surrounded me as they returned from their latest placements or holidays to begin their second year. I didn't know a soul and wondered if I'd be able to settle back into trainee life after the responsibility of being a specialist nurse in a hospital just a few months before. It was a good thing I'd taken a break.

I sighed again. 'You can do it,' I told myself while reassuring myself I would soon make friends. I always did.

Feeling more optimistic, I made my way to the reception, which was really just a window. I peered through the glass separating the receptionist from anyone approaching and preventing them from crossing into the hallowed land behind – a pretty small office, it has to be said.

The librarian lookalike came to the window and opened a small shutter.

'Yes?'

'Hello. My name's Dawn Brookes, I'm joining the September 1982 set today.' I smiled happily.

'Just a minute.' She leaned back and pulled out a list from a file, running her finger down it. Thankfully not too far – one of the advantages of having a surname beginning with B.

Her finger stopped. 'Yes, you are. Classroom 3 – over there, turn right.'

'Thanks,' I replied and crossed the room to where she had indicated. I made my way through yet more clusters of excitable girls – not one male nurse in sight – enjoying reunions. I found the classroom already half filled with nineteen to twenty-year-old girls; three older women, appearing to be in their forties, stood out among the group. Finding an empty desk, I sat down, plonking my crash helmet under the table. One of the older women seated nearby looked as bemused as I did.

'Hi,' I said. 'I'm Dawn, joining the set today.'

'Thank goodness,' she said, absently running a hand through her curly black hair. 'I thought I was the only one. Wendy, I'm Wendy. Are you doing the conversion, then?'

It always sounded like conversion should relate to a religious experience rather than a training programme and it made me smile. In spite of the fact that I had already done two years' SEN training, one year cardio-thoracic training, run wards and worked in intensive care units, this course would humiliatingly haul me back to square one. I had resigned myself to jumping through this hoop to get where I wanted to be, but didn't kid myself it would be easy. I wanted to be a registered nurse, and this was the only way.

I replied, 'Yes, I am. You?'

'Yes. It's odd being back in a classroom again – I trained years ago. They're all so young.' She laughed. 'I've been training some of these girls on the ward and now I'm one of them. Ironic, isn't it?'

'You're from this hospital then?'

'Yes, I've worked on women's surgical for the past fifteen

years. Decided it was time to take the plunge and do the conversion now my children are a bit older. I'm fed up with training people who then become senior to me as soon as they qualify.'

I had a lot of sympathy for Wendy because that was the lot of the SEN. Some of them became bitter about the injustice of the way the system worked. Others seemed happy not to have as much responsibility and to be more hands-on, but what was unfair was that one day they were senior enough to run a ward, and the next day when a staff nurse – even if newly qualified – came on duty, they would be treated like a student or worse. I hadn't had enough time to experience this frustration because I was still young and my feet had barely touched the ground after qualifying – I more or less moved straight down to London to undertake specialist training. I'd been so busy, but I am pretty sure if I'd stayed an enrolled nurse, I would have found it hard.

Enrolled nurse training never existed in the United States and no longer exists in the United Kingdom, and the qualification has been removed from the Nursing and Midwifery Council (NMC) register altogether. Enrolled nurses were given the option to convert in the 1990s through a much simpler process than the one I undertook; in fact, I was a tutor to many converting through a distance learning course in the late 1990s. Only a few enrolled nurses still remain who opted not to convert, biding their time until they can retire.

'Where have you moved from?' asked Wendy.

I explained how I'd been an enrolled nurse in Leicester, moved to London to do a cardio-thoracic course and worked at the London Chest Hospital up until three months ago when a friend and I had decided to tour Asia before I moved here. As I looked around and heard a few of the girls sharing their holiday experiences of Benidorm or Bognor, I sat back and sighed yet again. I didn't know whether to be smug or culture shocked about my return to the United Kingdom.

Later that morning, I asked the tutor, Mrs Crisp, if I would get a tour of the hospital. She laughingly explained that tours were only given at the beginning of the first year.

'Don't worry,' she told me. 'You'll find your way around soon enough.'

By lunchtime I was restless and needed a walk and a cigarette. My on-off relationship with smoking was back on, so I thought I'd undertake my own tour. The school of nursing stood in the grounds off one of three entrances from a road that spanned the west side of the hospital. I decided to follow an inside path running parallel to it and leading through the hospital grounds up the hill towards the rear. On my walk, I passed gynaecology outpatients and dermatology. I also saw patients and visitors making their way in to one of the main corridors that led through the hospital.

Unlike when I first started training, we didn't have to wear uniform when in "block" (as classroom training was referred to), so I sat under a tree, smoking my cigarette. I stayed still for a while, studying my surroundings and observing worried faces and ill faces. I watched people coming and going and wondered what troubles they carried with them as they entered and left the hospital. If you stand still outside a hospital, or even in a corridor of a hospital, you will see a multitude of stories unfold in a matter of minutes. It doesn't take a detective to work out what's going on.

Each face told its own story: an elderly man sat on a bench staring into space, probably having received bad news judging by the tear that fell unbidden down his cheek. Was it his news or someone else's that caused him such pain? A woman in her forties came out of the gynaecological outpatients department sporting a huge grin on her face as she fell into the arms of another worried looking man standing outside. Obviously she had had good news.

Inside the hospital, staff bustled along the corridors, all heading to some unknown destination, oblivious to the fact I was watching on. I saw nurses walking alongside patients heading to X-ray or theatre; porters chatting to patients as they wheeled them along corridors; doctors with stethoscopes hanging around their necks like a new scarf; admin staff wearing suits with badges pinned to their lapels. Within half an hour, I'd discovered where the large Nightingale wards were situated – they ran along the front and sides of the hospital, where the maternity unit stood near the top of the road, and casualty at the rear of the hospital. A woman was being shouted at by a man – presumably her husband – as children followed, most likely being dragged along unwillingly to either visit sick relatives or accompany one of the parents to an appointment.

Casualty backed on to yet another road. The hospital was huge, probably on a par with the Leicester Royal Infirmary where I had spent a large part of my enrolled nurse training, and the main building and its grounds were surrounded by four different roads. The main entrance to the older part of the building had been erected on the London Road, but only people who took the bus entered the hospital that way as parking was limited. The school of nursing was closer to the front of the hospital, but you had to leave the main corridor to get out to it or enter via the road I'd come in on that morning.

I had sufficiently familiarised myself with the layout of the hospital by the time I made my way back to the classroom for an afternoon of lectures and giggly girls. These young women would be responsible for caring for some of the people I'd observed going in and out of the hospital; I wondered what kind of nurses they would be. I hoped they would be caring, like the ones I'd worked with in London. I hoped they would try to understand the fear that many of the people coming in and out of my new hospital would be experiencing and that they would take the time to communicate compassionately with them. One thing I did know was that if they hadn't grown up already during their first year, they would do so pretty fast over the next few years. Some young women in this room would go on to great things; others would leave, get married or get pregnant; a small minority would become automatons who didn't give a damn about the people in their care. I would find out who would be who all in good time.

I was right about making new friends. A few weeks later it was as though I'd been with this set right from the start.

2

THE WEEK BEFORE: HOMELESS

It was all well and good doing a three-month trek round Asia, but now I was back in London, needing to move to a town forty miles away to start my RGN training next Monday. The small problem of where I was going to live occupied my mind as I dossed down on my friend Sheila's floor at the London Chest Hospital.

'Stay as long as you like,' Sheila had told me, but her real meaning was, *I know you have to be gone by the weekend so I'll put you up until then.*

It was great being back in London; I had thoroughly enjoyed the Asia trip, but there was no place like home – figuratively speaking, as the reality was I didn't have a home. The flight back from Karachi the day before had been a long one and I'd got the distinct impression that my travelling companion, Tina, was sick of the sight of me after three months living in each other's pockets. The fact that she hadn't offered to put me up in her flat spoke louder than words; it seemed she didn't care I might be homeless!

Travelling for that length of time with one person can be challenging, though, and I made allowances for that following her surprise outburst on the Tube on the way back from the airport. She had yelled at me over something particularly trivial and told me in no uncertain terms that I'd got on her nerves. I told myself, like Elizabeth Bennet in *Pride and Prejudice*, that it was good to have a short memory in such cases. I also reminded myself she was an only child and not used to sharing.

We parted ways with no real goodbye, both still a bit jet lagged. Years later, we did get back in touch with each other, after I'd moved away from London and Tina had married. We wrote to each other for many years, moving on to Facebook messaging in more recent times, both glad that our great adventure when we were young hadn't done irreparable damage to our friendship.

After Tina and I had gone our separate ways back in the early eighties, I decided to head back to Bethnal Green to see if anyone would let me stay overnight. I had been shocked by Tina's outburst, but I had bigger fish to fry as it was time to plan how to get to my new town and place of work. I only had a few days to work out where I might live.

Thankfully my old friends were only too pleased to see me on my return. I hadn't had the chance to get on their nerves for over three months, so they were happy to hear about my travels through Asia. My Australian friend, John, offered to put me up, but I thought staying with him in a tiny room and only a single bed might be challenging – for me, if not for him. We'd already been down that road before I left and it wasn't one I wanted to return to.

Sheila was on an early shift when I asked if I could stay an extra night while I sorted myself out, which was when she told me I could stay for as long as I liked. I heard her get up for work and climbed into her bed as soon as she left, exhausted and a bit jet lagged. I had heard that jet lag wasn't as bad going from east to west as it was going the opposite way, and so far that was proving true. Although I was still in a different time-zone, at least Karachi was only four hours ahead. Even so, I had been wide awake since 3am! It was difficult not making a noise in a room the size of a cardboard box, and to make matters worse, Sheila snored most of the night, but beggars couldn't be choosers.

I eventually got up at 10am after catching a bit of sleep, feeling ready for lunch. I found John in his room. He'd told me he had a few days off and wanted to hear all about my trip, particularly as I had stayed with one of his friends in Singapore. We spent some time catching up and I told him I really needed to sort out where to live before Monday. In typical horizontal Australian style, he reassured me it would work itself out.

'A bit like you telling your friend in Singapore we were coming to stay and us arriving with him not knowing who the heck we were sort of "work itself out", you mean?'

'He put you up, didn't he?'

I had to admit it had worked out, but with no thanks to John. At this moment, though, all I had in my hand was a letter with a start date for next Monday. The letter instructed me to arrive at the School of Nursing at 9am. Accommodation hadn't been an option for students undertaking an enrolled nurse conversion course – in fact, very little was offered to students undertaking the conversion course, if the sparse letter was anything to go by. Still, I was going to train as an RGN and that was all that mattered to me. I would be joining a group of students beginning their second year of training as my course had a year knocked off for good behaviour.

John couldn't believe the way the British system worked. 'Two years training as an enrolled nurse, two years working as a qualified nurse and one year training on a specialist course, and it counts for *one year*?'

'Yep, I'm afraid so, but it's only two years of my life.' Forever the optimist – no wonder I drove Tina mad on our travels.

I checked through my address book and decided there was nothing for it but to phone one of my ex-flatmates. She was married and living in a small village around fourteen miles from the town I would be working in, and she owed me big-time for the hours I'd spent painting flipping Artex all over their cottage walls before she and her husband moved in. If I'd known back then it contained asbestos, I wouldn't have been quite so keen to help.

The pips after I'd dialled from the phone box in the main hospital corridor told me it was time to put money in.

'Brenda, hi.'

'Dawn, is that you? It's absolutely delightful to hear from you. Are you back in the United Kingdom?' My friend spoke with a plum in her mouth and lived by the philosophy: why use two words when you can use twenty? Still, it was a good start.

'Yes, got back yesterday.'

'I can't wait to hear all about your travels. Oh wait until I tell Brian and Mummy you're back. You must come and tell us all about it, everywhere you went and who you met.'

At this point in the conversation I was recalling the time Brenda had gone away to the Cayman Islands, met a wealthy bachelor and broken off her engagement to Brian on her return home. Our friends and I had lived through every detail of the trip, from the daily temperatures to the colour of Bachelor Boy's socks; I felt I had been there myself by the time she'd finished. Thankfully she had got over the infatuation and married Brian who took her back with open arms, despite her infidelity.

I was hauled out of my reverie when she asked, 'When does your course start?'

'Monday.'

'That soon? Have you got anywhere to stay?'

'No, not yet.'

'Oh, you must come and stay with us until you find

somewhere. Brian will be pleased to see you; we have so much to catch up on. When can you come?'

I love you, I love you, I love you! 'Would tomorrow be all right?'

'Yes, of course. Are you getting a train? Brian can collect you if you let me know your arrival time.'

The telephone pips were now going demented so I put another coin in the phone.

'No, it's okay. I have a lift. Sorry, got to go, I don't have any more change. See you tomorrow, bye.'

Making my way back through the hospital corridor with a huge smile plastered on my face, I traipsed outside, through the courtyard that doubled up as a building site thanks to permanent renovations and a hospital extension that took longer to build than the Channel Tunnel, and upstairs to John's room, giving him the thumbs up.

'Will you be able to drive me to Brenda and Brian's tomorrow? It's about forty miles.'

'No worries,' he answered in the Australian drawl that I had grown to love. 'What we gonna do today, then, mate?'

We decided to go into the West End as it might be a while before I could visit London again. I would be back to living on a student nurse's salary and was stony broke following the Asia trip. We went to all my favourite places, including *My Old Dutch*, a pancake house in Russell Square that I adored. That evening I caught up with some more of my friends and we went to the local pub, *The Bonner*, for a few drinks.

The next morning, I packed up my "worldly goods", squashing them into the one bag I possessed. I'd bought it in Thailand – a multi-pocketed dark blue holdall with tan leather decorations around all of the pockets. I no longer owned a camera, having sold mine in India to raise some much-needed funds. With mixed feelings, I said cheerio to the few friends that were on late shifts or days off and jumped into John's battered old car.

I hated leaving London. Having been so happy in the Capital, first living in the East End, then in a flat in Stoke Newington, I had wanted to stay there forever. If I'd already been a registered nurse, I knew I wouldn't be leaving, but I needed the RGN qualification as much as I needed air to breathe, so the deed had to be done. This was my only ticket, but I still choked back the tears as John started the car.

Brenda came rushing out her front door as soon as John pulled the car up outside her house, a Victorian terrace about eight doors away from the village pub. I'm sure she and Brian had chosen the cottage based on its proximity to the pub as it took away all worries about drink-driving. It was before the days of mobile phones so she must have had telepathic senses, or been staring out the window.

Brenda didn't know John at all, but having been brought up with a father ranking highly in the RAF, she was used to making people feel at home. Having said that, she was also used to servants and a cook, but I didn't see any of those around. Within minutes, she had offered John overnight accommodation, which he gratefully accepted, along with a pot of tea. Pot, not mug; she was very British.

Brenda and I caught up on each other's news while Brian took John out to see his Austin Bentley sports car – the same car he and Brenda had driven away in for their honeymoon. After dinner, we all walked along to the village pub and spent a pleasant evening playing catch-up. John and Brian hit it off immediately; Brian was a few years older than me and Brenda, but nowhere near as old as John, and there was no shortage of conversation.

Brenda took me aside and asked if John and I were an item, so I explained that he had asked me out quite a few times before I went away, but there was a twenty-year age gap between us, not to mention there would now be a forty-mile distance, too.

'I like him, he would be great for you. So laid back.'

'I like him too, but it wouldn't work. I need to concentrate on my training over the next two years, and anyway, he's too old. When he's sixty, I'll only be forty.'

'Forever the pragmatist, Dawn. When are you going to fall in love?'

'Never, if I can help it. I don't want to give my love to just one person, I'd be claustrophobic.'

Brenda would never understand my philosophy on love, but she did understand about the gruelling training I was about to undertake. She was already a state registered nurse

(SRN) and registered sick children's nurse (RSCN) as she had trained for four years and obtained a joint adult and children's nurse qualification. We had met through a mutual friend when a group of trainee nurses were doing their adult placement in Leicester. She and my two other ex-flatmates had trained at Great Ormond Street, but we all went our separate ways after Brenda and Brian married. Sharon had stayed in London, but moved in with her boyfriend, and Lyn moved back into the nurses' home.

We reminisced for a while about the old days after the pub had closed and finally went to bed at around two o'clock in the morning. Brenda and Brian were working the next day, but had told me about the buses going into town.

'I think I'll need to buy a motorbike if I'm going to travel fourteen miles every day.' I was starting to worry about the distance because I hadn't passed my driving test and reality was sinking in. Before the Asia trip, my only experience of motorbikes had been as a pillion passenger, but Tina and I had hired bikes on numerous occasions while travelling in Thailand and learned on the job, a bit like nurse training.

'There's a bus every hour from across the road,' Brenda assured me. Before going to bed, she and Brian said I could stay with them for as long as I wanted to.

I heard Brenda and Brian get ready for work the next morning and waited until they left the house before rising. John had to get back to London and I saw him off. He kissed me before leaving and said, 'You've got great mates there,' and then I was left alone in a strange village, not knowing how I was going to manage the commute while working hospital shifts. My situation might be manageable for a short time, but certainly not for long.

Before going to bed the previous night, I had prayed for three things: that I would find somewhere to live quickly; that I would find a motorbike shop the next day; and that I would find a church to settle into. Not much to ask, surely!

By the time John had left, I was very much up and dressed, ready to explore the town where I would be working. Crossing the road to the bus stop about ten minutes before the bus was due, I waited in silence. I knew a little bit about the small village Brenda and Brian lived in from the times I'd stayed when we were doing up their cottage before they got married. It had typical village amenities, but I wasn't much interested in it as a place to live because it would be too far away from work.

The bus journey was straightforward enough, but took well over an hour due to regular stops on the way. It passed through several other villages, including Pangbourne where I noticed the weir that had inspired the author of *Wind in the Willows*. Brenda had told me to look out for it the night before, and as the bus stopped right outside the pub where the weir was situated, I couldn't really miss the place where Ratty had made his friends.

By the time the bus arrived in town, it was after midday. I didn't know the town at all, and had no intention of staying there after my two years' training. How little we know of the future! I got off the bus on a main road, a stop before the town centre as it happened, and spotted a motorbike shop across the road as soon as the bus moved on. One prayer answered, my usual optimism returned.

I crossed over the road, smiling, and saw a small round man with messy red hair wearing greasy blue overalls, bending down fixing something on one of the many bikes in the shop. He stood up and smiled a friendly smile.

'Hello, what can I do for you?' It was fairly unusual in the 1980s to find young women going into a motorbike garage.

'I'm looking for a small motorbike suitable for a learner,' I answered. Back then you could ride a motorbike on a provisional licence for as long as you liked, as long as L plates were on display. The engine size was restricted to below 125 cc, though.

He looked a bit askance. 'Have you ridden a motorbike before?'

Typical bloke attitude, I thought, but answered confidently.

'I learned in Thailand.' I assured him that if I could ride amongst kamikaze Thai drivers, I would manage in this town. Then I explained how I had just returned from a journey around Asia and was staying with friends in a village fourteen miles away, but was due to start work at the main hospital on Monday.

He wiped greasy hands down his overalls and smiled again. 'You're in luck, then. Me and my wife have a basement flat for rent.'

I gawped. He explained that he and his wife knew the village where I was staying because they went to church there.

'It will be a difficult journey from there if you need to work shifts, but from our house it would take you five to ten minutes to get to the hospital on a motorbike, and twenty minutes to walk.'

I couldn't believe my luck!

The man left a young lad in charge of the garage and walked me the five minutes to his house. As we entered through the front door into a long hallway, the mess struck me, but it could have been a lot worse. I'd just returned from places where people lived on the streets and washed in puddles.

He called his wife downstairs. A woman in her early thirties with long, greasy dark-brown hair stepped over toys and clothes, randomly strewn across the hallway, to reach us. They invited me upstairs as it was one of those houses where the lounge was on the first floor. I followed them through the obstacle course to a lounge even more untidy and cluttered than the hallway. The man introduced himself as Graham and explained that his wife didn't like housework.

Understatement of the year! The place was more like a junkyard than a house; if I hadn't been there with the owners, I would have thought it had been burgled. Clothes, toys and remnants of food were scattered all over the place; the three scruffy children and one scruffy dog I would meet later. But needs must. I was thankful that in India I had shared rooms with lizards and giant cockroaches; otherwise I might have run for the door.

We drank tea, certainly not made in a pot, and I didn't pay too much attention to the mug for fear of what I might see. Having said all this, I don't want to sound derogatory. They were really nice people who went out of their way to welcome me, a stranger, into their home.

After a while, they escorted me back downstairs and unlocked a door in the hallway that led down some steps into the basement flat. The flat, or rather, bedsit didn't look too bad at all; a lot cleaner than the house upstairs. It was a bit musty and damp, but it had a bedsitting room fully equipped with a Baby Belling cooker, and a shower room with toilet. I think sharing the toilet with the messy family upstairs would have been more than I could take, even though I had come to grips with holes in the ground on the Asia trip!

We agreed I could move in at the weekend and I paid a deposit. I don't think there was ever a contract; it was a handshake agreement without the handshake as Graham's hands were too greasy. Then I went back to the garage with him and chose a dark blue Suzuki 125 that was around five years old and within my price range. He said he would service it for me and have it ready for Sunday when I moved in. He also sorted out some L plates and a helmet that would fit on my head. I couldn't have been more pleased and felt like a huge weight had been lifted from my shoulders. Stage one had gone so much better than I could ever have imagined.

After leaving Graham's garage, I walked into town and ate a late lunch. I looked around the shops, found a W H Smith where I bought a map, and then headed back to the main road to get a bus back to Brenda's.

Brenda and Brian were flabbergasted when I told them the story that night. Brenda was disappointed that I wouldn't be staying longer, but understood it would be for the best.

John was coming back the next day for the weekend, and when I phoned him with the news, he said he would help move me on Sunday. Thankfully the flat was furnished because I didn't have much in the way of belongings.

John, Brenda and Brian helped me to move into my new flat on Sunday morning. It was more a matter of them wanting to see where I was going to be living than helping, as I only had the one bag! Brenda wasn't impressed with the hallway, and was even less impressed with the basement flat.

'It's damp and it smells musty. Are you sure you're going to be all right here? Who are these people? Don't they own a vacuum cleaner?'

I had to laugh. As she'd been brought up in a military household with a cook and cleaners, this was Brenda's idea of hell. I doubt that one shred of dust had been allowed to remain in her family home, and her cottage was just as tidy.

'It's only until I find somewhere else and it saves me travelling the fourteen miles into town every day,' I answered reassuringly. John didn't look any less concerned than Brenda, but he held his peace.

We went out for a pub lunch locally, and then Brenda and Brian headed back home and John left for London. I was pleased when they all left because the tension had been building in Brenda throughout the afternoon. I was beginning to think she might haul me into the car and take me back with her, or have me certified.

Graham and his wife, Karen, had stayed out of the way while I moved in, which was perhaps as well. Although I could see the mess whenever I went upstairs, it wasn't *my* mess. As with so many things, I have no regrets with regards to my short tenancy in the basement flat.

Graham had given me the keys to the flat and the front door of the house when I arrived. I noticed my Suzuki parked on the front drive and found the key in an envelope by the kettle, along with the ownership documents that I had to complete. I had sorted out insurance the day before, finding a broker in the town centre that Graham had told me would give me a reasonably cheap policy as he used them all the time.

I decided first to take a walk to the hospital, using the map I had bought. The letter from the hospital gave the address of the School of Nursing and I knew I would remember the building once I got there from my interview earlier in the year.

The interview stood out in my mind. I'd taken a Tube from Bethnal Green to Paddington, and then a train followed by a bus journey to the hospital, but just as I was about to enter the building, the heel of my shoe had caught in a drain and come away. I was running out of time and couldn't do anything about it, so I shoved the heel in my handbag and tried to walk as if nothing was amiss. The trickiest bit had been following a secretary to the interview room and entering without giving the game away. I was grateful that on concluding the interview, the tutors had dismissed me and chatted to each other while I made my way out of the room cautiously, trying to walk as if I had two heels.

Once outside the building, I had walked uncomfortably into town and found a cobbler who told me they could glue the heel. I ended up walking in my stockinged feet into a café where I sat for an hour before collecting the mended shoe. Thankfully, a few weeks later I received a letter from the hospital offering me a place, otherwise I might have been tempted to post a broken shoe to the interviewer.

Now, I wanted to know how long it would take to walk to the hospital, and to see if there was anywhere to park my motorcycle once I decided to ride it in. Following the map, I took just over half an hour to get there with a bit of stopping and starting to check directions. I figured it would take twenty minutes at a fast pace; it was about a mile from where I was now living. Not bad at all. It could have been a lot further away, so I was thankful for my little basement bedsit for now.

I located the School of Nursing through a side gate leading into the hospital grounds. It wasn't a big building and was locked up, so I was unable to enter. I walked along the road inside the hospital and noticed a bicycle shed on the right-hand side which might do for parking my bike – there was already a moped parked up.

There was no long-term parking on the road outside – the sign read "Two hours parking Monday to Friday". Alongside the limited parking area stood an old building with one entrance, but multiple windows. It stretched for a couple of hundred yards and had to be a nurses' home – it just had that look about it.

Having completed my task for the day, I decided to amble back to my flat and get unpacked ready to start training the next day. The thought cheered me up because I was missing London and didn't know anyone in this town, apart from the rather eccentric couple whose flat I was renting. There wasn't a phone in the flat and this was well before the days of mobile phones, so I felt isolated and alone with no outside contact. Graham had said I could use their phone upstairs, but I suspected that if I ventured up there, it might not be easy to escape again. And I was right – many a conversation lasted far longer than I would have liked when I did go upstairs during my tenancy. It wasn't that I didn't like them; I did, but the mess was unsettling. There was never anywhere to sit; food and drink spillages covering the floor stuck to my shoes – there was no way I was taking them off; and Charlene was always pleased to hand me the chubby six-month-old baby whose face was often dripping with something or other that ended up landing on my clothes. In spite of all of this, they were a happy family and the children didn't lack for anything (other than a wash).

But I digress.

I got back to the flat at around 6pm and unpacked the few clothes I had, hanging my one suit in the small wardrobe. The rest of the clothes I piled into a chest of drawers, and then I took in the details of the flat for the first time.

It was pretty dark as the only window was below street level. A Formica-topped table and two chairs sat in a tiny patch that constituted the dining section. In the main living area was a two-seater settee and a single bed. The kitchen had a few cupboards and one of those really old fridges that spent years destroying the ozone layer for future generations, but in my defence, I didn't know it at the time.

The walls were artexed, a fact I'd pointed out to Brenda and Brian, knowing how much they loved the stuff and hoping to distract them from the musty smell, but to no avail. It was all painted white while the floor was covered with an old Axminster patterned castoff that must have come from the same roll that carpeted the upstairs lounge and stairs. It wasn't fitted; rather it had been plonked in the middle of the floor, and the frayed edges suggested it had seen better days.

This carpet also accounted for the musty smell from rising damp. As soon as I sat down, I could feel the damp – I already knew it was damp because of the dankness in the air, not to mention Brenda pointing it out continuously before she'd left.

The window provided a view on to a concrete enclosure about eight feet below the level of the driveway. Light didn't really penetrate through the window, making it hard to tell whether it was day or night most of the time.

Everything seemed to stand still that evening. I was beginning to realise why John was worried about me staying in the flat and I missed my friends already, but I had to pull myself together. I told myself it was a roof over my head and I was starting a new job the next day, and Brenda had put a pint of milk in the fridge earlier and supplied me with a loaf of bread, some butter and a jar of coffee, so all was good so far.

3

GIVING BLOOD – OR NOT

During the second week of our initial block, a crowd of trainees went across the road to give blood as the blood transfusion crew was in town. After giving consent, and being told that my blood would need to be tested for infectious diseases which I presumed meant hepatitis B, I was asked to sit on a bed.

AIDs had hit the world's radar, but there had only been a few cases and it was not yet recognised as the danger it would later become. Terence Higgins had died of the disease in the summer of 1982 while I was on my travels, but the significance of his death was not known at the time. The disease became much more prevalent over the next few years and the HIV virus was identified in 1986 – the year I started midwifery training, as it happens.

AIDs was initially thought to be a disease confined to promiscuous gay men and drug addicts, so was largely dismissed as a low risk for the general population. Unfortunately, it didn't get the necessary attention until it became recognised as a heterosexual disease as well and after the first cases of contamination through infected blood were highlighted. In 1982 blood donors were not tested for the disease when giving blood and health professionals had no idea of the risks to them of this and other contaminants that were to arise from needle-stick injuries. Such injuries were extremely common for nurses – I had numerous during my nursing career – as we were still being taught to re-sheath needles after use before discarding them into a sharps container.

Not only were we in constant danger from infectious diseases, but the reporting of injury was appalling and generally not encouraged, so busy nurses and doctors just carried on with their work, hoping the cross-contaminated patient did not have hepatitis B. Later we discovered there were many more deadly contaminants, including HIV and hepatitis C.

Once the needle had been inserted in to my arm and the line attached, the nurse began the process of withdrawing blood and I felt all the life draining from my body.

'Am I supposed to feel as weak as this?' I asked as my legs and chest became heavy.

Without looking at me, the nurse answered, 'Don't worry, you'll be fine,' and carried on withdrawing blood.

'My limbs feel really heavy,' I said. I could tell that

something was not right as I was beginning to feel like I was sinking away.

Finally she looked at me, and suddenly a crowd of people was around the bed as she disconnected the line. She tilted the foot of the bed up to bring my head down and I felt someone mopping my brow with a cold flannel.

'Did you eat before you came over?'

'No, I came straight from lectures.'

A cup of tea and a biscuit later, followed by a lecture on the need to eat and drink before giving blood and a lot of ribbing from my newfound friends, I was feeling normal again.

'At least we can send your blood off to test your suitability to donate,' the nurse said.

A few weeks later I got the all clear letter informing me that I could give blood anytime and that my blood group was O positive. Have I ever given blood since? Not likely!

4

OPERATION THEATRE

Looking forward to getting back to where the action was, I woke up excited and jumped on the motorbike, revving up the engine. It purred into life with the same degree of excitement I was feeling, and I arrived at the hospital in plenty of time for my 8am start in theatre. In fact, I arrived a bit too early and had time to kill.

After doing a few laps around the hospital grounds at a pace any motorbike lover would be proud of, I parked my trusty steed under the forbidden bike shed near to the School of Nursing. I had come to an agreement with the head porter that he wouldn't tell anyone I parked there if I didn't let on he knew about it.

I made my way towards the hospital theatres. Anticipating new levels of responsibility, with visions of major operations taking place and surgeons thanking me for my expert assistance at the end of each shift, I knocked on the door to theatre. No reply – not a good start. I didn't dare walk through the doors into theatre from the anaesthetic room because everywhere would be deemed sterile and I was still in my jeans and t-shirt, holding a crash helmet under my arm, so I waited for what seemed like an eternity until someone came along the corridor.

'What are you doing there?' he yelled.

'I'm Dawn Brookes, student nurse. It's my first day, I was told to report to theatre at 8am.'

'You need the changing room entrance, back there.' He nodded his head towards a corridor on the left.

'Thanks,' I said and trundled off, feeling like an idiot already. 'Great start, Dawn,' I muttered to myself.

I found a door clearly labelled THEATRE STAFF ONLY and pushed it open slightly. A woman dressed in a navy blue uniform, obviously the theatre sister, saw me.

'Yes?'

'I'm student nurse Brookes reporting for duty, Sister.'

She smiled a genuine smile. One had to learn the difference between sisters' smiles; some reached their eyes, and others warned, *I'm going to eat you up and spit you out.* It paid to do your homework – it was a matter of survival. This woman wore the good type of smile and I immediately relaxed.

'Well, come on in, then. We don't bite.' She sounded harsh, but there was a jolly tone to her voice which was not at all frightening. I had met many ogre sisters before and immediately sussed she was not one of them, although she did do a double take at the sight of my crash helmet.

'You be careful you don't end up in here on the other side,' she warned.

'I'll try not to.' I didn't know whether to laugh or not, so held my peace.

'Right, follow me.'

She led me into a large room lined with rows of tall, narrow metal lockers. Some had keys to demonstrate they were not in use; others had labels on them and were clearly locked.

'Change into a pair of those.' She pointed to a pile of scrub suits on a trolley. 'And put some clogs on. What size are you?'

Not sure if she meant clothes or feet, I answered for both. 'Size 10 dress and shoe size 5.'

She chuckled. 'You nurses get smaller and smaller.' Looking at her size 22 frame and six-foot stature, I could see where she was coming from. She towered over me in every way. 'Clogs are over there. Once you've changed, join us in the office through that door.'

'Yes, Sister.'

I had to stifle a "yippee" as I looked at the blue scrubs I was about to put on. I'd only been in theatre twice when working at the London Chest Hospital, once to watch a coronary artery bypass operation where I bumped heads with a theatre nurse who was none too pleased, and once when I was ensconced firmly behind a screen at the

Brompton Hospital to observe paediatric heart surgery. This would be the first time I got to see things working close up and personal.

The scrubs fitted, apart from the trousers; they were too long so I had to switch to a dress instead. Trousers were always too long for me – they came in one length to fit the average height woman and I was five foot nothing. One thing I always carried around was a sewing kit in case I needed to turn something up, but I was happy to wear a scrub dress as my uniforms were all dresses anyway. I only ever wore dresses at work and to weddings; otherwise it was skirts or trousers that had been turned up to fit.

I found a pair of white clogs with heavy cork bottoms on a bench that was lined with at least thirty pairs in various sizes. On another bench I saw the white boots that surgeons wore. There were male and female changing rooms – thankfully, as they were very much open for all to see with no private cubicles or anything of that nature. Female consultant surgeons were a rarity, but there was one female gynaecologist, and as time went by there were more and more female registrars and house officers who would scrub up to assist with surgery or, in the case of registrars, carry out surgery themselves.

I found the office easily enough and was pleasantly surprised to find the day started with a cup of tea in Sister's office. This was something I can honestly say I'd never encountered in a hospital before. Sister Blenheim hadn't introduced herself, but I'd spotted her name from a surreptitious glance at the badge above her voluptuous right breast. The badge appeared to be seated on a large shelf, but it didn't pay to stare at nurses' badges unless you were a lecherous old man or an over-eager doctor! The badges were always placed above a breast on women, but some nurses placed them over the nipple. Whether by design or naivety, I never knew, but it could be embarrassing when you needed to know their name.

Sister hauled me back from my musings and told me to study an A4 sheet of paper attached to a clipboard hanging on the wall. It consisted of three theatre lists for the day, and it was jam-packed.

The other nurses on duty introduced themselves. There were six staff nurses and three student nurses on shift.

'Theatre operating times run from 9–5, Monday to Friday, for planned surgery. We have to fit emergencies in where we can and out of hours, but you won't be expected to work any late shifts or weekends unless you want to volunteer as an observer,' Sister explained before whispering conspiratorially, 'I wouldn't if I were you.' I felt a little disappointed, but thought it would be nice to have a few weekends and evenings off for a change, having already spent most of my adult life working shifts.

Just when I was feeling happy and jolly, my luck changed. I was allocated a rather fierce-looking staff nurse to work with.

'Staff Nurse Wright will show you around. You can work with her today,' Sister informed me. I smiled over at the staff nurse in question but she looked away, rolling her eyes in the process. I got it – not every nurse liked having students following them around, but to be fair, in those days, students didn't do much following; they did most of the work.

Staff Nurse Wright was around forty, I guessed, and rake-like with cropped dark-brown hair that did nothing for her dour face, other than to make it look even more sullen than it already was. She wore horn-rimmed glasses and no wedding ring.

What did I do to deserve you? I could imagine her thinking this, because I was thinking exactly the same thing. All the other nurses were laughing and joking, talking about their weekends and boyfriends, and I was stuck with Sourpuss!

Shortly afterwards, SN Wright, aka "Chirpy", got up and left the office. I wasn't sure whether I should follow or not as she could have been going to the toilet for all I knew! One of the staff nurses smiled at me sympathetically and nodded towards the door, so I followed after my new leader like a puppy dog that had been kicked.

'We need to get Theatre 1 ready for surgery. Fill that up.' Chirpy pointed to a bowl in the sluice area where she had led me after handing me a theatre hat to cover my hair. The sluice was adjacent to the theatre and was where the surgeons and scrub nurses got ready before operating. I obediently filled a bowl with hot water and Chirpy added disinfectant. We then spent the next forty minutes washing everything – and I mean everything, despite the theatres having been cleaned at the end of surgery the night before.

Who knew what dangerous microbes had marauded in the middle of the night? I began to visualise bacteria dancing around to disco music, having a theatre party after hours, and wondered if I would make a good cartoonist.

'Sister Blenheim,' I was informed by Chirpy, 'Will not tolerate any postoperative infections on her watch.'

My new leader, Sister Blenheim, was meticulous in every way, and so too were her staff. One thing I learned from hospital life was that a ward or, in this instance, theatre was only as good as the sister in charge – something modern-day hospitals could do with reflecting upon.

'Sister won't allow doctors or nurses to shortcut the rigid scrub-up times and no-one would dare to try,' one of the friendlier staff nurses told me later that day. 'Even the consultants who are bombastic demi-gods obey her rules of cleanliness and warn the junior doctors to do the same.'

After we had washed the theatre bed, all of the metalwork underneath, the theatre stools, anaesthetic trolleys, scrub trolleys, resuscitation equipment and the walls – yes, you heard right, the walls – the theatre was ready for the day. Just in time as we heard the first patient arriving in the anaesthetic room next door to the theatre. Two surgeons entered the sluice room through a different entrance, wearing white wellington boots and blue scrubs. They always looked strange in their *Ena Sharples* hats, but needs must.

Another staff nurse came through – I only knew who she was from her badge as everyone wore the same blue scrubs, which made identification difficult. I would be spending a lot of time checking badges as it was really hard to tell who was who once masks and hats were on, and I became very familiar with staff members' eyes when working in theatre. The eyes could tell me a lot about the person underneath the scrubs.

With an unnecessarily huge sigh, Chirpy pulled out a white theatre pack from a pile in a cupboard and placed it on the trolley in the main theatre.

'First op's a gall bladder,' she muttered.

Happy in your work, I thought sarcastically. This was going to be a long day if she didn't brighten up.

'Here, put this on.' She handed me a mask. It was even harder to recognise anyone now as everyone was wearing them, but Chirpy was easily identifiable due to her scowling green eyes and the lines on her forehead, not to mention her waif-like frame.

I peeped around the open doorway from theatre to the scrub room to see the doctors cleaning their fingernails and hands vigorously with a nailbrush and iodine. They washed and scrubbed to the elbows before drying themselves again. Chirpy pushed past me as though she were late catching a train as they donned their sterile green theatre gowns.

'You take that one,' she ordered. I had no idea what I was meant to do, but saw her tying up the gown at the back while the surgeon pulled on sterile gloves, so I did the same for the junior doctor and the scrub nurse. Chirpy only had time for the surgeon; all others were beneath her, it seemed, as she cold-shouldered them while oozing obeisance to the main man.

Once in theatre, everyone except for Chirpy carried on chatting as if nothing was happening, and I was pleased that I'd managed even this small task in spite of her. During surgery, everything in front of the surgeon and scrub nurse must be kept sterile, so they can only be approached from behind. In any other occupation that would just be plain rude, but woe betide a nurse who accidentally touched a gown in the wrong place. It was a frequent novice mistake; surgical registrars would laugh it off on the whole, but consultants often wiped the floor with the poor student nurse, taking great pleasure in doing so. The bigger the audience, the louder the dressing down. Unfortunately, surgeons were renowned for thinking too highly of themselves.

For the most part, the reputation was well deserved back in the day as they walked around followed by an entourage of junior doctors, rarely acknowledging the existence of patients or junior nurses. There were always the exceptions to the rule, and I did meet some surgeons who would smile and explain to a patient what the operation would involve, although I have to say that this didn't always go down well with the patient. Many preferred to be kept in the dark to revere the all-knowing surgeon; they didn't particularly want to be told he was going to amputate their leg or remove half their gut as if it was as easy as swatting a fly or buying a bag of chips.

There was no doubting the skill with which surgeons operated while talking about golf with the anaesthetist, who was equally blasé about it all. At the end of the day, routine surgery is just that, and most surgeons could do it with their eyes shut. The only fun some of them seemed to have was when someone dropped something so they could shout at them or if a junior doctor couldn't answer a question. Occasionally the scrub nurse would hand over the wrong instrument, which was almost a capital offense.

Nevertheless, it was all new to me and I watched operation after operation with wide-eyed enthusiasm, soaking the experience up like a sponge deprived of water. As I watched the surgeon hold out his left hand and the scrub nurse place an instrument into it without him even telling her what he needed, I soon realised that if that scrub nurse were to be in a village somewhere in the outback, she would be able to perform the same operation with almost the level of skill as the surgeons I observed. A sobering thought.

I say "he" for surgeon because the truth is that the majority were men; I didn't meet the female gynae surgeon until the mid-1980s, when they were still a rarity. Male nurses were becoming less rare, but I didn't come across any working in theatre. They tended to gravitate towards casualty or charge nurse positions, and men were much more likely to be promoted in spite of the nursing profession being female dominated across the board. There were, and still are, a disproportionately large number of men promoted to management throughout the NHS.

Although surgeons performed intricate operations with great skill while discussing golf and the price of whisky, if something went wrong, they would respond with speed and adept professionalism. During surgery, the surgeon would toss instruments and swabs backwards and forwards while the scrub nurse made sure instruments were placed meticulously to one side while the blood-soaked swabs were passed to assistants – in this first case, me and Chirpy – who would separate and lay them out on a towel on the floor to be counted later. After the surgeon had finished his operation, he would stop while the theatre went silent. The scrub nurse would count out the used and unused swabs to ensure all were present, and then she would do the same with the instruments.

'Ready to close,' she would say, and then conversation would resume as either the surgeon or his assistant (more often than not) would close the patient up again. The reason for this is obvious: no-one wanted to leave anything inside the patient that shouldn't be there.

I found the whole theatre thing fascinating, but my mum's dream of me locking eyes with a surgeon during an operation and the happy-ever-after ending never took place. But it wasn't unusual for a theatre sister and a surgeon to marry – or not. Some surgeons and/or theatre sisters got involved in extra-marital "open secret" affairs while others were fly by nights, but there were some happy marriages that began in theatres and, indeed, in hospitals in general. Nowhere near as many as portrayed in soap operas, though.

On my first day in theatre, I saw numerous bodily organs removed or exposed, and Chirpy had to nudge me a few times to get me to do some menial task – usually just when things were getting interesting. I did as I was told and thoroughly enjoyed my first day regardless. In between operations, all hell broke loose as we had to frantically clean and scrub again before the next operation while the surgeon went for coffee and the junior doctor wrote up the notes. If you ask me what I remember most about theatre, I would have to say cleaning! But that doesn't mean I didn't learn a lot.

It was during the third week of this placement that I was in orthopaedic theatre to witness an above-knee leg amputation. Orthopaedic theatre, I had been told, was like working on a building site as there was always the banging and clattering of tools and much of the operating equipment resembled a builder's toolbox, albeit a surgically sterile one. There were hammers, screwdrivers, chisels, files, but I would see even worse instruments/tools on this particular morning.

There is no way to describe an amputation other than barbaric. Thankfully, the patient was in a deep anaesthetic-induced sleep and had no idea what was going on. The orthopaedic surgeon looked at his trolley and examined various instruments that wouldn't look out of place in a torture chamber. When I say instruments, I mean saws. I have never watched horror movies that involve the use of saws because I have witnessed the real thing – except the patient generally survived, in my experience.

After the patient's skin and muscle was cut open, the surgeon selected a saw appropriate for the job in hand. I was the poor unfortunate who had to hold the leg up while he sawed through the bone, bringing forth a sound that is unlike anything else. Once I'd heard this unique sound, I'd remember it forever. The bed was high because the surgeon was tall, but I am small, and was trying to hold the dead weight of a man's leg at a forty-five degree angle.

The scrub nurse could see I was struggling. 'Rest it on your shoulder,' she suggested. Thankfully that worked, except that I now had a clear view of what was happening. As blood and bone spurted everywhere, I ended up looking like an extra in one of the horror movies I never watch. The assistant worked quickly to cauterise blood vessels, but not fast enough in my opinion, while the surgeon applied clamps that the scrub nurse handed to him. Thankfully, I was wearing the mask because an artery clamp came loose and I got showered before the surgeon managed to put his saw down and cauterise the bleed, applying another clamp. I almost dropped the leg, which would not have been good as it was only half off!

Deep breaths, I kept telling myself as I felt myself getting weaker. The leg belonged to a twenty-four stone diabetic man and there had been a lot of flesh to cut through before starting on the bone; even the surgeon was sweating.

At least he's getting his brow mopped, which is more than I can say for me, I thought.

Eventually the surgeon managed to cut through the bone and tossed the leg at me.

'Get that out of my sight,' he said as he rested, breathless, for a moment before starting repairs. I, on the other hand, reeled backwards under the weight of the leg and was about to end up on the floor, but was saved by – would you believe it? – Chirpy! She caught me and the leg in one swift movement and helped me dispose of it in a bag that would go to the incinerator.

She motioned me towards the sluice, and then, to my amazement, burst out laughing. We laughed and laughed until tears streamed down our faces. I think my tears were more of relief than anything.

Chirpy told me to go and take a shower and change my scrubs as I looked like a murderer. When I got to the changing rooms and saw myself in the mirror, I could see what she meant. I was covered in blood and I reeked.

Pleased I wasn't the squeamish girl who almost fainted on her first ward, I showered, changed and went back for more. Needless to say, Chirpy and I became firm friends after this incident and I grew to like her, even though she remained dour-faced most of the time. We had shared a moment, and those moments are all important within the stresses and strains of a nurse's life.

I was pleased to end my stint in theatres, not because it was boring or I was sick of cleaning – even though I was, but because I missed speaking with patients. In theatre, they were out for the count, or when I worked in recovery, they were too groggy to have a conversation with. I admired the surgeons and put up with their quirks, and I appreciated the skills the scrub nurses had developed, but I hadn't spoken to a patient for eight weeks solid and that just wasn't for me.

It was time to go.

5

WOMEN'S BITS

Female gynaecology was an early placement for me at the largest of the town's three hospitals. I had lived in the town for two and a half weeks, with two of those spent in school (block). At twenty-three, I was feeling much older than my years – it was the Asia effect, I told myself. You couldn't spend three months travelling Asia and not be changed, and I was still finding it hard to adjust to life in affluent England. Not that I was affluent at all – stony broke, actually, but that paled in comparison to whole families I had witnessed living on the streets in India and washing in puddles. I had seen a man dying on the edge of a busy road in Madras, which had to be one of the hardest things I had ever come across and remains forever etched in my memory.

By the end of the block, I had got to know quite a few of the girls in my set and found they were inclusive and fun to be around. Now it was time to get back to ward work.

Bridget was admitted to the gynae ward following a miscarriage. She was thirty-three, married with two young boys aged under five, and had been expecting the couple's third child when pains started in the night. Sadly, at sixteen weeks, she lost the baby and needed a dilatation and curettage (D&C) to scrape away any remains and prevent infection.

I knew immediately I met her that she was a Christian – I like to think it was a sixth sense, but perhaps the Bible on the side of her locker gave it away. It turned out Bridget was married to a church elder of a non-denominational fellowship in a suburb of the town. That was the new church sorted out for me, then! Bridget and her husband, Aled, became friends, and I'm pleased to say that the following year, Bridget did give birth to her third child, a daughter.

Gynaecology often created conundrums for us nurses because young (and older) women were admitted to the ward for a termination of pregnancy and could be given a bed next to women who were desperately upset following a miscarriage or who had been admitted for fertility treatment. All in all, it wasn't a satisfactory situation, and we did our best to separate people, but it was not always possible. The old Nightingale wards were often heaving and the turnover was high.

There were times when two women would get talking and both would end up upset. One can't underestimate the guilt that many women felt when undergoing a termination of pregnancy, and if they found out they were next to someone who was upset at losing a baby, their guilt could be multiplied. And vice versa, when a woman had just lost a baby, she didn't always understand why someone would want to terminate a pregnancy. Yes, there were some women who seemed to use termination as a form of contraception and one couldn't help but feel impatient with these, but they were in the minority. The majority were not in that situation and it was never my place to judge.

I am human, though, and I couldn't help feeling that some women were being pushed into aborting their babies rather than offered support to continue with a pregnancy. Pressure could come from anywhere: partners who didn't want children yet, parents of young girls, friends and occasionally counsellors who should have known better. Women who had doubts were the ones who struggled the most with guilt and passing judgement on them, as many anti-abortion lobbyists would do, was just not helpful.

Greta was one such woman, filled with guilt. She had been admitted for bed rest due to a small bleed and what we called a "threatened abortion", or threatened miscarriage. I found her in tears during the afternoon.

'Can I get you anything?' I asked.

She continued to cry, and then looked up at me.

'It's my fault.'

I knew immediately what she was talking about; I had read her medical history and seen she'd had a vaginal termination of pregnancy (VTOP) six years prior to admission.

'You can't think like that.'

'I'm being punished. I knew it wasn't right, but I went ahead and had an abortion anyway. They told me at the pregnancy advice clinic I was too young and would regret having a baby for the rest of my life if I went through with it. They convinced me I should go for an abortion.'

I couldn't believe what I was hearing; the advisory clinics were supposed to be impartial and, as far as I was aware, they were meant to support girls and women to make up their own minds, discussing the pros and cons of childbirth. Perhaps she was mistaken or even making it up so she could blame someone else, although she appeared sincere.

'I went for a pregnancy test and was a bit taken aback when told that I was pregnant. The woman who gave me the result was cold and heartless. She scorned me and I'll never forget her words: "What did you expect if you have sex without contraception?" She was right, but you don't always think logically, do you?

'The next thing I knew, I was receiving counselling for a termination. I told them I would prefer to keep the baby, but they said I was just feeling that way out of some misguided sense of doing the right thing. "Catholic guilt", they called it. They said I was too young and wouldn't make a good mother at my age; they told me I would be throwing my life away. I was only nineteen, but one thing they didn't tell me was that I was throwing someone else's life away: my child's. And now I'll never be able to have children. They didn't even give me the option to have the baby adopted, something I would have seriously considered.'

Greta sobbed some more.

This was a very thought-provoking conversation and one that I remembered for a long time afterwards. Thankfully Greta's pregnancy did continue and she was discharged looking much happier than when she had been admitted. I trust she went on to have a family and that her feelings of guilt were assuaged as a result.

Don't get me wrong, not all women showed such remorse, and some treated abortion as if they were returning an unwanted item to the shop. The majority were somewhere in the middle: rational women who, for their own personal reasons, decided pregnancy was not right for them.

Full disclosure here: I was a conscientious objector, which meant that I wouldn't be in theatre for a termination of pregnancy, but it didn't mean that I didn't understand why some women/girls made this difficult decision or that I felt I was any better than them. It just meant that I could not, in all good conscience, take part in the actual termination procedure, but I still had a duty of care to the patient. Unfortunately, some of my colleagues were more judgemental towards me than I ever would have been towards the people in my care. Like many workplaces, the sad truth is that the NHS could have an underlying culture of bullying, and being a conscientious objector could sometimes be enough to kick start a bullying mentality from other nurses.

'Nobody likes these do-gooder, holier-than-thou sorts, Dawn,' my colleagues would sneer. Bizarrely, I suffered for my choice more as a midwife than as a general nurse. I tried to explain my position, but some colleagues didn't want to know, so I found it was best not discussed. Life's complicated at times.

Phyllis was admitted for surgery following a diagnosis of leucoplakia of the vulva. A forty-nine-year-old Irishwoman, she was to have a total vulvectomy. If you don't know what a total vulvectomy is, be thankful because it means all your bits are intact.

Basically the whole vulva, including the clitoris, is removed and a woman is left with a urethra to wee out of and a hole for the vagina. Yes, you got it – female circumcision of sorts, only in Phyllis's case it was to prevent the spread of a very dangerous pre-malignant condition.

Phyllis took it in her stride, not at all concerned. She shared a house with a male friend and – not that it was any of my business – she maintained there was no sexual relationship and refused pre- and post-operative counselling. Gordon was a lovely, big teddy bear of a man with long beard and moustache, and their relationship appeared to be a full partnership without the sex. It worked for them. He visited every day and they chatted and laughed away the hours, both pre- and post-surgery.

'Not every relationship is about sex,' she assured me and I had to agree that in their case, it seemed to be true.

Phyllis and I became friends and I was frequently invited along to their house for dinner – maybe the only decent meal I ate in a month as takeaways and hospital food were my lot in life. Just in case you're wondering – their home was a one-bedroom bungalow. I'm only saying! Some people do sleep together for companionship, or it may have been good old Catholic guilt that prevented her from admitting to living with a man outside of marriage. They were of the older generation and, despite the sixties sexual revolution, not everyone was happy discussing sex openly. On the other hand, they could have been telling the truth – as I said, not really any of my business.

Gardinia had to be the most eccentric person I ever met, and as for her mother – words fail me! If ever women could talk, and I mean talk, these two would win any verbal diarrhoea competition. They didn't just talk, though; it was all politics mixed with New Age evangelism.

Gardinia was admitted for a hysterectomy as she had fibroids, and she happened to be in the bed next to Phyllis and a lovely thirty-three-year-old woman called Charlene. Charlene had three young children and a doting husband, but had tragically been diagnosed with metastatic ovarian cancer; she wouldn't live for more than a few months. If ever I have met an inspirational woman who knew how to laugh and joke in the face of adversity, Charlene would always have my vote.

The three women were total opposites in terms of upbringing, life and work, but they did what opposites often do – they got on like a house on fire. My life was all the brighter for getting to know them and we laughed the days away.

Gardinia and her mother were on a personal mission to free Nelson Mandela, a man I had never heard of who, they told me, happened to be locked away in a prison in South Africa. The first time I met Gardinia, it was to fill out her admission paperwork. I have no idea how asking someone for a few personal details can lead to: 'This man must be freed. We went to a march last week – look, here's a poster.' I had stared blankly at the picture, certain that I had only asked her if she was taking any medication at present. Perhaps whatever she was taking was hallucinogenic or psychotropic. I hadn't the foggiest what she was talking about, and talk about it she did.

To be honest, I couldn't bear to hear poor Nelson's name until much later in life when I realised he truly was a man fighting injustice. I still don't believe that fighting for a cause justified the ear-bashing this poor nurse received every time she met Gardinia and her mother.

In between the Mandela thing and the New Age homoeopathy, another thing they had going on, I could see clearly why neither Gardinia nor her mother had ever married. Not quite sure how her mother got pregnant, but there was never any mention of a father. Phyllis teased Gardinia mercilessly, which she took in good humour, and Charlene bantered away too once she was on the mend following major surgery.

I kept in touch with all three women after they were discharged from the ward, even meeting up with Gardinia and her mother at their large home in a small village in Buckinghamshire. Large it may have been, but it represented everything they stood for – cluttered, messy, disorganised, hippy but homely, and of course Gardinia drank black coffee while her mum drank herbal tea.

Charlene died six months after being discharged and we all attended the funeral at the request of her husband – a sad affair that has left a permanent cloud over my otherwise fond memories of female gynaecology.

6

IN THE STICKS

My community placement was out in the country, twenty miles from the nearest town. It was a good job I had a car by then, not that the powers that be would have cared either way; I would just have had to make my way there via a rural bus route.

I was given the placement address at the end of a training block on the Friday before I was due to start and told to arrive at a place called The Quarry Health Centre at nine o'clock on Monday morning. I left early, not knowing what the traffic would be like, and with there being no satnavs back in the day, I used a map for guidance.

I arrived at a ramshackle old building on the outskirts of what was supposed to be a small town, but I would argue was more like a large village. It took me a while to find the entrance to the health centre as it really was not obvious. I walked around the red-bricked building a few times, searching for an entrance, but found that every door was locked.

Just as I was about to give up, I saw a woman who looked to be in her early 60s wearing a light blue staff nurse's uniform.

'Are you the new girl?' she asked.

'Yes, I am. I can't seem to find my way in and I think I might be late now.'

'Don't worry about that, follow me,' she said kindly.

I followed her round the corner to where there was a hidden door. I say it was hidden because it was just a large plank of wood, painted brown and nestling into the brick building. She entered a code into a large metal security lock on the outside, which was obscured by black plastic, hence my not having noticed it before. Even if I had noticed it, I wouldn't have known the code, and as there was no buzzer, I wouldn't have been any wiser. It screamed, "Visitors not welcome!"

Once inside the building, I followed her up a flight of stairs and soon heard laughter and talking in the distance. She pulled open a large, heavy door and we entered a huge room with around ten medium-sized wooden desks where four groups of people huddled. I followed my guide as we headed to the far right-hand corner.

'Look what I found hanging about outside,' the kind staff nurse said, chuckling.

'Hello, you must be Dawn,' said a woman who appeared to be in her late 40s. She wore a navy blue uniform and I rightly assumed she was the district nursing sister. I was a little taken aback because it was the first time I'd been called Dawn since starting my RGN training, other than by other student nurses. Most qualified staff still referred to me as Nurse Brookes.

She smiled and gestured for me to take a seat next to her by tapping the chair.

'Would you like a coffee?' she asked. I knew from that moment I was going to like community nursing. Never did you arrive on a hospital ward to be offered coffee. It was always a quick handover and off you went to work. This team appeared happy in their work.

That morning, there were three staff nurses, the sister who introduced herself as Jenny, and an enrolled nurse wearing a green uniform. There was also another student I hadn't met before; she certainly wasn't from my set and the stripes on her hat told me she was a second year. The hats were good identifiers as first years had one stripe, second years two, and third years three. Qualified staff wore frilly linen hats. I was now a third-year, so proudly wore the three light-blue stripes on my cardboard hat.

Initially the conversation revolved around who had done what the previous evening before moving on to talking about children, grandchildren and pets. Noticing my bemusement, Jenny laughed.

'Don't you worry, we work just as hard as they do in the hospital, but we don't make out we're God's gift. Right, on to business then,' she said and everyone quietened down.

She pulled an A4 book towards herself and opened it up. I noticed there were columned lists with the names of each nurse present at the meeting written at the top of the columns. Patients they would be expected to visit that day were listed below, and I saw from the length of the lists that it wasn't going to be all tea and coffee! Each nurse had around 12 to 15 patients to see, with the majority of them needing to be seen by lunchtime. After that, I was told we would meet up again to share around any other visits that came in during the morning.

The sister, Jenny, carried a bleep and it didn't take long for me to realise that this would go off constantly all day long. She would then have to find a telephone to discover who was calling her and why. I was allocated to work with Jenny that day, although I would be working with the other nurses in the team throughout my placement, which would last six weeks.

Jenny gave me a quick tour of the facility, for what it was worth. Basically, the building consisted of the large room and a storeroom on the ground floor. Although it was called a health centre, patients were not seen on site; it was a satellite office housing healthcare staff. She explained there were four teams based in the office we were in, each assigned to different GP practices.

Rows of large grey metal filing cabinets lined the outer edges of the office, containing district nurses' patient records. This was long before the days of computers on every desk. The desks were rather cluttered with diaries, documents and letters overflowing from in-trays, though.

On Jenny's desk there was both an in-tray and an out-tray, each filled with sheets of paper and envelopes. The nurses on duty had grabbed their diaries and were frantically writing down their work for the day, along with the addresses of patients who were new to them.

After the tour, Jenny picked up her own diary and indicated it was time for us to go. I proudly donned my navy blue outdoor raincoat and navy blue hat, standard issue for district nursing; I had been itching to wear this outdoor garb ever since I'd been given it. Jenny walked over to one of the filing cabinets and pulled out a large pile of folders containing patient records, which she passed on to me. The files were thick and heavy, and I was holding around eight sets of notes which weighed me down slightly.

Jenny picked up her Gladstone bag, which made her look very much like something out of the 1960s, and I followed her out of the building.

'The storeroom downstairs contains lots of equipment for the patients that need it, but I'll show you that later. We really need to get on with our first visit. It's someone I haven't seen before and they live on a farm which I'm told is quite difficult to find.'

Jenny opened the boot of her Ford Fiesta and I gulped as I registered the contents. There was barely any room to add anything to what was already stuffed in there, but Jenny somehow managed to shove her bag towards the back in amongst the melee. It was like a mini hospital room. There were dressing packs, incontinence sheets, boxes of syringes and needles, and a huge yellow sharps box for contaminated waste. I wondered if it would pass any hygiene tests as I could see dog hairs spilling over from the backseat and decided not to dwell on it. I was to learn this was quite normal for district nurses and community nurses in the early 1980s.

'Put the notes in there,' she instructed, 'and you can put your handbag in there too.'

I wasn't at all keen to put my handbag in amongst this lot, but I was left with little choice so I gingerly placed it to the left of a large box containing who knows what? Then I got into the passenger side of the car after moving various items, including crisp packets, chocolate wrappers and other rubbish, off the seat.

'Sorry,' she said. 'We only got back from holiday yesterday and I haven't had time to clean the car. Only just had time to put all the stuff back in this morning before heading here. It's not always like this, trust me.'

I was relieved to hear she didn't take incontinence sheets on holiday and I wanted to trust her, but suspected that it actually was always like this. And of course, I was right; certainly for the four weeks I was working with Jenny, the vehicle was more of a train wreck than a car.

That aside, Jenny was perfect in every other way and, like all nurses of that time, she diligently washed her hands at regular intervals – not always in patient houses, for good reason. One of the major lessons about working in the community was discovering that sometimes you would have to take your shoes off after leaving the house rather than on the way in.

Jenny handed me her diary, started the engine and took off as if she was a rally driver heading for pole position. I fastened my seatbelt quickly, thankful that mandatory seatbelt wearing had just come into force for drivers and front-seat passengers, and gripped the sides of the chair as Jenny lunged through the gears, oblivious. She didn't seem to understand the correct way of slowing down; she would go from fourth gear to slamming on the brakes rather than waste time or energy moving through gears. I was once again grateful that I'd spent three months in Asia before starting the course because, in spite of Jenny's driving being reckless at best, there really was no comparison. In Thailand and India, it seemed compulsory for drivers to harbour a death wish.

Jenny also had a habit of turning her head to look at me when she was speaking for way longer than I felt was safe, irrespective of the fact that she was driving at a rate of knots. I soon discovered that community nursing was a lonely occupation in many ways, so almost all of the staff were pleased to have company in the car and someone to chat to. And chat they did!

I was pleased that Jenny did pull in to consult the map when it became clear she was not sure where she was going.

After satisfying herself she knew the route, she drove for another three miles.

'There should be a turnoff to the left after a shop,' she said. 'If you could look out for that and let me know when you see it coming. Apparently it's behind a green and we turn when you see a row of boxes, so it should be easy enough to spot.'

I was just wondering why people would leave a row of boxes out in the middle of nowhere when Jenny swerved quickly to the left, skidding as she did so. I once again held on for dear life.

'Didn't you see them?' she asked.

'No, I didn't see any boxes,' I answered, puzzled.

Jenny suddenly burst out laughing and looked at me.

'You don't know what boxes are, do you?'

Thinking she'd really lost her marbles and offended by her accusation, I was about to protest that I had not seen any boxes lying in the road when she continued.

'Box hedges, Dawn. You city people are all alike, no idea what goes on in the countryside.' She then regaled me with her opinion of "city people". I had to admit she was right about me as, in spite of my occasional trips into the rural world, most of my life had been spent in Leicester and London, neither of which could be considered nature reserves. I had in fact seen many box hedges in my life; I just didn't realise they were called "boxes" by people in the know.

We continued along a track of about a mile, consisting of

bumps and potholes which Jenny didn't seem to notice nor feel the need to slow down for. Her driving continued in the same manner in which it had started, and I would have loved to have given her a lecture on driving safely. She wouldn't have survived a day in the city. At least we city people knew a little about road safety.

It was a bright sunny day in early May. When we pulled up in front of the large farmhouse, we could hear dogs barking in the distance and I could see cows in a field off to the left. Jenny had parked in a large courtyard, if you could call it that, surrounded by barns and sheds.

Jenny got out first and kindly warned me to watch my step. I realised what she meant when I opened the car door. Having just about recovered from the bouncing journey along the drive followed by the emergency stop in the courtyard, I looked around and discovered large dollops of horse manure at various intervals along the way towards the farmhouse. It was like a game of hopscotch, making our way to the door of the farmhouse as we tried to avoid anything that we wouldn't want to stand in.

Jenny knocked on the door. There was no reply, so she just opened it and walked in.

'Hello, district nurse. May we come in?' she called.

We're already in, I thought, but didn't feel I should split hairs.

In the distance we heard a frail woman's voice and we headed towards the sound. The farmhouse was old but well-kept with lots of family photos, old and new, lining the walls.

I was a bit disconcerted when I saw a glass cabinet containing around five rifles, but when I nudged Jenny and nodded towards it, she just smirked and rolled her eyes, giving me that "city girls don't understand" look again, and continued through into the lounge.

'Hello, are you Mrs Benson?'

'Yes, Sister. I don't know why they called you, I am managing this leg just fine on my own.'

Jenny gave me a knowing wink and headed towards a large upright chair in which the woman sat. The smell in the room gave away the fact that she was clearly not managing the leg on her own.

Mrs Benson had a ruddy and deeply wrinkled face that told the story of an outdoor life. I looked at the letter Jenny had handed me after getting out of the car and saw she was eighty-six years old. She sat in the sturdy armchair, dressed in a long pink silk nightgown. Over that she had on a bright blue dressing gown. Jenny sat beside her on a wooden dining chair and motioned me to pull up another one from a nearby dining table.

'Well, now I'm here, Mrs Benson, I might as well take look,' said Jenny in a friendly voice that would have put anyone at ease. Anyone who hadn't spent any time in her car, that is.

'I suppose you may as well,' Mrs Benson conceded.

Jenny wrote a few notes down in her diary and pulled out a brand-new folder from the Gladstone bag before suggesting that I remove the bandages. Thankful for something to do, I asked Mrs Benson if I could go and wash my hands in her kitchen and, having been given permission, I returned a few minutes later and began removing the crêpe bandages that had clearly come from a first-aid kit. It was obvious from the discharge and the unmistakeable smell what I was going to find, and that it would not be pretty. Thankful for a previous experience involving maggots, I felt that nothing could be worse than that.

How wrong can you be?

After I'd removed three layers of crêpe bandages soaked in bodily fluids, some of which I suspected might be urine, the odour became so much worse that even Jenny began to look a little concerned. As I delved deeper and deeper through the quagmire of bandages, I eventually revealed a mass of slough with deep ulcers covering the whole of the leg from mid-calf down to the foot. The foot was gangrenous with the toes barely held together by exposed bone.

'Mrs Benson, is your daughter – the one who phoned me – around?' Jenny asked.

'Yeah, you should find her out in the milking shed cleaning up.' She nodded towards the backdoor.

'We're just going to go out and have a little chat with her, we'll be back in a minute.'

We left Mrs Benson's leg resting on a stool on top of a sterile sheet that I'd taken from the dressing pack Jenny had given me.

'She needs to go in,' Jenny said as we headed outside.

Understatement of the year, I thought. "Going in" meant

into hospital, and from what I'd seen, Mrs Benson would be very lucky to get away with a below knee amputation.

We eventually found Mrs Benson's daughter and Jenny explained the situation, suggesting that she go and prepare the old lady for a lengthy hospital admission and pack her bags. The daughter, Annette, explained that her mum had flatly refused to have anyone come out to her, especially the GP whom she called Dr Death. This was not for any reason other than she felt that all doctors were too familiar with death and she didn't want to be among those sort of people.

'She's always been independent, not been to a doctor in years.'

Annette told us she ran the farm with the aid of her nephew. She seemed genuinely concerned about her mother, and a little angry.

'I knew it!' she shouted to no-one in particular. 'I told her it would come to this. I told her she would end up in hospital, but she just wouldn't listen.'

Jenny nodded sympathetically and patted Annette on the shoulder before excusing herself to call the doctor and arrange admission. She asked for permission to use the farmhouse telephone to make the call. As Jenny left, Annette stopped suddenly with tears in her eyes and looked at me.

'She isn't going to survive this, is she?' Before I could bring myself to say anything, Annette pulled herself together and marched stoically into the house to tell her rebellious mother that she would have to go into hospital. I could hear the argument developing and left them for a while before making my way back to the room where Mrs Benson was still flatly refusing to be removed from her home of eighty-six years.

'I was born here, I'll die here. You're not moving me.' The old lady's jaw stood out, showing her determination.

Jenny returned and we breathed a sigh of relief. Annette battled back tears and went to pack her mother's bags. It was obvious that Jenny had come across this sort of situation many times before. She sat beside Mrs Benson and calmly explained that there was nothing anyone could do out here and that she would need antibiotics that only hospitals possessed. Carefully avoiding the subject of the life-saving surgery that would be required, she convinced Mrs Benson that the only way to treat this leg would be to go into hospital.

Mrs Benson wasn't daft, though. She asked plainly, 'Will I need an operation?'

Jenny then explained that she might need a small operation, but the doctors would need to decide that. As Jenny told Mrs Benson she would be home in no time, I stared at her disbelievingly, but managed to hide the look so that no-one else noticed. These were the days when health professionals were economical with the truth.

As we left the farmhouse, Jenny gave me a knowing look. 'What do you want me to do, tell her that she is unlikely to come out at all, and that if she does survive surgery, she'll be minus a leg?'

I silently got in the car. Not a great first visit; I felt truly sad that a woman who had managed to avoid doctors for most of her life would most likely end her days on a hospital ward or under the knife, and I still had the stench of gangrene filling my nostrils. At least it would take my mind off Jenny's driving.

I soon discovered that district nurses' rounds incorporated coffee breaks and our next visit was a regular coffee stop, a fix we both needed. As soon as we arrived, Mrs Blake put the kettle on while Jenny got ready to treat her husband's leg ulcers.

Jenny explained that it was always better to catch the ulcers early so that treatment could be started when they would be much more likely to heal. Mr Blake had venous ulcers covering the front of his leg, from the top of the shin down to and around the ankle, and Jenny proudly explained that these were much better now. I nodded and marvelled at her optimism.

After redressing the leg and drinking coffee accompanied by biscuits, we left the Blakes' house feeling much better.

7

DRESSINGS GALORE

Community nursing consisted of continuous rounds of dressings, mainly due to the scourge at the time of chronic leg ulcers, many of which would never heal. Treatments have moved on now, but back in those days there was little promise of healing once the ulcers had spread up the legs. Many years later, whenever I saw the Queen Mother on television, I noticed only the telltale bandages that covered her lower legs, a dead giveaway that she suffered from leg ulcers.

It was my third day of working with Jenny and I was getting the hang of her driving. Well at least, I was getting the hang of ensuring my seatbelt was always fastened and that there were no objects that could fly at me when she slammed on the brakes. I'd learned a valuable lesson on day one after I'd got fed up with carrying her diary on my lap and placed it on the dashboard – big mistake. She was about to fly around a bend when she'd spotted a pheasant in the road and screeched to a halt. The diary flew off the dash and almost decapitated me. Okay, I exaggerate slightly, but I did check my neck a few times that day to see if all was where it should be. The pheasant had given Jenny a long stare before continuing on its way, but it was nothing compared to my glare.

She'd laughed, clearly not noticing my pallor. 'I should have run it over. You can eat them if you kill them by accident, you know.'

Back to my third day. We were on our way to see a young paraplegic man with pressure sores to his buttocks. Daniel Gray, aged twenty-three, had been involved in a motorcycle accident and broken his back when he came off and was thrown against a wall. After spending some months in Stoke Mandeville Hospital, which specialised in spinal injuries, he had been discharged. He now lived in a small bungalow a few miles away from his family home.

Since his discharge, Jenny told me, he had gained weight and neglected to change position often enough to prevent pressure sores developing. His attitude was if you couldn't feel it, it wasn't worth worrying about. Life had dealt him a hard blow and he was very bitter about it.

Jenny explained that his family had told her he had always been a self-absorbed character and the accident had only added to his general belief that somehow the world owed him. The family relationships had completely broken down following his accident as he no longer tried to curb his behaviour and deliberately sought to insult or offend everyone he met, including the district nurses. He was wasting his time with Jenny; it was like water off a duck's back.

'Who's this now?' he asked, obviously meaning me.

'This is Dawn, a student nurse who's out with me. I can ask her to wait in the car if you'd prefer.'

'No, she might as well stay. I mean, I'm like a monkey in a cage, after all.' He performed a 180° turn in his wheelchair and headed towards a room at the back of the bungalow. We followed, but not before I'd taken in the mess surrounding me. It made Jenny's car look positively pristine.

Clothes littered the floor; Daniel obviously didn't feel the need to put them away after he took them off. Cigarette butts filled an ashtray on a table and stale cigarette smoke hung in the air. There was a settee, barely visible underneath crisp and chocolate packets. Dirty washing from the kitchen overflowed into the lounge.

We arrived in what turned out to be Daniel's bedroom where he heaved himself from the wheelchair on to the bed.

Jenny turned to me. 'You're in there.' She nodded towards the kitchen.

'You're kidding?' I mouthed, scowling. I was here to dress his backside, not to be kitchen maid.

'He won't let you do his dressing anyway, and no-one else will do it,' she said quietly, pleading with her eyes.

I sighed and stomped into the kitchen and began removing the crockery from the overflowing sink. Before I could even begin to do any washing up, I heard shouting and swearing coming from the bedroom, which made me smile. Perhaps I'd got the better share of this particular deal.

After filling a bin with chip wrappers, crisp packets and all manner of other nasties, as well as driving a few flies away from their feasts, I started on the washing up. Jenny was in the lounge by this time, picking up clothes, and she brought them through to put into the washing machine.

'Where is he?' I asked.

'On the bed on his side. It's the only time I can get him to relieve the pressure on his sores. He won't do bed rest, so we reached a compromise after everyone else who ever came here pulled out because of his rudeness: he stays on the bed while I clear up. It's not ideal, but even social and voluntary services have given up on him, and they rightly argue that he is quite capable of clearing up after himself. He just won't.'

'Can they do that? Social Services, I mean.'

'They say he's a danger to himself and to their staff. He's well able to look after himself if he so chooses, and his refusal doesn't constitute "need". He's his own worst enemy.'

'I can f***ing hear you in there.'

'Well, ain't that a shame!' laughed Jenny.

'Condescending cow!' came the retort.

This friendly (on Jenny's part) banter continued for an hour, until Jenny shouted, 'Cheerio, Danny. See you Thursday.'

'It's not f***ing Danny, it's Dan, you twat.'

Jenny put two fingers up on the way out, but obviously not in sight of Dan.

'Why didn't you warn me?' I asked when we got back in the car.

'Warn you about what?' She laughed at her own joke.

Following my introduction to Dan, who I'm pleased to say I never met again, Jenny took me to his polar opposite. A pleasant thirty-year-old woman had also sustained spinal injuries, but hers came after falling from a horse. The house she lived in was in the next village and couldn't have been cleaner. She lived alone as her husband couldn't cope with her disability and had left the family home a few years earlier, although he still paid the mortgage.

'Guilt,' suggested Jenny when I asked why.

There wasn't a bitter bone in Debbie Price's body. She radiated joy, demonstrating that we are all different. There's no point trying to understand why some people are pleasant and others are just plain obnoxious when they are handed the same cards in life.

We were there to change Debbie's catheter, and this time I was allowed to carry out the procedure. A long-term indwelling catheter had become part of Debbie's life and it was changed every eight weeks. Usually catheters were changed twelve weekly, but serious complications can occur from blocked catheters when someone has the type of paraplegia that Debbie had.

'If we leave it too late and the catheter blocks, she can get autonomic dysreflexia,' Jenny explained.

'What's that?'

Debbie took over the explanation. 'My blood pressure could go through the roof and I could end up fitting or even dying,' she said nonchalantly.

'Wow! Has that ever happened?'

'Only once for me, but it's pretty terrifying. I have to call 999 and take these tablets.' She showed me a packet of Nifedipine, an anti-hypertensive drug I was familiar with from my cardio-thoracic days. 'The quickest way to treat it is to deal with the cause, which in my case is either a blocked catheter or constipation. I manage the bowels myself with tablets.'

I smiled. 'That would do the trick.'

I had changed plenty of catheters during my nurse training course to date and as an enrolled nurse at the London Chest Hospital, but I'd never done this in a patient's own home. I looked around fearfully. Where was my dressing trolley?

As if reading my mind, Jenny cleared the top of Debbie's bedside table and gave it a wipe with a duster before opening a dressing pack. I gawped, as we hadn't swabbed the surface with a sterile cleansing wipe.

'We have to adapt when in people's homes,' she explained. 'Remember it's their own bacteria, not from a bunch of strangers. We make it as sterile as possible, though.'

I washed my hands and returned to open up the pack before donning sterile gloves, while Jenny removed the water from the balloon holding the old catheter in place, using a syringe to do so. She then pulled gently at the catheter; because Debbie couldn't feel pain, Jenny could cause internal damage if she was too rough. No need for worry, though, as the catheter slipped out with ease.

In the early 1980s women were not given local anaesthetic for catheterisation, the reasoning being that because the urethra is shorter than in men and there is no prostate gland involved, they wouldn't feel pain. It's true that some didn't, but some did. In this case, Debbie would not feel pain, but thankfully women are offered local anaesthetic in the modern era.

On a similar topic, female nurses did catheterise men in some hospitals, but there was no nationally adopted practice. In some hospitals it wasn't allowed. In the hospitals I worked in, it was to be introduced at a later date as the shortage of male nurses meant calling a doctor on to the wards to re-catheterise men at all hours of the day and night. Often the doctor called would be female, which highlighted the ridiculousness of the situation.

Catheterising women is, in fact, more difficult as the urethra can be hidden, particularly when women are on the larger side. I've spent many occasions delving (not literally) into the depths of darkness of a woman's anatomy with a torch in search of the pesky little hole that is the urethra. It is not unusual for junior nurses and medical students to try to catheterise a clitoris or shove the catheter into the vagina, thinking they are in the right place.

With only one hole, it is far easier to find the right place to catheterise a man. Erections, however, are another matter. It behoves a nurse to get on with the job as quickly as possible to spare any embarrassment on either side in such cases.

There were no such problems with Debbie's catheter. Once I had become used to the unfamiliar surroundings and adjusted to accepting the limitations concerning the lack of hospital equipment, it was a simple procedure. Many women with spinal injuries nowadays have suprapubic catheters inserted into a hole created by a surgical incision just above the pubic bone. Such catheters are less likely to cause infection and are often easier to manage for patients, particularly those who are sexually active. Sex is possible for people with indwelling catheters, but it requires a little more planning and effort. Sex for people with spinal injuries lacks the sensation of orgasm, but many men and women continue with sexual relations for the partner's sake and for the intimacy.

After leaving Debbie's home, I was feeling much happier.

'Talk about opposites,' I remarked.

'Welcome to the community, Dawn. The thing about hospitals is that you can get rid of your patients by sending them home. Out here, we are stuck with them, so we try to build up a relationship with the likes of Dan. He's unlikely to change until they bring in personality transplants, but there's not much point aggravating him, except when I get fed up with him. But I don't ever cross the line.'

Wise words from an experienced district nurse.

8

THE FALLOUT

One of my most bizarre experiences during the community placement came in the third week.

I had worked with most of the nurses in the team by then, including the auxiliaries, and experienced all manner of driving styles and vehicles. It's funny how we always remember odd things – I could tell you every make and model of car I sat in, along with their colours (not that there was much variety back then), but that would be plain boring. Describing the car boots and their contents would be a little more interesting, although the common theme was that no matter how tidy they happened to be, they were all jam packed with every piece of equipment that might conceivably be needed during a visit. This is understandable when you remember the nurses were making forty-minute round trips to visit people in outlying villages and farms.

The car interiors were also interesting. Some had baby

seats or crumbs and sweet packets littering the back, indicating the nurse had children or grandchildren. Others had dog hairs plus/minus a dog grill plus/minus said car seats, wrappers and so on. Some were pristine, indicating the nurse was possibly single or minimalistic.

The worst cars were those in which the nurse smoked, ashtrays overflowing with cigarette butts and the cursory 'You don't mind if I smoke, do you?' while lighting up fiasco. I had stopped smoking again myself the year before so I did still understand the addiction and the need to light up at every opportunity. Nevertheless, it was challenging, sometimes because I hated the smell, and at other times because I could have ripped the cigarette right out of their hand, depending on which way the wind was blowing in my world.

Cars and driving styles aside, the majority of the staff were a pleasure to work with and had built good rapports with the patients. Some of them nipped home for lunch – unheard of in hospitals – and others popped into the shop or post office to deal with household chores. I could see the attraction for married women with young children, but they did work hard. Even though it was only Jenny who carried a bleep, which went off constantly, district nurses worked weekends and late shifts as it was a seven-day service.

The patients were pleasant, on the whole, apart from the likes of Dan whom I never would have grown to like. Seeing patients dressed in their own clothes did make a difference to how they were treated, and how they behaved. In the community, to a large extent the patient was in control – it was their home and we were visitors with no right of access, except by invitation.

The homes we visited varied from the tidy to the downright infested. Dogs were as much a hazard to us as they were to postmen. Some dogs were friendly, while others were terrifying. I was always wary of the bigger dogs in spite of being a dog lover, although I was never attacked.

Some patients were chain smokers and we would walk in to a clouded room rather than a crowded one! There will be a lot more detail with regards to working in the community when I write about my days as a qualified district nurse, but suffice it to say for now that it was a very different experience to working within the safe confines of a hospital.

The district nurses planned their day around the patients they visited. For instance, people with possible infectious diseases were visited last thing, as were people living in the dirtiest houses or the heavy smokers. The reasoning was that the nurse could go straight home after that visit, get out of the uniform and take a bath – if they weren't going to Tesco first, that is!

But let's get back to the bizarre experience I alluded to earlier. Jenny thought it would be a good idea for me to work in a GP practice for the day and had arranged for me to spend the morning with a practice nurse. When we arrived at the surgery, there were two separate signs outside: DR M SMITH; DR F JONES, which I thought was slightly unusual, but thought no more of it.

We walked through the door to find two separate windows behind which receptionists sat within the same room, but manning their individual doctor's window. We took the window to the left, where Jenny said hello before leading me through the invisibly divided waiting room along a corridor to the left. By now, Jenny was watching my face and giggling.

'Okay, what's going on?' I asked when we entered an office, also separated into two halves.

'I'll tell you later,' she whispered.

She didn't need to; I'd already guessed, and the practice nurse confirmed my suspicions.

'They fell out five years ago. Since then, they won't speak to each other, and now the receptionists, secretaries, even the patients don't speak to each other when they're in this building.'

'So have the rest of the staff taken sides?'

'No. Outside, everyone behaves normally, but fear of losing their jobs makes them behave as if they have when they're in work. It's stupid – these two doctors are worse than children. I think the patients join in just for fun.'

'What did they fall out about?'

'I'm not sure, I expect it was something trivial. Dr Jones always did fly off the handle; I'm glad I don't work for him, he's always shouting at someone. You'll probably hear him bellowing sometime this morning. I think Dr Smith probably got fed up with his behaviour.'

For someone who wasn't taking sides, she was making it

clear whose side she wasn't taking! But then, who's going to bite the hand that feeds them?

Later on, when Jenny came to collect me from this rather peculiar environment, I scolded her. 'You could have warned me!'

'And miss seeing that look on your face? Not likely.' I had grown fond of Jenny, but she had a wicked sense of humour.

'I'm sure I've heard you call both of those doctors about patients.'

'Oh yes, the team works with both, but we have to be discreet because if one catches on that we're seeing more of the other's patients than theirs, they'll invent reasons for us to take on more of theirs. I work round it by sending a different staff nurse to each surgery to discuss patients so they never know what's happening on the other side.'

'Do you know why they fell out?'

'Money, Dawn, it's always money.'

'Or sex,' I said quietly.

'You're too young to know about sex.' She nudged me and cackled loudly.

I was going to miss working with Jenny and her team, but not the twenty-mile drive to work every morning, and certainly not Jenny's driving. I missed the hubbub of hospital life so it would be many years before I seriously considered working in the community again. Once I did venture out, though, I spent the final fifteen years of my nursing career *on the district* in one way or another.

9

MAT UNIT

The maternity unit was a large separate building with its own car park and ambulance bay, its entrance on the west side of the hospital. It was like a hospital within a hospital, with its own administrative offices, library, school of midwifery and outpatients departments on the ground floor. The labour ward and theatres were on the first floor, and antenatal and postnatal wards on the second.

I made a mistake in terminology on my first day and suffered a quick reprimand I wouldn't forget.

'We are not nurses, we are midwives,' said the rather rotund sister. The truth was that once nurses became midwives, they argued that midwives were very different to nurses, and who was I to disagree? In the early 1980s, a nurse who wanted to become a midwife did an extra year's training (later that decade it was extended to eighteen months, shortly before I began training to be a midwife in the mid-1980s). On completion of the training they became registered midwives (RMs), but also kept their nurse registration. Nowadays, many midwives enter through a direct-entry training programme.

As a student nurse, I found the labour ward placement particularly dull. Not because seeing babies being delivered wasn't fascinating – it was, and I did manage to see the required five births that were a mandatory part of my training in order to pass the placement, but we were always at the back of the queue when it came to seeing anything. Ahead of us were student midwives, medical students, junior doctors, and basically the world and its brother. On top of that, we were not allowed to *do* anything except check blood pressures, test urine and palpate the mandatory five pregnant abdomens, which made for long and boring shifts. I couldn't even speak to women in labour, perhaps because they had other things on their minds, but it didn't help the days go any more quickly on the ward. Years later, when I was a midwife, the labour ward was my favourite place of work and I was promoted to midwifery sister, working on one of the busiest labour wards in the country.

Each labour room had a door – obviously – and a small square window decorated with frosted glass stripes, allowing just enough clear glass for the midwife in charge to take a peek through without intruding on what was going on inside the room. One afternoon I was accompanying the midwifery sister along the corridor and we peeked into one of the rooms from which we could hear a lot of noise, although it wasn't unusual to hear the "cry of the banshee" coming from labour rooms. A father-to-be stood at the foot of the bed and the midwife was gowned up and proficiently delivering the baby while he looked on. Then I blinked, and he'd disappeared. One minute he was there, the next, he was gone.

The sister I was with chuckled. 'Whoops, there goes another one.'

Upon opening the door, we saw the woman who had just given birth cuddling her newborn. She rolled her eyes at her partner, who was still lying on the floor where he had fainted.

'I knew he shouldn't have come in. My mum would have been much more help.'

We handed the rather pale man a glass of water and helped him up.

'It's a girl,' Sister told him and I caught him before he passed out again. Eventually he sat up and rose from the floor, tears streaming down his face. He leaned over to kiss his wife and inspect his daughter.

'Don't tell your mother,' he said sheepishly.

'I wouldn't dare!' She smiled up at him. 'You tried, that's the main thing.'

After we'd left the doting couple, Sister told me that partners or other accompanying individuals were told that if they were going to pass out, they should leave the room as the midwife would not have time to deal with them.

'Mother and baby come first,' she said.

For the rest of the day I had visions of the disappearing man and giggled every time I remembered it. By the time I was on my break, I had embellished the story and was recounting it to my colleagues, alongside a practical demonstration to make it a real laughing point.

For student nurses, it was better and more interesting to work on the wards in the maternity unit. As well as being allowed to check the blood pressure of an antenatal mother-to-be, test urine and palpate abdomens, here I was also allowed to speak to people and listen to foetal heartbeats with a Pinard's stethoscope. Obviously, a midwife would check the latter before or after me.

Women were sometimes admitted for bed rest following a diagnosis of pre-eclampsia. Eclampsia is a dangerous condition where a woman can have a seizure due to high blood pressure, which in turn can damage the developing foetus. It was responsible for maternal and foetal deaths before the condition was better understood – who can forget the scene in the popular *Downton Abbey* series that demonstrated the horror of this condition far better than any textbook ever could? The pre-eclampsia condition was, and still is, taken very seriously, but thankfully I never witnessed an eclamptic fit during my student nurse days.

My favourite part of the maternity placement in the hospital was working on the postnatal ward as I got to be a lot more hands-on with both mothers and babies. I was taught to help mums with breastfeeding – not that I had a clue what to do, but I was slightly ahead of most first-time mums. The best people to learn from were the experienced mums who had just given birth to second or third babies, and in some cases sixth or seventh.

Many women in the early 1980s gave up quickly on breastfeeding as bottle feeding was deemed easier and was fashionable. The "breast is best" philosophy was in its infancy with an almost evangelical drive occurring a decade or so later. I secretly and rather selfishly loved it when a mother chose to bottle feed because I got to feed the tiny little babies, stashed away in the nursery while Mum had a kip. Some mothers opted to keep their babies by the bedside so they could feed them for themselves, but others were glad of the rest, particularly after a difficult labour. And hard labour delivering a baby was for many.

Four hourly feeding was the recommendation of the day. Feeding regimes, like many other health regimes, are an ever moving feast as new guidelines or the latest research is published. If a mother chose to feed her baby for herself, she would be woken up in the early hours of the morning to give the infant its four hourly feed, come what may. The majority of women who weren't breastfeeding opted to have their babies go to the nursery during the night so they could get some sleep, but the stalwarts persevered, much to the chagrin of the other women who would complain at being woken up by someone else's baby while the actual mother slept through the racket.

Babies got used to the four hourly feeding regime and would strike up with a cacophony of shrieks at the allotted time. Like an orchestra tuning up, they would cry out a universal chorus of discordant and chaotic wailing – not that orchestras tuning up are chaotic.

Visiting time was restricted to a couple of hours each morning and the same in the evening, and limited to two visitors at a time. In spite of this, the rules were occasionally relaxed to allow a third person in, but had to be curtailed when the noise of cooing parents, grandparents and small children in the postnatal ward became too much.

It was quite obvious who the new fathers were, not only because they beamed with pride at managing to father a small miracle, but because they had no idea how to handle said miracle. Some nervously took hold of the fragile being as if it was an egg that would crack at any moment; others picked it up and handled it as if it ought to be able to play football by now, and a midwife would quickly intervene and explain how delicate the baby was and how to handle it correctly. Yet others would hold the child at arms' length. One could never tell whether this was because they were worried about handling it or frightened of the curdled milk that was always lurking, waiting for the next shoulder to deposit itself on, which certainly wouldn't have helped the new fathers who looked like they had been out on the town, "wetting the baby's head" all night.

Inexperienced mums weren't always adept with nappy changes, either, and urine and other excreta was often deposited on an unsuspecting relative's hand or clothing. Disposable nappies weren't as commonplace as they are today, and so all new mums were taught to change and fold towelling nappies.

Personally, I enjoyed nappy changing; it gave me something to do, and once I'd mastered the art, I was allowed to demonstrate it to anyone willing to listen. New mums were like sponges, gazing at me and listening to my every word. The only problem was that sometimes pregnancy appeared to affect the memory and my every word went in one ear and out the other – a bit like the milk that went in one end of the baby and out the other at alarming speed!

Anyone who has worked with new mothers, or indeed been a parent, will know what I mean when I mention the "third-day blues", or "baby blues" as it was sometimes referred to. I had been working on the postnatal ward for – you guessed it – three days when I had my first experience of blubbering mums. It was as if someone had turned on an invisible tap and the women were unable to find the off switch. I might be exaggerating as not every new mum experiences the third-day blues, and its effects are as wide and varied as the mums themselves. Some women experience something far worse than this, leading to postnatal depression or puerperal psychosis. I'll discuss an experience I had of a poor woman with the latter in the next chapter, but for now, I'm simply talking about baby blues, which is a very mild form of depression resulting in mood swings following postnatal hormone changes.

Before undertaking my maternity placement, I had been

given lectures on pregnancy and childbirth, but mental health was skimmed over. Baby blues had been mentioned, but not in any detail. All I knew was that women could feel low for a brief period around the third or fourth day postpartum. What I didn't realise was how useless and guilty this could make a new mother feel or how easily a bout of tears could be triggered. Many women tried to hide their feelings, but they couldn't.

The guilt came from women believing they should be happy all the time because they had had a baby. These feelings, coupled with lack of sleep, pain from perineal suturing and/or caesarean scars, bruising and/or sore nipples, could lead to feelings of helplessness and inadequacy. Sometimes, it was the family that bore the brunt of these mood swings, and at other times a new mother might ignore the baby, almost blaming the newborn for how they were feeling. For most women, these feelings only lasted around a day or two, and nurses and midwives would provide reassurance during this time. In rare cases, though, a woman would become excessively paranoid and agitated.

Josie was one such woman.

10

TIRE EYES DO MATTER, DON'T THEY?

Josie was a twenty-eight-year-old first-time mother. Her baby, Christine, had been born normally following a lengthy thirty-hour labour. An episiotomy (cutting of the perineum with scissors) had been performed during the birth to prevent a large tear. Christine weighed in at eight pounds, three ounces and had a beautiful crop of black hair. Both Josie and Simon, her husband, were delighted by the birth of their daughter, and although Christine was a demanding and voracious feeder, everything appeared perfect until day three.

Josie was looking haggard and bedraggled. The other mums said she had been disturbing them in the night, then she started to imagine that all the other women were talking about her behind her back. By day four, she was becoming more and more agitated and paranoid, and her handling of Christine was a little rough.

Initially, the midwives had put her behaviour down to third-day blues, but now it was becoming bizarre. I was helping a mum breastfeed from the bed opposite when I saw Josie pick up Christine. Her eyes told me she was psychotic and, just before she could drop the baby on the floor, I dashed over and caught her.

Doctors were called, and then a specialist psychiatrist. Josie was displaying signs of a thankfully very rare condition called puerperal psychosis, where a woman becomes severely mentally ill following childbirth. The decision was taken to move both her and Christine to a mother-and-baby unit at the nearest psychiatric hospital for assessment and specialist supervision.

The psychiatrist called Josie's husband and explained the situation. I was chosen to escort her to the psychiatric hospital in the ambulance, along with Christine.

Josie was clearly bemused at what was happening, but not in this world. Almost as soon as we got into the ambulance, she turned to me and spoke.

'Tired eyes do matter, don't they?'

The thing was, she didn't say it once; she repeated it over and over again for the whole of the forty-five minute drive. By the time we arrived at the hospital, my brain was addled and I was beginning to feel like I was being hypnotised.

I was looking forward to being able to discharge my responsibility – I was way out of my depth – and get a lift back with the ambulance crew. Unfortunately for me, escort transfers could be a pain for nurses because sometimes we were taken miles away, and then the ambulance would be called off to another emergency and the crew couldn't wait.

This was one of those occasions.

'Sorry, love. We'll let dispatch know where you are.' I groaned inside, knowing this could mean hours before another ambulance happened to be in the vicinity, as they wouldn't send one especially to pick up a nurse.

I was led towards the mother-and-baby unit and things went from bad to worse. There was no psychiatric nurse available to admit Josie and I couldn't leave her alone with Christine as it wouldn't have been safe. After another ninety minutes of the 'Tired eyes do matter, don't they?' mantra, I was beside myself. As much as I felt sorry for Josie, I knew those words would be embedded in my brain forever, and I was right. As I write this, I am back in that small holding room, Christine in my arms, having to answer, 'Yes, they do,' every time I heard the question and Josie looked at me. I tried not answering, but then her eyes became wild and she looked like she might jump on me – or worse, Christine – at any moment.

'Tired eyes do matter, don't they?'

'Yes, Josie, they do.'

'Tired eyes do matter, don't they?'

'Yes, Josie, they do.'

'Tired eyes do matter, don't they?'

'Yes, Josie, they do.'

And so on, and so on.

Finally, when I felt I could stand it no more, a psychiatrist came in, accompanied by a psychiatric nurse.

'An ambulance is here to take you home,' the nurse said to me.

I leapt off the chair, thrust the baby into the astonished nurse's arms and ran for my life.

The tragedy of a woman suffering from puerperal psychosis is that prior to giving birth, they often show no signs of mental illness. The condition ranges from mild to severe, but women displaying symptoms invariably need specialist treatment. Most women recover after appropriate period of treatment. I'm not certain whether Josie was one of these, but there is no reason to assume she wasn't. The main problem is that around half of women developing the condition will suffer the same illness following subsequent births, but at least they are monitored closely throughout pregnancy and postnatal.

And just for the record, tired eyes do matter!

11

COMMUNITY MIDWIFE

Rosemary was a community midwife, and also a member of the church I had started to go to, although I hadn't got to know her through church. Because I worked the majority of weekends and late shifts, it prevented me from going out to too many social gatherings in the evenings.

Rosemary was one of the most bubbly people I have had the good fortune to work with, and a force to be reckoned with. From the moment she picked me up from the hospital reception, I knew we would get on. Her larger-than-life personality showed itself in every way, and because she was always happy, her demeanour would calm anyone's nerves. The women on her books were immediately put at ease on first meeting her.

Her driving was something else, though, similar to Jenny's. The district nurse and Rosemary could have been related, and I wondered if community nurses/midwives were actually frustrated ambulance drivers.

The difference between Rosemary and Jenny was that their car boots were complete opposites. Rosemary had a Gladstone bag, but the only other item she carried in her boot was a set of baby weighing scales. Her car, though not immaculate, was immeasurably cleaner than Jenny's and contained no dog hairs!

After being in the car with Rosemary for around ten minutes, I heard her laugh for the first time. Like her personality, that laugh was unforgettable.

The morning consisted of visiting postnatal mothers and babies. 'We visit daily for ten days, but can visit for up to twenty-eight days. If all is well we discharge to the health visitor between ten and fourteen days,' she explained. I was interested to see how new and experienced mums coped once they were at home as most of them were discharged from hospital between two and seven days post-delivery.

Rosemary's patch encompassed a suburban area of the town comprising mostly financially stable households. The first house we arrived at was on a relatively new estate where all the houses looked the same.

'Cardboard boxes,' commented Rosemary with that wonderful laugh I was already growing to love.

A bedraggled-looking man answered the door and almost hugged her. 'I'm so pleased you're here, we can't stop her crying.' As he led us through to the lounge – not that we needed leading, we just had to follow the wails from the unhappy infant – Rosemary mouthed to me that they were first-time parents.

A tired-looking woman of twenty-nine was pacing the room, frantically trying to calm the baby.

'There, there, everything's all right,' she said in a rather manic tone that didn't have an ounce of conviction. As soon as she saw Rosemary, she gave a huge sigh of relief. 'She's been like this all night. I've fed her until my nipples are sore.'

Looking at this frantic woman, I believed her. She still had her nightdress on, one breast hanging out of a nursing bra that remained unfastened. It really did look sore – raw, in fact.

'This is Dawn, she's a student nurse. Do you mind her being here?' This was a question Rosemary always asked, I discovered. In this instance, I would have been tempted to grab the screaming child from the mother's arms, but Rosemary's calm voice had the desired effect on both mother and baby.

'No, that's fine.'

'This is Mary, Donald, and this little mite is Joanna.'

What this conversation did, Rosemary explained to me later, was to distract Mary and calm her nerves. Once Mary was calm, Joanna, in turn, stopped crying.

'Babies sense stress in parents and they need to feel secure.' This statement turned out to be true in the majority of cases, as long as the baby was feeding enough, didn't have wind and wasn't wearing a dirty nappy.

Rosemary and I washed our hands, and then she took the baby and examined the umbilical cord, which had its clamp still in place as she was only five days old. Most cords dropped off after seven to fourteen days once they had dried out and shrivelled, but it was important to check that no infection was developing in the area. Rosemary also checked the baby's skin and felt gently over the two fontanelles or soft spots on her head. The fontanelles would gradually fuse together over time, but they were necessary, Rosemary explained to me, as they enabled the bones to move as the baby went through the birth canal and would allow the brain to grow.

After finishing with Joanna and holding her for a few minutes until she fell asleep, Rosemary laid her down in her crib.

'You're going to need to cream that nipple for a few days. Do you have any nipple protectors?'

'Yes, Donald bought some yesterday.'

'I don't think she's latching on properly. That's why you're sore, and probably why she's fractious. Dawn and I will go and see a few more people, and then come back and help you feed her.'

The relief on Mary and Donald's faces was priceless to see.

'Thank you, Rosemary.'

'No problem. You go and get washed and dressed while she's asleep. Donald will keep an eye on her, won't you?'

The anxious-looking man who had answered the door

now appeared much calmer himself and he nodded confidently. 'Of course I will. You go, love.'

Once outside, Rosemary explained that she needed to talk through some other things with the new parents and check Mary's perineum was healing as she'd had stitches. She would also ask about vaginal discharge and examine the uterus, referred to as the fundus, that would take six to ten weeks to return to normal size. I realised then that there was a lot more to midwifery than delivering babies.

'Midwife, Dawn. The term comes from the old English and means "with woman".' I could see how appropriate that term was, although it seemed from meeting Donald that new fathers needed just as much assistance post-delivery.

The morning passed by quickly. We visited another three babies and their mums, two of whom had other children and required little in the way of assistance. I observed as Rosemary discussed feeding, weight, maternal physical and mental health. Where a partner or parent was present, Rosemary included them, but also ensured she got time alone with each mother while they, or I, were left holding the baby – literally.

Rosemary explained before we visited the final couple with their first child that she suspected domestic violence, but the woman was unwilling to acknowledge this to her, in spite of multiple "accidents" during pregnancy resulting in bruises that could not easily be explained away.

'My concern now is for both the mother and the baby,' said Rosemary. 'After I've checked the baby over, I'm going to take Marion upstairs on the pretext of teaching you, so he'll have to stay downstairs and watch over Jake, the newborn.'

With this plan in mind, I was to ask lots of questions in order to distract the partner, who had managed to avoid meeting Rosemary antenatally, and come across as an overly keen student.

Rosemary rang the doorbell, but there was no reply. We waited, still nothing.

'Marion told me he drives a BMW so that's his car. We know he's in.'

As I looked at the BMW in the driveway and the large detached house, my expression must have been a dead giveaway.

'Domestic violence is not confined to the working classes,' she whispered while ringing the doorbell again, this time more persistently, keeping her finger on the bell.

I stepped back on to the driveway and saw a curtain upstairs move briefly. The man saw that he had been rumbled and answered the door shortly afterwards.

'I do apologise, I forgot you were coming this morning. Marion's not feeling so good, she had a fall in the night. Must have been tired, she's just gone back to sleep. Can you come back later?'

'I'm so sorry, Mr Fletcher, but we have to help someone with feeding after this visit, and then I'm in clinic all afternoon. Actually, if you don't mind, I'm desperate for the loo. Could I use yours?'

He looked uncomfortable.

'Nice to meet you, by the way,' Rosemary continued. 'We spoke on the phone. This is Dawn, a student nurse. Perhaps she could take a look at little Jake while I nip to the loo.'

'Of course. Come in. The toilet's through there.' He nodded to a downstairs toilet.

'Now you mention it, I'm desperate too,' I lied.

'You go down, I'll go up, if that's all right?' Rosemary's face was the picture of innocence.

Mr Fletcher coughed. 'Upstairs on the left.'

At that moment, the telephone in the hallway rang and he went to answer it. Rosemary shot upstairs like a panther and I went for my imaginary wee in the downstairs loo, being as quick as would seem appropriate so that I could distract Mr Fletcher when I came out. My distraction was not required, though; he was still speaking in angry muffled tones on the phone when Rosemary called from upstairs.

'Marion's awake now, Dawn. Come on up, I know you want to see little Jake.'

Mr Fletcher was too engrossed in his heated telephone conversation to pay us any attention. I walked into the bedroom and Rosemary motioned for me to close the door. The woman attending to her crying baby was sporting a huge black eye and multiple bruises to her upper arms.

Rosemary put her arm around her. 'You don't have to put up with this, you know. We can get help.'

The fear-filled eyes spoke volumes. It was not the first time I had come across domestic violence and sadly it wouldn't be the last. Women (and sometimes men) were beaten into submission, usually through verbal and/or physical abuse, until they felt useless.

'He doesn't mean it. Jake was crying and he hasn't had much sleep. He's under a lot of pressure at work.'

Rosemary sighed gently and said, 'And what if this anger spills over on to Jake?'

'He would never hurt Jake, he adores him.'

Footsteps coming upstairs warned us our time was up.

'Please don't say anything.'

The door opened and an angry Mr Fletcher filled the doorway. 'What's going on? I told you she needed some sleep.'

'Sorry,' said Rosemary. 'Little Jake was restless so we popped in and woke Marion by mistake. She's just been telling me about her fall in the night.'

Looking relieved, Mr Fletcher moved over to the bed and put his arm around his wife. 'She's got a bit clumsy since Jake was born, haven't you, love?'

Marion nodded quietly. After examining Jake, Rosemary spoke to the couple.

'Jake's looking well. I'll be handing over to Rebecca, the health visitor, in a few weeks' time. She'll keep an eye on Jake over the next few years.'

Rosemary looked sternly towards Mr Fletcher before turning and leaving the room.

'What happens now?' I asked as we got in the car.

Rosemary sighed deeply, exhaling a long breath. 'I'll report my concerns again to the GP and give a full handover to the health visitor, but without Marion's permission, I can't involve the police. And even if I do, they're not really interested in "domestics", as they call them. Obviously if child abuse is suspected, that's a different matter and we would refer it to social services. Not all abusive partners turn on children, but many do, so I suspect that will happen with Jake in the not too distant future.'

It was not easy working in the community and suspecting domestic violence, and even when we did complain to the police, the culture of the day meant that it wasn't taken seriously enough. Things are mostly different now.

After this visit, Rosemary had to switch back into midwife mode as we drove back to help Mary feed her baby.

'You're just in time,' said a delighted Donald, who answered the door immediately. 'She's just woken. Can I get you both a coffee?'

After what we had just been through, a whisky would have been more appropriate.

'We'd love one, no sugar for me.'

'Nor me,' I answered.

'Now where's that beautiful little girl?'

As I watched Rosemary happily demonstrating how to latch Joanna on to the breast and teaching Mary the art of breastfeeding, I drank my coffee.

'The nipples get sore when the baby isn't latching on properly. They're hungry little mites so they grab the first thing, often the nipple,' explained Rosemary. 'Unfortunately, they don't get enough food this way, so they get tetchy and you get sore.'

Rosemary applied the protector over the nipple, then showed Mary how to get Joanna to suck on the breast. As I watched and learned, I reflected – not for the first time – on how nursing and, it seemed, midwifery were art forms. We did everything we could to make the person in front of us feel like they were the only person in the world and that we had nothing more important to do that day than help them.

This ability to compartmentalise was learned by some nurses early on in their training. For some, it came naturally, and a few never learned it at all, but we were taught right from the start that even if we had stuff going on in our own lives to leave our problems at the door. The best in our profession have mastered this ability to switch off to what has gone before and deal with the here and now. That doesn't mean we don't go home and cry at night – I've been through enough examples of that – but it does mean that we are the best we can be when dealing with people who are at their most vulnerable.

12

TWINSET AND PEARLS

Health visitors reading this book might want to skip this chapter as they must be sick and tired of the joke. For those who don't know, though, nurses and midwives back in the day always referred to health visitors as the twinset and pearls brigade – because the majority of them wore a twinset and pearls and no-one knew why. This is no longer the case in my experience –maybe the teasing got too much for them in the end.

Trainee nurses didn't get to spend much time with health visitors, a day or two if we were lucky, but we loved it because we got the opportunity to work out of uniform. When my turn came, I met the health visitor at the front of the hospital as arranged and had to stifle a giggle as a woman in her forties with a mop of curly brown hair arrived to collect me. She didn't need to introduce herself because I recognised her immediately as she was wearing – you guessed it – a twinset and pearls.

After a cursory glance at my attire – plain beige pencil skirt and sky-blue blouse – she introduced herself as Barbara. Her grin told me I would have a good few days working with her.

'Health visiting is all about the promotion of health rather than caring for the sick,' she informed me. I soon learned that health visitors, like midwives, did not like to be called nurses, although they too were qualified nurses who had chosen to undertake a health visiting course, giving them the right to the title. To be honest, in their case, I agreed. The job was nothing like nursing.

For the most part, we visited mums with babies after the midwife had discharged them to the health visitor at 10 days, but parents with children under five also came under the jurisdiction of the health visitor. They worked closely with social services in cases when children were deemed to be at risk, and these cases were by far the most challenging part of their role.

On the first morning we visited around four mother and baby households. The health visitor asked if the mother had any concerns about the child and carried out developmental checks that included playing with toys where there were toddlers, something I was keen to participate in. There was more to it, obviously, as children had developmental milestones to achieve in order to be considered "normal". Those who didn't meet these milestones might be considered to have slow development and come under "learning disability" – now "special needs". Each parent had a Child Health Record book and most diligently produced this as soon as the health visitor walked through the door.

Although health visiting wasn't the most exciting of roles for a career nurse and adrenaline junkie like me, health visitors did sometimes have to deal with the most horrendous situations. They were often the first to pick up on suspected child abuse and became the villain in the eyes of the abusers for their part in involving social services and the law. Under child protection legislation, the health visitor was allowed – indeed, expected to breach confidentiality if they suspected abuse.

Student nurses are not taken into such households for two reasons. First, they would not be welcome, as often the health visitor wasn't welcome either, although on the whole, they were admitted. Second, the health visitor had to walk a thin line between trying to keep the family, including the suspected abuser, onside while reporting them. Dealing with students while this was all going on would be too much.

13

WATERWORKS

A urology ward is all about internal plumbing and catheters, but as with any other ward, there can be poignant cases. Problems experienced by patients admitted to a urology ward are caused by some abnormality to the urethra or kidneys. These abnormalities can be strictures, where there is a narrowing of the urethra, or blockages, either benign or malignant, or infection.

I worked on a male urology ward where the majority of men came in for prostatectomy, removal of the prostate gland. The prostate gland could become cancerous or enlarged for other reasons, and when this happened, surgery was common. Post-op, the men had urinary catheters that were attached to bags, which were in turn attached to catheter stands at the side of their beds.

The prostate gland is vascular and there was always a lot of bloodied urine afterwards. The men were encouraged to drink plenty of water to clear out any clots and get the urine flowing properly again, but I recall one patient, Mr Fallon, refusing. We tried everything we could, explaining how important it was to keep drinking water and how his catheter could block or he might get an infection otherwise, but he was having none of it.

'Leave it to us, Nurse,' whispered Charlie, another patient, when I emptied his catheter bag while looking dolefully at Mr Fallon's small but bloody offering.

Later, when I came back from the sluice, I stared in disbelief at Mr Fallon's catheter bag. It was almost overflowing, as were those of the other six men in the bay.

'What the...?'

'We had a drinking competition, Nurse,' said Mr Fallon. 'And I won.'

Charlie winked at me as I quickly went off to collect more receptacles to empty all their bags.

Sometimes the camaraderie among patients was just as good as that among nurses and they often helped each other with recovery. They would cry on each other's shoulders, help each other eat, encourage each other in so many ways that I was often left as proud of them as a school teacher would be of their class or a mother of her children. Sadly, though, not every day was fun and not every patient recovered.

A twenty-eight-year-old man called Steve had been diagnosed with testicular cancer, which did seem to affect young men. He was soon to be wed when he was first diagnosed, then the worst news possible came back and the doctor had to tell him, his fiancée and his parents that his cancer was incurable.

His fiancée, Sian, was determined to go through with the wedding, and she and Steve were married shortly afterwards in the hospital chapel, with his family and as many of us nurses who could attend supporting them. I will never forget Steve, a strapping six-foot tall carpenter, who never made it home following his wedding. His new bride stayed by his side, laughing and joking with him until he died peacefully on the ward two days later. Afterwards, she was finally able to shed the tears that had never been far away, as were his parents.

Nowadays he would have survived, or at least had his life prolonged, and his sperm could have been added to a sperm bank should he and his wife have wanted to have children, but treatments were in their infancy and there was nothing anyone could do at that time.

It was always a privilege to care for people through their lowest times and an honour to look after people as brave as Steve, Sian and his parents, but it also took an emotional toll. The night Steve died, I split with my boyfriend. We rowed over something really stupid and I know it was because I was feeling raw and angry with the world, but my boyfriend just didn't care about the people I looked after.

'Why do you need to get involved? Cheer up, it's no-one we know.'

'But I *did* get to know him,' I answered. 'Can't you see? I'm not sad for me, I'm sad for his wife and his parents.'

'Are we going out or not?' had been the response.

'Not,' I answered and he'd left, slamming the door behind him. That night, I realised I could no sooner spend another day with this man than eat bulls' eyes. When he called the next day, I was not available. I cried all night, but not over my broken relationship; I cried for the many Steve's and Sian's I had met and cared for over the past five years. It was as though a dam had burst and I wept and wept until the next morning, when I got up, went to work and did it all over again because I loved my job.

14

RESPIRATORY

During my placement on a respiratory ward, quite a few patients with cystic fibrosis were admitted. Cystic fibrosis is a rare and life-limiting condition, and although life expectancy has improved since the 1980s, sufferers rarely make it into middle-age. The men and women who were admitted during my placement were often younger or not much older than myself.

The most common complication for patients who had cystic fibrosis was a chest infection. They required, and still do require, gruelling chest physiotherapy with postural drainage, which enabled them to cough up the infected green sputum which lingered on their lungs due to the lack of ciliary clearance, as well as other things. Antibiotic therapy was advancing, but was still limited and not always able to treat the infections as well back then. The patients might also have accompanying complications, one of which was diabetes mellitus due to the pancreas and digestive system not working properly.

Charlotte, a young woman I had cared for during numerous admissions to the ward, was one such person, and to make matters worse for her, she was on insulin. We had become friends, inasmuch as nurses became friends with patients; when someone is around your own age, sometimes professional barriers need to be broken down.

Charlotte was frequently admitted with rip-roaring chest infections, and on one such occasion, she asked for my telephone number and I gave it to her, even though it was not wise or even permitted to give patients your phone number then. One night, she called me out of the blue. I hadn't heard from her in months and had long since moved on from the respiratory ward.

'I've stopped taking my insulin.' She didn't sound very well at all and her speech was slurred.

'Charlotte, you can't do that, you could die.' There was no point beating about the bush.

'I don't care, I want to die.'

'Look, Charlotte, you have called me so I need to send an ambulance out to see you straight away. Do you understand?'

'Suppose so.' She put the phone down.

I called for an ambulance and gave them the address. The next day I checked admissions and, seeing where she was, I went to visit her.

She looked up sheepishly from her bed. 'Sorry.'

'That's all right, but don't ever do that again. I might not have been at home. What would you have done then?'

'I'm not sure,' she said as she picked at the bed sheets. 'Probably called Mum.'

'Thank goodness for that, but please don't do it again. If you're struggling, you need to see your consultant or ring the ward. You know they care about you, as does your mum.'

'I'm only delaying the inevitable, though, aren't I? I won't live much longer anyway.' She was right. It was only a matter of time and I had no idea how I would have coped with the condition back then when patients were lucky if they made it into their thirties.

That situation gave me a wake-up call on the dangers of giving patients my phone number. That said, I don't know what she would have done if she hadn't had the number. I told the staff nurse she was having morbid thoughts and she told me they had already referred her to the psychiatrist for assessment, as they did routinely if someone self-harmed.

I didn't hear from Charlotte again.

The respiratory ward was also a lifesaver for people with severe asthma attacks. A common treatment included salbutamol tablets, although they are no longer used for treatment of acute asthma now. Another treatment that remains true today was a salbutamol nebulise. An old-fashioned remedy that some nurses swore by was tincture of benzoin, which was administered via a Nelson's inhaler, named after the doctor who had invented it in the 1860s. Tincture of benzoin was no longer used in the 1980s, although we still used the Nelson's to administer menthol and steam inhalation for people with chronic bronchitis or sinusitis. The menthol would soothe the inflamed airways and the steam would loosen secretions so that patients could breathe more freely and cough up sticky sputum.

A regular attendee was admitted once again on her wedding night following another asthma attack. Her new husband appeared by her side, suitably alarmed and embarrassed, and we nurses ribbed him mercilessly once his bride had recovered. He blushed and explained it was due to the stress of the wedding day and nothing else. Needless to say, we didn't believe him.

15

NURSING'S NOT FOR EVERYONE

The responsibilities of third-year students included training up the more junior students. There were numerous students on any one ward because, before Project 2000, students were part of the workforce and not extra-numerary. Teaching was fitted in among other ward duties and all of us had to take part, but training others was something I enjoyed, as I proved in later years when I taught both on the wards and in the classroom.

At one point during my training, I was moved back to a mixed surgical ward with twenty-six beds in a peripheral hospital to replace another third-year student who had been injured in a car accident and was not expected back for a few weeks. The ward included two side rooms and four six-bedded bays. On this particular day, I was allocated the right side of the ward; it was common practice at the time for one team to cover one side of the ward and another would cover the opposite side. Working alongside me was Gail, a first-year student nurse who was eight weeks into her first ward placement, Gwen, another first-year coming to the end of her placement, and a nursing auxiliary called Haley.

Surgical wards were always extremely busy with little or no let-up, and the term "deer in headlights" became a living reality that morning. Although I had no patients going for surgery, there were three patients for discharge and two due to be admitted to the ward. Gail appeared tense, but I remembered what it felt like to be a new student, so I tried to help her along a bit. She seemed keen to learn and did everything she was asked to do.

Breakfast was served to patients from a trolley wheeled on to the ward from the corridors leading to the bays and rooms. Gail was struggling to remember patients' names; in spite of being grilled to learn them ever since she'd started on the ward, she still didn't know who was in each room. Nowadays this is an all too common issue, but it was not acceptable when I trained. We had to know every patient's name and diagnosis by the end of a shift. Gail had been on the ward for eight weeks now so really needed to get a grip.

Once the breakfast round was finished, I left Gail and Haley to clear away dishes and make patient beds while Gwen and I sorted out the patients for discharge. When they'd made the beds, I asked Haley and Gail to help patients with personal hygiene. Haley had been on the ward for a few years, so was both adept and proficient at getting this job done. In the meantime, Gwen and I did wound checks and started an observation round.

After a couple of hours, it was time for breaks. I decided to take Gail with me, giving Haley a break as she was becoming impatient with the rather slow student. Gail was exceptionally quiet and it was difficult getting her to talk. After I'd persevered for a while, she finally spoke.

'I'm not sure nursing is for me. I freeze in front of patients,' she confided.

I felt sorry for her, but also felt she needed to lighten up, so I set myself the challenge of turning this situation around. She hadn't recognised the need to see the funny side of nursing and was taking herself and her job too seriously, which actually meant people weren't warming to her, and she in turn was clearly unhappy.

Once we got back to the ward, most of the morning jobs had been finished. Dr Curry arrived to write up the discharge medicines and Sister was in a mood. She was not at all impressed with the doctor as the medicines should have been prescribed the day before, but I shrugged my shoulders. At least they were done now.

I took Gail with me to the hospital pharmacy to get the drugs, explaining what each medicine was for and how important they were to the patients, but she really didn't seem to be with me. Her glazed look was becoming irritating, but I reminded myself what it was like to feel overwhelmed and persevered more slowly.

Relatives arrived on the ward and the discharged

patients left. The new arrivals weren't in yet; they were due to arrive between 2 and 4 pm for surgery the next day. I took Gail on a round, going through each patient's name, what they were in for and how many days it would be until they were likely to be discharged, showing her how to go through observation and fluid charts as I did so.

At 11.30, we had a spare hour. Going into the treatment room, I asked Gail to run through a drip and she looked at me, not understanding what I had meant. I tried joking with her as I did with the patients during our round, but it was like pulling teeth. The patients had tried too, but she hadn't responded, so I thought a teaching session might help build her confidence.

'Well,' I explained, 'the new admissions will be going for surgery tomorrow and will need to have IV fluids, so you need to know how to set a drip up.'

In the middle of explaining how to carry out the procedure, which involved her running the intravenous fluid through a giving set that would then be attached to a cannula in the patient's arm, I suggested she attach the end of the giving set tube to my arm with tape. As she did so, I looked up as a visitor came in to ask how their family member was doing.

'Not you too, nurse!' they exclaimed, roaring with laughter. While I explained it was a teaching session and laughed with them, Gail didn't know where to look. I then went on to explain to Gail that on occasions, blood transfusions were necessary and proceeded to teach her about them, but soon realised this was a step too far.

After lunch, I went with Gail to admit one of the patients, explaining to the patient what the ward routine was, who would treat them and how the theatre list would be compiled later. It was a simple task: there were numerous questions on a page that I asked and the patient answered, then I told the patient I would let them know an approximate time for their operation or what number they were on the list as soon as I could. I then made observations, wrote them down on a chart, and we left.

This time, Gail seemed to get it, and I was struggling to understand why she hadn't known these things already when she had been on the ward for a couple of months. When I told her the next patient was hers, I don't think she believed me.

When the second patient came in, I handed Gail the admission pack, telling her to come back to me if she needed anything. I had no way of knowing that this simple instruction would be enough to send her into a full-blown panic attack.

Minutes later, she came back into the treatment room, unable to speak, gasping for breath. I grabbed a paper bag, thankful that a lot of equipment came in paper bags, and managed to put it over her mouth and nose, telling her to slow her breathing down.

At last, she seemed to calm down, but it took an age.

Sister came in to the treatment room, demanding to know what had gone on. I explained that I had done an admission with Gail this afternoon, and had then asked her to do a second. Sister nodded, clearly understanding.

'Nurse Prentice, go to the kitchen and make yourself a cup of tea. I will see you in a minute.'

Gail, who had recovered from her shock and panic attack, quickly left the room.

'This is unfortunate, Nurse Brookes, but I fear Nurse Prentice is just not cut out for nursing. She has been here for several weeks now and has not been able to do much at all. Even taking temperatures at times seems to be too much trouble. The other nurses have had enough and, quite frankly, so have I. Nursing's not for everyone. Please admit the second patient yourself and I will speak to Nurse Prentice. I'll see if I can find out what's going on.'

'Yes, Sister,' I replied, completely flabbergasted by Gail's lack of ability to ask a set of simple questions and feeling a little bit guilty at having allocated her the job in the first place.

I saw Gail enter Sister's office rather sheepishly. Later, Sister let me know Gail had some personal health issues and would pause her training to restart again in six months, but she didn't give me any details. In the meantime, Gail was going off duty and would be on sick leave.

My chin hit the floor. What had I done? It was a heavy burden to bear, feeling responsible for a colleague's downfall. I struggled to work to the end of that shift, and in the end, Sister called me into the office.

'Put this behind you, Nurse, it was not your fault. If it hadn't been you, it would have been someone else. The senior nursing officer has been aware, almost from the outset, that there was a situation here. Has the rest of the work been done?'

'Yes, Sister,' I replied.

'Okay, Nurse Brookes, just write up the notes ready for handover. That's all.'

I did as I was told, realising that what Sister had said was true, but still feeling sorry it had been me who sent the poor girl into a panic.

It turned out Sister was having a bad day that day; they do happen. Another incident had occurred involving a work-experience schoolgirl who had been helping out to see how a hospital ward ran. Sister had explained that some of the patients were unable to eat or drink due to their surgery that morning, hence very large signs above the beds stating: NIL BY MOUTH. A nursing auxiliary had done the first round with the young girl, giving out tea and coffee. The next round, the young girl felt sure she could manage it herself and the auxiliary let her.

Sister was doing her round a bit later than usual, given what she called the "Prentice situation", and unfortunately – or fortunately, depending on your viewpoint – she went in to see one of the patients who was due to have surgery within the hour, only to find her tucking into tea and cake.

‘Cake’s lovely, Sister, are they home-made?’

‘No, they are bought in, but you do realise you’re due for surgery any minute, Mrs Knowles?’

‘Am I?’ she exclaimed. ‘What for?’

‘You’ve come in to have your gallbladder out.’

‘Really? Well I never!’

Sister looked at the observation chart and noted that the patient had a temperature of 39°C, but no-one had acted on it. Calling the senior student, Sarah, into the office, she asked her to explain. Sarah was unable to do so as she hadn’t known about it. Her first-year student, Brendon, had done the observations and not reported back to her.

‘You’re responsibility, Nurse, not his.’

Poor Sarah, I did feel for her.

‘Follow me.’ Sister led her to the ward desk. ‘Here’s the phone, Nurse. You need to phone Dr Curry, tell him what’s happened and get him to the ward – now!’

As Sarah grappled with the phone, Sister left her to it. Sarah then had to discuss with Brendon the importance of not just doing observations, but acting on the results.

Dr Curry appeared on the ward and was told about the patient’s high temperature and the tea and cake fiasco. He went and examined the patient and diagnosed a chest infection, explaining that surgery would not be suitable that day, then left to inform the consultant and the theatre team, kindly leaving out the fact that the patient had eaten. The surgery would have had to be cancelled anyway, even if the volunteer schoolgirl hadn't given food and drink to the elderly woman. The girl had no understanding of the impact of what she had done and Sister decided not to tell her. She was, however, never left to do rounds alone again.

16

BREAKING THE RULES

Sometimes nurses broke rules for their own personal gain, such as sneaking men into their rooms in the nurses' home or food from the food trolley into the kitchen on a late shift. I was as guilty as anyone of breaking these rules, particularly the latter when my overdraft was so large I was living on fresh air, justifying my actions by telling myself that the food would most likely be thrown away when it was returned to the kitchens. I *never* took food from a trolley until all the patients had been fed. This was in the days before outside caterers were involved in providing hospital food. To be honest, I don't think I would ever have stolen what they serve up as an excuse for food, but that's a different story.

Another absolute no-no was to become romantically involved with a patient, although some nurses crossed this line too. It was difficult at times for young nurses, who were wooed by patients of both sexes, to resist, and even some doctors could fall foul of this rule. There were many other rules, some sensible and some ridiculous, that we broke on a daily basis, and I will now confess to a couple of instances where I broke hospital rules.

Bill was a tramp – a commonly used term in the early 1980s for a homeless person – who was admitted to the surgical ward one day when we were on take, meaning we took emergency admissions via casualty and the community. I wondered why the ambulance crew thrust a folder into my hands, and then did a *Roadrunner* impression – I couldn't see them for dust as they left the ward.

Making my way towards the closed curtains, I soon smelled why they had left in such a hurry. I cautiously opened the curtains to find a man who looked like he was in his eighties, but was in fact only sixty-seven, sitting in the wheelchair that had been abandoned by the ambulance crew when they'd left the ward, telling him they had to dash off to an emergency. I glanced quickly at his folder and the ambulance crew's report.

William Yates, the record said, had been found under a bridge with bleeding to his head. A concerned member of the public had called for an ambulance. As I scanned down the notes, I found the casualty record was sparse.

Admit surgical ward for assessment by on-call SHO later. This was doctor speak for "We don't want him in casualty and no doctor is going to examine him until he's been cleaned up by a nurse."

I could see some old dried blood beneath cakes of dirt on the elderly man's forehead, but it was everything else that I saw that concerned me. His eyes had sunk into his skull; his once red beard, now black, and the multiple marks to his face and hands told me he was not the only admission. He had brought an army of little friends with him.

'Mr Yates, my name is Nurse Brookes. Would you mind if I took you to the bathroom so that I can help you change into some hospital pyjamas?'

'Name's Bill. Do what you want, but don't take me bag.'

He was hanging on tightly to an old sack – containing whisky, I suspected – but first things first. I called Tracy, a second-year student, and asked her to fill a bath and add cetrimide, a skin disinfectant, to the water. The smell told her the reason for my request and she shrugged her shoulders before dutifully heading towards the bathroom. I wheeled the chair from the side of the bed, already noticing a few escapees on the floor. As I headed towards the bathroom, I saw the ward domestic charge behind the curtains to start her scrubbing, and noticed that the rest of the ward staff and patients gave me a wide berth.

Sister scowled, not happy that this man had not been "cleaned up" before arriving on a surgical ward. She ran a tight ship and bacteria, let alone the goodies Bill had brought with him, were absolutely forbidden.

The bathwater was a lovely bright yellow and the smell of disinfectant almost helped to mask the odours emanating from Bill. The elderly man looked frail and was clearly tired, so didn't give us much in the way of assistance – or resistance, thankfully. Having donned gloves and aprons, we began the task of removing Bill's clothes. The threadbare coat was first off and Tracy held open a red linen bag to receive it. Red linen bags were for clothing and bed linen that was destined for incineration, and these clothes had only one destination in my opinion.

'Check the pockets,' I said to Tracy, who screwed her nose up at the thought while Bill sat dozing in the wheelchair. There were a few coins and an almost empty whisky bottle, along with a handful of mints that had turned black and one cigarette. The whisky bottle and the mints went in the bin and the coat finally made it into the waiting laundry bag.

With each layer of clothes that came off, there was more movement as fleas and lice made their escape. Finally, all the clothes were in the incinerator and all Bill's "worldly goods" sat on a shelf. These consisted of a few coins, an old penknife and a photo of a young couple on their wedding day.

Bill had woken by now and was looking suspiciously towards the bath. His body, still crawling with fleas, was red raw from bites and scratches.

'Don't worry, Bill. We'll help you in and then get you into a hospital gown.'

In spite of his emaciated frame, Bill managed to get into the bath with a minimum of assistance. The water was blackened almost immediately and the fleas that had managed to stay on his body floated dead in the water. Tracy washed his body while I secured the laundry bag so that none of the contents would be able to escape, sprinkling the top of the bag with a disinfectant that would kill any that did make it out. We emptied and refilled the bath while Bill was still inside and began work on his hair and beard.

'Do you mind if we get rid of the beard, Bill?' I asked. 'I want to see that handsome face underneath.'

He grinned a cigarette-stained grin, showing the few teeth that remained in his mouth, and his deep-set eyes finally smiled.

'Go on, then. Ya might as well, seeing as you've already got rid of all me clothes.'

A yellow plastic bag – again for incineration – was made ready to receive the hair from the beard as I began cutting it away to make way for shaving. I was trying to ignore the head lice that crawled around inside the matted hair and beard. As soon as I finished cutting the beard, Tracy filled Bill's chin and upper lip with shaving foam while I started on the equally matted hair that was down to his shoulders.

Once we had finished, the bath was littered with dead lice, so we emptied and refilled it for a third time. Next we applied head lice shampoo to his hair to kill off any remaining marauders. We washed Bill's skin gently and, once he was out of the bath, helped dry him.

As I dried his hands and feet, between the webs of his fingers and toes, I noticed the familiar tracks of scabies. I sighed heavily and pulled a bottle of treatment out of the cupboard. Bill was finally shiny clean and almost handsome as his aquiline nose was now visible.

'How do you feel?' I asked him.

'Terrible,' he answered. 'Where's my bag?'

I had removed a full bottle of whisky from the sackcloth and put it to one side. 'Sorry, Bill, I had to throw the bag out, but the whisky will be locked away until you're discharged.'

He grunted with disgust. 'Well that better be soon,' he snorted.

I took Bill back to the bed that he had been allocated while Tracy cleared up the bathroom. Sister was still glowering as I went past. It wasn't as if it was my fault, but that made no difference to her and she gave me a hard time all shift.

Bill only stayed for two days as there was nothing really wrong with him that warranted a surgical admission. The bleeding had been due to his scratching away at the infestation that blighted him. The social worker arranged for him to be discharged to a hostel.

'I ain't staying in no hostel. What do you think I am? I've got me pride, you know.'

'Well you can't keep living under a bridge, can you?' I retorted. We had developed an understanding and I'd grown fond of the belligerent Bill Yates. 'Anyway, now you're leaving us, are you going to tell me who's in that photo?' I'd been asking him for days, but he would just tap his finger on his nose to tell me to mind my own business.

He sighed. 'She was me wife.' He stroked the picture.

'That's us on our wedding day. She went to Holland during the war to find out if her family was all right. I was in the RAF and serving overseas or I never would have let her go.'

He bowed his head and mumbled the next few words.

'I returned home after the war to find she'd never come back.'

Tears fell down Bill's face. He looked up, sniffed, and then shook himself. 'Anyway, that was a long time ago, don't matter now.' He took the bottle of whisky and his photo and walked off the ward. I stared after him, tears falling down my face too.

Bill returned to his "home" under the bridge and I visited him most weeks, taking him to the hospital when I knew it was quiet for a weekly bath. Strictly forbidden, of course, but this was one of the rules that was meant to be broken.

Eventually, the social worker and I managed to get him ensconced in a small council flat with meals on wheels. The last time I saw him, he was living in a rather untidy flat, but at least it was warm. He was still getting his weekly bath, but this time it was arranged legitimately by social services.

I often wonder what happened to Bill and am always grateful to the servicemen and women who fought for our freedom during both world wars. He reminded me that many of them returned to find that home wasn't the way they had left it.

While I was working on the surgical ward in the peripheral hospital, Ray was admitted. A thirty-two-year-old alcoholic who also lived rough, Ray had been admitted to the medical ward first with pneumonia, but was transferred to the surgical ward for insertion of bands for oesophageal varices.

Alcohol abuse often results in huge varicose veins around the oesophagus, and if these burst – I have seen this happen once – the patient vomits copious amounts of blood and dies almost immediately. Banding is used to prevent the varices from bursting, but there is still a risk of more developing if the person continues to drink, which more often than not, they do.

I hadn't actually had much to do with Ray, apart from a brief conversation while I was checking his obs, and he was discharged when I was on a late shift. On finishing my shift, I walked along the corridor towards the changing room and heard a noise coming from inside the chapel. I looked inside and saw Ray sitting on the front row, crying. I couldn't leave him there this late at night, so I walked in and sat next to him.

'Are you okay?' I asked – stupid question as he clearly was not.

'I don't want to drink anymore, but I can't stop. If I go back to the hostel where I was, I'll just start again, I know I will.'

I sat quietly, waiting for him to continue.

'What will you do?' I asked finally.

'I don't know. Are you a Christian?'

'Yes, I am. Are you looking for someone to pray with you?'

Strictly speaking, I was not breaking any rules as I wasn't proselytising a patient. I'd found him in the chapel and assumed he had entered for a reason, and I was off duty so I offered to pray with him – not something I did every day.

'Would you pray for me now?'

I did pray. I asked God to help him overcome his problem with drinking. Then I had an idea.

'Why don't I take you to the YMCA? It's on my way home.'

He nodded and agreed to wait while I went and changed. I took him to the YMCA and paid for him to stay the first couple of nights, then I left him to it.

Nine months later, I received a phone call. I had been living in a bedsit for almost a year and now had a phone.

'It's Ray.'

At first I didn't have a clue who Ray was and must have sounded suitably confused.

'Ray from the hospital chapel. You took me to the YMCA.'

The voice on the other end of the phone was a far cry from the dejected voice of the man in the chapel.

'Ray! How are you?'

'Thanks to you, I'm great. I turned my life around, got a job and haven't touched the drink since we met.'

'Wow, that's brilliant.' I was delighted, but a bit hesitant, hoping the next sentence wasn't going to involve asking me for a date.

'I phoned because I needed to tell you something. You gave the YMCA your phone number when you left me there.'

That answered my unspoken question as to how he had my number.

'Anyway, I hung on to it until I felt that I was really making a clean break from the booze. That night in the chapel, before you came along, I prayed. I told God I wanted to give up the drink, and that if He really existed and gave a toss, He'd send someone to help me to prove it. Almost as soon as I finished that prayer, you sat next to me. I just wanted to tell you that you were the answer to my prayer that day. Now I'm happy, I've got a steady job and go to church.'

'Thanks for letting me know. I'm really pleased for you, Ray.'

'I'll always be grateful to you, and to God.'

We said our goodbyes and he hung up. I was left in awe. Reflecting on that evening nine months ago, I hoped that if the same thing happened again, I would behave in exactly the same way, even if it meant blurring the boundaries.

17

DOWN, BUT NOT OUT

Sometimes it's difficult to remember that nurses and doctors are human too. They suffer heartbreak, ill health, depression, and some even die young like those they care for. But being young and in the health profession, we student nurses often felt we were invincible. Occasionally we would be reminded that there is no such thing.

One of the saddest times of my training years came when a friend was diagnosed with lymphoma. Mark was just twenty-eight and loved life. We had got to know each other at church and were always talking and laughing together. We would cook for each other and he introduced me to Ethiopian food. I often teased him that he ate too much meat, and he teased me back that people frequently ate raw meat at home.

Then Mark started to lose weight and had some bowel

symptoms that he wouldn't discuss with me. He looked pale. It was obvious to me, having nursed so many patients with cancer, that something was seriously wrong, but I hoped it was something less dangerous.

One night he was admitted to hospital with severe abdominal pain and an emergency laparotomy (opening of the abdomen) was carried out to relieve a blockage. A week later he was diagnosed with lymphoma and told that his condition was inoperable and untreatable.

I visited Mark in a home where he was being looked after by a couple from the church and watched him waste away and die within a few weeks of diagnosis. I found it doubly difficult as I was working on a male medical ward at the time where there were numerous patients with terminal cancer. Caring for people all day and watching a close friend fade away at night was taking its toll and I was feeling like a miserable wreck.

It was one of the most difficult times in my nursing career and I struggled to be the happy but compassionate nurse I usually was when on the ward. I was emotionally drained after Mark died, but I had to struggle in to work each day as if nothing had happened. We were not allowed time off for bereavement except in the case of close family, and the reality hit me one night that Mark and I had had a friendship that most probably would have developed into a relationship had he not become ill.

I did manage to request a day off for the funeral by

changing shifts with a friend who knew about Mark. The day of the funeral came and his family had flown over from Ethiopia. Mark's body lay in an open coffin, as was the tradition of the orthodox church of Ethiopia to which his family belonged.

The hardest part for me was at the graveside. As the coffin was lowered into the ground, the family began wailing loudly and shaking incense balls. The latter I didn't mind, but the wailing was something I had never experienced, and is not something I would ever wish to experience again. And believe me, I was wailing inside. I was impatient with this outward display of emotion, but realised later that it was traditional for his culture. Almost as soon as the screaming and crying had started, it stopped again when the ceremony was considered over.

There was a dinner afterwards for the hundreds of people who had attended the funeral. Mark had become very popular within a short space of time and I will always remember the conversations we had, the mealtimes we shared, and that his life was far too short.

~

Ginny was one of the girls I had got to know through our training. She was a couple of years younger than me, but we got on well, often joking around in class when the tutors were trying to teach us something serious. It was our way of handling the pressures of learning anatomy and physiology while working like Trojans on the wards. Ginny and I almost always sat together in class.

We were in a two-week block of classroom teaching when I noticed something wasn't right. One morning, about a week in, I handed Ginny a drink at lunchtime. She took the drink and dropped it, spilling coffee all over the place. As she swore loudly, people turned their heads to see what was going on.

'Don't worry,' I said. 'I'll get some paper towels and clear it up, then I'll get you another one.' Ginny just stared down at the floor where the spilled coffee was pooling.

After I'd bought the second drink, I placed it on the coffee table in front of her. I was worried; I'd noticed she was becoming a bit vacant at times and very clumsy, but each time I asked if everything was okay, she said it was.

'What is it, Ginny?' I asked as I sat next to her.

'I'm not sure, I keep dropping things and yesterday I fell over. I think I'm just tired. You know what it's like – we work too hard and I've been studying night and day to get ready for finals.'

'That's probably it, Ginny, but have you thought about seeing a doctor?'

'What, and be called a neurotic nurse?' she exclaimed.

She had a point; it's difficult when you work in the health profession to strike a balance between neurosis and dismissiveness. Every ache or pain could be interpreted as a sign of some incurable disease, every symptom serious and every tear a breakdown. Some medical professionals develop a condition known as Munchausen's Disease where they imagine symptoms and spend their lives visiting doctors, even having unnecessary surgery. Others dismiss every symptom as nothing, not wanting to be labelled the neurotic nurse, and rarely go to see a doctor. Occasionally, they leave seeking help too late.

Ginny's symptoms were not imaginary, and if I had noticed them, things were clearly not right.

'I wouldn't worry about that. You never go to the doctor, so in your case the label won't apply. It might be worth going, just for a check-up and a bit of reassurance if necessary.'

'I'll think about it.'

Ginny didn't go to the doctor, and a few weeks later, she fell during a shift on the surgical ward where she was working. Only this time, she couldn't get herself up. She was whisked away to occupational health and referred urgently for a neurological assessment.

A few weeks later, I went to visit her in the nurses' home and she told me she'd been diagnosed with Multiple Sclerosis, a condition that consisted of relapses and remissions leading to disability, the severity of which depended on how bad the condition was.

'I've had to give up, Dawn. I won't be sitting finals. We can't have an invalid working on the wards, can we? That's what the senior nurse told the head tutor.'

I didn't know what to say. Ginny had wanted to become a nurse since she was playing with her first doll, whereas I'd just sleepwalked into the profession. I was gutted for her.

We said our goodbyes and Ginny's parents collected her later that day to return to Bournemouth where they lived. For a while after that, I felt like a neurotic nurse myself, but managed to get things back into perspective after a few weeks on the wards. After all, I had finals to study for.

~

I met Cameron when I worked at the peripheral hospital. As a pharmacist, he visited the ward daily, went through all the patients' drug charts and checked the ward stocks. We would always chat when he came along and he seemed to linger on our ward.

One of my new nurse friends was a charismatic girl called Rowena who invited me to the Christian Union she'd set up at the hospital. I was delighted to see Cameron there when I attended the first meeting. It was a fun time where, as well as Bible study, we played games, ate food and got to know each other.

Rowena was dating a guy from her church, but they were having difficulties with their parents. Rowena was black while Alan was white. In fact, he couldn't have been whiter with very pale skin and blond hair, whereas Rowena couldn't have been much darker in terms of skin colour.

The time came when they wanted to get married, but

both sets of parents were refusing permission on the grounds of race. They could have married anyway because they were both old enough, but they wanted their families' blessing and both sets of parents had reached an impasse.

Meanwhile, Cameron and I were getting to know each other better, and we would have the occasional night out as a foursome with Rowena and Alan. I felt sorry for them, but they remained bubbly and happy, determined to bring their parents round to accepting their choice of marriage partner.

The opportunity came for Rowena when Alan's mum was taken ill and had to have surgery. His dad had to keep working and they were struggling. Every day, before and after work, Rowena would visit Alan's home and cook for his mum. At first, Alan's mum would refuse to eat the food, but Rowena kept visiting anyway. She also cleaned and shopped for them while Alan's mum recovered.

One day, Rowena went to visit when Alan's mum and dad were both at home.

'all right, you can marry our son,' his mum said, smiling. After that, there were never any issues of race from Alan's family.

'One down, one to go,' Rowena told us at the CU meeting. 'This is the hardest part, though. My dad insists that "no white man will ever be part of his family".' We laughed as she mimicked her father's voice.

'What are you going to do?' asked Cameron.

'Alan and I are going to Rwanda for a fortnight next month.'

'But I thought you said your dad wouldn't let him visit?' I said.

'I managed to get the village elder to give permission. Dad would never go against the village elder.'

'What, for the marriage?' I asked.

'No, just for the visit. He won't interfere on the marriage front.'

Six weeks later, Rowena and Alan were engaged to be married. When we asked how Alan had managed to get her father's permission, she told us how he had visited her father every day, sat down on the floor with him, eaten things with his hands that he had never eaten in his life, and joined in all the village activities. At first, her father wouldn't even acknowledge Alan, but after a while he won over her mum, and once that battle had been won, victory in the war would inevitably follow.

'My dad thinks he rules the roost, but without my mum, he wouldn't eat! Besides, even my dad agreed in the end that Alan was as good as any black man he had ever met.'

The happy couple were married in the summer and moved to Wales shortly afterwards to go to Bible College before working abroad.

Cameron and I couldn't quite follow this love story. Although we did become romantically involved for a while, there just wasn't the spark. I felt like we were going through the motions and had been better friends than we were a couple.

With a heavy heart, I ended our relationship and

Cameron married another nurse a year later. I was sad for a short time and wondered if I had made the wrong decision, but the busyness of the day job took over and I threw all my energies into that, remembering to leave my problems at the door.

18

PRIDE COMES BEFORE A FALL

The junior house officers (JHOs) had only been working on the wards for eight weeks, but sometimes you would have thought they were superior beings as they donned their white coats and paraded around as if they owned the hospital. The white coats flapped as they wandered through the corridors with the *British National Formulary* stuffed into their pockets and stethoscopes around their necks. Some of them were great, others were lucky the stethoscope wasn't used to strangle them.

The senior house officers (SHOs) were not around so much when the juniors appeared on the wards, leaving them to manage unsupervised, and most of them did manage – most of the time. After all, the tasks they were given back then would now mostly be carried out by nurses.

As a third-year student nurse, I had enough to think about seeing to patients without having to watch JHOs with a superiority complex swanning around. I remember one particular ward, a female surgical ward, had twenty-eight beds and was busy all the time. Patients generally stayed on the ward for around ten days, and admissions and discharges had to be managed in a timely fashion.

But one day was an exception to this rule and the ward was unusually quiet. I was on a late shift and started at 12.30pm. After the handover, there was not a lot to do.

Sister told me to use the time wisely and take the opportunity to teach one of the junior students. This was to help prepare me for my forthcoming management assessment. On my management assessment day, I would have to run the ward, but I would also have to teach. Today, I would be part of the team that sat at the nurses' station and delegated work for a change.

The phone rang. Usually the senior nurse would answer it, but Sister looked at me.

'Go on, Nurse Brookes, answer the phone and deal with whatever it is.'

'Yes, Sister,' I replied as I took the call. 'Benson Ward, Nurse Brookes speaking.'

'Staff Nurse Jacobs in casualty here. Have you got a bed for a forty-seven-year-old woman with abdominal pain?' Knowing how many empty beds there were on the ward was important as casualty staff would expect swift transfers of patients.

'Yes, we can take her, what's the diagnosis?'

'SHO thinks she's got ulcerative colitis. Currently

dehydrated and in a lot of pain. Intramuscular meds written up, she's had some metoclopramide and is on an IV drip. She'll be with you in the next half-hour.'

'Okay,' I said and put the phone down.

'Well,' said Sister, 'What's happening?'

I repeated the information and suggested that my student could prepare the bed for the patient and together we would admit her.

'Very well, Nurse.'

That seemed to be that. I went out to the ward to find the first-year student nurse, Rose, to explain what was happening. The patient duly arrived and was settled into a bed. We checked her blood pressure, pulse, temperature and respiratory rate, requested she provide a urine sample and took down details for our nursing notes. Once she was admitted, I went to phone the JHO on call to get him to come to the ward to clerk her in.

Dr Baines was one of the most arrogant house officers I had come across. He was around my age, but there the similarity ended. He was always in a hurry, always abrupt, and rarely deigned to lower himself enough to acknowledge any of the nurses, except for Sister.

He arrived on the ward after an hour and asked where the patient he was to clerk was. I noticed he was unusually sombre and his porcelain-like skin was red from the neck up; he was clearly embarrassed about something. I asked the most junior nurse available to accompany him behind the curtains. Usually I would have taken pleasure in this, knowing it would annoy him, but on this day he accepted everything without comment.

Something had obviously happened to him and I was intrigued as to what had caused this change in his behaviour. He wasn't friendly by any means, but he was certainly subdued and not his usual obnoxious self.

Sister and a second-year student left the ward for their evening dinner break. While they were gone, I was in Sister's office, writing up the nursing notes and night report as part of my management preparation. Dr Baines came in and coughed sheepishly before explaining the treatment he was recommending for our new patient. Curiosity was killing me now as I looked at this difficult man who, at that moment, looked like a child about to cry.

'Are you all right?' I asked, knowing full well he wasn't. 'You seem upset. Has something happened to you?'

He threw himself down in the chair opposite Sister's desk and sighed.

'I've made a bit of a balls up and am in the doghouse.'

'What did you do?'

'I clerked a patient in on Taylor ward. He had severe abdominal pain. I prescribed intramuscular analgesia, told him he had appendicitis and that he would need surgery tonight.'

'Okay, following you so far. What was wrong with that?' I was puzzled because it all sounded reasonable and his SHO would have approved his decision. 'Was it the wrong diagnosis?'

'No, it was the right diagnosis. I told the patient what would happen next,' he said.

I was still confused. Nothing he'd said so far seemed wrong and the patient needed to know what was going to happen to him.

'I told the patient, which was fine. He had had surgery before so knew the nurses should be coming to get him ready, but nothing had happened so he asked the staff nurse why because he was still in agony. She told him that as far as she knew, he wasn't going to theatre. The ward sister read my notes and then called me. I got a blasting for not telling the nurses about surgery, and she wanted to know why I thought that she had psychic powers that would tell her when someone was going to theatre.'

Stifling a giggle, I encouraged him to go on. I knew I shouldn't be, but I was enjoying this.

'So the patient wasn't prepped. I then got it in the neck from the theatre sister because they hadn't set up for surgery. Then the anaesthetist shouted at me as there could be no anaesthetic without him. Finally, the SHO yelled at me because I hadn't told him and he'd been told off by the registrar because I was his responsibility. He told me that without a surgeon, there could be no op. Then he told me my communication skills were appalling and went into a tirade about all the complaints he was getting from ward staff about my behaviour.'

'Really?' I couldn't help myself. As much as I had sympathy for him, I just had to laugh. It was too difficult to contain. Eventually, he saw the funny side too. He had learned a hard lesson that day. Had he been a bit nicer, he would have still been in trouble, but not quite as much as he had experienced.

It was always a pleasure when an arrogant doctor or nurse was pulled down a peg or two.

One of the student nurses in the set, Wilma, seemed to have a chip on her shoulder. Nothing was ever right and she was constantly complaining that she was passed over for the nicer jobs on the wards.

'I'm just as good as everyone else. What's the matter with them?' By "them" she meant the senior ward staff.

There was no doubt that she was intelligent and would be able to pass the written examinations. The truth was that there were doubts about her practical skills and her attitude, both of which she would require when she became a staff nurse.

I happened to be working on the same ward as Wilma and found myself on the same shift. I was preparing five patients for theatre, administering pre-meds, along with helping the staff nurse do the medicine round. I was also delegating work to the nursing auxiliary and a first-year student, who were making beds and giving out breakfasts.

I went to break with Gracie, the first year. On our arrival back on the ward, we saw our staff nurse talking to the other staff nurse, who was working the early shift. It was a little odd as it wasn't patient mealtime or handover and there was still a mountain of jobs to get through before lunchtime.

Wilma, looking rather sheepish, was then led into the treatment room by the staff nurses. I wondered what was going on. The next thing I knew, the JHO was called to the ward and the staff nurses went with him in to Sister's office. Wilma was left standing in the treatment room, so I asked her if everything was all right

She stared at me. I wasn't sure whether she was upset, angry or a mix of both.

'What's happened?' I asked.

'I'm just as capable of giving injections as you or anyone else on this ward,' she snarled. 'There were two left to be given, one to Mrs Smith and one to Miss Finch. Knowing I would not be trusted to give or check the injection, I picked one of them up and gave it to Miss Finch. Unfortunately, it was morphine that should have been given to Mrs Smith. Now the JHO is up to sort out this mess which wouldn't have happened if they had bothered to include me in the first place. It's their fault, not mine.'

Her face was beetroot red and she stormed off, back on to the ward. How do you deal with someone like that? I was glad this wasn't my management assessment day or it would have been left to me to sort it out.

Miss Finch was assessed by the JHO and was no worse off for the error, but it could have been much more serious had it been a different drug. The staff nurses were also at fault as controlled drugs should not have been drawn up and left unattended in the treatment room, not that it would have stopped my irresponsible colleague, who should have checked the charts and been accompanied by a qualified staff member anyway. I knew heads would roll and was glad to get back to my side of the ward.

The staff nurses were disciplined and received warnings, and they had to be retrained in the handling of controlled drugs. Wilma was severely reprimanded and failed her ward placement as well as receiving a verbal warning. She later failed her drugs assessment and decided to jump before she was pushed. A decision, in my opinion, that improved the safety of patients everywhere.

19

MANAGEMENT ASSESSMENT

The day of my management assessment arrived. I didn't know why I was so nervous as I'd managed wards as an enrolled nurse and on night shifts; it's something about having your every move watched that sends shivers down the spine.

I had to wait fretfully through the morning as I was on a late shift. I would be watched for the first half of the shift, so it was by far the hardest assessment other than finals. Waking early, I went for a three-mile jog then showered, changed and had breakfast. I tried to study, but nothing was going in; I just had to wait it out.

I knew the patients on the ward well. The consultant would be doing a round, which I hated, but it was all part of the job so wouldn't be too onerous.

When I arrived on the ward fifteen minutes early, Sister greeted me.

'Nervous, Nurse Brookes? Surely not. No need, you will pass with flying colours. Just keep your head when all around are losing theirs.' She chuckled at her joke.

I listened intently to the handover. Did I hear everything? Did my notes tell me everything I had to do? Taking a deep breath, I headed out to the ward with the clinical tutor who would be assessing me in tow.

Heather, a second-year student, would be my support. I knew she was good so had no worries about her ability. We went around the ward and checked patient charts; I had to verbalise everything I was doing to the tutor so that she knew I understood. I checked that observations and drips were up-to-date and requested changes where they were needed, then checked on the patients who were due for discharge.

One patient was for transfer to another hospital nearer home, and three were for complete discharge. It would be a busy shift as the morning staff had left everything for me, as was often the case when someone was doing a management assessment. The JHO had written up discharge medicines and letters, so I was grateful for that.

Heather and I sorted out the patients for discharge, cleaned the rooms, made the beds and did obs on the rest of the patients. The great thing about doing a management assessment was that I got to delegate work to the ward sister and I had given her one side of the ward to look after, while Heather and I took the other.

The consultant, Mr Hart, arrived for his round at two-thirty and Sister grabbed him on his way in to tell him I was doing my management assessment. Patients and staff closed ranks whenever a nurse was doing an assessment – it was wink-wink, nod-nod as we headed off on the round. I wasn't sure if Mr Hart would be better or worse than normal, but hopefully Sister had warned him to go easy – especially if he wanted his tea and cake at the end of the round.

It was going well until we came to Mrs Beck, an eighty-year-old lady who had had surgery, but was at risk of developing pressure sores. As the consultant went to examine her, the bootees that she had been wearing on her ankles were in the bed. Sister apologised to the consultant for the mishap.

'Nurse Brookes, you really must manage patient care better,' she snapped. So much for the consultant going easy; Sister had temporarily lost it, while Mr Hart didn't seem at all concerned. At least the observations were up to date.

The round continued uneventfully, then I answered the office phone to a nurse from casualty.

'We need to send a female patient to you, she has appendicitis and may need surgery. Another one is coming to you with cholecystitis, should be with you within the hour.'

As I took the details and thanked the nurse before putting the receiver down, I could hear the clicking of Sister's heels approaching. Why did she have to wear loud heels today, of all days? Normally they were quiet. Perhaps she wanted me to know she was coming.

'Nurse Brookes, when are you planning to do your teaching session?' What a time to ask. Gathering my thoughts, I looked sheepishly at the clinical tutor, who silently continued writing notes.

'About 4pm,' I answered. 'I will be teaching the first years how to admit a patient to a surgical ward and what they need to know regarding an individual patient's surgery. There's a patient coming in later for drainage of a pilonidal sinus tomorrow. I thought that might be appropriate.'

'Okay, Nurse, I'll get back to my work then.'

I looked at the clock and realised it was time for break, so I asked a staff nurse to cover my patients while Heather and I went. Thankfully, the clinical tutor didn't accompany us so I got half an hour to de-stress.

When I got back, the two new patients had arrived from casualty. I had to assess who should be seen first. The patient with cholecystitis had been given buscopan, an anti-spasmodic, and morphine and was settled, but the appendicitis patient was in pain. I asked Heather to admit that patient first while I bleeped the JHO to let him know the patients had arrived and that the appendicitis patient was in pain.

Sister must have overheard me speaking to the doctor because she was on my heels.

'Nurse Brookes, are you going to let theatre know? Is the JHO on his way? What medication has the patient been given and why? Is it enough? Think, Nurse, this patient needs you now. What are you going to do?'

I had felt fully in control of the situation, but now my head was spinning. I went into the office to get notes ready and thankfully the clinical tutor didn't follow me. By then the JHO had arrived and asked why I was in a quandary.

'Don't worry,' he said when I explained. 'She's not going to theatre now. That's my decision, not hers. Sister's testing you, trying to make you panic to see how you'll react when everyone around you is stressed. Stay strong.'

I remembered Sister's words from earlier and now her harassment made sense.

Sister and the clinical tutor came at me again. This time I was prepared. 'No decision has been made to take this patient to theatre as yet,' I heard myself say in a quiet, calm voice. 'Therefore she will be assessed by the JHO and I will monitor her condition and inform the JHO of any changes. In the meantime, the patient with cholecystitis also needs my attention as she has a fever. Her temperature is 39°C. I need to go and see her.'

I walked out looking calmer than I felt with palpations in my chest following my near-miss. Somehow, I had to keep my cool; I did not want to fail the assessment and have a repeat of this.

Once the ward was in order, and Heather and I had given appropriate treatment to the new admissions, I took the first-year students to the patient who was due for surgery tomorrow for the teaching session. At 5pm, Sister called me into the office.

'Just a few questions, Nurse Brookes.' For another hour, I

was grilled on every subject common to the surgical ward, as well as some complicated issues such as complaints from patients and junior staff. She asked me about the medicines used and what side effects might be experienced by patients to ensure I knew all about these. We discussed surgical procedures and I felt like I had been dissected by the end of the hour. Sister and the clinical tutor then dismissed me and stayed in the office before calling me back half an hour later.

I had passed my assessment.

I went out to tell the staff nurse and Heather, pleased to be able to tell someone.

'Congratulations, Dawn. That's the final milestone before your exams. Why don't you go to break and get a drink? You need it, I can tell.' I thanked the staff nurse and made my way down to the canteen, beaming from ear to ear.

Almost there.

20

FINAL PLACEMENT

At last, after a long road to qualification, I was on my final placement. After all the hard work that had gone into getting to this stage, including prior to my two-year conversion course, it was so good to be on the last leg. Somehow, I had always hoped I would get there, but never for a minute really thought it would come true.

It was my final week and I was working a split shift. No-one liked working split shifts; it felt like you might as well work the full twelve hours rather than have a few hours off in between. I had worked the morning part, which ran from 8am until 1pm, and the shift had gone well; all the patients on the ward were stable. There was no ward round due that day, so there were no consultant airs and graces to worry about. Some consultants were totally unreasonable and expected silence during their rounds, and some wouldn't do a round unless Sister was present.

On this particular day, I went to the hospital canteen prior to the second half of the shift and sat with a mug of coffee, thinking about what I would be doing after my holiday. Finishing up my coffee, I sighed and got up to go and see what the evening shift had in store.

Staff Nurse Loftus would be in charge – a quiet and efficient member of the team. We were due to be working alongside a first-year student called Carla. For some reason, she always looked scared to death and I couldn't help thinking she was going to be one of those who would drop out of training fairly quickly. There would also be two second-year students who were good workers, Mavis and Jo. During handover, we were told all the patients were stable, so we were looking forward to a rare busy but non-dramatic evening.

Once all the patients were settled and had evening drinks, it was time to write reports. I was twiddling my thumbs, wondering what to do next when I had an idea. I was due to leave the ward at the end of the week and there was a male nurse, Jack Maynard, who always ensured everyone who left was dumped in the bath fully clothed. It was a ritual that only occurred on this ward and only when Sister was not on duty. It would be my turn in a few days' time because Sister was off all week.

Perhaps the time had come for payback.

While Staff Loftus and Carla were at break, I hatched a plan with Mavis and Jo who would be working on Friday. Our only problem was that Jack Maynard was small in stature, but rotund, so our task would be difficult; we realised we didn't have enough brawn to manhandle him down a corridor. After considerable thought, we decided that one of the JHOs might just play ball.

As it happened, a patient rang his call bell to say he wasn't feeling that well. Mr Buchanan was suffering from a chest infection and did appear to be getting worse. His temperature had gone up from earlier and was reading 39°C, his heart rate was also high at 110 beats per minute and his respiratory rate was 24.

'I'll be all right, luv, don't worry about me,' he insisted.

'You have a high temperature, Mr Buchanan,' I explained. 'I need to call the doctor to check you over.'

'I don't want to be any trouble.'

'It's no trouble, Mr Buchanan.' *In fact, it's perfect*, I thought. Although I didn't wish the man to come to any harm, it was convenient.

I contacted the switchboard and asked for the JHO to be bleeped.

'Dr Connelly, the JHO, is on call and is coming to see Mr Buchanan,' I told my co-conspirators. 'We need to act quickly because Staff Loftus is due back any minute. Whoever doesn't get sent to break will need to ask him.'

Mavis looked concerned. 'What will happen if something goes wrong? We've still got a year to go.'

'The only thing that could go wrong is Staff Maynard snitching on us, but then we snitch in return. He's got too much to lose.'

'It's not that; it's just if harm comes to him, and then Sister finds out, we would be in trouble.'

'Yes, you're right,' I heard myself say. 'But this is happening with or without you, and think of all those girls he's dumped in the bath before.' Looking at Jo, I asked, 'How about you, are you in or out?'

The grin from ear to ear told me she had no issue with the plan. So, our plot was hatched. All we had to do was carry it out.

Dr Connelly duly arrived on the ward to examine the patient. It worked well because Staff Loftus sent me and Mavis for break so Jo was left behind. I suspected Mavis would have chickened out. When we got back to the ward, Dr Connelly had been and gone, having prescribed an intramuscular injection of amoxicillin for Mr Buchanan. Jo gave us a thumbs up on our return, so we were committed.

On Friday, my last day, I was excited for oh so many reasons, but mostly I hoped that my colleagues wouldn't back out of our plan and that it wouldn't be me who ended up in the lukewarm bath.

Jack Maynard was on duty and I could see his glee mounting at the prospect of dunking me as the day drew on. Mavis bleeped Dr Connelly, who arrived and hid in the bathroom. Maynard, true to form, wasn't willing to do any of his own dirty work – apart from manhandle student nurses, that is – and had ordered Jo to fill the bath ready. The time came and he grabbed me. He pushed me towards the bathroom, but as soon as we got in there, he was grabbed from behind by Dr Connelly, causing him to let go of me. The four of us then lifted him and dropped him unceremoniously into the colder than usual bath. We also shot a few syringes of calamine lotion at him for good measure and poured talc down his uniform.

He actually took it all in good humour and smiled sheepishly as he walked down the ward, dripping wet, with us following him and patients and visitors cheering us on. He did have the last laugh, though.

'Right, you lot, clear that mess up before any of you go off shift.'

We were an hour late leaving, but it was worth it and, apart from a few splashes, I was relatively dry. Thankfully, neither the Senior Nurse nor Sister ever found out, and Mavis and Jo didn't suffer any backlash from their part in my grand scheme.

~

A week later, a friend called me to let me know there was a letter from the English National Board for Nursing and Midwifery waiting for me. It had been sent to my old address, and she wondered whether it was my results.

'Yikes! I've been waiting for that, I did give them my new address.' I could feel my heart pounding through my chest.

'Do you want me to open it?' she asked.

I grimaced. 'Yes please.'

I waited for what seemed like an eternity, but was just a few seconds.

'Dear Miss Brookes, I have pleasure in informing you...'

Shrieks of joy from both ends of the telephone. I had done it – I was a registered nurse at last.

THANK YOU

Thank you for reading my third memoir. In order for me to gain feedback on whether you have enjoyed this book, and to hear any other thoughts you may have, I would love you to get in touch via either an honest review on Amazon or any other platform you use, or the contact form on my website. I am always looking to improve as both an author and a human being, and with that in mind I would appreciate your comments.

Dawn Brookes

To get a FREE eBook, receive news and updates about my work, sign up for my newsletter

Connect with me via social media:

Facebook

TikTok
YouTube
Twitter

ALSO BY DAWN BROOKES

Coming Soon

Can I Come In? A District Nurse's Story

Rachel Prince Mystery Series

A Cruise to Murder

Deadly Cruise

Killer Cruise

Dying to Cruise

A Christmas Cruise Murder

Murderous Cruise Habit

Honeymoon Cruise Murder

A Murder Mystery Cruise

Hazardous Cruise

Captain's Dinner Cruise Murder

Corporate Cruise Murder

Lady Marjorie Snellthorpe Mysteries

Death of a Blogger (free eBook when signing up for my newsletter)

Murder at the Opera House

Murder in the Highlands

Murder at a Wimbledon Mansion

Carlos Jacobi Series

Body in the Woods

The Bradgate Park Murders

Children's Picture Books

Suki Seal and the Plastic Ring

Gerry the One-Eared Cat

Danny the Caterpillar

Ava & Oliver's Bonfire Night Adventure

Ava & Oliver's Christmas Nativity Adventure

Jesus feeds a big crowd

Jesus heals a man on a stretcher

ABOUT THE AUTHOR

Dawn Brookes is a fun-loving, light-hearted person, with a creative side.

Dawn holds an MA in Creative writing with Distinction. She writes across genres but has developed a passion for memoirs and cosy mysteries.

She worked as a hospital nurse, midwife, district nurse and community matron during a career spanning thirty-nine years. Before turning her hand to writing for a living, she had multiple articles published in professional journals and co-edited a nursing textbook published by Palgrave Macmillan.

Dawn grew up in Leicester, later moved to London and Berkshire and now lives in Derby. She holds a Bachelor's degree with Honours and another Master's degree in education.

Dawn has a passion for nature and loves animals, especially dogs. Animals will continue to feature in her children's books as she believes caring for animals and nature helps children become kinder human beings.

Dawn is now writing full-time.

ACKNOWLEDGMENTS

I couldn't have written these books without the help and support of my two best friends Ruth and Sue. Thank you for all the prompts and reminders that helped get this done.

Thank you to friends & colleagues for your ongoing patience.

There are so many people who have inspired and encouraged me over the years, and too many to mention, but here are just a few. Thank you again to Gail for suggesting nursing as a career path. Thank you to my friend who encouraged me to move to London. Thanks to Mr Robinson; your belief in me brought me much happiness, and helped build my confidence in my ability to study. I know there are many others and I thank you all from the bottom of my heart for being friends and colleagues.

As always, thank you to patients, past, present and future; I hope that I have helped some of you. I have learned so much from so many of you; it was always you patients who made it worth getting out of bed in the mornings.

The biggest thanks goes to patients, past and present, because without you the world would have been a poorer place. Some patients referred to in this book are no longer with us but you are forever in my heart. I hope that you are now in readers hearts too even though they will never know your true identity.

Printed in Great Britain
by Amazon

56728411R00341